WORKING IN HOLLYWOOD

★

WORKING IN HOLLYWOOD

★

Alexandra Brouwer
Thomas Lee Wright

Crown Publishers, Inc.
New York

Published by Crown Publishers, Inc., 201 East 50th Street, New York, New York 10022

CROWN is a trademark of Crown Publishers, Inc.

Manufactured in the United States of America

Library of Congress Cataloging-in-Publication Data

Brouwer, Alexandra, 1955–
    Working in Hollywood / Alexandra Brouwer, Thomas Lee Wright.
        p.   cm.
    1. Motion picture industry—California—Los Angeles. 2. Motion
pictures—Production and direction. 3. Hollywood (Los Angeles,
Calif.)—Industries. I. Brouwer, Alexandra. II. Title.
PN1993.5.U65W75   1990   89-22092
384′.8′0979494—dc20   CIP

ISBN 0-517-57401-2

Designed by Shari de Miskey

10 9 8 7 6 5 4 3 2 1

First Edition

Contents

234456

5 · THE TALENT

6 · THE LOOK

7 · THE ARTISTS

8 · THE MOVERS

CONTENTS

CONTENTS

Introduction

This book was conceived in a darkened theater. The movie had just ended. The music swelled. We sat mesmerized, still in the emotional grip of the film we had just seen. And then, ever so slowly, names began to roll down the screen, followed by a list of job titles: boom operator . . . foley artist . . . best boy . . .

At the time, we were working for room and board at an old-folks' home in downtown Los Angeles, as a luncheon waitress and a night desk clerk, hoping somehow to "break in," to get a job in the film business.

We had recently tried to explain to our parents and friends back home why it can take months, even years, to find a job working in the movies. No one seemed to understand that Hollywood is often an enigmatic place, even for those who spend most of their time here.

We watched the end credits with interest, thinking maybe we'd find something we might be able to do one day. Most of the terms up on that screen meant absolutely nothing to us at the time: sound mixer . . . timer . . . dolly grip . . . property master . . . matte artist . . . negative cutter . . . script supervisor . . .

Who were those people? And what tasks did they perform to make that movie possible?

We've watched movies all our lives to escape, to flesh out our feelings, to heighten the emotions of our daily lives. We go to find out how other people live and to lose ourselves in other worlds.

The movies answer our hunger for drama, for color, for release, for validation.

What about those who make it their life's ambition to satisfy that hunger? How do they create those moving images? What kind of time, labor, money, and collaborative effort go into making a movie? What does it take from the conception of an idea through the nuts and bolts of planning to the shooting, cutting, and final release of "the picture"? How is one accepted into the union or guild, the exclusive club to which one must belong in order to work in most jobs in this industry?

In the following pages, the unsung workers behind the camera tell their individual stories—the deal makers, laborers, craftspeople, technicians, artists, executives, and other creative talent. Each one speaks in his or her own voice about personal and professional concerns, imparting information and sharing anecdotes.

Every interview includes two fundamental questions: What does your job entail? What is the best way to get started in your particular line of work?

This is a book about people who work hard. Like Americans in any other industry, people in the film business report to an office or job site each day, look forward to paychecks, take care of families, pay mortgages, worry about unemployment, and strive to improve their personal situation on a daily basis. And most who arrive here hoping for a job are happy to find any kind of niche in the industry.

How many among us know what our true calling will be when we first embark upon our professional life? And that's the way it goes in Hollywood. People come here with the dream of being part of the world of moviemaking. Some succeed in finding a place. Others, after long, arduous struggles, take the bus back home.

This is not an industry that provides job security.

For those who work at the studios, there is the constant specter of a change in management that will completely realign personnel, negate promises, and shut doors of entire departments.

For those who work outside the studio system, in the challenging gyre of independent production, there is no guarantee of your next gig. Independent productions spring up virtually overnight and, very often, dissolve just as suddenly.

The studio employee punches a time clock, toiling daily for a given number of hours in the century-old Hollywood tradition. The employee on an independent production has a job only for as long as it takes to complete the motion picture.

Unlike the old days in Hollywood, there is no longer a formal system of apprenticeship. What you do and how well you do it is dependent largely upon your own initiative and the people you come to know as you acquire personal battle scars in the moviemaking wars.

Job titles and descriptions in this industry vary widely depending upon whom you work with and for. The job descriptions in this book are based upon generally understood definitions supplied by trade unions and culled from actual interviews we have done.

This book could have been divided into three sections—jobs pertaining to preproduction, production, and postproduction. Articles and books have often structured their presentation in this fashion. We believe it is a false structure because so many jobs in the moviemaking process overlap two or more phases of production.

Instead, we have chosen to divide those in our book into chapters according to joint goals and similar functions. We have allowed our interviewees to define themselves and what they do in their own voices. Because each individual in our book brings his or her own unique perspective, it can safely be said that if we had interviewed different people, this would be a different book.

We have endeavored to assemble the top people in each of sixty-four different categories—with over a dozen Academy Award winners and nominees among them.

For many of the jobs, of course, no Academy Awards are given, which is another reason we have written this book—to give credit to the unsung heroes who toil behind the scenes in motion pictures.

Each interviewee has overcome personal and professional challenges to become established in the industry.

Those who work in the trade or craftsman capacity on movies have had to earn the right to belong to a union. People like Meta Wilde, one of the founders of the script supervisors union, and Cecelia Hall, the sound editor on *Top Gun*, have revolutionized the place of unions in the industry, earning respect and increased visibility through their efforts at organizing and standing up for themselves.

Throughout the book, you will find that unions are a double-edged sword. On the one hand, they have an expensive hold on movie production that is difficult to ignore, requiring membership for certain jobs while at the same time making it difficult to acquire the experience that would allow someone to become a union member. On the other hand, once you have achieved membership, the union guarantees that you will always have a certain level of salary and medical benefits. A union card, however, does not guarantee employment—it merely protects and preserves the safety and income of the industry worker at those times when he *is* employed.

Again, the film industry is not about job security. And one of the major challenges of anyone entering the business is simply to find jobs on a consistent basis.

Other challenges recur in our book—barriers of gender prejudice and tolls taken on personal lives by the unusual demands of a career in filmmaking.

Very often people in the film business are doing one job while waiting to do another. For Hollywood is truly the land of dreams. Indeed, it has been called a dream factory. But there are certain realities that go along with the pursuit of this dream, and in the following pages we have endeavored to highlight the signposts along the road to that dream.

No matter how you plan to enter the industry, there are certain givens that you should be aware of. So often, as we have read in novels by Nathanael West or F. Scott Fitzgerald, naiveté and innocence can be the greatest nemesis of a healthy person's fresh ambition.

If nothing else, the people in the following pages, each one of them, knows a secret—a secret revealed in his or her own way: *how to survive in Hollywood.*

Yes, these people are survivors. And they are dreamers. And those who have chosen to work in the motion picture industry are employed making movies that are meant to inspire dreams.

The determined dreamers who come here still arrive from all around the country.

We dedicate this book to them.

ALEXANDRA BROUWER
AND THOMAS LEE WRIGHT

WORKING IN HOLLYWOOD

★

1
THE HELMSMEN

A movie can begin in many ways. The initial idea might originate with any of the four people in this chapter. But the idea cannot be acted upon, nor the movie made, without their mutual cooperation.

Although there are some in this book who might be left out of the process, and a movie could get made without them, such is not the case with any in this first chapter.

They are the helmsmen, the leaders of the production. They cause a film to happen.

They are the indispensable ones. Their efforts make the employment of others possible.

Without the participation of all four, a studio cannot make the movie.

They depend upon one another for everything pertaining to the production. And the future success of their communal enterprise is completely dependent upon each one carrying out his self-appointed task.

Head of Production

The Head of Production supervises every aspect of the filmmaking process on behalf of the financing entity, from generating ideas and developing scripts, through the packaging and production phases and actual shooting of the movie, and on into the postproduction, marketing and release of the feature film.

Michael Medavoy

MIKE MEDAVOY is the longest-tenured head of production currently in the motion picture business. Born in Shanghai, China, in 1941, the son of Russian immigrants, he moved to Chile at age eight. Movies became a way to "transport myself to almost any world," particularly the elusive and much-dreamed-of United States. His family finally did come to America when he was sixteen. After graduating with honors in history from UCLA, Medavoy got a job in the mailroom at Universal Studios "clearing $67 a week, married and with a baby on the way." Six months later he got a slot in the casting department and rose quickly to become a casting director at Universal. After a year he was hired by Bill Robinson as an agent trainee. Two years later, in 1967, he joined General Artists Corporation (which eventually merged with Creative Management Agency) as a vice-president. In 1971 he became vice-president in charge of the motion picture department at International Famous Agency, where he represented such talent as Jane Fonda, Donald Sutherland, Gene Wilder, Jean-Louis Trintignant, Michelangelo Antonioni, Karel Reisz, Steven Spielberg, George Cukor, John Milius, Terence Malick, Raquel Welch, Jeanne Moreau, and Francis Ford Coppola. While at IFA, Medavoy was involved in packaging *The Sting, Young Frankenstein, Jaws,* and others.

He joined United Artists Corporation in May 1974 as senior vice-president in charge of production. During his tenure there, UA was awarded three consecutive Oscars for Best Picture for *One Flew over the Cuckoo's Nest, Rocky,* and *Annie Hall.*

In 1978 Medavoy left United Artists together with four of his colleagues to form Orion Pictures Company in partnership with Warner Communications, Inc. In 1982 Medavoy, three of his partners, and Warburg Pincus Capital, Inc., purchased a failing distribution entity, Filmways, Inc., and restructured the company to create Orion Pictures Corporation, a company publicly traded on the New York Stock Exchange.

Medavoy and his partners led Orion to its fourth Oscar for Best Picture with *Amadeus* and the fifth in 1986 for *Platoon*. In addition, they have been responsible for more than two hundred feature films, including *Network*, *Apocalypse Now*, *Carrie*, *Raging Bull*, *Black Stallion*, *Coming Home*, *Terminator*, and *Robocop*.

THE PRODUCT we manufacture—film—is unlike any other. It is not like refrigerators or a pair of shoes, where it's the same mold every time. It's more like a living organism. Yet it must operate like any other business; that's why it's called Show Business. What you have here is a different set of rules with every film whether it's comedy or drama or fantasy. And the vision is never of your own choosing, but rather a combination of the director's, the writer's, the actors', and, in some instances, the producer's. In the making of motion pictures, the head of production is the captain of the studio production process.

What the Studio Does

How does a studio function?

First, it selects (and I want to emphasize the word *select* because we are selectors, not producers) the creation and purchase of film material—scripts, books, and ideas.

Second, we select and help engage writers, directors, producers, and actors.

Then we [help] select, support, or supervise all the preproduction elements, selecting key crew such as art directors, cameramen, etc., and supervising budget preparations, legal, accounting, physical housing, and support of all the people who participate in the making of the film. We are involved in labor relations, governmental regulations, payroll, transportation, stage, props, sets, wardrobe, dubbing and editing rooms, and finally, the marketing and distribution of all films made by the company.

Why Films Get Selected: Weighing the Investment Versus the Risk

A major motion picture company has to have a program of fifteen pictures per year, and a reasonable average for such a slate of pictures will cost the studio somewhere between $200 to $250 million today. It is therefore the principal theory behind every major studio to minimize its risk and maximize the upside potential. How do you do that? Obviously by making as many commercial movies as you can, and as inexpensively as you can (without losing quality) by laying off the risks to known ancillary avenues such as video, cable, television, and satellite—worldwide. In the final analysis, you must be lucky enough to select more winners than losers. Not only are large amounts of dollars necessary, but most companies work with borrowed money— therefore, interest and overhead must be factored into the decision-making process.

Think about what it costs not only to make a film but to market a film, including interest. The industry average today is $19.6 million per picture, and that does not include the cost of marketing, which on a broad release picture (and a lot of pictures are released broadly today) runs anywhere from 7 to 10 million dollars a picture—and that's just to open and pre-open. You can imagine the stakes that are involved.

As head of production, you are constantly assessing what you think a particular movie is worth and what returns you can get back in all gauges. What do you expect to get from its foreign distribution, what do you expect to get from its domestic distribution, what do you expect to sell it for when you sell it to television, what do you expect to get from cable and television syndication? and so forth. You take all those numbers, you add them up and you say, "Okay, we *feel* . . ." It really becomes a gut instinct that is usually based somewhat on a priori knowledge (and on experience) that this film will do "X" and that you won't have a disaster on your hands. The idea is to make sure that no *one* film can sink the year or, for that matter, the company. A couple of bad years for a company can and usually does end a number of careers.

The main question is "Is the reward worth the risk?" Often what happens is that studios are prone to spend money for expensive pictures because the rewards are greater. Some studios would rather spend $30 million and make $100 million than $2 million and make $5 million.

The Filtering Process

The process is basically the following: an agent, lawyer, or some other individual who represents a particular client submits a script to one of several production people at Orion. It gets evaluated by the staff and filtered to the top.

There's no question in my mind that the most important ingredient in the chain of events that leads to a film getting made is the script. And then for a film to be successful, a whole series of events has to take place. The *concept* has to be right because the first question anybody asks when deciding to go to a movie is "What's the movie about?" The second question is usually "Who's in it?"

Depending on who presents it and how it's presented, the script goes through several channels before it reaches those particular people who make the decision. If a script comes in the mail, even though it's represented by an agent, it usually hits a reader. If the reader's report is interesting or if in reading the reader's report you gather that there's an interesting idea, or if the reader points out that the writer is someone to reckon with, the next step is either an assistant reads it to verify it or one of five or six people, including myself, will have a chance to pick it up and read it. The volume of scripts that comes in per week is so large that it's really impossible to give every script the kind of attention that you might ideally hope for.

After a script's been read, filtered by the sieve so to speak, a decision is made rather quickly as to whether it is something interesting or not, and the next step is taking into account the "elements" that are presented.

The word *element* is often used in the business to characterize either an actor, a script, a producer, a director, or any and all of the above. The thing that usually makes you read a piece of material faster is when it has an element attached that you like—in other words, an actor or a director or a very good writer or an important producer. Chances are those projects will get read first and be given more special attention than if they just come in the mail.

Taking into account desirable elements is part of "packaging." Packaging is trying to fit together as many elements, preferably finding the story, the director, the stars most sought after at that time, and arranging financing, salaries, and percentages for all concerned. Making sure that everything is in place to make the movie.

When I first started as an agent, there were two things said to me that still stand me in good stead. One was "If you want to be a successful agent, you have to learn how to package a movie," because that's where the big money was. Number two, "The best way to package movies is to control the material."

The five major elements that need to be in place before we decide to go ahead and make the film are the script (and a clear idea of what changes it might need); then we need to know the producer, the director, the principal members of the cast, and the budget. We have a responsibility to ourselves as well as to our partners and stockholders to attempt something that will be financially rewarding.

What a Studio Looks for in a Story

If you ask me about what kinds of movies to make, the word *entertainment* is a given, but the idea should be fresh, the characters interesting, and the subject universal, whether it's a drama, comedy, or any other genre. Interesting characters, unusual and yet contemporary—in the sense that they reflect something that all of us are feeling. Hopefully, the story deals not only with the gut—what goes on inside of somebody emotionally and viscerally—but also engages the intellect.

Following a trend is probably the most dangerous thing you can do if you make movies. The fact is, if you make a program of pictures, out of the twelve to fifteen pictures, you'll have a turkey or two in there, and then you'll have some that'll do well. The one rule that I have kept in mind, and that our company has kept in mind, is that we never aim at *Star Wars*, never aim at *Jaws*, never aim at that picture that everybody says, "That's going to be the picture that's going to explode and risk your company's treasury." There is one rule in the business: There are no rules that decide success—it's all an educated gamble.

Captain of the Selection Process

My primary responsibility is to see that twelve to fifteen movies a year are made at Orion. In order to build a program of movies, you must first put into motion your three summer films—then your Christmas films. These films must be strong enough to compete with other such big films or potentially successful sequels in the marketplace.

I believe in the team concept. Finally, however, somebody has to say "yes" or "no." In my production team, I believe in allowing people to express their strong likes or dislikes of material or of a package or of any of the things that play a part in trying to make a movie. And therefore I have a very open and accessible office. Anybody can walk in—certainly any of the people who work for us—and express their views. I prefer people who don't necessarily agree with me and who will present an argument contrary to the conclusion that I might have arrived at. This allows me to see the other side of the equation.

I'm sort of the captain of the selection process, the captain of the filter. Finally, it boils down to selecting the right *people*. You're selecting people you trust, whose vision you think is interesting, to convert the words on paper into images.

I work closely with my partners—Arthur Krim (chairman), Eric Pleskow (president and chief executive officer of Orion), Bill Bernstein (executive vice president of business affairs), along with my production staff headed now by Marc Platt (senior vice president of production). None of the decisions are made unilaterally and lots of thought goes into them. The final decision obviously falls on the chief executive officer.

Personal Taste

I've never felt that there are any rules in selecting what films to make. There's no question that personal taste and experience play a part in those decisions. Personal taste drives you to certain things that many other people may have passed up. If we try to be anything other than what we are, we usually fail. You might still fail by being who you are, but you're more likely to succeed if you follow your instincts. Whenever we've attempted to do something that we really didn't feel deeply about, we usually failed. I think that in almost every instance, except one, those pictures that won Academy Awards for us—whether it's *One Flew over the Cuckoo's Nest, Rocky, Coming Home, Network, Platoon,* or *Amadeus*—were all films that reflect the personal choices and personal taste of those involved in each project. The people involved were passionate about what they were doing.

In most instances, these projects were turned down by everybody else, but they represented to us, either consciously or subconsciously, some feeling that "this is a story worth telling."

The object of every studio is to work with the more talented filmmakers—Miloš Forman, Phil Kaufman, Jonathan Demme, Stanley Kubrick, Steven Spielberg, George Lucas, to name a few—because in the final analysis, you're in their hands. It's their vision that makes the film whatever it finally becomes.

What's obvious is that if you make fifteen films a year, you can't do everything, you can't be everywhere. The staff and myself have this constant problem of having to find and then select fifteen films a year. We're usually working a year ahead of schedule. That means that you really can't try to figure out what the audience is going to like. We very quickly make films that *we* think are interesting, have universal content, and can be in the marketplace and compete with all the other forms of entertainment offered to the public in a given week.

Relationships

Relationships play a big part in Hollywood filmmaking. The way a particular picture is viewed will vary from studio to studio. A particular actor may be more "bankable" at one studio than at another. Stars may be worth more in terms of what you might think their marketability is because you may already have a picture in production with them and therefore know enough about what their next picture is going to be. Such was the case with Dudley Moore, who did *Ten* for us and then *Arthur,* and again with Sylvester Stallone, who did *Fist* before *Rocky* was released.

The choice to make both *Platoon* and *Amadeus* had to do with the fact that we had relationships with the makers of those films and they felt comfortable with us. In both cases we thought that the investment was covered. These are projects that came to us and were co-financed by us.

In the case of *Platoon,* we consciously decided to put up x number of dollars and to pick up all the foreign rights and the domestic theatrical distribution rights in the United States. In the case of *Amadeus,* Saul Zaentz, who had done *One Flew over the Cuckoo's Nest* and *The Unbearable Lightness of Being* with us and who therefore had a history of quality films with us, had prefinanced the film and basically came to us and sold us the domestic rights.

What will push it over the top can be any one element or combination of elements. In *Annie Hall,* Arthur Krim and Eric Pleskow had had a longstanding relationship with Woody Allen. He's had a free hand and has made every film he's decided to make.

Mississippi Burning came to us as a script. Fred Zollo, the producer, and Chris Gerolmo, the writer, gave it to us. It originally had John Schlesinger attached as director. John Schlesinger has done many films with both Orion and United Artists, and is almost a member of the family. And had John Schlesinger not decided to do *Madame Souzatska,* he would have been doing *Mississippi Burning.* I gave the

script to Alan Parker, thinking that he'd be the right director for it—
and the rest is history.

Rocky was a script that was turned down by everybody. We had a
deal with Irwin Winkler and Bob Chartoff, and they were in the
process of making a film for us called *New York, New York* that we
were very excited about. They brought *Rocky* to us, and Eric Pleskow
and I sat with them in a meeting, and after knocking down the budget
to $1.2 million and crossing it with *New York, New York*—thinking
that *New York, New York* would be a big hit and that *Rocky* would
barely get by—we decided to give the picture a go. And it became a big
phenomenon.

Network came to us because of a relationship we had with Paddy
Chayefsky dating back to *Hospital*. That picture was shared with
MGM. They became the point people. But we co-financed it and were
very proud of the film.

Apocalypse Now—I had a relationship with Francis Ford Coppola, the director, and John Milius, the writer, which dated back to
being their agent. It was a lengthy negotiation. Arthur Krim and Eric
Pleskow were both involved in this because it was a very expensive
film. And it was also presented in a very different manner. The one
thing we always had at United Artists and at Orion was flexibility in
deal making. The picture was going to cost, at the time, about $14
million. It wound up costing $30 million. As it turned out, the film
did become successful and everybody made some money on it, including Francis, but it was a very big risk.

Raging Bull was one of the last films we approved at United
Artists before we left and formed Orion Pictures. It was a labor of love
of Marty Scorsese and Robert De Niro. Marty had just finished two
films for us—*New York, New York* and *The Last Waltz*. The decision
to do that film (and to do it in black and white) was a difficult one, but
the budget was controlled, and I think it was a great film. There's
always a struggle within yourself when you do something that goes
counter to what the audience is expecting—in that instance, doing it
in black and white. But in the final analysis, we decided there was a
majority of valid reasons for doing it, not the least of which was our
trust in the filmmakers.

Coming Home was done as a labor of love by Jane Fonda, Waldo
Salt, Hal Ashby, and Jerome Hellman, all of whom had relationships
with us for years. Jerry Hellman had been with United Artists going

back to *Midnight Cowboy*. Hal Ashby, Jane Fonda, and Waldo Salt were all ex-clients of mine.

So deciding how and why pictures get made, as you can see by that list, has much to do with personal relationships and the passion of those who make the films. We have relationships with many of the creative people in this business and basically keep an eye open to find material as well as new talent.

Timing also plays a large part in filtering down and finally selecting which movies we choose to make, figuring out what hasn't been done, making "original choices." Timing *along with* luck. The industry has plenty of examples of pictures that have been turned down by one studio, that have been passed off to other studios to become big hits—*Star Wars, Midnight Cowboy, Last Tango in Paris*. The list is endless.

We attempt to schedule the release of as wide a variety of movies as possible. There will be comedies, dramas, horror films, and musical films if we can find them. We don't do just one type of picture. If you look at this year's schedule (1988), there's everything from *The Unbearable Lightness of Being* to *Monkey Shines*. And if you look at our record, you'll see *Terminator* and *Robocop* at one end of the spectrum and *Platoon* and *Amadeus* at the other.

Stepping in on the Line

Whether or not I personally get involved in the actual moviemaking process has to do with the particular film and the individuals making that film. We (meaning myself and my partners) get involved when we're going over budget. And if we sense some kind of weakness, we usually try to shore it up. I don't claim to have all the answers, but I think I have had the good fortune to work with some extraordinary people and to have learned a lot from them. But the philosophy that Arthur Krim, Bob Benjamin, and Eric Pleskow started with at United Artists many years ago was that you let the creator create. Once you've made the decision on the people you are trusting, you have crossed the Rubicon, you live by that sword. Interference often makes filmmakers and films worse. Most pictures have to have *one* point of view—and it should be the filmmaker's.

We try to give the creative people as much freedom as is reasonable within the confines of cost controls. We also make suggestions. If we find a cinematographer we think is terrific, for example, then we'll suggest him—and in some instances try to get the cinematographer the job. But we won't drive somebody down their throats. Every so often we will run into somebody who needs that kind of help—that's when we step in and give our input to the director, producer, or writer. There is always somebody in this business who is starting, and that person needs and often welcomes help.

Every picture has a different dynamic. Of the two hundred films that we have been involved with, every one has presented a different set of problems. Sometimes the problem is in the script, sometimes in the producer's inability to handle a difficulty. Sometimes there's a disagreement between the producer and the director, and we'll step in and try to help resolve it.

What It Takes

The common rules of behavior and how we deal with other human beings basically define our ability to succeed or not. Because the stakes are so high in this industry, people are not normally trusting, and you have to win their trust.

Outside of being lucky and persistent, I think that my strength was to see changes before they happened. That's what made me a successful agent. I wound up representing people who later on became major forces in the industry. The ability to get along with talent makes it easier—I had achieved a reputation for supporting artistic and talented people.

While it was a great training ground, the agent's responsibility basically ends when he makes the deal for the client, which is when a studio production chief's responsibility begins.

A head of production is responsible not only for the financial aspect of filmmaking, but also for the artistic outcome. Hollywood is a very unforgiving town; you can't make too many mistakes or you will simply be out of a job. I don't think anybody really wants to be known as someone who does schlock. Obviously, nobody starts off wanting to do garbage, but sometimes it turns out that way because this is a very complicated business and subject to many often uncontrollable variables, and then, of course, everyone has his own taste.

The final variable that dictates your success (or lack of it) is the often unpredictable reaction of a movie-going audience. I always feel that underestimating or catering down to an audience is the wrong thing to do. I think the general audience is more intelligent than most people will give it credit for, though I'm sure there are people who disagree with that.

Setting Priorities

The pictures that are immediate are the ones that get priority. If one is to be successful in this business, it has to be a seven-day-a-week job—and no less than twelve hours a day—constant dedication, that constant thought, constantly thinking about shifting moods and changes, constantly reading something, and knowing what your opposition is doing.

You're dealt certain cards. You come to your office and there are ten scripts that everybody kind of likes. You read them and you say, "Okay, let's make that one and that one," and, "Let's see if we can put that together," "Let's see if we can get a cast for this." In a perfect world, I'd be able to concentrate on each one of these and really make each one a jewel, but I can't. There isn't enough time. I'm interested in what happens in the world, and I want to go beyond the insularity of certain kinds of moviemaking. I think that in this town I've created a consciousness by getting involved in politics and being known as someone involved in civic matters.

I feel that people must give back what they get. I've been very lucky. A long time ago I made a conscious decision to help others, whenever I could. That's why I've taught a class or two at UCLA. That's why I feel an obligation to help people get started.

The Orion Family

There is a fairly systematic hierarchy to try to cover all the bases—everything from readers of scripts in the story department to executives who attempt to bring in and evaluate material. They're only as good as we allow them to be and as they have talent. I think the group of people I have now is probably the best I've had in a long time—maybe even ever. They're hungry, they're competitive, they're intelligent, and they have some experience.

There is a very familial relationship between the four of us who head Orion—Eric Pleskow, Bill Bernstein, Arthur Krim, and myself. That's not to say there haven't been some real tensions, but then I guess this is true of all families.

12

The building of Orion has been a monumental task. I don't think that I ever thought that it was going to be this difficult, but I suppose anything worth doing is usually hard.

I would like Orion to continue to be a major force in the industry. We've accomplished one goal in that respect, but there are several others to accomplish, among which are stronger earnings and expanding into other fields, such as television, television syndication, and cable, so that we are not totally dependent on just our movies being successful.

Advice

You can't get a degree in "head of production." If you want to be in this business, you have to love seeing films. And you have to be as passionate about making them.

I try to think of how lucky I am to be a part of something like this. If you think about the monies involved and the responsibility, it can get scary. And, of all the professions in the movie industry, producer and head of studio have the shortest lifespan. I've been doing this for fifteen years—longer than anybody—and have loved almost every minute of it.

The beauty of the relationships we have at Orion is that we have had our successes, we've had our failures, but through it all, we've stuck together. There have been many times when I'm sure any one of us would have liked to have gotten away from it all, but in total we're all proud of our accomplishments.

Postscript: *In February 1990, Michael Medavoy left Orion to become chairman of Tri-Star Pictures.*

Producer

The Producer finds and/or develops the material to be made into a movie, often participates in the hiring of the screenwriter and director, arranges for financing, oversees all financial and technical aspects of the production, and monitors the release and exploitation of the film.

Kathleen Kennedy

KATHLEEN KENNEDY spent five years working in television while simultaneously pursuing a telecommunications/film degree at San Diego State University. After "testing the waters" in nonunion television and wearing many different production hats (including camera operator, news production coordinator, videotape editor, assistant director, director, and producer), Kathleen decided it was filmmaking that she really wanted to pursue. Her "foot in the door" in the film industry came through a college roommate working with Producer John Milius, who told Kathleen that a production assistant, "someone who runs around and gets coffee and answers phones," was needed on *1941*, a film that Milius was producing and Steven Spielberg was directing.

Proving her production talents on *1941*, Kathleen was promoted to associate producer by Spielberg on *Raiders of the Lost Ark*. Toward the end of production on *Raiders*, Spielberg asked Kathleen to co-produce a picture that he was preparing, at the time still untitled. That picture eventually became the highest-grossing film in the history of motion pictures—*E.T.* She has gone on to produce and/or executive produce such films as *Back to the Future*, *Indiana Jones and the Temple of Doom*, *Poltergeist*, *The Color Purple*, *Who Framed Roger Rabbit?*, *Gremlins*, *Young Sherlock Holmes*, *The Money Pit*, *Batteries Not Included*, *An American Tail*, *Innerspace*, and *The Land Before Time*. In early 1988 she became president of Steven Spielberg's film-producing company, Amblin' Entertainment.

First Break

AFTER THREE weeks on *1941*, the producer called me up and said, "Steven needs somebody to help organize the special effects. Can you do that?" I thought, If I say yes, I'll either sink or swim, but if I say no, I may lose my only shot. So I said yes. Of course, there's something about being twenty-three years old that allows you to do that.

I come from a very small town, Weaverville in northern California, of one thousand people. Going to someone's Beverly Hills home—forget meeting Steven Spielberg—*that* in and of itself was incredibly intimidating. I was in a bit of a fog walking into his house, but he was very warm and made me feel comfortable.

He had little pieces of paper, backs of envelopes, tops of newspapers, anything he could get his hands on, on which he had written these notes and camera shots, drawn little figures. And he said, "Can you take these and make some sense of it?" He said if I wanted to work at his house, that would be fine. If I wanted to go back to the office, that was fine, too. "Just call me from the office if you have any questions."

The only thing going through my mind was, I can't work here because he'll figure out I don't know how to type. So I gathered everything together and headed back to the office. I poured myself into this, all day, all night, going through, redrawing the little drawings, calling him a few times to clarify things I didn't understand. And I made these little booklets, which I had stacked up on his desk when he came in. He was blown away. It seemed to me a certain amount of common sense, but for whatever reason, he had never had anyone organize things for him in that way before. From that point on, he gave me little jobs to do, things he wanted me to take care of.

When we finished *1941*, Steven didn't have a producer working with him on a regular basis. His assistant had just left, and there was no one in the office. He asked me to work with him. This was right in the beginning of preparation for *Raiders of the Lost Ark*. I met Frank Marshall, whom I'm now married to, who had been prepping the film for a year and a half. When I came on board Frank was the only person on the picture. There were only the three of us. Steven had us doing everything, including building little models to set up the truck chase. I remember deciding between us who gets the passenger carrier, who gets the motorcycle, and taking them home to work on them over Thanksgiving. I was just having a good time. I didn't think about where it was leading. When Steven asked me to produce his next film, what later turned out to be *E.T.*, I was shocked. It seemed to come from out of the blue, but I think it was because he felt confident about the way I got things done for him. He had come to rely on me to get things done. And that is basically what a producer does.

The Meaning of the Word

"Producer" seems to be the most abused title in the business. Unlike writers and directors, who had gotten organized early on, producers in the thirties and forties (though many were creative) were primarily businessmen, and many were studio heads.

Today, it's a title that often ends up being given away—sometimes in lieu of money. Somebody's friend had an idea but doesn't really know anything about making movies, and in order not to have to pay exorbitant rights—payments, whatever—he is given a producing title and a nominal amount of money. There are what I call "broker producers"—people who package or get financing together. And there are line producers who come on in preproduction and leave the picture before postproduction and are nonexclusive in the postproduction phase.

So the term *producer* can refer to a number of different functions. I can only speak for how I, as a producer, have come to function in this operation. The way the relationship between myself and Steven and Frank evolved has led to us getting involved in every single aspect of producing.

We are also fortunate because we do not have to go out and raise every dime to make our movies. The tremendous luxury we have is being able to pick up the telephone, call a studio of our choice, sit down with them, present a piece of material, and, for the most part, they're more than happy to make the film with us. It still doesn't make the process easy—the work still has to be done. But there's something very satisfying about being able to put most of your time and energy into the creative process rather than into running around trying to raise money. I have tremendous respect for producers in the independent world, because they've got to do it all—raise the money, keep costs down, plus struggle with the distribution, which is also an area where we don't find ourselves doing a lot of struggling. It gives us a great deal of freedom.

Taking all that into account, I tend to drift toward things that I like to do. The things I don't like to do—one of them being postproduction—Frank happens to love. He does most of that. Steven, obviously, has a tremendous amount of clout in the decision-making process. I address that to some degree, but my heaviest input is in the development process.

Finding and Developing Material

This company always looks for a good story. That sounds very simplistic, and the obvious reply is, "Well, doesn't everybody?" But you'd be surprised—it is the most difficult thing to find. There is a great deal of pressure now to develop material around certain casting and packaging possibilities. I understand the need for that in some cases. It can be a valuable way of developing the material. We happen not to have those sensibilities. We tend not to use the television approach because television is almost entirely packaging. *Ideas are most important* to us.

It can be an idea that originates within this company among the three of us. It can come from somebody on the outside who comes in and pitches. It can be a book or a script that has been submitted to us.

We're fairly strict about how material gets in. We tend to be as selective as possible, otherwise we'd be inundated. We used to have a strict policy where we did not accept any unsolicited material. It's a very unfortunate position to have to be in because it doesn't allow the people who are not *in* the system to get access to us. But because we have had lawsuits on every movie we've ever made, we've had to very carefully institute a system that effectively screens a certain amount of material. Now we send out a "submissions release" to anybody who sends us a screenplay who is not represented by a bona-fide agency, which protects us to some degree. And in some cases, we have to say, "No, we won't accept it," and if they say, "Well, how do I get it to you?" then usually my advice is, "Try and get an agent." I realize the catch-22 inherent in that, but we came to a point where we had to draw the line.

In the last three years, our development staff has increased to about five people, which includes three full-time and two part-time readers, and that helps get through the volume of work. And then we have a fairly informal system of sitting around and talking about who likes what and keeping track of what writers we like and pinpointing certain projects that we know we are very definitely moving forward on.

Making the Picture

On pictures that we are executive producing—such as the sequel to *Back to the Future*—I will get involved, as will Steven and Frank, in the script and casting phases. But once we move into production we don't come in "on the line," the way we do with anything that Steven directs. On pictures we executive produce, we'll bring on a line producer to do the budget, and we'll hire the production manager, who then gets involved in hiring the crew and setting up a schedule. We'll oversee the project in an executive capacity by working with the director creatively on the screenplay and the cast, but once the picture goes into production we back off. Unless a serious problem arises, that picture should be proceeding the way we and the director want it to in preproduction. There should be no real need for us to be wandering around making production decisions.

In the postproduction phase, we'll come back on board to get the promotion and merchandising campaigns going and work through to the overall distribution and selling of the picture. We work very closely with the studio publicity staff and/or outside agencies that may or may not be brought in for one sheets (publicity/advertising posters) and any other element involved in selling the picture.

We get very involved in the score, which is probably one of the most enjoyable parts of making the movie—sitting on a scoring stage— especially if it's John Williams and an eighty-five-piece orchestra.

We also get very involved in looking at rough cuts. The preview process, depending on the picture, requires varying amounts of time. If you're doing a comedy, you usually find that you want to preview that picture at least four or five times because audiences can really help you with timing. If you're doing a picture like *The Color Purple* or *Empire of the Sun*, the audience is not *vocally* going to tell you much. Consequently we rely more on our own gut reactions and don't do a lot of previewing with those kinds of pictures.

We get involved with everything that happens with the foreign markets. We pull in all the dubbing directors. We listen to all the voice tests, then screen and choose every voice that's replacing a major actor in the picture. And we oversee the mix. Often when pictures are dubbed in foreign countries, they will boost the dialogue and kill everything else. We want to ensure that there's a balance in the final mix. That's certainly a side of things that most producers do not get involved in. That usually becomes a studio function, a distributor function, but because we feel that creatively we have invested so much time and energy in the movie, we want to take responsibility for that phase.

When Steven directs a movie, the process becomes different.

When we do step in on the line—something I'm doing somewhat less of since I've become president of the company—we remain involved in all the preproduction aspects with the script and casting. But then we continue to stay very involved in hiring the crew and supervising the day-in, day-out process of making the film—which we don't do in an executive producer capacity.

What Is Looked For

The execution of those ideas that we decide to make into a film becomes crucial. You can have—on the page—a beautifully described sequence of events, but in order to make a good script into a great movie, you need individuals who then take that script one step further and bring in fresh ideas, many of which you may not be able to use, but some of the best you can take off the top.

There again we have the luxury of being able to attract some of the best people. We also sit in the fairly good position of being able to work with, in some cases, very high budgets, which allow us to experiment and do the kinds of things that many people only dream of doing. But we recognize the responsibility inherent in that, so we try to go after the best people available. There's really only a handful when you get down to the technical side of getting a movie made—directors of photography, even to the extent of a really good prop man and everyone in between. *All of those people* make a huge difference because they all have a creative contribution.

When Steven directs, he is completely open to ideas from anybody. You never know when the best boy's going to walk up and say, "Have you ever thought of . . . ?" If you're not open to that, then you shut it off and it never happens. All it takes is one little suggestion sometimes to make a shot extraordinary. A terrific example is in *Raiders of the Lost Ark*, when we were running a bit behind in our shooting in Tunisia. We had a three-day shoot planned for a sequence involving a swordsman, and at lunch, Harrison Ford and Steven were talking about what they were going to do and how hot it was and when could we get out of here. And they came up with the idea of shooting the swordsman. Immediately three days were gone and we had one of the funniest moments in the movie.

One very important aspect of producing is always staying on the case. I used to take common sense for granted until I finally realized that there are a lot of people who don't have common sense. Once you come to that realization, you stop assuming things. The incredible thing about making a movie is that it's over a period of time and you can *never* let up. What I mean by "letting up" is the minute you start to say, "Oh, it's good enough," you're in trouble. You've got to constantly, with each phase of the process, be paying attention to every minute detail. That's why in the key categories in filmmaking, you need to absolutely rely on good people. They're the ones who have to be constantly coming to the director saying—when there's time—"Hey, wait a second, this doesn't work, this would be better." And for us, too, one of the most important functions a producer can provide is coming up with alternatives, *not* just describing what's wrong.

Prioritizing

I think of making movies in three phases. There is the preproduction phase, the principal photography phase, and the postproduction phase. Your priorities completely shift depending on what phase you're in. Now because many of our movies overlap, I find myself having to be somewhat schizophrenic. I try to set aside creative thinking time, which is crucial during the preproduction phase. You can get very caught up in an activity trap of trying to get your phone calls made, trying to get everything read. I'm finally at the point, after three or four years, where I feel I have a very good staff and am very comfortable delegating.

Ultimately, the most important thing about what we do is putting in the time with the writers and the directors and the actual production of getting a movie made. I have a loose priority system—with those movies we're about to start on rating top priority. Everything else I tend to focus on depending on my particular passion.

I try to maintain relationships with people on the outside as best and honestly as I can. If I really don't think I've got time to spend with somebody and it's frankly not a priority, I'll tell them that. It is very easy to keep people hanging because you don't want to hurt their feelings, but ultimately you waste everybody's time, so I try to be up-front right away instead of trying to string people along.

Staffing

I always look for someone who has certain organizational skills. But I've learned over the last few years that people are only as good as you train them to be. When things don't go right, you have to take the time to sit down and explain, "I know you were trying to do this, but here's how I need to have it done." That is the way you progress with someone.

The two people I have now did not have a great deal of film background. It was frustrating in the beginning for all concerned, but in the long run it was easier than if I'd had someone who might have known a great deal about film but had set ideas about how things should be done. I would take a phone list and say, "Do you know why this person called?" And if they didn't know why, we'd talk about it—who they were, what it was I was involved in. The perfect working situation is for me to have my assistant listening in on everything I say and do because I don't always have the time to go through everything with them a second time. Some employers are threatened by that, but I feel that the best people are those who are motivated to move beyond their particular position because they have been stimulated and have a desire to learn even more.

I will, however, forewarn them, "I'll teach you everything I know, but I want you here for two or three years." That's very important to me. As much as they may look at me—especially women who come into this company and think, If she did it, I can do it—I have to remind them, "Yes, you can, but not necessarily here. Here is where I've invested years to get to where I am, and in order for you to start the way I did, you have to find a Steven Spielberg who has no one. You have to find a new, relatively unknown filmmaker or a small nonunion company to make your break and then work your way up." Unfortunately, when they come in here—it's sort of starting at the top, and there's really nowhere to go. Unless Frank or myself walk out the door, they're not going to produce Amblin' movies. It's always a difficult thing to prepare people for because they don't want to believe it. They think, If I can just get my foot in the door, that's it. It's certainly a great overview, but it isn't necessarily *it*.

I think a secretarial or assistant position is one of the most valuable positions to be in. In fact, it's unfortunate that most guys probably feel uncomfortable going in and taking a secretarial job because it is one of the best places to start. If you get in as a secretary or as an assistant with a producer or director, you're the *only* person who has access to the entire filmmaking process. That is, of course, if you hook up with someone who allows you that opportunity. If you have someone who shuts you out, then it can be just answering the phones and bringing in mail and coffee.

21

Teamwork

I was extremely active in sports when I was young, played on the boys' football team in sixth and seventh grades as a quarterback. Only because it was a little tiny town and it boiled down to "If you can throw the ball, then you get the job." And I could throw the ball. Sports gave me a tremendous insight into how business works. Not just because it's a male-dominated arena and therefore gave me a window on understanding how men think, but because I really think that's how business works.

Women who have made it in a managerial capacity have those values of wanting to include their staff in on what they do. When women do not make it, it's usually because they do not understand teamwork. Those women tend to operate on a very one-on-one basis. They especially get threatened by other women. There tends to be a notion of "It's up to me. *I'm* going to succeed. *I'm* going to make this work." There is a tendency to veer away from involving everyone in a team effort. That's changing gradually. I like to believe that people like me and Lucy Fisher and Dawn Steel and Sherry Lansing will be the role models who will make men feel more comfortable with women in that capacity and who will inspire other women to strive for more. Hopefully, now, the socialization process is changing and little girls are being given that access to team sports. I'm not saying it's the only way, but it certainly is a very valuable way to understand that you need *all* those people to get across the goal line, not just one outstanding athlete.

And in that same vein, I find it much more dynamic to have both men and women working creatively. If men and women are going to see movies, then shouldn't they be made by men *and* women? I don't agree with the "male voice" and "female voice" theory. That's like saying that a screenplay depicting a woman's story should only be written by a woman. When it comes to creativity, it crosses genders. I don't think you can identify certain characteristics that are *only* in women or *only* in men. I've found men who have incredible insight into what I consider to be female traits. And vice versa. It's all in your ability to observe. The most creative people are those who have an uncanny ability to observe other people and what's going on around them.

Advice

Many young people coming out of school don't have any idea what they want to do. Nor should they necessarily. There are always the Stevens who started making movies when they were eleven years old, but the majority don't really know—in any occupation—what they want to do. *Even so,* it's very important to focus in on certain immediate goals.

There seems to be that impatience with many of the students I talk to coming out of film school. All they talk about is wanting to be a producer, a writer, or a director. On top of that, they really haven't done any research to find out what those jobs are all about. They haven't broken things down to figure out, "Okay, in paying dues, what kind of a job should I be thinking of going after in order to get there?" They're only looking at the end result, and they have no idea what the course of action should be to get there. That is when the obnoxious traits come in—being aggressive, energetic, and enthusiastic over nothing tangible. For somebody in my position, what do I do with this person—this bundle of energy with no direction?

I have never had someone come in here and say, "You know what I'm really interested in is distributing movies." They just want to *make* them. Yet there is a vast number of interesting opportunities in the marketing area. They aren't looking at all the different avenues in the film business that may eventually give them the opportunity to produce or direct. Writing I put off to the side because all you need is a piece of paper and a pencil. Anybody who comes in and says, "I really want to write," is ridiculous. Then I say, "Go write."

But certainly with producing, you can go many different ways. And the challenge for the enthusiastic person breaking in is to ask themselves, What's a job that could lead me there eventually?

My advice is that a production assistant position is an excellent opportunity to get into the business, *but* the PA position is there for one reason. It's like the mailroom job you read about in the Selznick days, which still exists, but without quite the glamour it used to have. It's the opportunity to meet people, to get an overview of the business and to get a sense of where you might want to go. And I don't think anybody should stay in a PA position for more than a year. At that point, they should have a fairly good idea of where they want to be heading.

In my case, the whole television experience gave me a very interesting overview of many different areas within the business which are quite applicable to the job of producing. At the time, I didn't know exactly what I wanted to do, but now I realize that my education, which was predominantly telecommunications, journalism, and an emphasis in management, did not necessarily focus on any particular job, and my background in television has helped me tremendously.

From the time I was sixteen, I was always in a huge hurry. When I was a sophomore in high school, all I wanted was to be in college. Finally, one of my college professors, who is now in the film business, said to me, "You should slow down for a minute here, you don't need to be in such a hurry." This was good for me. I backed off, got involved in my job in television, started to feel I didn't have to speed through school. I came very close several times to just dropping out. It is difficult to work full-time and try to stay in school. And since I was working in the business I had essentially decided I wanted to be in, there were moments when I thought, "This is a waste of time." But looking back, I'm really glad I stuck with it. I appreciate now that I took the time to finish. I *am* still in a hurry, but I tend to be meticulous, too. So even if I'm racing, I won't do things halfway.

Screenwriter

A Screenwriter creates the characters, dialogue, dramatic situations, and written aspects of a film story. The screenplay he or she composes is used to attract talent to the project, to raise funds for its production, and as a constant blueprint or reference guide for all those involved with the making of the motion picture.

Alvin Sargent

ALVIN SARGENT grew up in a suburb outside of Philadelphia. He left high school during World War II to join the Navy and later entered the UCLA theater department. In the fifties he sought work as a television actor in New York "without much success." Moving to the West Coast, he landed a job selling advertising space for a trade paper, got married, had two children, and worked for nine more years selling advertising. He was thirty-five years old when a friend gave samples of his writing work to a man named Sam Adams, who became his agent. He soon won assignments writing for television shows like *Ben Casey*, *Naked City*, *Route 66*, *Alfred Hitchcock Presents*, *The Nurses*, and *Mr. Novak*. Eventually, through Alan Pakula, whom he had met earlier working in a Los

Angeles theater, Mr. Sargent was given the assignment of writing the movie adaptation of a book called *The Sterile Cuckoo*. He subsequently has gone on to write, among other films, Academy Award–winning screenplays for *Ordinary People* and *Julia*, and, most recently, the screenplay for Orion's *Dominick and Eugene*.

Getting Started

I WAS in the Signal Corps in the navy and learned Morse Code. There I learned to type. Once out, I found myself a small typewriter. I didn't think of myself as a writer so much as a typist. I made rows of soldiers with Ks and 7s, men with top hats with Ns, Ms, and Ps, and one-legged women with Ws and Is. Then I'd compose little playlets, and scenes to go along with them. It never occurred to me to make a career out of writing. After all, I was making a big $100 a week selling advertising at a Hollywood trade paper in 1962. I was there nine years.

I was introduced to Sam Adams, who was just starting as an agent. I had written a few scenes. Just a hobby. Bits and pieces. Sam took my work to the producer of a television show at Fox called *Bus Stop* (based on the play). Sam said, "I can get you a job as a story editor on this show, do you want it?" I thought, "Hell, I'm secure, I'm making $100 a week as an ad salesman, I've got two little kids and a new house. I'd better not. Besides, I don't know anything about editing other people's work." Sam said, "I can get you an eight-week guarantee for $250 a week. Take it." I was thirty-five years old. It was now or never. I bit the bullet. Eight weeks! I'd certainly be there longer than that. I wasn't.

I didn't even know what a story editor did. All I remember is that anybody who came in with an idea, any idea at all, impressed me. I was in awe of the writer's mind. Whatever they offered, I said "Wonderful! Wonderful!" They must have thought I was some sort of a nut. I was never even introduced to the producer. Eight weeks later I got the boot. Two months after that, so did the show.

I waited. Checked the want ads. The trade paper didn't have my old job available. I did some writing exercises, stared into the hills, played with my babies, and wondered what time would bring. Three months later the money was gone, and then, on New Year's Eve 1962 a call came from Sam. "I got you a rewrite on a *Ben Casey* TV show." *Ben Casey!* TV's big, hot drama. Me? *Ben Casey?* Something in me stirred, something out of my education as a child in movie houses believed I could write what had to be written for the screen. I did a fair job. Good enough to get another assignment. From time to time I began to think of myself as a real writer. I worked in television with some very smart people, patient people, good teachers.

After five years of writing dramatic TV Sam called. "Got you a job. Rewrite a movie." Something called *Gambit*. I got a credit. I was in the feature business.

Then my friend Alan Pakula, whom I'd worked with in the late forties at the Circle Theatre in Los Angeles (I was an actor then) called to ask me to adapt a novel he had optioned called *The Sterile Cuckoo*. It would be Alan's first directorial work, my first solo screenplay credit, Liza Minnelli's first starring role. It was nicely received.

Learning the Language

Growing up in Pennsylvania, I would go five, six times a week to the movies if I could. The language of movies became my second language: the cuts, all the story telling devices, camera angles, transitions, flashbacks, long dialogue, short dialogue, no dialogue. When I left the movie theater and came into the bright daylight, I was never as at home as I was inside that theater. Security was knowing I could get back into a movie house.

Writing a movie is simply going to the movies. Nothing more, nothing less. I am always the audience, watching the screen. If I can see the movie, hear the movie, then I can be writing the movie. There is nothing more to put into a script than what is exactly seen, exactly heard! The screenplay is a work of pure objectivity born out of pleasant and painful invention.

The Process

You're a writer. You write. I usually write at home. I've worked at the studios, but it has never felt comfortable. Too much like college. Not that I went to one. I only had a high school education, but quit to go into the navy. It's only recently that I have left home to write in a studio. Only recently have I had any connection with anyone on the film other than the director. The fewer contacts with producers, executives (a few exceptions), the better. Privacy is important. Keep your work to yourself or share it with one you trust who can be a sounding board and with whom you won't feel you've given away the power of your ideas. It is a delicate thing, the work, the private work. Don't ask it to be born too early. It will appear when it's ready. You need, though, to encourage it and, at times, take the whip to it.

The screenplay is a blueprint. There's an exactness about it. It is architecture. It is not prose. Do not write poetry. It is not a poem. It is not a novel. Don't try to impress anyone, or yourself with your poetic directions. Be clear. Be simple.

I've never thought about directing, though I feel I'm directing when I write. I am the first director. As for being "the" director, I would do it if I didn't have to show up everyday. But I don't get things right enough the first time. There'd be too many takes, and I don't enjoy being on the set. I've worked on the set, and there's little more tiresome in life than hanging around while a movie's being shot.

I've actually collaborated twice. I do not operate well in a collaborative situation. I can't be free. I can't take the necessary chances and learn from my mistakes. I can't be foolish and outrageous. Alone is best, with your own toys. Naked.

On Being Rewritten

A reality of this industry for a writer is that you can suddenly be rewritten. (I've done it, it's been done to me once.) Have something as important in your life as your writing, something to retreat to, because it hurts. And it's angering. And sometimes you have to swallow your pride because you've failed or you've been led to believe you have. But if you write your own original work, you can own it and fight for it. You can peddle it, but the moves are yours to control. How deeply you believe in yourself, your work is gauged by what you're willing to give up or your need for money.

I like to listen to other people's comments on my work. I'll try almost any idea that somebody I'm working with or not working with throws at me. Insight pops out of the minds of the most unlikely people.

I've been fortunate that most of my work has not been tampered with. But when it has, and I am in disagreement, then there is a battle at hand. What began as a private struggle so many months or years ago, in an empty room with ten reams of paper has graduated into a full blown war.

You need a strong ego. I don't know how you can survive without one. As a writer, you stand alone. Your ego is you with your typewriter and your pieces of paper. I still use a Standard manual machine. I thrill at how it slides around the table. Sometimes it falls off or tries to. It's a real friend, the right machine. It's a musical instrument. I have six of them. And each has slid off the table at one time or another. One died.

My confidence grows or dissolves with each day's work. As I work and start to see "it" happening and realize that I'm moving somewhere, that there's some kind of real life, then it's a good day.

But when it doesn't seem to be working for a long time, or you just can't find a truth, then the terror sets in. You must not stop. You cannot give in to anxiety. Maintain energy. Drive. Rage. Whatever it takes to keep writing. Do not masturbate when writing.

Even though you can't immediately solve problems, that doesn't mean the work isn't alive. You have to go *back*. Back to the beginning. The process is to move into it, come up to it, step by step, find out where you've hit it wrong, what's dishonest. Where you've gone wrong usually involves a matter of honesty. You've been dishonest either to the character or to the structure of the piece. Or just to the nature of the style of the piece.

Everybody has his own process. Now I guess people's minds are working a little differently with word processors. Like everyone, I write on matchbooks and all kinds of loose pages, napkins, etc., but finally put it on the typewriter. I've been collecting some old pages of my scripts with scribbled-in corrections, massive markings, filled with the emotion of that day. They are so alive. Filled with energy. I believe that a page of writing has its own energy, a pure energy. When a director can transcribe that energy to the screen, then he can make happen what the writer has intended. Too often the director and other craftsmen ignore or dislodge the writer's energy and an original concept is slain. I'm not very orderly, so I create great confusion—more now than ever. This has not been to my advantage. However, strangely enough, out of the confusions, the ruins, comes the structure.

On-Screen

Seeing my work on screen never means as much as it does seeing it on paper. Nothing is as fulfilling to me as *doing* it, writing it down.

Because I know things I've written, and sometimes they are hard to touch, to get on-screen. However certain filmed sequences do get it fully, actually capture the page. That's exciting, to see the original work, "life" as I perceived it.

But in terms of, "Hey, there's a movie and I wrote it," that's never been a major thrill. I am extremely grateful to be successful at this—and to see the films *made*. But when the writing is successful, that's much more exciting to me than when the film is successful. I'm disappointed if the film doesn't work, and I'm happy when it does, but it's the writing itself that renews my courage. *Encourage*—a great word when it is born of oneself.

I don't think winning an Oscar for me was the ultimate in recognition. When I heard my name announced, I went back to being an actor. I was going up on a stage in front of millions of people. It's exciting, and you want to win. But if you don't win, well we, most of us, start out getting used to losing, so we're mostly more ready to lose than to win. Of course that attitude will never get a screenplay written.

Adaptation

I don't think an adaptation is much different from writing an original screenplay. Once you have the material that you're going to make this quilt from and sew together, then the process of telling the story, writing the screenplay, is essentially the same. I can't see any difference. Again it's understanding architecture.

If you are using outside material—then maybe the challenge is a little different in the sense that you're confined to certain things. But once you start seeing/hearing the movie, the process is, essentially, the same.

Mostly, I have adapted. And there is, of course, often immense original work in some adaptations. But sometimes I feel like a legitimate crook.

Julia

With a book, mostly you use pieces of it. Very much of *Julia* is suggested in the book. Sometimes I use just one line from original material; it gives me a sense of something and it can explode into a large piece of the story. I would go over and over that novella, search for things that felt strong for me, moments I finally knew would end up being somewhere in the movie. I came to know these characters and slowly created my pieces of the quilt, patches of scenes slowly leading to a structure.

Lillian Hellman and I became pretty close friends. She was tough, very smart and loyal, and usually difficult, even unkind, but always alert and extremely insightful.

In *Julia*, she wanted Hammett served well. She never liked the search for the baby. In my script, Lillian (Jane Fonda) returns to Europe to search for Julia's baby. Lillian and I had a terrible argument over that. She lost, but she was, in retrospect, more right than not. The sequence, while it was not dishonest, lacked something. It needed more. It lost style, it was not designed well on paper. She was pleased with the way Hammett was written, scenes not in her book at all. Lillian made a suggestion for the last scene, wrote a page, and I used it. Hammett's scenes, I think, and she agreed, were the freshest work in the screenplay.

Ordinary People

The origins were Robert Redford's and his strong attachment to the book and, particularly, to the character of the mother, her need for control. He has always said the theme of the movie is "communicating."

When he sent me the book, I had great admiration for the story, but I didn't want to write it. I didn't know if it was just going to be another soap opera, melodrama. I finally agreed to have a go at it and tried all sorts of outlandish approaches, ways that were far removed from the structure of the book.

I think the first scene I wrote, just to get loose, was of the house burning down and the family standing out on the front lawn, total chaos. What a mess. The Christmas tree had caught fire. It was a form of therapy for me, to get me going, to show me a way. Of course, the house never burned. It took me about fifteen months to write the first draft, I worked with Redford for a little time at the beginning. He kept me straight, kept me from burning down houses.

Finally, I went away and came back with the screenplay about a year late. Then we worked together—writer and director. He was wonderful, he knew what he wanted it to be. We both understood this movie. Then I went off again, reworked it, came back, and we worked on it again. Delicate work sometimes, sometimes harsh strokes, sometimes oh, so delicate. Delicate moves in the midst of harsh exchanges. The structure was always right. Choices of new scenes and subtleties were the issues. A hard, satisfying time.

Commercial Concerns

I can't think about the commercial concerns when I'm working. Again, I am the audience. I know when it is doing its job. When it is solidly right, there is a golden alarm that goes off in your head and you have earned a glass of scotch. But it takes time to know. The golden alarm doesn't go off as often as it used to. The standards get tougher. Less scotch.

Sometimes I've had to change a script to fit an actor. A lot of the changes I've had to make have been pretty true to the screenplay. And when it is, I always think it's better for it. But some actors change things. Often they have wonderful ideas—brilliant—and they execute them brilliantly. Extemporaneous, an important word . . . as an exercise. But extemporaneous dialogue is almost never successful. It is my pet peeve. The results are usually "cute" and represent a refusal to honor the script. (Though I must admit, some scripts shouldn't be taken seriously.)

Advice

You must write everyday. Free yourself. Free association. An hour alone a day. Blind writing. Write in the dark. Don't think about what it is you're writing. Just put a piece of paper in the typewriter, take your clothes off and go! No destination . . . pay it no attention . . . it's pure unconscious exercise. Pages of it. Keep it up until embarrassment disappears. Eliminate resistance. Look at it in the morning. Amazing sometimes. Most of it won't make any sense. But there'll always be a small kernel of truth that relates to what you're working on at the time. You won't even know you created it. It will appear, and it is yours. Pure gold, a product of that pure part of you that does not know how to resist.

Finally, think of a screenplay in two ways. It takes the form of a joke or a dream. Dreams and well told jokes are always beautifully designed, exquisitely cut. We hear, see, only what's necessary. There is never any deadwood. Never a dull moment. Always unpredictable, always the surprise. The audience cannot sit there and write it before it comes on the screen. That is my guide. The architecture of the dream, the joke.

Director

The Director is head of the production unit and is responsible for directing the actors and for translating the screenplay into cinematic images in accordance with his vision. He or she works closely with the writer, production designer, and director of photography in this translation, with the casting director in the selection of the actors, with the sound department on the sound, with the editor in the assembly of the film, and with the composer on the score. The Director depends upon the producer and production manager for the financial and technical aspects and on the first assistant director and script supervisor for the organization of the set and logistical aspects of accomplishing his task. All crew members ultimately answer to the Director.

Taylor Hackford

TAYLOR HACKFORD first began to view film as a serious medium when he was a prelaw international relations major at USC. In the late sixties, a time when politics, cinema, and contemporary music came together to express social and political foment, Taylor found himself drifting away from the course laid out for him. Upon graduation, after serving as student body president and being accepted into law school, he opted instead to join the Peace Corps and go to Bolivia. There he started a Peace Corps newspaper and got a taste for expressing himself in a public medium.

On his return to the United States, he attended law school for two weeks, realized he no longer wanted to be a lawyer, and quit. Forfeiting all of his tuition monies, he obtained a job in the mailroom of KCET, Los Angeles's public television station. At the understaffed station, Taylor was asked if he could shoot film. Never having done so, he said, "yes," got a book, and taught himself how. In time he got a chance to do a little bit of everything—edit film, write, appear on-camera, associate produce, and then produce cultural and music shows. He eventually made documentaries, won a few Emmys and Associated Press Awards and a Peabody Award for television journalism. During this time, he also frequented movie houses, viewing some six to ten films per week, catching up on foreign and American classics as well as contemporary releases.

After seven years at KCET, Taylor's career was very much in the vein of hard-news investigative reporting, but he found himself losing enthusiasm for straight reportage. The station, which had received backlash from corporations due to Taylor's documentaries dealing with illegal American business practices, began to opt for softer programming. At this crossroads, Taylor decided to see if he could make it as a filmmaker, quit KCET, and, after six months of unemployment, got an assignment to do a short film to be used in high school for sex education classes. Rather than doing a straight documentary, he wrote, produced, and directed *Teenage Father* using actors, which won him an Academy Award for Best Short Film and serious attention from the Hollywood film community. He was hired to rewrite the screenplay of *The Idolmaker* and subsequently to direct it. Since then, he has established himself as a major Hollywood director with such films as *Against All Odds, An Officer and a Gentleman, White Nights,* and *Everybody's All-American.* He also co-produced *La Bamba* and will be executive producing his new mini-studio New Visions Pictures' first slate of films: *Rooftops, Defenseless, Confidence, The Long Walk Home,* and *Queens Logic.* Hackford assures us that this is a temporary sojourn as a movie executive, and he plans to return to directing after he successfully establishes his new company.

THE ESSENCE of feature filmmaking is leadership. Directing a film is not a solitary art form like being a painter, alone with a canvas, or a writer at a typewriter. In order to get your vision onto the screen, you need to use the talents of other people . . . to collaborate. No one can do it by himself. So as a director, what you really need to be is a leader, a decision maker, and also a keen judge of talent.

The Foundation

Everything in the film industry is based on source material. It is the director's medium, but the writer is the one building the foundation, and if you don't have that foundation, I don't care how brilliant the filmmaker, how fantastic the cast, how spectacular the cinematography and production design, it will be an unsatisfying film because it will be based on a faulty foundation.

The age-old battle between the screenwriter and the director is very real. Faced with this conflict, the director has three choices: (1) work out a collaborative relationship with the original writer; (2) bring in a new writer who shares the director's vision; or (3) rewrite the script him or herself.

My first feature, *The Idolmaker*, had an existing script, but I came in and wrote two drafts. I was the final screenwriter. On all my other films, I've worked in collaboration with a writer. Douglas Day Stewart, who wrote *An Officer and a Gentleman*, had worked and reworked the script for five years before I saw it. I then added my own perspective before we shot. However, with *Everybody's All-American*, we stayed very close to Tom Rickman's first draft. *Against All Odds* and *White Nights* I developed from scratch collaborating with Eric Hughes and James Goldman.

Despite the inherent problems of fusing two creative points of view, I would personally always prefer to collaborate with the writer. Unless it's an incredibly personal piece, most writers are better at putting words on the page than I am. However, I feel that I am much better at guiding them toward what will work best on the screen.

Finally, if you get something on paper you're happy with, you're ready to go out and try to match the unique talents of other artists with the qualities of the script. The production designer comes first, and he or she should be involved with the director on the next rewrite of the script.

Working with the Production Designer

Production designers are architects, painters, builders. The crucial time spent with the production designer is the transition from literary to visual conception. This work must take the inspiration off the page and actualize the environment. Hopefully, the production designer will introduce a new point of view, propose visual ideas you never even considered.

Everybody's All-American covers twenty-five years—a huge challenge, and a production designer's nightmare. You don't just jump from 1956 to 1981, you stop at eight or nine time periods along the way. Every time you stop, there are major design changes. America changed its appearance drastically over those twenty-five years. Franchises didn't exist in 1956; foreign cars were barely on the road; hairstyles, clothes, everything changed.

Moreover, production designer Joe Alves and I had horrific design problems—like seeing Gavin Gray, the Gray Ghost, the greatest running back of his generation, performing heroic acts in the middle of a football stadium with eighty thousand cheering fans rooting him on. That's not an easy shot. Are we going to matte it? Are we going to shoot it for real?

You try to solve these problems with your designer and his or her collaborators: costume designer, prop master, special effects coordinator, construction team, etc. It's initially a very close collaboration; then you send them off to build the city. That's the thing—you hire people who are masters at what they do and let them do it—let *them* hire their own army. However, the director must constantly check in and evaluate the progress. Adjustments are easier, and much less expensive, if you can make them early. *Early* is the key word here. Going through the script with your practical collaborators before you budget can make the difference between whether a project gets done or doesn't. Therefore, design problems must be solved in the final rewrite.

The Production Manager

Filmmaking is accomplishing the impossible, but there are always limits. Any amount of time and money can solve a problem. But the questions are do you have the time *and* do you have the money? Certain scenes may be just too impractical to shoot, or if shot, may cause you to lose what are truly essential scenes. It's a medium in which someone will finally tell you, "You've spent enough on this." That *someone* is your production manager.

The PM is very important because he or she has the fiscal command of the picture. I do often use a line producer, but still the production manager is the person who actually writes the checks, deals with labor problems, and oversees all the location deals and logistics.

I always hire production managers who have been first assistant directors because they've been out on the battlefield and understand the practical realities of production. Sometimes you can't choose the most economical solution to a problem because it might inhibit the creative process; for instance, an actor may be in the middle of a scene and won't be able to re-create the emotional circumstances of a performance on another day. If that's the case, you may decide to go into overtime regardless of the costs. In *White Nights*, when Mikhail Baryshnikov was dancing with an injured achilles tendon, we had to shoot only when he was healthy, regardless of budget constraints, or we wouldn't have gotten the dance sequences. A production manager who's been on the floor and has worked with talent will understand this, while an accountant may not. Whether it's a student film or a feature film, it always comes down to the practical realities of your budget.

On the other hand, I have never come in *under* budget. I'm not saying that you should aspire to coming in over budget, but in a strange way, if you come in under budget, you're either not pushing your full potential or somebody has done a bad job budgeting the film.

Every minute of time and ounce of energy that I spend shooting is amazingly precious. I'm not Clint Eastwood. I don't quit early. He's finished by noon and that's fine, but his philosophy of filmmaking and mine are different. I'll go until the last ray of sunlight; they have to yank the camera away from me. It's not indecision—I know what I want—it's a different style. To me, if you go home at twelve noon, you're missing major opportunities to try and get something a little bit better on the screen.

Working with the Director of Photography

The visual concept of the film, which was first defined by the writer, director, and production designer is difficult to finalize without the director of photography. I like to involve a DP as early as possible. I look for a great painter, someone who paints with light. I happen to like natural light keys.

It is wonderful to develop a look with your DP that incorporates the unique nature of a geographical location. For instance, in *An Officer and a Gentleman*, Don Thorin and I wanted to use that overcast, natural diffusion that's created by all the cloud cover and rain in Washington state. On *Against All Odds*, I worked with Don again. It was a very bright picture. I wanted to do a film noir in the sun, a dark film in mood and timbre, set against Los Angeles' sunny landscape. When we shot in Mexico, the light was even more intense—that's the style I was looking for.

On *White Nights*, I worked with David Watkin, who has in many ways defined contemporary key lighting. We tried to portray a Russian reality, the white nights in Leningrad, the midnight sun.

The challenge on *Everybody's All-American* was to create a realistic look while jumping through hoops photographically to complement what makeup artist Dick Smith had conceived. Dick had aged Dennis Quaid and Carl Lumbly to fifty years old, and DP Stephen Goldblatt had to painstakingly light them. If he made one mistake, it would have looked phony and we would have lost the entire essence of the scene.

Those are all challenges that are fascinating to deal with in collaboration with your cinematographer. That's the good part. The unfortunate part is that directors of photography are too often only interested in the photography of the picture, in painting with their light. They tend to lose sight of the fact that a picture has a life of its own, not just a photographic life.

I've found that on a film the real conflicts tend to be between the director and the director of photography. The DP feels that everything must wait until things are just right photographically, while you, the director, are saying, "Wait a minute, this is also about actors and drama. If you spend all night lighting and then you give me the set at 5:30 AM but sunrise is at 5:45, I only have fifteen minutes to shoot the entire scene, and you've had ten hours to light it—what's that about?"

I feel that one of the worst things that has ever happened to the film industry is the commercial. Directors of photography are absolute kings on commercials, which are essentially a noncontent form. It's totally photographic, so DPs get spoiled. They work short days, take three-hour lunch breaks, spend hours lighting a hamburger, and get paid immense amounts of money. You then bring them back to feature filmmaking and say "Hey, there's got to be *life* on the screen, and we've got to move fast because this is a film with many dramatic scenes." They have trouble changing their work style.

The director is faced with a very difficult dilemma. If a DP is too fast, chances are the photographic look is not going to be good. And you want it to be good. But you *don't* want somebody getting bogged down and spending forever lighting. Therefore, you've got to achieve a certain rhythm and pace. It's realizing how much time you need to give your director of photography and, at the same time, knowing when to say, "You've had enough time, let's shoot it. You can piddle around and tweak lights for another four hours and you still won't be happy." On the big shots that make a difference and establish the atmosphere *give* them time. On the other less crucial shots make them *move*.

As with the production designer, you hire the DP and let him hire his people—gaffers, grips, electricians, camera assistants, and operator, with the understanding that, ultimately, they all work for the filmmaker. But in too many instances they work only for the director of photography. Of course, I don't want shoddy work, but *everyone* is making compromises. As the director, I want more time with the actors; I want more set ups, but I have to compromise. The photography department must also.

The Sound

Sound is usually the forgotten department, and that's a big mistake. Except for *White Nights*, I've used Jeff Wexler on all my movies. He has a strong ego, and I give him a real say in the filmmaking process. He takes pride in his sound, and with Jeff and his boom man Don Coufal, you only have to do minimal looping. That's important to me. I believe in production sound over looping because I always go after performance. If I'm out there on location creating a little bit of reality, I'll be damned if I have to go onto a looping stage six months later and try to re-create that. You can't do it. You can get terrific looping jobs, but it should be a little Band-Aid here and there, not whole sequences of replaced dialogue.

Casting Directors and Actors

I believe I'm an actor's director, and in each film, I attempt to get the best performance ever given by an actor. However, it's not me up there on the screen. I can only guide someone with real talent into a memorable performance. The task of finding the acting talent for a film is probably only second in importance to the script process.

A director needs a collaborator with great taste (not necessarily exactly like his or hers). You want a casting director with enough moxy and backbone to stand up and say what he or she thinks. It's not like I'm the master and whatever I say is right. Although, I usually know what I'm looking for. I have no trouble making decisions, but I like to have people say what they believe. I want someone who will say, "I believe you're wrong. This person is terrific for the role." It may cause me to reevaluate and see something. I have this kind of relationship with Nancy Klopper, who has cast all my films since *An Officer and a Gentleman.*

I have a very stringent attitude about casting. You may have a brilliant actor, but he may not fit a particular role. It's matching an actor's unique talent with the specific attributes of a role—something like a chemistry set.

For example, in *An Officer and a Gentleman*, the role of Sergeant Foley, eventually played by Lou Gossett, Jr., was first written "white." The writer, Douglas Day Stewart, had a white drill instructor when he was in Officer Candidate School, so he wrote the character white. I looked at all the available white actors, but unfortunately, either they weren't right or we couldn't afford them. So I found myself with a brilliantly written role and no quality white actor to play it.

We therefore changed direction and opened the role up to ethnic actors. Clearly there are many black and latino Marine DIs, so we were on realistic footing. This was a brilliant turning point because we got Lou Gossett, Jr., one of this industry's best actors. He played the role, exactly as written, without changing one line of dialogue, and won the Academy Award for his performance.

The First Assistant Director

In a first assistant director, I want someone who can deliver the set to me with all the elements ready at the same time. The AD must be strong but diplomatic, moving actors and crew along even if they don't want to be moved. It's a very delicate balancing act because the pushing must stop short of alienating cast and crew and still carry out the director's game plan.

The assistant director schedules the picture and is therefore responsible for keeping things on track. If that timing is off, and the actors come to the set but the camera department is not ready, then everything falls apart. That's chaos. A first assistant director has to be able to dance—to understand exactly what the director wants and then orchestrate it.

To me, it's the most difficult job on the set—difficult because, although the AD is not actually making the film, he or she must control and deliver all production elements for the filmmaker. Sometimes, in fact too often, ADs don't accept the full responsibility of this relationship. There's both a technical and creative facet to the job. The technical side is extremely difficult, but many more ADs can fulfill this requirement than can truly understand what their director's creative approach is. If you can find someone who can juggle both facets effectively, you've got a very rare collaborator.

You also want an AD to have the strength to tell you the truth—to let you know when you're heading for trouble even if you're in the middle of a sequence and don't want to break your concentration. Directors can get very myopic, trying to win the immediate battle but losing sight of the war. Your AD must sometimes interrupt and say things like, "If you do three more set ups, we won't finish today, and tomorrow this location evaporates," or "There are fifteen hundred extras out there and they're hungry. If you work on, they'll mutiny, and we won't be able to get them to do anything this afternoon." This is valuable information that a director must focus on, and it's the AD's job to make sure he listens.

The Script Supervisor

The other person I need right beside me at all times is the script supervisor. You need somebody who is hyper-aware, serves as your eyes and ears, points out what you miss and does so diplomatically. He or she must be able to walk up to the actors and say, "You had the cigarette in your left hand, not the right . . . you sat down after your third line and crossed your legs after your eighth line."

Everyone challenges the script supervisor—the director, the director of photography, the actors. It's a tough job because you've got to be right all the time or everyone will lose confidence in you. After the first couple of weeks of shooting, you can make a mistake or two. But before that, everyone is saying, "Does this person really know what they're doing?"

I had an impossible situation on one film. I went through three script supervisors—I fired them all. Their mistakes cost me financially and creatively. I had shot lists, but we went through several incredibly exhausting, difficult days. Everyone was exhausted and wanted to go home. One day we wrapped and were driving home, when suddenly I realized we dropped a shot. It was disastrous. We couldn't go back. The script supervisor's excuse was, "I was tired and did not look at the shot list." That's just not acceptable. The script supervisor is everyone's backstop.

The Editor

The editor is your closest and certainly your longest collaborator on a film. You do a movie with an army of people, and then, when you finish shooting, that army disbands. You are left with one person—your editor. The two of you spend probably twice as much time together as you spend with the crew during production.

I look at every frame of dailies. I make selections while I'm looking at dailies for the editor. I tell him which takes, sometimes even which parts of takes, I want. Often, I'll say, "I want the first three lines of take one, the last four lines of take six, and the middle of take three." In other words, the editor gets very specific notes from me.

On the other hand, I don't look at cut footage while I'm shooting. Occasionally, if there's a problem, I'll look, but rarely. Nor do I usually have the editor on the set with me. I hire great editors, and I want them to cut a rough assembly while I am shooting. When production is wrapped, I don't look at anything for two weeks, giving them time to finish their cut. I also want to get away from the film. I've been so close for so long, and I need a break to regain some objectivity.

I've been fortunate to work with great cutters. Fritz and Bill Steinkamp, Peter Zinner and Priscilla Nedd, Shelley Kahn, and Don Zimmerman. I have great respect for their work. Invariably, they find things in the footage I never thought of. But also, there are sequences they don't understand because the design was specific, and they couldn't know what was in my mind. At that point I say, "All right, pull it apart, reconstitute the footage, and I'll show you how I want it cut."

Once they've delivered the rough assembly, they never get me out of the editing room. I am *there*. I go through every outtake. I go through all the possibilities, and we work in a very collaborative way. We spend days, weeks, months on the last "rewrite" of the script—the one in the editing room.

Music

Music has always been a crucial element in my life, so why shouldn't the characters in my movies share my love of music? My concept of film music doesn't just involve the composer; it also incorporates songwriters. I try to underscore dramatic scenes with musical collaborators at the earliest moments of the filmmaking process. At this point, when I get the script and start conceptualizing scenes, I already know the people I want to work with, and I get them started developing musical themes and songs.

On Being a Filmmaker

I went to a film festival once where Andrei Tarkovsky, the Russian film director, said, "The moment the first film was shown and someone charged admission was the perversion of the art of filmmaking." It was a provocative philosophical statement, but total fantasy. The reality of this industry—whether Russian or American—has always been *entertainment*.

I strive for artistic perfection, but I don't call myself an "artist." I'm a "filmmaker." Inherent in the term is that you're trying to say something . . . with integrity, and at the same time, you're trying to entertain. People have to be motivated to drive to a theater, pay for parking, tickets, and even sometimes a babysitter. Every feature filmmaker has to recognize this, and to ignore or deny it, to me, is idiocy.

The thing that you learn as a filmmaker is that you can't go out and say, "What's the most commercial flavor of the month, and I'll try and do it." The successes that I've had as a filmmaker have been those films that everybody has passed on: "Don't do it, it's not going to be commercial." My biggest grossing film, *An Officer and a Gentleman*, only got made at the last second because of a loophole at Paramount. They needed an extra film. The head of the studio told me that *Officer* would never be successful, and that *White Dog* was a much better bet. "*White Dog* is *Jaws* with a dog," he said, "and this little romantic movie you're making nobody will want to see."

The bottom line is, you don't know, and they don't know. You can't run out and make what is commercial. You've got to make what inspires you.

Two Hats

Having produced many of my own films, I have found that there are moments of true conflict between the producer's and director's hat. I've found I always make the decision in favor of the director.

On *Everybody's All-American*, the budget for the movie came in at more than Warner Brothers wanted to pay. They said, "We will agree to make the film, but we will not give you any contingency. You will have to guarantee completion of the film." On a $22.5 million film that means that if you go 1 percent over budget (the normal allowable contingency overage is 10 percent), you will spend $250,000 of your own money. I chose to go ahead and make the film, guarantee completion, and put my fee up because I wanted to make the film. In retrospect, I was probably crazy, but I'm proud of the film, and it wouldn't have gotten made without this commitment.

I make very good money and am not ashamed of that fact. But I'm not doing this because I want to get rich and retire. I'm doing this because I love making films. It's a privilege. We're all overpaid in this industry. What it's about is getting the work on film because twenty years from now, when you walk into a theater and you look up at the screen, you're going to have to face the music. Film transcends time. You live with it forever, and it keeps coming back to haunt you or pat you on the back. When I work with actors, I say, "You want to argue about the size of your mobile home? Twenty-five years from now, when you walk into a theater and look at this performance, you're either going to be proud of it or not. You're not going to give a shit about your mobile home."

Advice

Make sure you've got a little experience in your life before you go out and make a film. Film school is fine. But too often film students only have old films to use as a frame of reference; they are trying to make a sequence as good as that scene they saw in that 1935 or 1956 movie. The filmmakers who founded this industry—whether it's John Ford or William Wellman or Fritz Lang—all did other things. Lang was an architect, Wellman, an aviator, and Ford, a cowboy. They had real experiences before they made films. I wouldn't trade a day's experience in the Peace Corps for the finest education in film school.

Also, read some great books, and expose yourself to all kinds of media and real life. When I was trying to break into feature films after being at KCET, everyone in the Hollywood community saw me as a documentary filmmaker—"You might be able to get terrific moments of insight from real people, but that's not like working with actors," they said. When, in fact, many of the finest European directors—

Fellini, Bergman, Goddard, John Schlesinger—started in documentaries. In this country, for some reason, American filmmakers don't, and Hollywood doesn't, have an appreciation of the documentary.

I spent hours and hours looking at film. But I also spent hours and hours living and looking at real life. That is what I try to infuse into my filmmaking. The only thing filmmakers can do is use what they've got. I think it's better to develop a wealth of experience and talent and have something to say before you pick up that camera and try to say it.

2
THE DEAL

It has been said that Hollywood is more concerned with deal making than moviemaking. Certainly more deals are made than movies.

Through the web of agreements and contracts that precede the launch of a production, the three people in this chapter act as guides. And in the wake of a completed project, they meticulously keep files and records because the legal ramifications that emanate from the making of a movie can continue for decades.

Agent

An Agent represents writers, directors, producers, and actors by seeking employment for them and negotiating their contracts with studios and/or with one another.

Jeremy Zimmer

JEREMY ZIMMER, son of a novelist and grandson of producer/ MGM president Dore Schary, was twenty-one and running a valet parking service outside a Boston restaurant while concurrently managing the parking concession for the Boston Red Sox when a mugger knifed him. For six long weeks in the hospital, Jeremy thought about what to do with the rest of his life. Through his grandfather's connections, he landed a job in the mailroom of the William Morris Agency in Manhattan, where he pounded the streets and rode the subways making pickups and deliveries. When an opportunity arose to become secretary to one of the agents in the motion picture department, he landed the job, fielding three hundred phone calls a day and sending out forty scripts. After becoming a junior agent, he accepted an offer from ICM (International Creative Management), the largest talent agency in the world and one of Hollywood's most powerful, and worked his way up through the ranks there to head their motion picture packaging and literary departments. Recently, he left ICM to become a partner in the prestigious Baver/Benedek Agency.

T HERE ARE two aspects to a day in the life of an agent.

The first, the more overwhelming, is the reactive aspect of the day. At any given time you're in the middle of fifty, seventy-five, one hundred pieces of potential commerce, ongoing interactions: submissions of material you're waiting for responses to, deals you're in the middle of, people who want your clients, clients you're trying to acquire for representation. People are constantly calling you about things that need to happen. You're spending your day *reacting* to a tremendous amount of input.

The other part of the day, the more difficult and ultimately more important part, is *proactive*. Proactive means *you* determine something is going to happen and *you* go about making it happen. The best agents are the proactive agents. The best moves are the proactive moves. That's not to say the reactive aspect is unnecessary. Any time you reach any degree of success, you have to be reactive because when you have a client list that's at all desirable, people are calling wanting them and you're responding, reacting to those requests.

My day starts at about eight o'clock in the morning and ends at about seven-thirty at night. And it doesn't really end at seven-thirty at night because it's a highly social business, so I'm either at a screening or at dinner or something. And if not, I'm at home on the phone—with clients, friends who are buyers, other people who are in the business, talking about what happened, what's going to happen, and so on.

It's hard to define whether or not my job eclipses my "personal life" because the business is all-consuming. My friends are all in the business. So who knows when you turn the clock off from business to social? I don't think you ever really do. My wife works with me as a development executive. We spend our weekends reading scripts and talking about them. I don't know where it ends. I don't *think* I'm working when I'm asleep, but I probably am.

Client/Agent Relationship

When you're a young agent, you judge a client by reading a piece of material, or seeing a movie or seeing a performance, and believing that it's excellent. And that you can sell that person.

When you get older and more experienced, more factors come into play. There's a high time-versus-revenue coefficient that operates in an agent's life. As you become a more successful agent, your time becomes more valuable. Therefore you've got to evaluate the level of client that you get involved with. That's not to say you don't make the time to read the work of a new writer, or see the work of a new director that you just love, and don't spend time trying to get him off the ground. You do that. But you've got to make more critical evaluations, and you have to pursue a higher level of client. You can no longer be strictly in the research and development business, which is what new client business is. R&D doesn't pay, although it does pay off in the long term.

Once you become more established, your company is paying you more money, your big clients are paying you more money, their time demands are more excessive, and your time becomes more restricted. You can't spend the same kind of time on R&D. It's extremely time-intensive. To launch a new client takes a lot more time than it does to service an established client. And as clients make more money, they're paying you more and they expect more. You sign a guy who's making $100,000 a year. Two years later he's making $2 million a year. He's gone from paying you $10,000 a year to $200,000. It's a tough check to write, and you've got to upgrade your level of service to accommodate the level of compensation.

Once clients become really big, the work comes to you. What you have to do then as an agent is suss out the great opportunities. Be *proactive* as opposed to *reactive*. For every ten choices that are offered to a client, there's probably something better for the client to do that *isn't* being offered to him. For you to earn your money, you have to find the thing that is not being offered to him—that's a better career opportunity. Otherwise he can hire a lawyer to make deals.

We do, of course, rely on lawyers to execute the paperwork. The relationship with a lawyer is symbiotic until it becomes antagonistic. Hopefully you've got a good team. The agent procures the work, is involved in the highlights of the negotiation, and then the lawyer consummates the deal and supervises all the contracts. That's what happens in the best of all worlds. The problem in our business is that an agent takes 10 percent, a lawyer takes 5 percent. In my opinion, lawyers feel they have to justify their existence more than an agent does because, for the most part, contracts are not that involved—until a guy becomes a company and he's got all kinds of production operations going on. But in simple service-for-hire agreements, the lawyer's job is overseeing, especially at a large agency where there is a business affairs department. So it becomes a function of how these two guys work together. If the agent starts to fuck up, the client will tell the lawyer. And if the agent and lawyer work well together, the lawyer will protect the agent. If they don't, the lawyer is going to help the client find another agent—thereby getting points from the new agent.

Stages of Negotiation

First of all, you've got to get the deal. Somebody's got to have said, "Great, let's do it." It's kicked to business affairs. At that point it's been positioned to some degree, hopefully. If they want you, you have told them how difficult it will be to get your client. If you want it, you have told them how enthusiastic your client is. At that point you then try to either manifest your will upon them or deflect the will they're manifesting upon you. If they know that you need it more than they need you, then they're going to win. And if you know that they need you more than you need it, you're going to win. If you understand that, you understand the basic tenet of the negotiation.

As in any battle, there are sides and there is a battleground. And it comes down to whether you can take a bigger piece of their battleground or they can take a bigger piece of yours. At the end of the day, where do you end up? Do you end up with them in your backfield, or are you in theirs? And I look at the whole thing as a 20 percent swing on either side, which gives you a 40 percent shift. If you're completely successful, you end up 20 percent over where it should be, maybe more, maybe 30 percent. Some cases when they really need you and you've got them over a barrel and you really feel like it, you can ram it home. *But* the guy you ram it home to, whom you hurt, whom you leave bleeding, is the same guy you're going to be looking in the eye next week, saying, "Hey, I need a favor, can you help me out?" And if you've left him bloody the last time, he's going to drill you. So you've got to hold that in your mind, too. This is *not* a one-day skirmish. This is a lifetime event. The whistle never blows here.

It is absolutely possible for both sides to be pleased at the end of a negotiation, when everybody in the negotiation knows all the permutations and angles—what it could be, what it should be, and what it shouldn't be. And in that situation when you've got the leverage and you push it just a little bit out there on the edge to take just a little more, the other guy knows that and he's not going to hold it against you.

Client List

I try to have a balanced client list—clients who do different things and do them well. Some guys do comedy real well, others drama, action, and so on. What's most interesting is that the guys who do comedy real well want to do drama, the guys who do drama real well want to do comedy, the guys who do action want to do drama, and nobody wants to do what they do. Everybody wants to do what they don't do. Nobody wants to be typed.

Power of Agencies

The power of agencies and studios fluctuates. Right now, end of 1988, it's going back to the studios because what you've got is a tremendous contraction in the industry with the loss of several of the minimajors and Wall Street drying up in its enthusiasm for the motion picture business. The studios are again becoming more powerful. You've got the six or seven majors, less jobs, less development, so the majors have got more power. It's just the law of supply and demand. When you've got Dino de Laurentiis and Cannon and Lorimar and whoever else out there, it's a party. Everybody's competing for the same talent. So all of a sudden, Rob Lowe is making $2 million to do a movie. But then boom, everything dries up and you can't get Rob Lowe a job.

Packaging

Packaging is like laying down carpet. The carpet comes to you from the store all rolled up and you have to hold down all four corners at the same time. If you can do that, you can package a movie.

Packaging has a lot of negative connotations. Debra Winger ran around screaming about how she was "packaged" in *Legal Eagles*. But packaging *can* benefit everyone.

Packaging is assembling elements that make the financing of a motion picture possible. It starts with a script. You need actors, a director, producers. If the elements—writers, producers, actors, and script—are put together in a way that everyone sees as a good opportunity for them, that's terrific. A positive scenario in packaging would be that you have a director who's got a wonderful script, yet with maybe too tough a subject for the studios, and he sees an actress in it who would both be right for the role and make the film more desirable for financing—so you go to that actress and ask her to be involved prior to the picture being financed. That's packaging to the benefit of everyone. It's packaging like that that results in great movies.

The negative side of packaging has to do with a certain degree of insecurity in our business. People look to agents for career management, and if you act in the interest of one client to the detriment of the interest of another, then you're not doing a good job. You're packaging in the negative sense of the word.

Studios don't really package in the sense that agencies do. We package those elements I have just spoken of. Studios finance the development of the script. If they believe a script is good, they say, "Let's see if we can put it together"—in other words, put together a package that's good enough to justify their spending the money. Some studios are much more element-dependent than others. Disney, the most successful studio right now, believes enough in their scripts and ideas to say, "We're going to make this movie, let's see who we can get." *Most* studios say, "Let's see who we can get, then we'll see if we want to make the movie."

Packaging notwithstanding, it's got to be a good idea and it's got to be a good script—most important, it's got to be a good script. To me a good script goes beyond the setup, is well motivated through the second act, and has an ending that is both surprising and powerful. The biggest problem is usually the second act of movies. Everything's a good idea. Sometimes you get away with just a good idea. *Three Men and a Baby*—good idea, the story sucked, but somehow it worked—the magic of Disney. But apart from those flukes, you've got to have more than just a good idea and a big action climax, you have to have a second act that pulls the audience through the movie. Otherwise you're in trouble.

The Future

I love being an agent. I'm good at it. The more I do it, the more I realize that. And the more you deal with the studios, the more you realize what a tough job that is and how ultimately unrewarding it is because unless you're one of the guys pushing the button, you have no power, you have no vote. And yes, the possibility of running a studio is very intriguing. But I know that by the time somebody's willing to offer me that job, I'm going to have outgrown it.

If you look at the guys who have long, important careers in this business, most of them have it because they stay somewhere for a long time and get really good at something. The guys who bounce around just bounce out.

The idea is, if you get really good at something, you have a skill, and that skill is applicable elsewhere. But once you're really good at something, and you're at a place that works for you, it's not about money. The money comes. With success comes money and power. So then it's about what do you do every day when you wake up. And it seems to me that what I do every day is as interesting as it could be.

Survival

The secret of surviving in this town is having good instincts and trusting them, not being afraid to learn more—realizing that the only thing that's certain is change, and understanding how to use change and uncertainty to your advantage. By the mere fact that we are in the center of the information flow at the agency business—we know everything that's going on and what everybody's doing to everybody—we have power. And because we know what's going on, we can allay or deal with the uncertainty that everybody else has. And if you have good instincts, are smart, and have access to good information, then you've got all the ingredients of the pie. You can figure out how to put it all together. Without one of those ingredients, you're kind of lost.

I think the reason I was able to move up was that my superiors saw certain aggressive instincts in me, good instincts about the business, material, and human beings—who will fit with who under what circumstances, when somebody means what they're saying and when they don't. How to get somebody to see your point of view. As an agent, you have to be an effective communicator and a good, logical thinker. I think you have to be a tactician. And you have to have a certain degree of passion and anxiety about what you do. Otherwise, go sell commercial real estate, make more money, have less pain.

Advice

There's only one way. You've got to work for an agent. Be a secretary, be a runner, whatever. And you've got to know about the movie business.

I'm on the training panel here interviewing all the prospective trainees. All these kids come in here, and I ask them, "Who's your favorite director?" or "What were your favorite films in the last five years?" and they say, "Gee, I don't know." Or I ask them, "Who directed *Blade Runner*?" They don't know. That doesn't cut it. I can tell you with about 80 percent accuracy who directed every movie released by a studio in the last five years, probably 50 percent accuracy who wrote it, 50 percent accuracy who produced it. Why? Because I go to the movies and I pay attention. You've got to inform yourself. You've got to know what's going on.

Business Affairs Executive

A Business Affairs Executive negotiates deals with writers, directors, producers, and actors for their services on behalf of the studio or production company he works for.

Wm. Christopher Gorog

After living the life of a ski bum in Colorado and earning a film degree at San Diego State University, then experiencing a brief award-winning career as a documentary filmmaker, CHRIS GOROG moved to Los Angeles, where he enjoyed a meteoric rise in the business affairs arena of Hollywood. At the age of thirty-five he is president, co-owner, and chief operating officer of ITC Entertainment Group, a company that has been involved with the production of many motion pictures, including *On Golden Pond, Sophie's Choice, The Muppet Movie, Without a Clue,* and numerous television productions.

Chris began his career by working seven years at Walt Disney Studios and witnessed firsthand what took place through multiple changes in management, an experience that gives him a unique perspective on the many faces of Disney in the 1980s.

IF I'M making a deal for a writer, Joe Smith, to write an original screenplay, and he's accompanied by his longtime associate, Herb Schwartz, to produce, I hope to negotiate with their one agent, instead of two, for Joe's screenplay fee and for Herb's development and producing fee. And the dynamics of that are superficially very easy. I want to pay absolutely the least amount I can get away with, while the agent wants to leave my trousers around my ankles.

Then the fun begins.

A lot of people have certain wise old adages about deal making and negotiating. For instance, you have to know precisely where you want to be, where you want to end up, before you enter a negotiation and so forth. I don't know what deal-making philosophy I subscribe to, except that I am fearless in a negotiation if I know exactly where the marketplace is with respect to that particular deal.

If I know what a competitor would pay for the same thing, then I know where I'm going, and I don't have to arbitrarily fix a price. Absolutes just don't make sense in a business as crazy as ours.

In other words, if you determine that the total, all-in compensation for the writer you really want is $150,000 and after you work for fourteen days getting there, they won't settle for less than $157,500, you're an idiot to walk away.

It's an approach to a negotiation where you've done all your homework before you pick up the phone. You have the security and the ability to move fast on your feet, make changes in your game plan, and make a good deal.

I do set an absolute ceiling in my own head, but it can be violated. And I always take personal pride when I can bring it in considerably below the ceiling. But that's just an intellectual game you play with yourself; nobody else knows that. It's how you keep yourself sharp.

Old Disney

When I came into Disney, which was 1978, it was a very confused company. It was still on the preferred-buy list of all the brokers and still viewed as a blue-chip glamour stock and a very stable company, and of course they had the cash cows of the parks.

But everybody in Hollywood, in the entertainment business, had totally written it off as not even a player. Being a young person in an organization like that was kind of the good news and the bad news.

The bad news was that this wouldn't be an environment where you could learn from all the smart, with-it, hip people who were working there on all of their very exciting projects with the contemporary talent of the time. But the good news was that they desperately needed to be doing that, and they desperately needed to be shown the way.

And because Disney was so insular and so family-driven—that is, family members at top management, family members below them, the sons, daughters, cousins, and so forth—they really had come to fear the outside.

They feared contemporary Hollywood and the furor surrounding all the new, exciting filmmakers. And they just didn't comprehend executives who were in the limelight and things like, at that time, executives leaving United Artists to form Orion Pictures or leaving Fox for the Ladd Company.

Had it not seemed so foreign to them, they would have gone out and bought those executives, they would have approached Alan Ladd or Mike Medavoy or Frank Price and said, "Why don't you come in here and straighten everything out for us and make us competitive?"

But they didn't because they feared what they didn't understand.

Frontierland of Opportunity

This environment created a wonderful opportunity for young people like myself. Because the Disney organization couldn't ignore the fact that they needed to change. They knew they were creatively bank-rupt and that they really had a problem on their hands, but they would not and did not consider bringing in seasoned outside talent.

They had been surviving off formula comedies since Walt's death, and each comedy they released did a little worse than the one before it.

They had totally lost their credibility with exhibitors and with the moviegoing public. There was a creativity gap at Disney, because ultimately the merchandising, Disneyland, the parks, everything was fed by successful theatrical motion pictures, including their television operation, their Sunday night show.

They promoted a young guy by the name of Tom Wilhite, who was in charge of publicity, to head of production. And everyone seemed to think that yes, this was a pretty talented young fellow, and he was given the total production reins for motion pictures and tele-vision at this historically great studio.

Although he didn't have the right to green-light pictures, effec-tively they were rubber-stamped. So Tom was out there with all the resources of this wonderful institution, a great deal of money behind him, and he got to do whatever the hell he wanted to do.

The Birth of Business Affairs

Well, along the way Tom needed business affairs support, some-body to do all of the deal making for all of these young up-and-coming writers, producers, directors, and actors he wanted to be involved with.

But Disney was totally out of step with the rest of Hollywood in how they conducted business; they did not even have a business affairs department. They operated their studio the way all the major studios did through the fifties and early sixties, a period of time when the studios had all of the power and the talent had very little.

As the talent got a lot more power, in the late sixties, where a picture like *Easy Rider* suddenly became a phenomenon and people realized studio backing and major stars weren't necessary to have a successful film, talent suddenly became, among other things, a lot more expensive.

Since all that talent had sophisticated agents and entertainment lawyers representing them, the studios had to convert, they had to have the same types representing them.

The way Disney had been able to survive without a business affairs department—and this is all after Walt's death, mind you, before Walt's death you didn't need anybody else—was that they only worked with talent that was on the way up and therefore didn't cost anything, or on the way down and therefore didn't cost anything. So whether it was a writer/script deal, producer/director, the agent would say to the creative buyer, "I want forty grand," and he walked down the hall to see Ron Miller, and Ron Miller would say, "Thirty-five," and that was the deal. And two years later a contract would come out of the legal department.

We couldn't do that anymore under this new regime because we were working with all the talent that routinely got deals that were competitive, and suddenly you needed somebody who could play in that world.

Well, my *real* break happened, not when I got my job at Disney, but when this transition took place.

The Deal Maker

I had become a student of deal making, just because I was interested in it and attended all of the seminars in Los Angeles, USC, UCLA, the AFI, all about the business of filmmaking, packaging, co-production deals, distribution deals, profit participations, net profit, adjusted gross, modified gross, rolling break evens, all of this crazy stuff.

So at this odd time in the universe, when somebody needed to do this, I walked down the hall to visit Ron Cayo, who was head of business affairs for the entire corporation. He was the corporate deal maker, he did the little deals, stuff like EPCOT and Tokyo Disneyland! He never was involved in anything that wasn't in the multimillions of dollars.

And I said, "Mr. Cayo, the company is changing, there's going to be a lot of deal making going on, you need a business affairs department, what you should go do is get out there and hire a seasoned veteran. You're going to have to pay them, at least, $150,000 a year at today's market prices. But since I know you're not going to do that, I nominate myself to be the deal maker for motion pictures and television."

He thought about it for twenty-four hours, and he called me back and said something to the effect, "Okay, kid, you're on."

56

So I became the deal maker.

The wild thing is, I became the *only* deal maker, and the deal maker at the highest level for our motion picture and television company.

I was called the manager of business affairs and was solely responsible for all of the above-the-line deal making for everything we did: the features, the TV; ultimately when we set up the Disney Channel, I was responsible for getting those deals done; when we dabbled in radio I did that; when we dabbled in live stage on Broadway I did that. It was the learn-while-you-earn program, never earning very much but learning a great deal.

It was a wonderful time because I was too inexperienced to be fearful of it. It's the arrogance of coming into a situation as a film student. You've studied film, you've studied filmmakers, all of the current happening talent is on the tip of your tongue, you're with it, you're in the soup; and you have no doubts whatsoever about your ability to make a contribution in that organization. If I had been surrounded by a lot of people who knew considerably more than I did, it would have been intimidating.

But I genuinely don't feel that Disney suffered an ounce by taking me on in that capacity because I took the responsibility painfully seriously and did an enormous amount of homework and was as buttoned up as anybody in town when I got on the phone to make a deal.

If I hadn't made a specific type of deal before, I would call somebody who did that more often than anybody in town, introduce myself, ingratiate myself with that person, and shoot the breeze about that deal and what the pitfalls were and how you could get burned.

And I developed relationships with the heads of business affairs, both in the feature side and the television side, at every major studio in town.

They were probably a bit bemused about this new guy Disney had turned the whole thing over to . . . who would call and say, "How the hell do you make this deal?"

There is a business affairs underground, if you will, that says business affairs executives can freely trade any information in the world about deal making and talent with each other on a confidential, not-to-be-repeated basis.

And they would always drop what they were doing, I didn't have to wait for call-backs. I'll never forget their kindness and the time they took.

So I just grabbed hold of a wild tiger and held on tight. And then the change began.

Tom Wilhite made some movies, had some bad luck; that was *Tex, Tron, Trenchcoat*—huge failure—*Something Wicked This Way Comes*—huge failure—*Return to Oz*, and unfortunately he never had the opportunity to enjoy the success that was rightfully his with *Splash*.

Splash was the success that Disney desperately needed. Not only did the movie make a great deal of money for the company, but it also said, "Look, Hollywood, these guys did it. This is with Ron Howard directing, and this crazy young kid, Brian Grazer, producing, and these two fresh-faced actors and actresses you haven't seen before, Tom Hanks and Daryl Hannah, and you guys didn't do it and Disney did. Ha, ha." As a matter of fact, that movie was initially developed at UA, and they dropped it, and then it went to the Ladd Company, and they dropped it, so Disney finally did something right.

In any case, Tom Wilhite was gone by the time the movie came out, replaced by a fellow named Richard Berger, who came over from Fox. And then Richard was unceremoniously tossed out when the company was taken over by the Bass brothers, who installed the Michael Eisner/Frank Wells regime.

The New Disney

It was a whole new generation. The new management had established an outstanding track record of hit movies at Paramount.

Prior to the Eisner/Wells management team, I had gone from manager of business affairs to director of business affairs to vice president of business affairs, all the while being the one and only business affairs executive.

There were maybe seven feature films made, and when I left I had personally handled ten network television series, including the Disney Sunday Movie deal with ABC, which was the largest series deal in the history of network television in terms of the license fees—$65 million a year to Disney.

And I worked for Michael Eisner, Frank Wells, and Jeffrey Katzenberg for about seventeen months and had a great time. I viewed them as the guys on the white horse coming in to rescue the studio.

Disney company stock was trading at something like $60 per share when they took over, so I went and took a second mortgage out on my house and invested it in Disney stock. I figured anything above a hundred would be the cream. The stock went to $140 and split four to one, and made me, in my world, a step ahead and made a lot of other people more than a step ahead.

Two Labels

There were many things the new management had going for them. They had inherited Touchstone Pictures, which was what the Disney people finally had done to rid themselves of the cross they were bearing of the Disney label. The Disney label is like the Good Housekeeping Seal of Approval: we shouldn't screw with that, we shouldn't put it on a movie like *Tex*, which among other things had teenagers drinking beer. We shouldn't confuse that small but loyal audience we have.

Unfortunately, most of the motion pictures that mainstream distributors release throughout the world cannot go out with the Disney name, because of profanity, because of sex, because of violence. And this caused a terrible struggle internally for years at Disney.

There was a legion of people who said, "Let's just get a second label. We should make Disney movies for the Disney label, and we should make other kinds of movies for another label." And they went out and gave some image marketing firm way too much money to come up with "Touchstone," which is fine, it doesn't matter.

The point is, it doesn't matter what you call it, they just needed another avenue to release pictures. And you'll note that there aren't too many Disney movies being released through Disney right now. The Paramount team is having just as much difficulty finding commercial Disney-type projects as their predecessors had.

The thing that they're not having any trouble doing at all is repeating the incredible success they had at Paramount with mainstream, highly promotable, light comedies for young adults.

Leaving Disney

When I was at Disney, I considered myself part of the "new" breed in Hollywood—one of those young people who are sort of transient among studios and just sort of pursuing their own career goals and hopefully making a contribution along the way. I never expected to be *in any one place* for seven and a half years. But it turned out that the learning curve for me at Disney was always a rocket to the moon. There's no place that I could have done any better.

I was offered jobs along the way where I could have gotten a little more money, but I never would have had all of that responsibility and opportunity to learn.

I didn't have any desire to leave until, ironically, the Eisner regime got situated with their layers of management underneath them.

As the company became so large, announcing a slate of ten to fifteen motion pictures every year, announcing major prime-time series television goals, announcing interest in making numerous overall writer/producer deals, entering made-for-syndication programming, the sheer volume of the activity and deal making required many levels of executives and hierarchy and administration and things that were foreign to me, because my whole period at Disney was a bit like running your own store.

What I had gotten good at was making decisions on my own that I felt were the best decisions for the company. And that's not the way a major organization like today's Disney runs.

So when I was given the opportunity to come to a smaller company like ITC, to be a major entrepreneurial player, I felt that I was back where I should be.

Throwing out the Book

At a smaller company like ITC, where I am now, the rule book, thankfully, is thrown out. We work with an impressive array of talent, and we make some very peculiar deals.

I've got a talent deal in-house for one of the biggest feature stars in the world, hands down, who is a $2.5 million-plus player.

He'll be working for almost no money up-front for the picture and then has an extremely accelerated adjusted gross position that essentially makes him like an equity partner in the movie. He's putting himself on the line. He's donating his craft with the possibility of making a lot more money than he otherwise would should the picture become successful.

And it's very competitive, not only for us, but for talent and producers and packagers.

And if you throw out the rule book and state directly, "Look, I understand that your client routinely gets $125,000 for a first-draft screenplay and $50,000 for each subsequent revision applicable against

$250,000 and 5 percent of the net, and we deeply respect that, but we're not going to pay that, not because we don't respect him and he hasn't earned it, but simply because we don't want to."

And if your client has sufficient interest in this material and wants to play ball and have some fun, and we've got some other knuckle-heads involved in this project who are deferring a substantial amount of their up-front compensation, here's a way to make a different kind of deal.

Difficult Deals

The most difficult deals are those that require very heavy up-front cash compensation, like $5 million or more for a top actor—Steve Martin, Chevy Chase, Bill Murray—and require adjusted gross participation from first dollar or after cash break. I wouldn't have wanted to be the studio on *Ishtar* with Beatty and Hoffman; you go and front these guys millions of dollars, fund all the negative cost, and then you start peeling off hundreds of thousands of dollars in participations on a picture that's totally in the crapper, it's a tough row to hoe. But it's a different business.

Information on someone's latest deal is freely exchanged on a confidential basis. You could get the same information from the agent, who clearly knows it backward and forward, but the funny thing about agents is, I don't understand it, but they have terrible, terrible memories. And I know it's just coincidental, but it seems that, more often than not, they add money to the previous quote.

And sometimes they feel guilty about it. Whenever you hear, "It was something in the neighborhood of . . ." or "I think it was . . ." or "I don't recall specifically, but . . ." you know, it depends on the deal, but if you're in the $200,000 range, you can figure 25 to 50 percent has been added on.

Market Price

So this business affairs underground is the only way to stay sane and try to determine what the market price is for talent that, in all honesty, can be a bit nebulous.

I had a conversation with one of our creative vice presidents here at ITC a couple of weeks ago who was a very strong advocate for a young male actor to star in one of our movies. I had determined, in my infinite wisdom, that the number for this guy was $175,000 and that that was probably $25,000 high. Period, over and out.

And she was making a very vocal case for "the number is whatever you want to pay, and why is it 175 and not 225?" And I became, after listening patiently, a bit enraged. I said, "For God's sake, that's why I exist. That's why we negotiators exist, because we're attempting to put some semblance of reality and logic on these proceedings."

The annoying thing is that what she was saying is true! Because all it takes is some bozo at another studio to pay him $225,000, and that is the market. The market becomes what people will pay. Along the way, you try to outsmart everyone and really try to put a value on that piece of talent.

And to a business affairs guy, writers, directors, producers, actors, people with credits are numbers—cash and points, profit participations; they *do* become commodities, which is not a very attractive way to put it, but it's the only way that we can stay sane, because we have to measure this piece of talent against that.

We have to put them on a scale and say, "Well, I agreed to pay this guy $500,000, and I agreed to pay this person $350,000, why did I do that?"

If you don't have a reasonably good answer, it's hard to justify why you're here. And the business affairs executive's role expands when you get outside of just purely the numbers game in calculating when a profit participation will kick in and how that's going to affect the overall economics of the movie.

It becomes incumbent on the person who runs business affairs to say, "Well, now wait a minute, this fellow Mike Cimino, now I've heard about him," and be an advocate of the business position for the company and say, "In my best judgment, it's highly unlikely that he'll be respectful of the budget," or "Maybe he'll be *real* careful next time because he learned one hell of a lesson, didn't he, but we want written guarantees," or whatever your view might be.

Weighing the Elements

Producers, unfairly, are the second-class citizens.

Writers would say *they* are. But as a buyer, I don't think writers are. I think a good script is gold. And they may not be paid enough in their view, but they certainly are appreciated and respected enough.

Nothing goes into production without a script that somebody respects, appreciates, and thinks is commercially viable.

Directors, probably because of the star/director syndrome in the seventies, may even be overvalued in terms of the hope that by getting a million-dollar-plus director it's going to bless the whole project and make it good. It's very difficult to beat a bad script, very difficult to beat bad casting. But if anybody can beat it, it's the director, and maybe that's why the premium is paid to a director.

But it's the producer who's a second-class citizen, and I think the reason is that nobody knows what a producer is. Anybody can define a director's job. Anybody can define a writer's job. But I doubt that you would get two similar definitions from any two people in Hollywood as to what a producer is.

Producers are everything from a star's personal manager, trying to extract some extra bucks for himself and get his name on the screen and that's it—and believe me, there are many, many examples of that kind of thing—to the other end of the spectrum: a creative idea finder, developer, packager, entrepreneur, alternative financing expert, line producer, "get the camera trucks there on time" guy. This kind of person is an aberration and worth his weight in gold. They're special people, seasoned, well experienced.

To make the definition of producer less complex—if one were to try to build a guild around producers, there should be executive producers, who are creative packagers, and there should be producers, who get the camera trucks there on time—and never the twain shall meet. That's the sanest way to run a movie.

A lot of the confusion in creative direction and financial and line production management of the movie happens because nobody knows what their role is, what's expected of them, what they can get away with, and what they can't.

That fogginess causes producers to become second-class citizens, and the good ones have to bear the brunt of that.

Goals

I didn't have the five-year Dale Carnegie goal list. For all of my career, all I wanted to do was hold on to the tail of the wild tiger and do the job, gain the industry's respect, learn more, and survive. And everything else would come, and I knew that, and it did come.

The last ten years have just been one crazy, challenging ride. Within that context, my goal was survival and doing an outstanding job. And I could not come in to work every day, negotiating for a living, if it wasn't fun.

It can be a burnout job. For me, it's emotionally involving. I suppose the best, the longest hitters, as business affairs executives, are those who can remain detached.

But for me, the only way I can get on the scoreboard is to get excited about something.

Advice

My advice for people who want to break in will sound corny, but I believe it very firmly. And that is to believe in yourself.

Interestingly, the names of people I became familiar with ten years ago who were fringe nobodies, who were just like me with a little outline under their arm that wasn't particularly well written—the only thing these people had going for them was their passion for succeeding in the business and their belief in themselves—I see their names every time I turn on the television set or go to the movies today. Somebody's an executive story editor for a dramatic series, somebody's producing a feature film.

These people have made it in Hollywood through tenacity. They felt the scorn of the executives reviewing their material. They were met with ridicule. They sat in outer offices and had their meetings canceled and suffered the humiliation of never getting their calls returned.

For whatever reason, they've made it.

Frankly, I think the only thing you have to do in Hollywood to make it is have a fierce desire. You have to find your way, but you do have to really want it because there's a hell of a lot of people standing right behind you who want it very badly.

Hollywood is a transient place. There are some old Hollywood families, and you can point to some dynasties—the sons and daughters of Kirk Douglas, Lloyd Bridges, Martin Sheen, and the like. Maybe they have gone on for a generation or two.

But I think Hollywood and the next generation is whoever else wants to come out here and scrap around.

This is the last frontier. There's no place in the world like it.

Entertainment Attorney

The Entertainment Attorney prepares and sometimes negotiates details of contracts and analyzes legal situations in order to protect his or her client whose services are required on a movie. Responsibilities include ensuring that contracts accurately reflect the deal negotiated by the client's agent with the financing company as well as giving the client legal advice on other aspects of the client's professional life, such as investment and tax matters.

Tom Hansen

TOM HANSEN grew up in Los Angeles' San Fernando Valley, where he spent most of his childhood and adolescence in a darkened movie theater. A child of the sixties, he quit college and his political science major to "bum around." He worked in a warehouse, drove a truck, bought and sold a couple of sailboats and made enough "dough" to travel around Europe for a year and a half. On returning to the United States, he realized he was more interested in fiction than political science, enrolled at the University of California at Santa Barbara as an English major, then switched to film when a fledging film program was established there. During his last year of college, he discovered the field of entertainment law, thought it sounded like an interesting way to make a living, and applied to several law schools. He obtained a scholarship to study law at the University of Southern California. After his second year there, he got a summer job at Kaplan-Livingston, Goodwin, Berkowitz and Selvin, a prestigious Los Angeles law firm, where he was immediately apprenticed to the head of the entertainment department. Upon graduation, Tom was offered a full-time job there. Three years later, when the firm went out of business, he went to Ziffren, Brittenham and Gullen (now Ziffren, Brittenham and Branca), another preeminent Hollywood entertainment law firm. There he learned what kind of lawyer he really wanted to be and, six years later, decided to go into business for himself with two other entertainment lawyers, who, like himself, found that their interest lay with representing the next wave of creative talent, the emerging filmmakers. Together they formed Hansen, Jacobson and Teller, where Tom has been a partner since 1987.

THE ADVANTAGE I have as a lawyer, which is extremely appealing to me, is that I have control of my own destiny. I don't work for anybody. I have clients, of course, but there is no one client on whom I'm dependent for my livelihood. So I have the opportunity to exercise my own best judgment almost unfettered. Obviously, I have a job to do and clients to keep happy, but I'm not so slavishly beholden to anyone or anything that I ever feel I can't give my best advice.

My love for film has stood me in good stead. While I never pursued a hands-on filmmaking career because my interest always was more in history and criticism, I now find that this background has been enormously helpful. My practice has evolved towards representing directors. Having the ability to talk about films in a historical context, to understand the language of filmmaking, to understand how the camera works, and how a film is put together gives me an immediate common language with my clients.

I am passionate about film and know it reasonably well, and, completely apart from its being an advantage, it's who I am and what I do and the reason I do this. If I had just wanted to make money, I would have gone to Wall Street and sold widgets.

The Route: Becoming a Certain Kind of Lawyer

I received great training at Kaplan-Livingston. It was a wonderful "blue chip" Westside firm. Eric Weissman, the head of the entertainment department to whom I was apprenticed, represented quite a few directors: Alan Pakula, Mark Rydell, among others. I was immediately immersed in that end of the entertainment business. After the firm dissolved, I went to Ziffren, Brittenham and Gullen, which was and is, as far as I'm concerned, the premier entertainment law firm. I had been out of law school for only three years. I had one or two clients. It was a fabulous opportunity for me. At that point the firm was emerging as a force to reckon with. As Creative Artists Agency has set the tone for how agencies should work, Ziffren, Brittenham have set the tone for how a law firm should work. They are extremely efficient and they understand the business. They are not the type of lawyers who will spend endless hours working on less important boiler plate provisions. They are bottom line and very businesslike. They understand where the substantive points are and they move to them immediately. I was schooled exceptionally well there.

I was given the responsibility of running important accounts. I did a substantial amount of work for people such as Jim Brooks and the Zucker Brothers. I was very much part of their lives. But I found I also wanted to develop the young filmmakers, the people who I thought were going to be the next Jim Brooks, and this was just inconsistent with what the firm wanted me to do. As I continued to work there I kept struggling to attend these new clients and simultaneously do my work for Ziffren, Brittenham, and it was very difficult. So two years ago we formed our own, new firm. My partners were former partners of Tom Pollock's (of Pollock, Bloom and Dekom), and Tom Pollock's leaving to head Universal was an obvious time for a transition for them.

The Spectrum

There are several different kinds of lawyers.

I am a transactional lawyer who concentrates primarily on the seller side. My main clientele is composed of writers, directors, actors, and very few producers. I represent virtually no buyers, meaning no studios, no production companies. I am seldom in a situation where I am representing an entity who is hiring an actor or hiring a writer. I am almost always, because of my inclination and because of the way my practice has developed, on the side of the seller.

There are entertainment labor lawyers who deal with the guilds and with the various union problems, there are entertainment litigators who do lawsuits, there are entertainment specialist tax lawyers. There are also buyer's attorneys—for example, a project attorney at a studio or a lawyer at a firm who is primarily involved in representing buyers. A lawyer who is representing buyers in a firm usually is doing more than merely the day-to-day production work.

On the simplest level, as a project attorney, if you have a picture that gets green-lit, there are a myriad of contracts that have to be dealt with: the actors' contracts, the writer's contracts, the director's contracts. There may be location releases, and contracts for using a popular song. There are the contracts for the use of commercial products in the movie. There are very complicated insurance issues and there is errors and admissions insurance, which is for defamation and breach of invasion of privacy. The lawyer is involved in making sure that the script has been reviewed by the proper people, that any names that could be problematic have been changed or removed. For instance, if they put a phone number on the side of a cab you have to make sure the phone number is not actually in service. You have to file the copyright. You have to make sure that the screen and ad credits are consistent with the contractual requirements. Those are all the production lawyer's responsibility. That production lawyer can either be at a studio or at an outside law firm engaged to do that. Most of the firms that represent more in the buyer arena are also frequently involved in the financing arrangements if it is a complicated deal. It may be a separate foreign deal or a separate video deal for a certain amount of money. There may be a separate theatrical distribution deal, and the lawyer has to coordinate all of those deals so that they all mesh. Very important. Very complex. Lawyers often represent a bank in those transactions because a bank may be loaning against the money that is expected to come in from the picture. There is another thing called a completion bond that is similar to a completion bond for a large construction project. Under this arrangement the bonding company guarantees the picture will be delivered or the bank will be paid off. The buyer's lawyer spends a lot of time with those kinds of things, protecting the investment and making sure the money flow is appropriate and that the contracts pursuant to which the picture can be made are all in place. The firms that have traditionally been more buyers' firms are some of the larger firms, such as Loeb and Loeb and Mitchell, O'Melveny and Myers.

The Seller's Lawyer

The "boutique" firms—Ziffren, Armstrong, Hirsch and Levine; Gang, Tyre, Ramer and Brown; Bloom, Dekom and Hergott—are thought of more as sellers' firms.

My involvement, as a seller's lawyer, depends on the client and the agent. There are some clients who don't want as little as a business-related phone call to be made without my knowing about it. There are other clients who think of me more as someone who makes sure the paperwork is appropriate and that everything is done correctly.

I have a good relationship with most of the agents. I think the agent and lawyer or law firm working together can end up helping each other enormously in making better deals. Most of the agents that we work with bring us in fairly early.

Say we are representing a writer. That is probably the simplest kind of situation. Normally what will happen is the agent will be canvassing the waterfront trying to find out if there is either an assignment for the writer or a studio that is receptive to an original idea the writer wants to write. Once the studio has said, "Yes we like this idea" is usually when I come in. The writer, agent, and I will get together to talk about the kind of deal we should ask for: how much money we should be asking for, what the special provisions are, whether the writer would like to be a co-producer, whether to share the turn-around, and similar kinds of provisions. We'll look at the past deals, come up with numbers, and usually the agent will take the first salvo with the studio. Sometimes we're on the phone with the agent, sometimes not. Sometimes we play good cop/bad cop with an agent. Sometimes I may have a strong relationship with someone at the studio that I can use to get what we need to get done. So once the deal is done, depending on the agent and the studio, a deal memo may be prepared by us, or we may prepare a memo to the file memorializing the deal.

Next the contracts come in. My job is to go through the contracts to make sure that they accurately reflect the deal, that all the additional provisions that are really substantive and often not talked about in the first go-around are included. Such provisions include a sequel remake provision and a provision to make sure that the writer is paid even if the studio doesn't ask for the second set of revisions. I also spend a fair amount of time going through the net profit definitions, that is, the long form provisions that define how profits will be calculated. Then I get the contract signed, and off it goes. That's *that* part of it.

The other part that goes along with this is that of representing the client in other, nonfilm-related concerns, you maintain their corporation, you help them buy a house, you help them with a will or with an estate plan, and you give them advice about potential tax issues. You are really a personal lawyer for somebody who happens to be in the entertainment business.

With the more complicated deals—such as the one we are doing currently for a prominent director to do a very interesting television deal—there are more complex interrelations and ramifications. On a deal like that, the agent, another attorney who is representing the other partner in the deal, and the business affairs representative of the agency all get together and spend an enormous amount of time kicking around a proposal. Once that has been done, my partners and I usually—and in this situation in particular—draft a very detailed memorandum, which is then circulated among all of the same people. For this deal, we all then got a chance to take a shot at the document. We all gave ideas. That memorandum was then sent to the potential buyer. This is a deal where, because of the complexity, the lawyers are involved from the beginning, will continue to be involved and will be as active in the negotiation as the agents will be. The complexity of the deal often influences whether or not the lawyer(s) will be involved at a very early stage.

The Rules of the Game

You have to be mindful of the politics of the business and at the same time realize that you are representing a client. Your primary allegiance is to the client. You find yourself having to be particularly attuned to this when, for instance, a large agency has a packaging commission in a television station, and where there is an enormous amount of money at stake. I don't think the agencies act unethically by any stretch of the imagination, but there is a natural momentum in a large deal that sometimes has the tendency to carry the smaller players along with it. I think part of my job is to be aware of that and to use my influence to make sure that the individual client doesn't get sacrificed to this rolling snowball.

Lawyers tend to have very stable lives with their clients. People don't change lawyers as often as they change agents. Agents are very predatory with one another. Lawyers have traditionally been much less predatory. It is a tiny little business. There are rules of ethics about soliciting other people's clients. There is really much more of a code of honor among lawyers. Although, it would be naive to say that lawyers don't covet other lawyers' important clients, lawyers don't cold call other people's clients and say "your lawyer did a bad job on this deal." And that does happen with agents.

I also think lawyers stay in longer because a lawyer has a more circumscribed job, one with definite parameters. And if a lawyer makes a mistake, or does something poorly, or is dilatory in his or her work, it's relatively apparent. An agent who has a very amorphous job with no real boundary lines has more opportunity to be blamed or to be perceived as not having done his or her job well.

One of the most difficult situations a lawyer can find himself in is when a lawyer and agent share a client who goes to the lawyer for advice. That agent may be someone with whom you have a strong relationship, someone you may actually be good friends with. And that mutual client comes to you for advice, often to help them find another agent—that can be a painful situation. Again, you have to keep in mind that your main focus is to represent that client and do what is in the client's best interest and, ultimately, avoid doing something that protects your own interests but is *not* in the best interest of the client.

Negotiation: Fighting the Good Fight

People get paid the big bucks for shrewd judgment. Any lawyer and any agent can be as technically good, as glib, or as appealing as any other lawyer or agent, or better, but what gives a lawyer the edge is his or her judgment. You have to be able, under the circumstances, to decide "is this in the best interest of my client?" That is my job. I understand that I swim in a shark tank. I seldom get angry. I seldom lose my temper.

Anger, very often, is used as a tool in getting a movie made. However, it is, I believe, an ineffective tool. I can be emotional about something, but I understand it's a business and is not personal. People can and do take what happens in this business very, very personally. I like it when somebody else gets mad because that means they are losing control. What Rudyard Kipling said about "keeping your head when those about you are losing theirs" holds true. People who are mad make mistakes. There is a judgment line—you get to the point where there is a potential damage to the client. Your relationship with your client is not based on what you say or how aggressive you are, because deals blow all of the time. Your relationship is dependent on whether you are perceived as having been honest, having been reasonable, and not having been a complete jerk. You can be as tough as you want, but if you are straight about it and you don't play games everyone will respect you and they'll do business with you again. Where you get in trouble as a representative is when you are perceived as having been dishonest or duplicitous.

Building a Reputation

Diplomacy is an important part of the job, but the more important part is honesty and delivering when one's word has been given.

And, ultimately, if you're a representative, your reputation in the community is more important than your representation of any one client. Clients do come and go, less so for lawyers than agents, but your ability to function effectively is based on your reputation—your reputation for honesty, intelligence, and integrity. And if you have that, you can accomplish so much more for a client. I can get people to pay without signing papers because I say "I'm going to handle it." I can get people to give me access to material because I tell them "it won't leave my office and it's confidential." I can get people to do favors for me because they know I'll return them and I will treat them fairly. That's a big advantage, and I learned that from Ken Ziffren and Skip Brittenham, who people say are tough and difficult, but who are totally honest and have integrity. If a client tells them to do something that they think is inappropriate, they won't do it. And if they lose the client, that's just how it goes.

If you operate at a certain level, there is an enormous amount of honor. Now completely apart from whatever altruistic motives you may have, if you are operating at a high level it is very important— from a business point of view—that people believe you. Very important. There are a very small number of people at the top. In the scheme of things, there are only thirty or forty people separate and apart from the clients who make this work: five or six lawyers, five or six agents, and five or six studios, which comprise 80 percent of the business. And the majors have consolidated their positions even more than before. It is very important that Mike Ovitz (head of Creative Artists Agency) can believe what Jeffrey Katzenberg (president of production for Disney) says to him. So at the top level, there is an enormous amount of straightforwardness.

When you start getting involved in the netherworld, it gets difficult. The "Wannabes" you have to stay away from completely, particularly as a lawyer, because they'll use up all of your time. But even in the independently financed world because there is money coming in from all different sources and it is a puzzle that has to be put together, you are often in a situation where you are being told by the people who are involved, "all the money's together, everything is here, we're making a firm offer to your client, do you accept?" and it doesn't mean anything. That's the area where I've had most difficulty.

There is *difficult* intellectually and *difficult* emotionally. You want to concentrate on the difficult intellectual deals. I did a deal with Ken Ziffren that was really a series of deals for someone who had gone through transitions from having been a producer to second-in-command at the studio, to the head of the studio, then back to producer again—all of which took about three years and a million negotiations. It was for me a landmark because it marked the point where I began to get the confidence to do it on my own.

The Golden Child was another real breakthrough negotiation because it was a big sale, a big deal. It involved a writer out of relative obscurity going into a huge deal with a movie getting made and his being promised to be the director, then not being allowed to do it and so getting a big settlement because he wasn't. That was a difficult negotiation, and I think it marked my emergence as somebody who was, maybe, *somebody*. Those two deals were difficult intellectually.

Difficult emotional negotiations—the ones that last for months and months and you get the deal done and as soon as it's done, the people renege—those are the nightmares, those are the ones that take their toll. Those are the ones to avoid.

Keeping a Personal Life

I'm fortunate in that I grew up here. My oldest friend has nothing to do with the business. He has been my best friend since I was eleven years old. My dad was a mailman. I'm from a completely working class family, and I have a support system that is separate and apart from the business.

I live with an agent. She's very ambitious and, in a way, it is an ideal relationship because each of us is very dedicated to the relationship but at the same time we have our careers. She has formed her own agency. It would be horrible to have one career that was successful like that and one that wasn't. It just wouldn't work because the other person would be sitting at home pining.

There is an enormous amount of socializing in connection with the business, so we make a point about not going out on weekends. Weekends are sacred time. We try very hard not to plan any business-related activities. We hang out with the dogs, and I surf.

Surviving

My ideal and the paradigm for this whole thing is the Ziffren firm, which is about twelve to thirteen lawyers who are all partners and who form a very cohesive outfit. They do well financially, and they seem to have a pretty good time. The thing you have to be careful of when you are a lawyer is getting burned out. It is very stressful and you can alleviate some of that stress by having fantastic people working for or with you. But you can't alleviate it all. There is a metaphor, attributed to Gary Hendler, who was a lawyer and quit, which I think is perfect. He said, "If you're a lawyer in the entertainment business you are like a rock in the ocean, constantly being hit by these waves. It is not any one wave that knocks you over, they just all wear you down."

After a number of years, if practicing law does not continue to be intellectually stimulating, people get tired of it. And that's why some lawyers become producers and studio executives.

At the other end, if a lawyer retains a passion for films, loves movies, has rewarding relationships and accumulates a certain amount of power in the field eventually—and it certainly happened to Tom Pollock—people think of him or her as a person who could possibly run a studio or production company.

Advice

The difficulty with breaking into entertainment law is that it is a mature business, meaning that things are in place and ossified to some degree. There are fifty or sixty lawyers in private practice in Los Angeles. There are another hundred or so jobs at the studios and networks. There are probably in the entire United States 300 or 400, if you put music in there, maybe 500 lawyers dealing in entertainment. It is a tiny little bar and a tiny little business, and in the scheme of things, if you compare what a motion picture grosses in a year to Exxon's gross profits, a year's worth of a film's profits is like a day's worth of Exxon's. There are expanding technologies, but the software business, which is the business we're all in, is not expanding exponentially, so the jobs are primarily to be filled because of turnover. And there is not that much turnover.

There are very few entry-level jobs. When we look for somebody, we're looking for somebody who has three or four years of experience. Because we're busy, we don't have the time or inclination to train anybody. There are very few entertainment law firms that will take entry-level people. So it is very difficult to get in. It helps to have fabulous law school credentials to get in the door of the few law firms that still have an entry-level program. All the "kissy points"—good grades, prestigious schools—matter, unfortunately. They are not the only things that matter, but they do matter. Certainly if you want to go to the studios, there are a couple of studios that will take people with no previous entertainment experience, such as Disney. But they usually want someone who has had good corporate experience, or good litigation experience, someone with some legal background.

You can try to pound your way into an agency. Surprisingly enough a lot of people with Harvard MBAs, Yale degrees, and law degrees are going to work at the agencies. The future seems to be heralding the era of the agency. The agencies wield enormous amounts of power and there are enormous amounts of money to be made, and being an agent is a much more respectable job than it used to be. Creative Artists Agency has brought a very corporate, organized veneer to the agency business. The kids in the mail room and the young agents are all extremely well educated, focused, and motivated people. They are not unlike people you would see at IBM or any other major corporation. It is not the "Sammy Glick" era any more.

In considering a potential employee, I think people respect somebody who is willing to work hard and whose record indicates their ability to work hard. We have a young man that works for us now who comes from a working-class background, got himself into Dartmouth, got into Harvard Law School, got on the Harvard Law Review. That record indicates, if nothing else, a willingness to work, and that's very important. This is a hard business. People put in long hours, and you have to be very dedicated. This is not a business for dilettantes, and it is brutal to them.

If you don't feel passionate about the product, it's the wrong business to be in because that's what drives it. Unfortunately, there is a disturbing trend in this business to give people few chances. If you are one director and you make one bad movie, whoop, you are history, you are gone. It is understandable because the costs and risks are getting increasingly staggering per picture.

The passion must be there. Several years ago, I represented—in fact still do represent—a very wonderful director. I had had one of those days where everything went horribly from moment one. The last meeting of the day was about this particular director. It was a very tough meeting, and we were negotiating like crazy, emotions were running high. I felt just beat to death, and on the way home in my car at 9:00 P.M., I was thinking, "Why do I do this? Why do I go through this bullshit? I could be a bicycle mechanic, I could build boats, I could do all sorts of other things. I don't have to do this." I dragged myself into the house and flicked on the **Z** channel—the dear departed **Z** channel—and on it, about a third of the way through, was one of this director's movies. It's an exceptional movie. I watched it for ten minutes, and I said, "That's why I do it." You go through all this craziness and, every once in a while, something really wonderful comes out the other end, and you're a little tiny part of it, and I'm proud of that.

3
THE GUARDIANS

Without a screenplay, there can be no movie.

The Story Editor culls through reams of material in search of what he hopes will be a hit movie.

The Titles Registrar protects a very important element of the movie—its title. A successful title can be worth millions by attracting an initial audience to a motion picture in newspaper ads, on posters, billboards, and theater marquees.

The Script Supervisor, like a staff sergeant in the army, rides herd over the most minute details of a script that need to be kept on track in the feverish course of making a film—matters of continuity and shot selection (scenes to be shot and others that will get away because of time and money limitations)—and jealously guards the treasured intent of the screenplay while standing at the ready at the director's right hand.

Story Editor

The Story Editor supervises a staff of analysts who read and evaluate the screenplays, books, and plays submitted to the studio and cultivates relationships with the publishers and agents who make those submissions. He or she prepares development notes for the writers and producers who are creating projects for the studio. And the Story Editor usually functions as a member of the "creative group"—the core of executives who select, develop, and supervise the movies on the studio's production slate.

Dan Bronson

After receiving a doctorate from Princeton University, DAN BRONSON taught English and American literature at Prescott College in Arizona and DePauw University in Indiana. A lifelong interest in the movies led him to create a film program at DePauw and eventually won him an internship at Universal Studios, where he was apprenticed to legendary film editor Verna Fields and Directors Guild president Gilbert Cates. He subsequently worked as a story analyst at Universal, Fox, and Paramount, as associate story editor at Filmways, and at the time of this interview, he was executive story editor at Paramount Pictures.

MY BACKGROUND is not in film. It is in literature. Shakespeare, English literature, and American literature. As a matter of fact, I've always been in love with language. That's what got me into teaching in the first place. There were things in F. Scott Fitzgerald that were so vivid I felt compelled to study his work.

I remember the opening of *Tender Is the Night* and the bright tan prayer rug of a beach spread out in front of the hotel of strangers. And it just seemed absolutely right. Not only could you *see* that beach stretched out before the pink facade of that blushing hotel, but you knew what the novel was all about—the worship of wealth. The tan prayer rug and all the corrupt people.

Well, that kind of thing got me very excited and sustained me through a rather long teaching career. But as I worked my way further and further into that career, I got back to my first love, which has always been film.

I discovered that there is another kind of language—a language every bit as exciting as the words that F. Scott Fitzgerald put together. I made this discovery while I was watching Kubrick's *2001*, in partic-

ular a scene I'm sure you must remember. The apes touch the mono-
lith and they begin to evolve, they begin to learn to use primitive tools.
There's that one magnificent scene, after the ape has ironically taken
his first step toward civilization and learned to kill with a tool. He picks
up that thigh bone and he crashes it down, again and again and again,
on that pile of bones, and they shatter and fragment and fly all around.
And finally, in a sense of elation and triumph, he throws it up end over
end and, cut to, as the bone comes tumbling down, a nuclear satellite
circling the Earth. My God, hundreds of thousands of years of evolution in a split second on a screen. That's when I thought, *yes, I want
to know about that, too.*

I started working with film and had a very hard fight of it at this
conservative little institution in Indiana, which thought that film was
something akin to underwater basket weaving. It took a long, long
while. We slipped film into our interim semester, a winter-term course
between the two "academic" terms. And then, finally we got an in-
troductory film course and then a film program. It grew and grew.

My perspective on film until I made the move to Los Angeles was
very much an academic, intellectual, and aesthetic one, the kind of
thing I was just talking about with that wonderful, wondrous cut from
2001. I taught film as a visual art, essentially a silent medium. I spent
a lot of time looking at early film and at the vocabulary of film that
evolved during the silent era. I felt that I could teach my students most
of the techniques of contemporary cinema just by looking at the silents. And then we discovered the terrible setback of sound and
watched film work its way back to what is essentially a visual medium
in films like *2001* and *Psycho*, which are half silent.

Then I came to Hollywood. I joined the film "industry," the film
"business." Not the film "art." Nobody ever calls it the "film art." It
is the film *business.*

I spent six months as a studio intern at Universal. I accepted a
position as a story analyst in the studio story department, resigned my
tenured professorship, and found that because a strike was about to take
place, the union roster had not gone down to the level anticipated. I
couldn't take my job because there are all these wonderful catch-22's
in Hollywood. You can't have a job without being a member of a
guild, but you can't join a guild unless you already have a job. Well,
for four months I sat there and wondered how things were going back
there with my paycheck at the university as I sat around unemployed
in Hollywood.

Finally I got my position as a reader, and I experienced a rather abrupt shift of perspective. I was forced to see films as "product": "Now we have to get a certain amount of product out there in the market. We've got to feed our distribution system. We've got to feed that product out there . . ." I came to look at screenplays as "properties." Okay? Now these are things you *own*, like your house or your car.

So we talk about product. We talk about properties. If we talk about "art," we lose our jobs, because they think we've gone soft in our heads.

It's very obviously the entertainment *business*, the entertainment *industry*. And this was something I found very difficult to accept. As a matter of fact, I winced when my first employer said, "Look, Dan, any picture that makes money is a good picture."

I remember sitting through *Smokey and the Bandit* and looking at all these morons around me laughing at this ludicrous nonsense on the screen. But boy, did *Smokey and the Bandit* make money! And now I was being told that *Smokey and the Bandit* was a good picture?

But, in a sense, my employer was right. Because if a picture doesn't make money, people find themselves out of work. This *is* an industry. This is a business. And it's a very volatile industry, one that's very quick to respond to successes and failures in the marketplace. And the gentleman who told me any picture that makes money is a good picture is someone who had grown up in a Hollywood family. His parents had been story analysts, story editors, and writers all their lives. And he remembered, his voice trembling a bit as he told me about those days when his parents used to come home and he could tell from the expression on their faces that they'd been laid off. Or that the studio (RKO) was "going under." Or whatever. Disaster after disaster after disaster.

I myself have been out of work because of an actors strike, a writers strike, and fear of a directors strike. So it is an industry, it is a business. And when films fail, people suffer. People are out of work. So it's very easy to denounce these commercial assholes in Hollywood who have no taste and don't give a damn about anything but the profit-and-loss sheets. But, in actual fact, there's more to it than that.

There's a lot of commercial assholes out here, there's no question about that. But at the same time, there are people who are quite rightly concerned about keeping the studio afloat and keeping people working.

What a Story Analyst Does

The question that I always ask myself when I am evaluating a project is this: If it were my ten million dollars, would I be willing to spend it on this project?

The answer is usually "no." The answer is very frequently "no."

Story departments, by the way, have really become clearinghouses for the studios. They get an enormous amount of material.

Studios are structured in a fairly conventional way. There's someone at the top who is probably the only person who can say yes to putting a project into production. One person. Below him, there are a series of creative vice presidents or vice presidents for production who supervise development projects. Their names never appear on the screen, but they're the ones responsible for these things being there. They look around for material. It's submitted to them by agents, by producers, by directors. They're getting work from an enormous number of sources, and of course, they convey the impression that they're going to read all these things and evaluate them themselves.

They almost never do. They don't have time. They're too busy. What do they do? They send it down to the story department. The story editor assigns it to a story analyst, who writes a synopsis and an evaluation or comment. It's called coverage. They "cover" the screenplay or the book or whatever's submitted. Then they send it back to the studio executive.

Now ninety-nine times out of a hundred, it'll be with a negative recommendation. Every once in a while, it will go down with a "yes." If it's earned a yes, perhaps an executive will read the project. Perhaps. Not always. And if that executive happens to like it enough, he or she may go to the single person who can say yes and say, "Hey, I've got something terrific, let's go with it. . . ." Chances are, that executive will be shot down. The top executive will reject the material.

But every once in a while, it happens that a project gets on to the development or production list at a studio. Perhaps one in ten of the projects on the list actually show up on the screen.

That's the process. That's where the story department fits in.

What a Studio Looks for in a Screenplay

Well, what do you look for if you're a story editor or analyst? You're inevitably concerned with basics like character, dialogue, plot and structure, visual potential, and, finally, commercial prospects. There are other things, but those are the main ones you deal with in almost every piece of coverage.

Let me return to this idea of the difference between the academic perspective and the industry perspective. I received a screenplay about a year ago that was very obviously a new version of *Smokey and the Bandit*. I hated it. However, I realized it was much better crafted than the original *Smokey*. It was actually funny. The characters were better developed, and it had a much tighter story.

And, of course, Hollywood is nothing if not imitative. Mostly it imitates itself and its own successes. So I found that I had to give this screenplay a "maybe" even though I loathed it.

All right? There's one example of the kind of compromises that you find yourself forced to make in this business.

Then I came across a beautiful screenplay. It was owned by a major producer who had had some of the largest successes of the last ten years. It was a western in which there were really only three characters who counted—a buffalo hunter, a black man, and an Indian girl. It was a meditation upon the meaning of the West, upon frontier freedom, its strengths and possibilities and its limitations. And I laughed and I cried as I read this thing. And I tensed up with excitement. My God, it was wonderful. So I recommended it, only to be told—I was still new at this—that westerns were "out." Okay? Nobody's doing westerns anymore.

Well, actually, there were a number of people trying them. At that time, *Tom Horn* had just wrapped. *Cattle Annie and Little Britches* had just gone into production. And, of course, there was *Heaven's Gate*. There were a lot of westerns being tried. But at my studio they said it couldn't be done. The western was dead. And, of course, they said, when you look at the reception of the movies mentioned above, there's no chance for the genre currently.

That's another example of the startlingly different perspectives you come across out here.

Another project I dearly loved, Philip Caputo's *Horn of Africa*, was something I read when it was still in galley form. It's a brilliant book, a contemporary *Heart of Darkness* concerning a mercenary mission to a remote province of Ethiopia. It's a masterwork, and the author is a contemporary Conrad. It has everything a movie should have. The three best characters since *Deliverance*. Wonderful dialogue, dramatic action, spectacular highly visual backgrounds.

Unfortunately, the studio I was at when I covered this project had just committed itself to a number of very expensive failures. So the word had just come out, a week before I got this thing, that we were not going to commit to any more big-budget films. So I had to praise *Horn of Africa* but recommend against it due to budgetary considerations.

There are a lot of frustrations in life out here. Production costs are one of them.

Recently I came across a novel by a very famous older novelist. It had been adapted by a skilled screenwriter. I loved it as a book, but it was a slow, probing psychological study that simply didn't have enough action sequences or vivid-enough characters to justify filming. I had to recommend against it. Well, there we go. Projects that I myself respond to with great enthusiasm, I have to say no to or find that someone else will anyhow.

As literary works, certain stories or novels may be masterpieces. Yet as films, many of them haven't got a chance, for a variety of reasons. This new perspective on film has caused me some pain as I sit watching movies. I go to the revival houses a lot.

Recently, I caught *Slaughterhouse Five* for the first time. Billy Pilgrim coming unstuck in time. It's astonishing the way this fragmented story comes together in a beautiful mosaic. It's really a wonderful experience. I love the way it's cut. The editing is so tight. There's a scene with Billy in a freight car, peering out from under a blanket on his way to Dresden, and there's a cut to match later with him peering out from under a blanket at this nurse. Well, the cut ties the two sequences, which are vastly disparate in time, and it shows you that he's in a prison no matter where he goes. This kind of imaginative filmmaking really turns me on. But if it had come to me as a screenplay, I probably would have said upon reading it, "Look, this is much too fragmented to hold the attention of a mass audience." Brilliant, but it will not be a commercial success.

That pains me, but it's my job as a story analyst.

One of the first questions you ask yourself as a story analyst is: Is there a character the audience can relate to? Is there someone you care enough about to watch his story from beginning to end? This does not mean that he has to be a moral man or someone like you or me, but he must be sympathetic, someone we can relate to.

I thought *Thief* was an absolutely brilliant film that introduced Michael Mann as a major director. But it's highly uncommercial. An unsympathetic central character. A man who lives outside the law believing in nothing, capable of anything because he knows that nothing matters. It's not the sort of character that goes over well in today's conservative society. I'm delighted to have seen this film, delighted it got made, but I'm just glad it wasn't my studio that made it because it lost a lot of money.

The films I most admire are entertainment that becomes art. They're entertainment first. Films have to be that if the studio that makes them is going to survive.

It's terribly exciting to work within the commercial limitations of the marketplace, as Hitchcock and Shakespeare did in their times. I look to Ford and Hitchcock for examples of this kind of film. Hitchcock to me is the supreme example. Until the last years of his life, virtually all his films made money. He was a man with obsessive themes always expressed in highly commercial, exciting ways. He was Shakespeare as far as I'm concerned. It seems to me that film is what we have in place of drama in Shakespeare's day.

That's what it's all about. And you feel like beating your chest and screaming if you manage to beat the system, if you manage to make it work for you, if you go along with all the rules and somehow still manage to make your own movie, to make your own statement. It's that possibility, no matter how remote, that keeps a lot of the most creative people out here trying to make movies.

Unemployment may be a constant reality out here. It's very different from the academic world, where they have this beast called tenure. You have quite the opposite out here. You have total insecurity. It's terrifying, but it's very exciting at the same time, and I'm really glad I made the move.

Current Trends

I find that the most successful films are very often the most original films, the ones that are unlike anything you've been seeing in the last few years. Science fiction was dead until *Star Wars*. Suddenly science fiction is really *hot*. That's what happens. And what people fail to realize is that it's the originality of the project as much as it is the public demand or appetite for that particular kind of movie that's responsible for the success of the film.

You know, we had a whole series of "disaster" films. That was very, very big. Everyone wanted to do a disaster movie—earthquakes, plane crashes, fires. We've had this *Halloween* thing, horror movies. For a few years now, we've been tormented by this sleaze. I used to love horror movies. I still do. I think *Psycho* is a masterwork of cinema. But I'm beginning to have serious questions about the genre.

Let's see, sword and sorcery was in, now it's out. Westerns are still out. It's all nonsense, really. As far as I'm concerned it comes down to whether or not you have a terrific story told in a terrific style. If you've got that, none of these preconceptions really apply.

Submitting Material to a Story Editor

I don't think writers should send a treatment or synopsis with a screenplay when submitting to a studio. They'll read the treatment instead of the screenplay. There are some people who've been readers for thirty or forty years. They learn to skim. They learn to read just the dialogue. One of the tricks that you learn as a screenwriter is to keep the prose descriptions as brief as possible because chances are that the reader who looks at your material won't read them anyhow.

Readers get tired. And if they see a synopsis of a work inside the pages of the screenplay, they'll read the synopsis and write their own synopsis on the basis of that. I've seen it happen many times. It's a fatal error to include a synopsis. Bad strategic move.

Reader's Burnout

Story departments are ordinarily pretty efficient. When I read a screenplay that's good, I can usually tell in a page or two that it's special. They are that rare, good screenplays. Reading can be very depressing. You read such garbage. I mean, ninety out of a hundred screenplays are total shit. You can't believe how bad, how unprofessional, a lot of these things are even though they're submitted by agents. There's another 9 percent that may be competent but don't work for one reason or another. Then there's that one percent that actually may do it for you.

You get tired of reading all these scripts. You feel contaminated after a while, like you want to take some sort of spiritual bath. It would be very nice, I suppose, to be a powerful producer who only has to read so far and say, "Okay, I'm not interested," or, "I'll take it." But if you're in a story department, your responsibility is to the executive, and there's always the possibility, however remote, that the screenplay will take fire on page ten. Or page fifty. Suddenly it shifts gears and there's something there that will work. Usually it's the other way around. It's beautiful for the first act and it dies in the second and third.

As a reader, your responsibility is to find something of value if it's there, and that means reading it from beginning to end. And I try to read *every* word of a screenplay when I'm given an assignment.

The Ones That Got Away

One of the first things you learn when you start reading in Hollywood is that you can never get in trouble by saying no. Now of course this has serious repercussions. Everyone is scared. There's a tremendous amount of fear and paranoia in the studio structure in Hollywood. Everyone lives in fear for his professional life. It's silly, and people do some silly and sometimes reprehensible things as a result of this terrible fear.

You know, a Hollywood friend once told me that the awful thing about paranoia is that it's *real*. If you are driven by fear, if you live in that kind of atmosphere, and you're told that you'll never get in trouble by saying no, well, what are you going to do? You're going to turn down everything that comes to you. And that's how a lot of story people make their living. But don't tell anyone I told you!

The point is that you can get into trouble for saying yes if you're in a story department. If you do say yes and the film goes on to become *Raiders of the Lost Ark*, everyone forgets that you were the first to say yes and everyone else takes credit right on up the ladder. If it's a tremendous disaster, everyone looks around for the reader who said yes to this project. It was his fault.

As far as I'm concerned, there's no reason to be in this industry if you haven't got a passion for film. You've got to *act* on that passion. And if you find something you believe in, you've got to go out on a limb. And if your head rolls, it's going to roll into another studio. It's okay if you lose your job, you expect to lose it, and as a matter of fact, you wear it as a badge of pride because it means you took a stand on something.

You simply have to go and fight. That's what it's all about. And there's not enough of that out here, and that's one of the reasons that we have the kind of appalling films we so often see today. There are very few films in the last three or four years that I care about seeing again. And I never thought I'd hear myself make that kind of statement because I love movies. I'm a junkie. I've got to have my fix of film every week. But it's been pretty impure stuff lately.

How to Prepare Yourself to Become a Story Editor

A good story analyst knows how to write well. He or she has a literary background, knows something about the history of film, knows contemporary movies. He or she knows the current state of the industry, reads the trade magazines, and has some sense of current events, of what's happening in the country today. You've got to know the inside of the industry on the one hand and your audience on the other. Most of all, you've got to know story. You've got to know why one story *works* . . . and another *doesn't*.

Postscript: *Subsequent to giving this interview, Dan Bronson left his studio job to pursue a full-time career as a screenwriter. His adaptation of the novel* The Last Innocent Man, *which starred Ed Harris and was produced by Home Box Office, received critical acclaim. Dan Bronson has also written projects for Interscope, Disney, Paramount, Tri-Star, MGM, and Orion.*

Titles Registrar

The Titles Registrar is a paralegal or lawyer employed by the studio who is responsible for registering the title of a project with the Motion Picture Association of America (MPAA). This provides a limited form of protection for a film project's title, ensuring that no other signatories to the Motion Picture Association of America title memorandum agreement can use that registered title during the time that the original registering company is in the priority position.

Dan Furie

DAN FURIE got a summer job in the legal department at Paramount through the placement office at the University of Southern

California between his second and third year of law school, and he continued working there on a part-time basis during the school year. Shortly thereafter Dan became the titles registrar at Paramount and was able to use the position to become a project attorney for the company.

Even though his father is noted director Sidney J. Furie (*Lady Sings the Blues, The Boys in Company C, Iron Eagle*), Dan has avoided using his father's connections to get ahead.

 ITLES REGISTRATION started in the twenties when there was havoc in terms of people using titles. The majors got together and decided, "Hey, this is ridiculous, we need to come up with a system." In coming up with a system, they decided they didn't just want the right to use a title, they wanted to make sure that they were the *only* company who could use the title.

Titles registration, as it exists today, is a means of getting limited protection for a film title rather than relying on the protection provided by the law of unfair competition and the concept of "secondary meaning." It is only a *limited* form of protection—for a number of reasons. One, it only protects the use of titles vis-à-vis those companies that are signatories to the Motion Picture Association of America (MPAA) title memorandum agreement, which includes the major studios and some independent producers. It offers no protection to independent producers or companies that are not signatories to this agreement. The protection is a result of everyone agreeing that the system exists. It is not a legal mechanism per se.

Two, protection is granted only for a limited period of time unless a picture is produced.

Secondary Meaning

Your title is truly your own only after it has acquired so-called secondary meaning, meaning that the public identifies that title with your particular product—in this case your film. Until that time, you really do not have any means of stopping the other person from using the title.

Secondary meaning usually attaches to a title after the film has been released and people out there say, "Oh, yes, that's that movie with so and so. . . ." For example, *E.T.* definitely has secondary meaning. Sometimes secondary meaning can attach based on publicity for a film. For example, when the public knows that this *E.T.* is a Steven Spielberg film, it's possible that the film could acquire a secondary meaning prior to the release.

Two Types of Title Registration

The two categories for titles registration are the *copyrighted work* classification and the *original feature* classification.

The *copyrighted work* classification applies to titles where the person registering the title has the rights, or is negotiating for the rights, to a previously published work. Once your rights terminate or expire— let's say if you have an option on a book that expires—then you have no further right to maintain that registration. You are in priority as long as you own the rights so you can effectively block anyone who just dreamed up the title on his own. The only way those people can use that title is with your consent, and that consent is called a "waiver."

The title has to be exactly the same as the published work. For example, *Love Story* was a book by Erich Segal. Paramount would register that title in the classification of a copyrighted work.

The title of a published work gets a greater form of protection than an original title because it is presumed to have a connection to the published work in the minds of the public.

The original feature classification includes everything else. These titles have to wait in line because theoretically any one of the signatories could dream up a title and stake a claim to it.

How Titles Are Registered

Titles can come to me for registration through anyone in the company—from a creative executive, from a producer, from an attorney, from a business affairs executive . . . whoever thinks about it first.

We have some systems in place to ensure that all *real* titles, meaning other than "working" titles of projects "in development," get registered just in case someone else comes along.

There are cards that the MPAA provides that are very simple to complete—you fill out the date, you list the name of the title, and you mark the classification, whether it be copyrighted work or original feature, and just mail the cards in to the MPAA. Then the registration is published in the TRRs, or title registration reports, which are issued daily, except on holidays.

Protests and Transfers

When a title is registered, all other companies have a ten-business-day period in which to protest the title based on similar titles that they may want to use.

For example, Paramount registers *Love Story*—someone else may have *A Very Special Love Story*. That company would then send a letter to Paramount and to the MPAA saying, "We hereby protest your registration of that title because it is confusingly similar [or words to that effect] to our title that we have previously registered." And that freezes Paramount from using that title until they either negotiate with the company that made the protest or take the matter to arbitration at the MPAA.

Obviously we prefer to negotiate with a company because arbitration takes time and energy and some expense. Most companies cooperate whenever they can because they know that they will want similar treatment if they need to clear a title. The other thing to note is that generally the major studios will not negotiate until the other title, for which the person is requesting the protest be removed, is a green-lighted "go" picture, which means it is in either preproduction, production, or postproduction. Studios don't want to have to deal with the issue until it is a real controversy, and it is not a real controversy until the other side wants to use that title for a "go" picture. When companies cannot come to an agreement through negotiation, the dispute goes to arbitration.

You try to develop a sense of what kind of protest could withstand an arbitration. You don't want to just fire off protest letters willy-nilly because you do tie up someone's title when you protest, and while it's not that much of an inconvenience, after a while you can build up resentments. It would be comparable to an attorney in court saying "Objection!" every five minutes. You try to use some discretion.

However, once the deadline has passed, it's too late to block the other company's title. So you do err on the side of protesting because it is very easy to withdraw a protest. You just send a letter to that effect.

Upward Mobility

It is valuable, as a project attorney, to understand the titles registration system. Titles are very important to companies. They spark interest in a film and help attract audiences.

We usually don't confer with creative executives on the daily protest letters. They assume you're doing your job. To the extent that things are going along smoothly, nobody pays attention. That's true on the lawyer level generally, not just titles registration. And in a corporation that's to be expected. On a general day-to-day basis, you're not noticed unless you're screwing up.

For the most part, title registrars at the "major" studios are not lawyers. They are paralegal-type people who usually do credits as well as titles, under the supervision of a lawyer. There is upward mobility in terms of what a paralegal can accomplish—such as doing more in credits, contract administration, casting administration. It is conceivably a foot in the door for a move into publicity or a low-level creative job.

As a way to becoming a project attorney or some other kind of entertainment lawyer, if you have a law degree, being a title registrar is a way to get into the studio. But there may be a lot of clerical work. When I started, I did my own typing, photocopying, and filing. You have to be willing to get down into the pit and do the dirty work.

Eventually, maybe, it will pay off. It happened for me. I think if you are diligent and subtly make people aware of what your goals are, they'll think of you when they need someone to fill that position.

At the moment I am content to work as a project attorney. I suppose at some point the learning curve will flatten out, and then I might be ready for a change. As for the creative area, the films I'm interested in tend not to be commercial, and right now I don't want to mortgage my life-style to the vagaries of that area.

Script Supervisor

The Script Supervisor serves as an indispensable aid to the director, maintaining an up-to-the-minute accurate shooting script and recording in meticulous detail all information related to each take, including the date, time, and length of the shot, scene and take number, lenses, t-stop, camera placement, frame rate variation, and printable takes, as well as any notations on dialogue, action, props, set dressing, costume, hair, and makeup in order to provide continuity during shooting and to facilitate editing.

Meta Wilde

META WILDE recently received the prestigious Lifetime Achievement Award from the Women in Film Organization as well as the Crystal Award in 1985 for Outstanding Woman in Film.

She is the founder and first president of the Script Supervisors Union. Her lifelong relationship with William Faulkner is the subject of her critically acclaimed memoir, *A Loving Gentleman*, and her work, at age seventy-seven, with John Huston on *Prizzi's Honor* was the culmination of a distinguished career that spans more than fifty years in the film business. Her credits include such classics as *The Maltese Falcon, Old Acquaintance, Now, Voyager, To Have and Have Not, The Big Sleep, Rio Bravo, Who's Afraid of Virginia Woolf?, The Graduate, Catch-22,* and *Carnal Knowledge.*

MY FIRST job as a script supervisor was with Howard Hawks. I was his secretary for four years. There were no script supervisors as such—just people who helped out on the set.

We actually created the job. On *Barbary Coast*, Howard took me down on the set with him to take notes and work with Eddie Curtis, his editor, or "cutter," as it was then called. Eddie sat down on the set with me—and in those days we had different lenses than we have now—and showed me what a 28-millimeter would do, what a 35-mm, 40-mm would do—what a 2-, 3-, 4- and a 6-inch lens would do according to where the subject was in front of the camera. This was the beginning of what eventually became the job of script supervisor.

So I was down on the set doing that every day as well as doing Howard Hawks's personal secretarial work, taking care of his wife's bank account, hiring the washerwoman, taking his children to their grandparents' house.

I made so many mistakes back then! I remember very clearly one day, Howard Hawks was on a boom, high in the air looking down on a big set. There was a communications system on the boom, sort of a PA system. And he said, "Meta, what angle did I want?"—or something to that effect—and I was going through page after page and I couldn't find anything. I finally had to say, "Mr. Hawks, I don't know," and he called out, "Bring me down!" And he came down and said, "Give me the book, Meta," and he went through the book and said, "Here it is." I really learned the hard way. I was young. I guess he took that into consideration.

Eddie spent about six weeks telling me about geography and logistics and how the camera functions on-screen—things like an over-the-shoulder or "Now the camera is looking from right to left" and "When you reverse that angle you have to go left to right" and "There's a certain line beyond which the camera cannot go without putting people on the wrong side." I learned how the director thinks and how the actor thinks. I learned certain technical things, for example, how fast film runs through the camera.

The Job

What started off as just taking notes on the set has now become very specialized with a system that is quite rigid. There are certain things you must do and certain forms you must turn in to the production office and to the editor—and information that must be sent to the various departments.

Certain "rules" like script supervisors having to be on the set when the director is on the set did not exist when I first started out. It makes sense because at any second he may want you. But it certainly is hard on your bladder! If he says, "I'm sure I did that close-up last week," I have to find the day we shot it, how many takes, which takes were printed and which takes were held (in other words, saved for possible printing later on), and how long the takes ran. You can't be too far away from the director when he's on the set because he wants that information and he wants it now.

Script supervisors should never leave the studio until they've seen the dailies. They could show you something for the next day's work. You could possibly have made a mistake you weren't aware of. Dailies will help you prepare for tomorrow.

Script supervising is more difficult now because the lenses have changed. We zoom a lot now. I have to depend more on the "focus man," who stands on our side of the camera, rather than the "camera operator," who stands behind the camera. After the last rehearsal of a scene before shooting, I'll ask the focus man, "What is your focus?" and he'll say, "We're going from 125 to 280 and back." So then I will know what's happening on the screen.

Our work is crucial to the editor. I have to know all the scenes that are shot, the scenes that are left out, and how you segue from one scene to another, how the scenes are juxtaposed. It's fascinating how an editor can really remake a whole picture. He could almost make a love story out of a horror movie if he wanted to by his choice of cuts.

In terms of how I stand in the hierarchy, I think we rank above the second assistant director and a little below the first assistant director. We give information to the second assistant, we take information from the first assistant, and we all cooperate at the end of a day—how much we have accomplished, how many minutes, how many pages, how many scenes, how much left to do, and so on.

I'm sitting in the background viewing any discussion between any of these individuals. I can influence the decision of the director, if I feel comfortable with him, and say, "In my opinion take three and take six would be best," so he may then say, "Print three and six, but hold five and seven."

If a director were to say, "I know I made a close-up. I think it was a three-inch lens and it was about four or five feet from the subject, and I'd like to see that cut in," the editor can go to that can because I have a record of the day it was shot, the number of the scene, the slate number, and which take it was. I also have a record of the set description, the timing—in other words, how many minutes each take is—and the footage.

Providing Continuity

Our title is a misnomer. I never really liked the idea of being called a script supervisor. But this is what we ended up with. The British title "continuity" is more accurate. We keep everything in continuity. And I have sometimes had screen credit in that way.

Here's how continuity works. Wardrobe has to put the right costume on the actor in the wardrobe department before they come to the set. Once they get on the set, I'm responsible for what happens in the interior of the scene. If they walk in a room and take off their overcoat and hang it on a rack and take off their hat and put that on a table, and take a cigarette case out of their pocket and open it and take out a cigarette and light it, I'm responsible for keeping track of what they did and in what order they did it in.

The next day we might go outdoors to shoot exteriors. If we have to shoot him coming out of the house, I'm in charge of knowing how he was dressed when he left the room in the interior scene from the day before.

I'm not in charge of the fact that he has to be on the set with the right outfit. However, if I notice that he had on the wrong outfit, I would go up to wardrobe and say, "Are you sure you checked page five on that? According to my notes, he should have on the blue-striped suit and not the brown suit." Now I don't have to do that. That's their responsibility. But wouldn't it be mean if I didn't?

I depend on other crew members to come to me and help me. Very often I will say to a gaffer, "You know, that key light was on the left side of the subject," and he'll say, "You're absolutely right." Three weeks later he'll come over to me and say, "Meta, did you realize that when he sat down he had his gloves in the right hand and not the left?"

We all help each other. I'm only one person. I can't see everything, so I have to be friends with everyone, and moreover I want to be. This is a question of getting into your act on-stage—with everybody.

When I go onto a new set, when the day is just starting, I usually try to get there fifteen or twenty minutes before anybody else. And I will go into the room and see that this is a bar . . . the exit light is on . . . five booths . . . two people sitting at the bar . . . a bartender behind the counter . . . three men on stools. I'll sit and try to see everything.

I'll make a mental note of everything. Then when we block the scene, when the rehearsal starts, I can fill this all in. And it begins to be almost a photographic memory for each set. I can almost recall sets and scenes that we shot forty years ago. Now that doesn't apply to westerns when you're out in the desert with the sun and heat and so few frames of reference. But it is particularly important, say, in dining room scenes. There are twelve people at the table, and you have to keep track of the glasses that are being emptied and the cigarettes that are being tapped out.

Without my finished script, marked as it is with notes on the actual day-to-day shooting, it would be very difficult for the editor to put the film together.

Above and Beyond Normal Duties

Often we are used to cue action. In the early days there used to be dialogue coaches. Now that job is virtually nonexistent.

When I worked on *Who's Afraid of Virginia Woolf?* for Mike Nichols, I was reading off-stage lines in every close-up. If Elizabeth Taylor was tired and didn't want to do the close-up, I would play the scene off with Richard Burton, and vice versa. When Richard would go to have a drink or go to sleep or something, I would play Richard's part to give Elizabeth a semblance of what was happening.

On *Prizzi's Honor,* I read all the off-stage scenes for Jack Nicholson. All those bedroom scenes. As a matter of fact, I was quite upset one day because Johnny Huston's driver came up to me after I'd finished one of those scenes and said, "The way you read those lines!" indicating that it was very erotic and sexy. I said, "Now that's just acting and there's no reason for you to come and compliment me. That's just a job I'm supposed to do."

Some actors have impeccable memories, and I don't have to be quite as worried about them. Bette Davis, for instance, worked out the sequences in her particular role at home and marked it in her script. So if she came in the house with a fur scarf around her shoulders and gloves on and a hat, she knew when she came in that she took the hat off first, then the fur, then the coat, then the left glove and then the right glove. After a while, I never had to worry about Bette.

A director can benefit from my viewpoint. For instance, when I first read *Prizzi's Honor,* I told Johnny, "This script is too long. It is never going to play in two hours." He said, "Oh, yes, every page I can bring in in a minute's time, sixty seconds." I said, "Well, I know how Jack Nicholson speaks and I know that the feeling of the picture is such that you're not going to come in under a minute a page. Even at sixty-six seconds a page, it's not going to come in." "Oh, you're wrong, you're wrong," he said to me. So when we actually finished the picture, it ran two hours and thirty-nine minutes. We had to cut it down. That's the reason we had to lose a lot of wonderful scenes. It broke his heart, too.

Politics

The clerical work is something you get after a while. It just becomes second nature. Having done it so many years, I don't even have to think about it. It takes time and effort. But it is not as important in terms of keeping a job, in my opinion, as being aware of the political situation on the set and then "playing the game"—doing what you should do when you should do it and keeping your mouth shut when it should be kept shut and knowing when to back off and when to come forward with your concerns.

It's not a small job, learning to walk softly and please everybody as well as do the work. It's also a job in which you should have your mental faculties at the ready. Often when young people come in, they make mistakes because of a lack of seriousness. It's such an enticing, exciting business—"Oh, we're going on location!" So they get to New York, they're in a hotel. They do the day's work. Then they're alone—not at home, with friends or family. All of a sudden the guys in the company say, "How about let's go out tonight?" and inevitably it leads to drinking, late hours, getting distracted from the job. This doesn't happen with the pros, the old-timers—they simply say, "Look guys, gotta work. Saturday night or Sunday morning, I'll go out and have a drink with you. But I'm at the typewriter."

And I don't mind, haven't minded all my life, because I expect to be paid on Thursdays and I want to turn in the job that I'm being paid for. A lot of younger people don't view it that way—they see it as a stepping-stone—"I'm only doing this for now, I'm going to direct," or "I'm going to write." I've never wanted to direct, although script supervising is excellent preparation for that. Directing is a hard goal for a woman. Even today it's still a man's world. I know that. I'm not a fool. It's twice as hard for any woman.

Work is work, and I have a rapport with some of the people I work with, but I have another life totally apart from the business. I studied music all my life. I prefer moving in different circles, which I hope doesn't sound snobbish or arrogant.

Change

Hollywood has changed radically. There are no longer the major studios as we once knew them. There were eight "majors," and when you worked in those studios you were part of a family. And you knew that you were going to have a job. And you knew when someone's grandmother had died and when babies were born, and you attended birthday parties, picnics, and festivals.

Back then, when I finished a picture, I knew I would be assigned another picture right away. And I would run into some of the people I had worked with before. I wouldn't always remember the names—there were as many as four thousand people at a studio at one time!—but I did remember the faces. Policemen knew you, writers who came on the set knew you. Now the studios are run by businessmen for the most part. Certainly they are not run by creative people anymore. They are interested, first and foremost, in the box office. Money.

Warner, Thalberg, Goldwyn—of course, they were interested in money, too. But it was much more than money. It was a whole new industry. It was a pioneer mentality. Everything was a discovery, brand-new, of vital interest. There was a constant feeling of communal excitement.

I did feel that recently when I was reunited with John Huston on *Prizzi's Honor*. I had worked with John twenty-four years ago on *The Maltese Falcon*, and it was most nostalgic to bring back the old days.

The Union

During the mid-forties, I was working with other people who were all interested in trying to have some structured organization. If it could be said that anyone sparked that interest and carried it through, perhaps I did, but there were many others who were just as eager.

There was a lady, Thelma Priest—a professional secretary who agreed to work with us and very graciously opened her home to maybe ten or twelve of us every week. We'd talk about what we would like to do and what we would like to be and how we would like to talk to the producers. Then she would serve hot chocolate and tea and cookies or something. It wasn't long before I began to realize that we were simply not going to get anywhere as a small group of women and maybe one or two fuddy-duddy men.

We asked the producers to meet with us and negotiate with us. They agreed to give us a night, and we invited them for dinner, which we all pitched in and paid for at The Old Skandia, a small restaurant with a big wood-burning fireplace. We thought we were doing a big thing by getting the producers to come and meet with us there. We sat in the cool of the evening and outlined some of the things that we wanted. And they said, "Well now, girls, you don't have to worry about anything. You're going to get what everybody else gets." So we went along with that for a while until we found out we were *not* getting what everybody else was getting. We were still small fry, the bottom of the barrel, low man on the totem pole. That's when I decided to activate the people in our guild and ask them to affiliate.

What I did, in effect, was to campaign. I telephoned, wrote, pleaded, and begged with everybody in the group of our so-called guild at the time to vote for affiliation with IATSE, the International Alliance of Theatrical and Stage Employees, which is affiliated with AFL-CIO nationally.

Now the problem was that some of those people were older than me, and they all said, "The producers have been very nice to us. They've met with us and they've tried to help us and have always said they'd treat us well." Those were the ones opposed to affiliating with the union. But there were newer, younger people coming in. The industry was growing. All the studios were opening up. Our job was becoming more familiar to directors and producers. Instead of asking for secretaries to come down from the office to the set, they started having what was called a "script girl" or a "script boy" or a "script clerk"—whatever the director felt like calling us.

I even remember on one occasion that Michael Curtiz called across the stage yelling, "Script girl!" and I answered, "Yes, directoooor!" And he said, "She called me director!" I said, "Well, you *are* the director. You called me a script girl. My *name* is Meta." As you can see, I was sort of a maverick in those days.

Eventually I got to calling people in the middle of the night or any time of day I could get them. I'd say, "Please come to my house Sunday morning," or, "Please come by on Saturday night." And I would serve cheese and crackers and wine or whatever I could afford to spend. In those days I was making $42.50 per week, six days per week.

And we'd have general membership meetings. This went on for ten years because I kept getting opposition from the older people. Although there were vastly differing opinions, one thing we all wanted was recognition that our job was a highly responsible and important position, that we were not just "secretaries."

We petitioned for years to other guilds, thinking they would want us to be affiliated with them. We petitioned the Directors Guild, which said no. Mainly, I think, because we were females for the most part. We petitioned the editors. They turned us down. We really were on our own because we were a very small group. On a movie set, there were hairdressers, costumers, several makeup people, but only one script supervisor. It's difficult when you are so few in number to wield power in the labor force.

When I became the first president of our union—Local 871—we only had about 120 people. We have since grown to over 200. Still, we are one of the smallest unions. And many of those are inactive and don't pay dues. Our 200 people as a unit do not have enough power. If the directors had taken us in as they did the second and third assistant directors, they would have had to negotiate on our behalf. Apparently they didn't want to lose points for their own people, for television directors, documentarians, and the like. We were always the last priority, even though when we're on the set in production, everybody is always saying, "You kids are so underpaid, why don't you do something about it?" But when the chips were down, they refused to help us. Do you think all those people would walk a picket line for two hundred script supervisors? I don't think so. That's why they'll never help us. So we have to help ourselves.

Recognition and Wages

We were fighting for two main things—recognition of our capabilities and wages.

The respect for the position was something that took many years to earn. When I did *Come and Get It,* which starred Frances Farmer, there were three or four men in the company who were called script boys. I think at least one was a *grandfather,* and they were still called "boys." In the South, if you talked to a negro, to a "nigger," as they called them, it was, "Boy, come over here." It was that kind of attitude, and in fact today there is some of that mentality with some of the young directors, an attitude I abhor. People are on that set because they are needed. They have work to do, they contribute to the making of the film. And I don't understand why anybody wants to denigrate someone else's work. They may not be as important as the writer, the director, or the producer, but the stars and the creative team need those people there to supervise continuity, to operate the camera, even to push the door back and forth or to drive a truck out to location. They are there because they should be.

We finally became part of IATSE in 1957 and quickly blossomed to our present number. Over the years, of course, you have some attrition. People move away, die, withdraw, decide they don't want to work at all anymore. Presently, business as it is, we have as many as fifty people out of work at any given time. It fluctuates. Also, by gender, we are not just a female organization anymore. We are now made up of about one-third male members and two-thirds women.

The biggest benefit of being IATSE is that if you are ill, you can go to the Motion Picture Association hospitals and when you're old live in the Motion Picture Home. A lot of people don't realize when they're forty-three or fifty-one that the time is going to come when they're sixty-five or seventy or eighty.

I'm just damn lucky that people still want me to work for them because I'm so old now. It's incredible that I worked on *Prizzi's Honor* when I was seventy-seven years old. I still love to work, and I feel if people are still with it and still have all their marbles and can still function efficiently, there's no reason why they shouldn't just keep on working.

I don't think the younger members appreciate all the things we went through in those early days. Furthermore, they don't come to union meetings. The last membership meeting we had, out of two hundred people in the local, twenty-two people showed up. We needed twenty-five for a quorum. So we sat and waited for an hour while some of the members called up their friends who were script supervisors and said, "Please get dressed and get over here." On the other hand, when a grievance comes up, they expect the union to fight for them and get them the money they have missed.

The Future

I will concentrate on my next book. But I will also take a job if it comes up, as long as it's not in the jungles of Latin America in hundred-degree heat or a grueling schedule of all-night shooting on the subways of Manhattan.

I would like to add one final thing. With all the disadvantages, with the troubles and heartaches and some of the unpleasant, unhappy experiences, I think that all the years I've spent in the industry add up to being a rich and fulfilling life. And I'm grateful I've had it.

4
THE MONEY

Money flows when a movie gets made.

The Production Manager represents the needs and interests of the producer and the production in general. All checks are signed by him, all financial decisions are filtered through him. He finds himself frequently at odds with the Auditor, who monitors the spending of every cent in the best interests of the studio or financing entity.

The Auditor makes sure that every dollar is spent as originally intended. Quite often the Auditor is the one who has estimated what the final budget should be before the cameras start to roll.

The two positions in this chapter go head to head, working in tandem, while a film is being made.

Production Manager

The Production Manager is hired by the producer to coordinate and supervise all administrative, financial, and technical details of a motion picture production. He or she usually prepares the production breakdown—isolating each factor in the script—such as cast and crew needed in each scene, exterior or interior, day or night, length, cost, and complexity of each scene—and scheduling the most efficient and cost-effective order in which to shoot. The Production Manager also hires the crew and makes all the first contacts for dates, locations, and fees. During production, he or she approves changes in scheduling and the budget, serves as intermediary between the producer/management and crew, and oversees the activities of the entire crew.

C. O. "Doc" Erickson

C. O. "DOC" ERICKSON is something of a legend in Hollywood. He came out to Los Angeles after his discharge from the army at the end of World War II and managed to get a job in Paramount's budget department. From there he moved into set estimating, eventually making his way into the production department in charge of allocating stage space to the various production companies. In 1953, when Alfred Hitchcock came over to do *Rear Window*, Paramount was in the midst of a production boom, and not having an available production manager, Doc was assigned to production-manage the picture. "Hitch" took a liking to Doc, and he ended up doing Hitch's next four Paramount pictures—*To Catch a Thief, The Trouble with Harry, The Man Who Knew Too Much,* and *Vertigo.*

Doc left Paramount in 1959 when the studios began to lose their former control and producers were going independent to hook up with John Huston on *The Misfits* and *Freud.* He was then asked to production manage *Cleopatra,* the most logistically challenging feature of the day. Today, he's had twenty-five years of successful production managing, and more recently executive producing, on such pictures as *Chinatown, Urban Cowboy, Ironweed,* and *Phantom.*

PEOPLE OFTEN confuse producing and production managing. It's always gratifying, as a production manager, to hear, "Well, *you* really produced the picture." But producers do something quite different these days. Producers are usually involved in putting a project together. There was a time when producers were hired hands, as were production managers.

In this day and age, producers are *out* there looking for stories, writers, directors—trying any which way they can to find a project that they can then take to the "money," whether it's a studio, independent money, a bank, whatever, and get something going.

The producer is the first and foremost person in that activity. He's the one with the energy, foresight, or the talent, creativity, and *salesmanship* to convince somebody to make the project, whether it's a short story, a book, or a completed script. He has to sell somebody on it.

That's quite different from being a production manager. The production manager is only involved in the physical making of the movie. And his expertise lies in knowing how to put together a package of people to make the movie in the best fashion. The production manager is *interfered with* at all times by the director and the producer and everybody else, but mainly the director these days. That's because the director has become the person who has to have "approval of" everything from soup to nuts. This is not said in a complaining manner—it's just as a fact. The director is, after all—once the producer has involved him in the project—the man who has to deliver the picture. It's *his* vision that will appear on the screen.

I'm basically a facilitator, walking two tightropes. The first is between director and producer. The other is between the producer and director *and* management—whoever is putting up the money for the film. Now, if it's an independently financed film, it's quite different from a studio that has a hierarchy of people who are constantly involved in what you're doing. And you've got to report in and check in and make sure that you're not upsetting the applecart.

The director is reluctant to get involved in the nitty-gritty details of budgeting. The production manager works with the producer to establish what's affordable. The director will get involved to the extent that he'll say, "Okay, I don't need ten thousand extras—I can do with four thousand," or he doesn't need three cameras, he can do with one camera. He wants to know the broad strokes—"Am I okay on this?" or "Why is this costing so much?" or more often "Why can't I have . . . ?" He should be keeping his eye on the ball, the business of directing, and leave the budget responsibilities to the producer and production manager.

The day-to-day activity of making a movie, from a production manager's standpoint, is fairly dull and dreary. It's being here early in the morning, making sure that nobody's missing and answering all questions: "Why isn't this ready? Why didn't that happen?" "Who did that to whom?" "Did you hear about . . . ?" and "Guess what he wants now?" I find that tiresome.

The creative part of production management is in the planning of the movie. There you *can* have some influence over the producer and the director. Taking the script home and making a board and a schedule and a budget and thinking about where to make the film. Getting together some of the creative members of the crew like the production designer and the director of photography. They will listen to you when you say, "Forget about that production designer—I can tell you what he does, and you don't like that," that kind of thing. *But* if the director has made his choice already, then you're wedded to it and you've got to walk that tightrope again. And you've got to make it work.

There's no thrill in coming in under budget. In the planning, you can talk about things that really affect the creative making of the movie. You're trying to find a way to make the picture—*not* for less money necessarily, but to make *more* picture for the same money.

The thrill is going a little bit over budget—and having everything that the producer and the director and the studio wanted on screen.

That's the prebattle planning. Once you go into battle, you're dealing with the daily logistics of making a movie. It's a loose framework of authority. The production manager *is* responsible for signing that piece of paper saying "It's okay to do this" or "The budget has been increased to accommodate this," and he does that knowing that he's already got or can get approval from the producer and/or management. If he thinks the expenditure is going to meet with a "no," he can still try to convince the producer by going to him with the individual—that art director who wants to add another wall to the set—to present his case. Or find another way for the director to shoot it.

Or you can simply do what management expects you to do. And that is to say, "No, you can't have it. You must realize that there's a limit to the budget." And you might win that one. And have to give on something else. But at least you're setting up a pattern. And saying, "The sky is *not* the limit. There's a limit well below it. Think twice before you ask for these things."

That's the day-to-day aspect. The propmaster wants another prop man: "I've only got one. We've got this big set. It's a restaurant scene— got to put meals out on the table. I need more help." If you know that

person, you respect him, or you've worked with him before and understand what he's saying—fine, get another man. You don't even
quarrel. But if you think, Wait a minute, this guy's putting one over
on me. He doesn't need another man. It's his brother-in-law he wants
to bring in for the day, then you resist it.

And that's not to say I don't make mistakes or misjudge people.

Then and Now

It's not fair to say that the people nowadays are not as bright or as
talented or as motion picture–oriented. It's a different world. This new
generation—they know better what pictures are going to sell. If it were
left to those of us who came out of the dark ages, we'd just be remaking
Parlor, Bedroom and Bath probably.

There's a line out of David Mamet's play *Speed-the-Plow:* "You
know what we want to make—anything that anybody else made last
year." That's what it's all about. Joe Mankiewicz—an old friend I've
made a couple of pictures with—said he'd gone in to see Louis Mayer
about a project he wanted to make right after Warners' big success with
Forty-Second Street. Mayer was reading the reports in *Variety* as Joe
presented his project. Mayer said, "I don't care about any of your
projects. I want another *Forty-Second Street!* I want a *Forty-Third
Street!*" And he's chasing Joe down the hallway—"*Forty-Fourth Street!
Forty-Fifth Street! Forty-Sixth Street!*"—yelling all the way.

That's what the business has always done.

Studio Support and Restrictions

On an independent picture, you deal with less people because
they don't have the staff—the legal, the music, the art, the postproduction departments—that you have in a major studio. In the studio,
you have a lot of bases to cover. That's not bad because they give you
a lot of help. But it forces you to make sure that you are keeping
everybody informed of what you're doing. You are not as free to strike
out on your own with some decision, which you could do on an
independent where you only have one or two people. The producer
might be the one person, or there's just one more phone call to make
and that's it.

Freedom has been more and more restricted in our area over the
years with the change in the contractual situation favoring the director

over the producer. It's troublesome from time to time because you have less freedom to put together a crew.

I get to select my production coordinator. And *maybe* the craft services man. But even that's not always so. The director may have one he likes from the last picture. You *might* get the transportation coordinator if the director was unhappy with the one on his last picture. And that's about it. The assistant director is absolutely a choice of the director. And he insists contractually on the right to approve almost every key position there is. The director of photography. And then the DP says he has to have his grip and gaffer and camera operator. On and on . . . there's not much left.

Postproduction for me is very unimportant since any major studio or company has its own postproduction department. I've followed a few pictures all the way through, and it's very dull for me. My credo is, once they've wrapped, finished shooting, move on.

Executive Producer

People tend to feel that you are a little bit more important than the production manager. But basically the job is the same—you're dealing with the physical side of making the movie. Nobody's interested in what *I* think of the script. It gives you a few things—insures that your name in the credits is ahead of the producer. It makes your mother feel good. It almost always insures your name in the paid ads and on the billboards. It gives you more prestige.

I'm not belittling the title. It does boost you a notch or two. But I find I do principally what I've always done. Maybe you get it done a little easier because "Oh, that's the executive producer talking—pay attention," and you are accorded a certain amount of respect.

Screamers

I don't know whether screamers are in or out these days. I don't know how to scream, and I am currently working with people who don't know how to scream, either. It's possible to be firm and know what you want and not put up with any nonsense without being a screamer. In the early days, people like De Mille—though I never worked directly for him at Paramount—just struck fear in the hearts of anybody connected with the show. You really trembled when he came on the set; you never knew whom he was going to strike out at.

Today the director probably has more power than De Mille had, at least contractually. But they're a different breed.

Unions

They're being pummeled. They've lost all their clout. Whether they can ever regain it, I don't know. All the things that individuals and unions fought for for so many years—decent wages, decent hours, health and welfare, pensions, and so on, whether they've led to increased costs or exorbitant costs—management was only too eager to give them in return for labor peace. They didn't want to stop work. They wanted to get those movies made. "What do you need? Another 10 percent? We'll give it to you!"

Now suddenly management wants to take much of it away. That's an oversimplification, and I would hate to be sitting on either side of the bargaining table. When I started at Paramount I was in the office employees union, which was just an association. It meant nothing, we had no bargaining power, we were given whatever management wanted to give us—which was a dollar an hour. Forty bucks, $32.50 a week net. As I progressed into different areas, I eventually became a member of the Directors Guild of America, as all unit production managers have been since 1963. I'm very happy to be a part of that group because we have considerable clout. More clout goes to the directors than to us, but we tag along.

The Future

I look forward to more of the same. I like doing what I'm doing. Packaging, the creative end—I don't begrudge anybody the task of putting a picture together. Walking around with a script under your arm for a year or two, hoping that somebody will agree with you and say, "Aha, you've got just what we want" . . . that's not fun. I just hope there are a lot of people out there with scripts under their arms who get them made. And need somebody to help them. I'm here, ready.

As far as selecting or getting work—you always want to be doing that "other picture." Oh . . . that looks interesting, why didn't they call me? I think that's human nature. It's important not to wait for that more important picture to be offered to you. I've always followed the rule of "just take the first best offer." I haven't been unhappy doing that. Maybe I've missed opportunities to work on more important pictures. But . . . maybe not. That more important, more prestigious potential Oscar picture that you're waiting for sometimes never gets made.

The Toll

If you resent getting up in the dark and coming home in the dark . . . and missing your kid's birthday party or graduation or being out of the country at Christmas . . . you can't think about it. If you do, you're finished.

Auditor

The Auditor is responsible for keeping track of all financial costs and transactions incurred in the making of a motion picture. He or she works closely with the production manager in preparing a preliminary budget and monitoring the budgetary status of the production.

Sandra Rabins

SANDRA RABINS began her career in Hollywood as a secretary to a studio vice president of finance. She soon assumed additional responsibilities as auditor on such complicated motion pictures as *Flashdance, Explorers, Terms of Endearment,* and *Witness.* At the time of this interview she had just completed drawing up the budget on Paramount's $25 million feature *The Golden Child.*

MANY PEOPLE ask why a motion picture production requires the services of an auditing or accounting person at all. After all, if the financing studio has a payroll department, an accounts payable department, and other accounting functions as part of its production support services, then why not make all payments associated with the film through those studio-based departments?

There are some very compelling reasons for a production auditor to be assigned to a motion picture project. First, the sheer volume of accounting transactions that take place during production really requires the full-time attention of one individual. Without the auditor on staff—someone like myself—whose job it is to keep track of where all the production company's funds are going and how they are being spent, money can easily end up going out in all directions and being unaccounted for.

In addition, the auditor is needed to collect the show's financial information from the many possible and varied sources that exist. This is particularly true of a picture that is done on a studio lot rather than shot on location. When a film is produced on a studio lot, payments are being made by numerous sources that are not immediately under the control of the auditor: studio payroll and accounts payable departments, and so forth. The auditor is the member of the production team who must keep track of *all* sources of payments and their amounts in order to give to the production's management and the studio's executive management an on-going and accurate financial analysis of the film. If the production had no such person, payments could be duplicated or not made at all, and it would be very difficult to determine the current cost and the estimated final cost of the film.

The Budget

One of the key responsibilities of the auditor is to prepare an initial production budget. The purpose of the production budget is to identify all the costs that are likely to be incurred during the making of a motion picture. A budget is comprised of a "chart of accounts." The chart of accounts lists key departments involved in the production process, their support staffs, equipment, purchases, and rentals that are needed by them in the making of the film.

To successfully budget a motion picture, I have found that the auditor really needs to understand the unique role that each of the various departments plays in the production. Especially, the auditor needs to learn what function each of the various departments performs for the movie, what equipment they typically might use, how large a staff they usually require, and any union requirements that must be adhered to by the production. For example, if the script for a production I am involved in is a "period" picture, which requires that a large number of very intricate or detailed costumes be manufactured, I know that I should either become familiar, or renew my familiarity, with all of the major costume houses in the Los Angeles area that cater to the motion picture industry. For pictures like this where the manufacture of costumes can become a substantial part of the show's wardrobe budget, I always try to determine—or know where to find out most quickly—the current market rates for all of the specialized services that these costume houses may provide to the picture. And if any of the costume houses the costume designer is considering using has any unusual billing procedures that the show must follow, I'll make a note of that as well since it may affect the budget figure for the show's wardrobe account.

Set construction is another difficult area for the auditor to budget. The auditor should ask *many* questions of the construction crew and the production designer prior to preparing the budget for the construction of sets. Some of the questions I usually ask are, What is special or unique about any of the sets for this picture? Will they be built on a studio sound stage and remain there, or will they be constructed at the studio and then transported to another location? How many man-days of painters, plasterers, laborers, and so forth, will be needed to complete the sets? This information all translates into preliminary budget figures. The old saying, "Ask and ye shall receive," is especially true when formulating a motion picture's preliminary budget: ask as many questions of as many knowledgeable people as you can, and you'll receive valuable information for your budget.

Reading a Script with the Budget in Mind

I initially read the script to understand the film—its story, its locale, its unique production requirements that may have an effect on the cost of making the picture. After reading the script several times, I then review a breakdown board that has been prepared by a production manager or a first assistant director. A breakdown board defines the number of shooting days, the number of locations, the cast members and on which shooting days they are needed on the set, and any other daily requirements of the film: what stunts are to be performed on which day and by how many stunt people, what props, special costumes or vehicles are needed on a particular day. As I read and reread the script and become increasingly familiar with the story and with all the production elements that will be needed for the film to be produced, I will continue to discuss the project with as many key individuals involved in the project as I can: the producer, the director, members of the production crew if they have been hired at this point. Sometimes I will even meet with the writer or writers to get their thoughts on the translation of their script into a film. Again, the more people with whom I can meet to discuss the concept and scope of the film and its production requirements, the more complete and accurate the budget I am developing is likely to be.

In some cases, however, I have been in the position where I am asked to prepare a film's budget before a director or a producer has gotten involved in the project. This is the most difficult budget for any auditor to prepare, since the ideas and input of those key individuals who will actually make the film cannot be included yet in formulating the budget. In these cases, I rely on my past experience on other productions, on my own concept of how the script will be produced, and on the thoughts and ideas of everyone with whom I have been able to discuss the project, including the studio's production executives (if the film is being produced by one of the major studios) to identify as many of the costs that the project is likely to incur.

The script, the script breakdown, and the thoughts and ideas of key individuals involved in the project are the raw materials for the production's initial budget. When analyzed and compiled, these then become the production's *preliminary* budget. The preliminary budget allows the studio's production executives and/or the film's producer(s) to see an approximate dollar amount for all the individual elements of the film as well as an overall price tag for the movie. This preliminary budget information may help sway the decision as to whether the financial backer(s) want to proceed with the project at all, or if they will ask for changes in the script to be made to alter the scope or "appetite" of the movie to reduce the cost. As more of the key individuals who will be involved in the project are identified and come on board, the auditor will gather more and more information to be included in the budget.

In preparing a production's budget, perhaps the easiest costs to figure are the above-the-line costs. Budget figures for above-the-line talent—all cast members (except stand-ins and extras), producers, directors, writers, bit players and stunt people—are negotiated and agreed to in a contract or, more frequently, a deal memo. If the production company will be paying for housing or living expenses of any of the above-the-line talent, these costs will also be specified in each individual's contract or deal memo. The "day-out-of-days" log is the source of information for budgeting cast, bits, and stunts costs.

I recall, for example, being asked by Paramount to prepare a preliminary budget for the film, *Top Secret*. The film's script contained many gags and bits, which took place in a wide variety of locations in an even wider variety of countries. It was quite a challenge to figure out how each of those gags and bits were going to be shot—and whether the studio's art department could "cheat" a location so that the scenes could be shot locally rather than taking the production overseas—so that we could budget the picture at a reasonable enough cost to get the film made!

When a film I am involved in is being produced by a major studio, I may receive budget information from many different sources at the studio. Whenever I receive such detailed budget information from the studio's various departments, completing the budget becomes much easier than it is without this detailed information. In completing the production's overall budget, I will verify and include the information I obtained from each of these studio sources. Unless the producers of the film change the entire concept of the film or unless they decide to film the movie on location after the auditor has budgeted it for a Los Angeles location, an experienced auditor's initial instincts—and the careful analysis of the detailed information provided by the studio's departments—are usually most accurate.

I have found that overseas productions are the most difficult to budget. Whenever an American production company is filming outside the United States, different concerns must be included in the budget to accommodate the special requirements of the production location. For instance, if a feature film is shooting somewhere in the United Kingdom, the auditor must be knowledgeable in English tax regulations. For example, what are the procedures for the recoupment of the British VAT tax. In addition, customs issues in each country are slightly different; the auditor must research the applicable customs laws and taxes for his or her specific locations because they may have a dramatic effect on the film's budget.

Aside from tax and customs issues, staffing the production crew on an overseas production may be different depending on the country in which the film is shooting. English crews, for instance, are staffed in completely different ways from American crews. One example is the buyers on British crews whose job it is to purchase what is needed to prepare the sets for shooting. In a standard U.S. crew, of course, these purchases would be made directly by the set decorator and the prop master. The auditor needs to be familiar with these crew staffing differences, especially in the show's set dressing and prop accounts, since they can also have a dramatic effect on the budget for the film.

PreProduction

Once we've gone through perhaps as many as twenty different versions of the budget, we are *hopefully* ready to finalize and lock the budget from any further changes or additions. At this stage, the final budget figures are submitted to the studio's production executives and/ or the producer for their final approval and sign-off. Following the acceptance of the final budget figures by these individuals, the auditor's primary responsibilities shift away from projecting the movie's *probable* costs to tracking the film's *actual* financial status.

Preproduction is a very busy time. The crew members are hired; major purchases are made in preparation for the film to begin principal photography; if necessary, arrangements are made to rent equipment or other items that are either not available or too costly to purchase (specialized or unique items of set dressing or action vehicles for a film taking place in the mid-1950s, for instance). Crew members are traveling to vendors and suppliers all over town, trying to make arrangements for and acquire whatever is needed by the film so that principal photography can begin on schedule. Of course, sometimes things don't always go as smoothly as they could: needed items sometimes just aren't available when the production requires them, vendors sometimes won't provide goods or services without being paid on the spot (rather than billing the production), and so forth. As the preproduction phase of the project goes on, the number of accounting and financial transactions involved will increase.

Production

By the time we have completed the preproduction phase, the entire crew has been hired; all major roles in the film have been cast; wardrobe has been either purchased, manufactured or rented; the show's major sets have been constructed and dressed for the camera. The cameras are ready to roll—and costs will be *really* rolling in to the auditor's office.

The auditor always works closely with the production manager in controlling the production's costs. Given the volume of the production's bills and invoices that the auditor must review, code, and discuss with the production manager, this is when he or she spends a lot of time becoming intimately involved with the show's books. The auditor and the production manager jointly approve all charges that are being made to the show. The auditor is responsible for making sure that any show charges are financially accurate: Is the cost accurate? Is the production receiving an agreed-to discount from the vendor? Is all the petty cash that was advanced to the key crew members being accounted for? The production manager ultimately approves the bills or invoices for payment by me on behalf of the production. If the production is shooting at an out-of-town location, per diem and living expenses are paid by the auditor.

Another of the auditor's key responsibilities during the production phase is to track and report significant cost overages or underages in any of the production's accounts and to report these to production management—the movie's producer and production manager as well as to the studio's executive management, if appropriate. I may also report to the production's management and/or the studio's executive management any current problems—or problems likely to occur in the production's future. For example, if shooting is going over schedule substantially or if the postproduction schedule is going to be affected by delays in production, I will communicate that to the post-production department as well as to the production executives.

I think it's important for the auditor to visit the set once or twice a week during production. By keeping in personal contact with the crew members, seeing how set construction is going, getting a feel in person for how much film the director is shooting in a day, I have had a much more accurate understanding of the production and its possible problem areas than I would have had if I had just stayed in my office. For instance, on the film *Annie*, the sets were becoming bigger and increasingly more and more complex. If the auditor hadn't visited the set and seen the problem with set design and construction brewing, he would never have been able to alert the production's management to the issue.

The Cost Report

Preparing the weekly cost report, which is based both on the final budget that was begun by the auditor early in the movie's evolution and the literally thousands of invoices that have been received, processed, and paid by him or her, is probably the auditor's most important tool in reporting the financial status of the picture to the producer(s) and to the financial backers of the film. In essence, the cost report is the picture's financial report card: it lists each account in the auditor's chart of accounts, what the approved budgeted amount for each of those accounts is, and how much has been spent to date in each of those accounts. The cost report allows the production's management and studio management to see instantly where there are cost overages and where an account is under budget. Key production decisions—dropping scenes from the script, reducing the number of extras that will be used in a crowd scene, and so forth—will be made based on these cost reports. Of course, the auditor will be asked to generate many other financial reports in addition to the cost report in the fulfillment of his or her job responsibilities during the production phase.

Postproduction

After principal photography has been completed, the movie enters the postproduction phase. The auditor who worked on the film during production will sometimes remain with the project as it goes into postproduction, especially if there will be major visual effects or other time and money-consuming elements in the postproduction phase. In other cases, two or three weeks after principal photography on the movie has been completed and the majority of the bills have been paid by the auditor, another auditor may take over the responsibility for the show's finances.

During postproduction, the auditor is performing the same role as during production: paying bills and invoices, monitoring, tracking, and reporting the financial status of the film. There are some unique requirements, however, which he or she must fulfill during postproduction. Cast lists and labor hours must be created for use later on by the film's distributor in calculating residual payments; vendor 1099 statements must be prepared for those vendors with whom the production dealt who do not qualify as corporations, a comprehensive vendor listing must be generated to record all the businesses from whom the production purchased or rented items.

Becoming an Auditor

There is no one right way to become an auditor. Working as an assistant on a few shows under the guidance of an experienced auditor is an excellent way to learn the intricacies both of production and of production accounting. Obviously, a more-than-passing familiarity with standard accounting practices is pretty much a prerequisite for this position, but you definitely don't need to be a C.P.A. to be a top-notch auditor. I also think that having good people skills—the ability to sit down with a producer or a unit production manager, or anyone else involved in the making of a film and satisfactorily resolve an issue—is vital to the success of the auditor.

So after I have gone through bottle after bottle of eye drops as the budget goes from revision to revision to even more revisions; after I have drunk the equivalent of the total annual export of coffee from Uruguay during those long days of production when it seems no movie, especially the one I have been working on, could possibly generate as much paperwork as it apparently has done; and after I have seen the project go through all of its phases and finally see it projected on the screen as a movie, I have my moment of satisfaction. But then, of course, it's on to the next project.

By *when* did you say you needed the budget?

Postscript: *Since this interview, Sandra has gone on to become vice president of Motion Picture Production Finance for Walt Disney Pictures, Touchstone Pictures, and Hollywood Pictures.*

5
THE TALENT

In this book we have no chapter dedicated to actors and actresses—the paid performers who appear before the camera. They are given more than sufficient attention in other media. Those who *help* the performer, however, are quite often ignored, not only by those who need them most, but by the public at large. In this chapter we talk with those who assist actors and actresses in the successful completion of a motion picture performance.

Although all of these professionals are there to support the talent, each of the people in this chapter possesses unique gifts and talents that can supplement and enhance the performance of an actor or actress, thereby improving the quality of the motion picture in general.

Casting Director

The Casting Director finds, auditions, and negotiates for the services of actors and actresses in a motion picture. He or she breaks down the script by role, characteristics, and age, compiles lists of potential candidates, checks their availability, contacts their agents, and schedules interviews, auditions, and call-backs. The Casting

Director works closely with the director and the producer in narrowing down choices and making deals for the final cast.

Janet Hirshenson and Jane Jenkins

JANET HIRSHENSON, born and bred in the San Fernando Valley of Los Angeles, got into casting while supporting herself with temporary secretarial work. One of her assignments was answering phones in the casting offices of Rastar films. There she met casting director Jennifer Shull. The two hit it off immediately. She became Jennifer's assistant and three years later cast her first movie.

JANE JENKINS came to casting as an actress from New York. A youthful marriage to an actor made apparent the fact that "somebody in the family should earn a living." She began getting jobs in production first in New York and then in Los Angeles. While working in production, she had an opportunity to watch the casting process from start to finish. "A flashbulb went off" in her head, and she realized that she had much to offer in the casting arena. She called a friend, Ralph Waite, to see if he could help her break into casting. He suggested that she cast a low-budget independent film he was writing, producing, and starring in. Jane became an "instant casting director" on *On the Nickel*. After this first trial-by-fire assignment, Jane met with a number of casting directors, one of whom was Jennifer Shull. There was an immediate rapport, but no work was available. Some months later Jane got a call from Jennifer Shull to help cast a movie.

When Francis Coppola asked Shull to head the casting department at his Zoetrope Studios, Shull insisted that Jane and Janet join her. Two years later when the studio folded, Jane and Janet decided to go it alone and rented a small casting office. Together they formed The Casting Company and since 1981 have cast over forty films, including *Godfather III, Air America, Ghost, Parenthood, When Harry Met Sally, Lord of the Flies, Mystic Pizza, Tucker, Planes, Trains & Automobiles, Beetlejuice, Willow, She's Having a Baby, Ferris Bueller's Day Off, Stand By Me, Clue, The Mean Season, Body Double, The Sure Thing, Red Dawn, The Outsiders, Rumble Fish, Hammett,* and *Night Shift.*

JANET: Casting used to be a very male-dominated area, and women got into it I think primarily because they could be exploited inexpensively.

JANE: And because you start off generally as a secretary—that's the way you learn.

JANET: You can't tell somebody how to do it. You have to work in an office to see what the process is. After you're there for a while, you start absorbing, learning the SAG rules and how to draw up contracts.

JANE: The advantage I had was that I knew a lot about actors from my prior existence as an actress. It's a purely instinctual area. It's governed by your own tastes. The way you accumulate knowledge of who's out there is from watching television, movies, and plays. You know how many phone numbers you know without even thinking about it? It's sort of the same thing. The actors who spring out at you from anything you see, whether it's a play, a television show, a movie—somehow that person you find the most interesting miraculously gets stored in some recess of your brain.

JANET: Then it becomes activated—we have files, tons of pictures. We have to have not only the leads, but the smaller parts in mind. We go through our files. Also breakdowns come out on every project.

JANE: The breakdown is a service that a very clever young man, Gary Marsh, started in this town about ten or so years ago. It has revolutionized the way business is conducted. The agents used to come to all the casting offices years ago in the dark ages, try to get the scripts of the current projects and pitch their actors on a face-to-face, "hi, come into my office, have a cup of coffee, tell me who you've got" basis. Gary Marsh's mother was an agent who didn't have time to go over to all the casting directors' offices and read the scripts, so she sent her son, who made notes about all the characters in the scripts, what page they appeared on, whether it was a leading character, down to the little bitty parts, how many lines they had, and he wrote a little synopsis on the story. This became so invaluable to Mom that she sent him out all the time and he started a business, the Breakdown Service. Now agents hardly ever leave their offices and they all subscribe to the Breakdown Service, although they do still like to read the scripts to get a more personal viewpoint.

Once we give the script to the Breakdown Service, they send this information out to all the agencies who subscribe. That along with courier services like the Go-Between has changed the way business is done in Hollywood. Everything is sent to the office—that person-to-person exchange has all but been eliminated. The breakdowns go out in New York and several other cities. They also have a "hinterland" service that goes out to Seattle and smaller towns. They have an international service that extends to cities like London.

JANET: Once the agents receive the breakdown, they'll send pictures of clients they think are appropriate for the part. You'll get stacks of pictures. Most of the people you're not going to know. Some will look interesting, like they'll fit a part, and you bring them in. Or you'll find someone who may be completely wrong at that moment, but we like them, we'll read them, and there may be something about their persona that will make me want to keep them in mind for a future project.

JANE: It's very unscientific, though we try to be organized about the whole process. There are people who become television stars or movie stars or commercial stars. There are people who do very well in commercial acting but don't seem to be able to break into television, film, or theater. And that's because whoever is hiring is looking for performers who "fit" one of those given mediums. It's very biased. Fortunately, Janet and I are very much in sync. We have always had a symbiotic relationship and been very much in agreement, which is why we've had a successful relationship for the last ten years.

It's the kind of thing you look for in an assistant. There's no training. There are a number of other casting directors who have also had experience as actors, and I suspect that those people bring their own inclinations and what they've learned as actors to the process. And for every casting director who ever worked as an actor or actress, there are as many or more who have never experienced being an actor. Casting is like that line about art: "I don't know anything about art, but I know what I like." When you read a script and digest who the characters are and you meet various actors to read for those parts, one or two or three people walk into the room and you'll gasp, "They've got it!"

JANET: It also depends very much on who the producer and director are. You have to get into their psyches. You have to get a connection with that person. You have to see what they want.

JANE: Ultimately, we as the casting directors and probably just about everybody who is working on a film is there to serve a director's vision. In features, which is what we do primarily, we have to work through with the director what his vision is—what he wants to appear on screen.

JANET: And he or she may not be sure sometimes. That's where you can help and even bring in something off the wall that he might be open to.

Nuts and Bolts

JANE: Most people perceive casting as just putting together lists of names and that's the end of the job. Putting together lists of names is just the beginning. If, for example, you think that Paul Newman is perfect for a particular part, you had better have ten or twenty other ideas because in that caliber of actor—Paul Newman a) may not be available, b) may not be interested, and c) may not want to do it for the amount of money that is in the budget. Then, even though he might be the perfect person, you have to come up with another perfect person and not marry yourself to one particular idea so that everything else seems absurd after you've lost Paul Newman.

You check availability. Most actors have agents or lawyers or some representative who can tell you if an actor is available for the work. You call the representative, who will then say, "Yes, he's available," or, "No, he won't be available until the spring of next year," which is often the case with a number of successful stars whose careers are booked well in advance. You can't rely on that handful of well-known name actors. That's why there are always new names emerging. Because after you've gone through the list of those ten famous guys—none of whom are available or affordable—there's got to be somebody standing in front of the camera on the appropriate day saying those words.

You figure out the monies involved. The amount of money that any given actor gets is usually negotiable, usually dependent on any given project, who's involved, and how much they want to do it. People who get exorbitant sums of money for one project might easily be willing to work on a particular project for less money because they love the material or the part or the writer or the director. A particular actor may have a set established price, but I never want to eliminate anyone because that person just might want to do it for less. Chances are an actor is not necessarily dying to work for no money because he loves the material.

Finding out the availability, the price, and the interest is the simplest step. You just call the agent. Sometimes you *want* somebody who's a five-million-dollar actor because the studio feels that they won't be able to get the picture out there and that an audience won't be available unless you have a major star. So it really depends on the nature of the material and who's involved, who's producing, and who's directing, as to "Do we need a star name, or do we need to populate this film with fabulous actors?"

JANET: It could be that unless you get one of these five top people, you don't make the movie.

JANE: And there are some scripts that are so very specific that unless you have Steve Martin or Robin Williams, then you don't have a film that you can sell to the audiences.

JANET: Or you really can't go with an unknown person—instead of Paul Newman—you need somebody of that power with those characteristics. Coming up with brand-new, incredible forty-five-year-old talents out of nowhere—not so likely. We would love to clone a few of those.

The Eight-by-Ten and Résumé

JANET: In going through pictures and résumés, it is the picture that first draws you and holds your attention. You see a light in the eyes, something that makes you focus in on *that* picture. *Then* you turn it over and look at the back and see what this person has done, what kind of training they have, if they've done any professional work. Very young actors don't usually have a lot on their résumés, and it is their picture that "sells" them.

JANE: If I were to advise an actor what kind of a picture to select, it would be to have just a plain headshot that captures who you are. Not a glamour shot, not three days' worth of *Miami Vice* beard—just the shot that captures *you*. It's not a bad idea for an actor to have several different pictures because any given human being has a maternal or paternal aspect to them, a businessperson aspect to them, and we all are made up of any number of different aspects that add up to our personality. But if you can't afford to have five different pictures to show the different sides of you, a simple, straightforward "I'm an intelligent human being" or "I'm a character person" or "Jewish harried housewife person" or "grandmother" person or whatever—the casting director needs to know what it is that she's looking at.

And then the résumé tells you really how serious an actor is. And if all they've done so far is study—depending on where this actor has gone to study their craft—that can tell you a lot about the seriousness of their intent. Then, of course, with age comes more experience, more credits. We don't really expect a teenager to have a long list of credits.

JANET: As to stretching the truth on résumés, I have often been able to spot it—many times it's been things I've cast. And maybe they did do a certain film, but they were an extra and it's become a "featured role" on the résumé.

JANE: It's not important to us—it doesn't affect how I react to their reading—it is silly, and it does lower them in my esteem. I would rather people just be honest, even if they haven't had a chance to gather many credits or to get their SAG card. It's pointless to lie about what you've done. If I see a résumé filled with all this incredible work and the actor who comes in is very inexperienced—it won't help. If an actor comes in and is extraordinary or just perfect for the part, then it doesn't make any difference. We want good people. Sometimes there is a part—there are sixty thousand actors in this town—and we can't find the right person. Or there are a couple that are right, but they're not available. The reality more often, though, is that there are more actors than there are parts.

JANET: If you don't have the training, you may get *a* part because you're extraordinarily cute, but eventually you're going to need the goods and the training to substantiate that. It's a dream when some incredibly beautiful woman walks in who is incredibly talented; you'd give your eyeteeth for that, but that natural actor is rare.

Breaking down the Roles

JANET: We start off with the leads—determine whether they're "name" or "nonname." If it's name, then we make some lists, we call for availability. If it's nonname, then we bring in pictures.

JANE: When I'm reading a script, I make notes of every speaking role. I will figure out how many characters there are in a movie—the leads and supporting roles. The description that a writer has made of a particular character is sometimes very pertinent. Other times a writer has decided that this is a "fat black man," and it could be a thin Chinese man or anything else. Depending on how important it is for a character to really meet the description that a writer has created, you begin to get a feeling for the principal characters—through who they are, what they do and say, who they know, all those material hints a writer gives you. Sometimes you very quickly visualize the actor for the role and think, God, I know who's perfect for this. Other times they've left such an open canvas that it could be *anyone*, and you haven't a clue as to whether a character is fifteen years old or thirty, blond or brunette. There are inevitably those characters you have to sit down and discuss with the director: "Okay, who is it? Who do you want and why?"

JANET: You start having meetings immediately. You have to pretty quickly go through all of this with the director because you don't have a lot of time—just a day or so. Then you've got to come back with some ideas and discover things like the director hates that actor.

You pull out specific scenes from the script or "sides" for all the different parts and bring in the appropriate actors. Generally for the leads with a well-known actor or actress, you don't read them—you offer them the part.

JANE: There are exceptions. It was reputed that Glenn Close auditioned for her role in *Fatal Attraction* because she wanted to show that it was a role she could do—she hadn't done that kind of role before. A smart actor will want to do that.

There's a challenge to choosing the leads in the sense that it's not just any star in a storm that you're looking for. It's the *right* star. There are those parts where you find someone who is just beginning to get to that level of stardom. The right movie at the right time that gets the right sort of attention can bring a good actor into stardom. You don't control that factor, but you can help.

Ultimately it's left to the audience as to how well any particular film does. If the actor in that film is what the audiences have acclaimed, then that leap can be made. It's chemistry—that something you cannot hold in your hand—charisma—and the right timing.

When we hired Michael Keaton in *Night Shift*, he had not made a feature film, had been in a couple not-very-successful television shows, a couple of guest appearances. There were several more well known actors that were seriously talked about for *Night Shift*. It was a difficult role to play. The character as written is a very irritating human being. You can get very quickly burned out on a character who is constantly irritating you—you just hate the person—you needed an adorable little puppy dog that kept peeing on the rug, but you just didn't have the heart to beat him. We considered a number of other actors, but Michael was just the "rightest" person for the part. The producer and the studio felt they needed a marquee that would read "Henry Winkler and So-and-so." The only known entity was Henry Winkler, and Henry was not a big movie box office star, he was a television star, so it was a real risk to hire Michael, who was an unknown. Michael was so right for the part and so endearing, that that character jumped off the screen and was the impetus for a very successful career. Again, with *Beetlejuice*, Michael had had a couple of successes right after *Night Shift* and then did a couple of films that weren't enormously successful. *Beetlejuice* turned all that around again. Now *Clean and Sober* has proven that he can also be a serious dramatic actor.

JANET: Casting people to type is very boring. You want to be as imaginative as possible.

JANE: So that using this roly-poly comedic actor as an undertaker is frequently an interesting twist in perceiving how the character could be played. It depends on how willing the director and producer are to take a risk. Particularly if an actor or actress has become established as a particular character—as in a television series—the producer and director might be afraid that audiences won't "buy" that person—the "Oh, there's Archie Bunker!" syndrome. Breaking out of type can then be tough. You need a very bold, adventuresome producer or director who is willing to take the risk. You can only push a director or producer so far.

Francis Coppola and Fred Roos took a marvelous risk in casting

126

Martin Landau, whose career had been going nowhere for the last several years—doing B movies and European things—and when his name was brought up for the role in *Tucker*, there were a number of other actors, more well known and more prestigious in terms of their marquee value. Francis and Fred were in tune with actors. They knew who Martin Landau was, that he was a very well trained actor and that he had had a long and serious theater career as well as a prestigious film career and that it was just in the last few years that he had fallen on less visible times. Actors come in and out of favor like the flavor of the month at Baskin-Robbins, but they weren't intimidated by the fact that he hadn't had any recent big successes. They felt he was the right person to play that part and took the risk of casting someone who was not a big star at the moment in a very substantial role.

Auditioning

JANET: If it's someone whose work we know, we don't need to preread him, we'll set him up to read for the director. If it's someone we don't know or someone we're unsure of for the particular part, then we'll bring him in to read for us. We'll go through the pictures and pick the people we think look interesting for this part—purely off an eight-by-ten. They'll come in, you chat for a minute—we give them as much time as we can. Generally they have the scene from the day before. We don't just give them a scene and say, "Here, read this." That doesn't do anybody any good. We set up the office to be conducive to doing good work.

JANE: It's not a very comfortable situation, no matter how well prepared you are—the least that we can do is make it as painless, comfortable, and supportive an environment as possible for actors. When they walk through the door, hopefully those actors will have had time with the material. They'll know what the story is about and what their character is. Now when you get down to Cop Number Three, who simply says, "Don't come in here," you don't need to go into a great deal of the motivation, plot, and where this character fits in. But if it's a supporting part that does have some influence on the story, it is an actor's job to find out as much as possible—they should know whether they're coming in to audition for a sit-com, a feature film, a comedy, a filmed play, or a soap opera. Janet and I never ask people to read unless they know what it is they're reading because there're any number of ways to approach any piece of material, given the context it's been written in.

JANET: In a smaller part, you may not be able to tell from the lines if it's a comedy or a drama. It may not be a particularly funny line, but it is a comedy that you're reading.

JANE: The actors' agents usually have a script. Occasionally there will be a project where nobody will see the script. We have worked on a number of projects that have been "secret." When we were doing *Willow* nobody was allowed to see a script. *We* did not read the script. We were simply told what the story was about and the characters we were casting. And we in turn explained our interpretation of the story to the actors. It was very complicated because there were all these strange characters and creatures, and it took place in another century or planet, and there were little people and giants and death-dogs and fairies and brownies and dwarfs. There were specific scenes written just for the purpose of auditioning. That and what we gleaned from the writer, producer, and director were all we could give to the actors.

Most of the time there is an opportunity to read the full script. If not, then Janet and I usually give a thumbnail sketch of what the story is about. We meet a lot of actors on any given day, and after you've told the story thirty-five times, you begin to get bleary-eyed.

JANET: So we also often make synopses of the scripts. Especially when you're down to Cop Number Three, they're useful to have.

JANE: The most important thing actors can do is to take the time to find out what it is that they are here for. If their agent hasn't been able to inform them of what the project is and all the pertinent information, it's still their obligation to find out.

JANET: They can ask the receptionist if all else fails.

JANE: Because to have an uninformed actor come in and not know why he's here or come in dressed totally inappropriately—for the part of a ditch digger, he's dressed in a business suit—doesn't help the process. It hinders him, it wastes our time.

Assuming he's acquainted with the script and the role and after answering any questions the actor may have, we'll plunge into a reading. If the actor has taken the wrong tack altogether, but we think that there's something interesting about him, we will ask if he

128

can do it again with a different point of view on the scene. Some-times he'll live up to our expectations of what the part should be—he's the one who'll get to come in for step two, meeting the director. The number of call-backs is dependent on how complex the part is, how secure or insecure the director is, whether you have to match that particular part to other parts. You're looking for people who look like they can work together or a family, or if you need a particular chemistry.

JANET: Sometimes an actor will just walk in and you will know that she's totally wrong. Sometimes she'll look nothing at all like her picture, which is a big mistake actors make—glamour shots where they need a fan blowing to make them look remotely like their picture. She is not a beautiful woman, which is what the part may call for. She'll get her two minutes, we'll still read her, and maybe she's a good actor anyway and you file her away for something else.

JANE: If an actor walks in and the desire to get the part is so intense, it's palpable, I usually tell him to just relax. That desperation doesn't help at all. The best thing an actor can do is relax and be himself, which is much easier said than done, and it comes with experience. We've had new actors walk through the door and you literally see their knees shaking and their hands trembling. Their feel-ing is that we're in charge of their lives and we can make or break their careers—which is *not* the case. *Nobody* can do that, and if I don't see their talent, somebody else will.

JANET: It's not a power trip. And if someone is into the power of it, I think they're in the wrong profession.

JANE: In auditioning, I approach it all from the point of view of an actor, which is the only way I know how to read a script. I try to put in the appropriate dynamics—which isn't always easy when I'm read-ing a male part in a love scene. I try to give someone as much to respond to as possible. There are a lot of casting directors that are simply not good readers and read a passionate love scene as if they were reading a telephone book. It is the *actor's job* to get past that and do his or her part. And if they're fortunate enough to read with someone who can give them something to respond to on an actor-to-actor level, then that's icing on the cake. It is *their* job to act as if I have read this passionate love scene as if I am indeed Harrison Ford or the most beautiful woman in the world or a three-year-old son—whatever the part requires.

JANET: I advise an actor to dress simply when coming in to audition. Some people will come in with too many props or get hung up with miming things. They should do whatever makes them feel comfortable—walk around—but it should be simple.

JANE: If the part is for a psychotic killer, you don't come in as a psychotic. And I prefer not to be thrown up against walls. One of the most telling experiments we conducted was in a little movie we cast in which there was a very intense and funny and complicated love scene between the boy and girl in the movie where they went from the kitchen floor to a couch that had a plastic cover on it to frolicking and rolling all over the place, and in the process of auditioning both young men and young women for the parts, I was alternately either the boy or girl myself.

People would come in and say, "Uh, how are we going to do this?" because it was such a physical scene. I said, "We're going to do this by *not* rolling around on the floor, by *not* touching each other, and for you to think of this all as just your close-up. I need to see all of that stuff happening in your eyes. You don't have to grab me, you don't have to kiss me, we don't have to roll around on the floor." When it comes to actually getting all of that crazy, rollicking stuff on film, eventually what the audience is going to see is a close-up where perhaps the other actor is going to be standing next to the camera and not actually rolling around on the floor with you. As a film actor you have to get beyond the physicality of it all because so much of film is in the expression and the suggestion and the close-up. And it's amazing how much passion you can evoke with just your eyes.

JANET: Sometimes a new kid will walk in and you just feel chills, "He's got it," before he even opens his mouth. This is a star. On the other hand, some actors are terrible at auditions. They don't do readings very well or are very shy. Sometimes you get past it, sometimes you don't. If there's other work of theirs that you've seen, that helps.

JANE: But if the actor has not been in the fortunate position of your being able to see other work of his so that you know what he is capable of doing and if he's a very shy person and not very good at auditioning, sometimes you miss out on somebody who is very interesting because you don't see it. You can only see what he or she gives you.

JANET: There have been times when I'm not sure—it's an awful reading—but I think there's something there, I'll say, "Look at this, come back again." You give them the material and let them spend more time with it. And we go out to see whatever they might be in—a play, another film. We go to plays and films all the time as a matter of course.

JANE: If the play warrants it. It's very difficult to convince us to see a one-man show, for instance. There's a lot of "showcase workshop" productions in Los Angeles that are staged really to advance the careers of the actors involved. And usually those productions are pure vanity. We don't go to those as much as we used to because the level of intent isn't very pure. But there is a lot of wonderful theater being done by actors who are simply interested in doing good theater, and usually the production is much better and the intent is on a higher level.

JANET: Certain schools will do wonderful showcases. Milton Katselas, the acting teacher, consistently exhibits good work. We tend to go to those because we can find some interesting people there.

JANE: There are so many actors, we just can't get to them all. We will talk to an actor who doesn't have an agent if his picture strikes us as interesting or if he happens to be right for a particular part. An actor has to make every attempt to get himself an agent.

JANET: But we can't get into referrals—it's not our business. It is a business, and most agents are looking to bring on new clients whom they feel are going to make money for their office. They're not looking for yet another unknown actor; they want someone who will have something to offer. But you will meet those individuals who have a lot of charisma or character or promise, and occasionally I will refer them.

Negotiation

JANE: There are so many variables in casting that I think even most producers don't understand exactly what it is they hire us to do. Once you start making some choices, then the whole negotiating process of actually hiring any given actor becomes enormously complicated. Although usually the legal departments of studios make the exorbitantly expensive deals, frequently those deals are made with a great deal of input on our part because the lawyers aren't familiar with all the ins and outs of a particular actor's wage history. We negotiate deals up to the money break, anything under $40,000. Anything over $40,000 becomes a "Schedule F" player according to the Screen Actors Guild. How much you pay an actor is based on a number of things—how much that actor has made before, how much money is in the budget, whether it's a part that an actor is dying to do or a part that you have to pay him to do because you want that particular actor. Sometimes we're pushed into a corner and left without much negotiating power, we have nowhere to turn, there's a deadline and they need somebody on the set tomorrow. With all those parameters, you make the best deal under the circumstances.

We are employed by the producer, and the money that we're spending is not ours to give away freely. An actor's agent says, "We want $500,000 for that part," but the person has never done anything that warrants that kind of money. You have to negotiate a salary that's commensurate with what that person's made previously, what the part is, how important the part is to the film.

JANET: Salary is only one part of it. Then you come to billing, which can be a killer—the size and positioning of someone's name, his or her credit, comes in to play when negotiating.

Flexibility and Limitations

JANE: Movies sometimes can take a completely different direction. For instance, in the movie *Burglar*, which was written for a guy, Whoopi Goldberg suddenly became the star. *Beverly Hills Cop* was originally developed for Sylvester Stallone, and then it would have become an action-cop-adventure. The whole tenor of the movie changed when they cast Eddie Murphy—it was now a comedy.

JANET: You have to be ready to take a new direction and come up with alternatives. An actor can pull out a week before or two days before you need them, then you have to scramble to find a replacement. There is always an alternative.

JANE: There have been actors who have been fired in the middle of shooting and another actor has come in to replace them, and usually the original actor was the one everybody thought was perfect for the part. Three days into filming, they realize, "Oh, we made a terrible mistake." It's really unfortunate that something of that magnitude happens because it's a very expensive problem. But it happens with regularity.

Originally, Harvey Keitel was hired for the part that Martin Sheen took over in *Apocalypse Now*. And originally Eric Stoltz was hired in the part that made Michael J. Fox a star in *Back to the Future*. And those mistakes were collaborative mistakes, so there's never any one person who can be blamed. An actor is only a human being. An actor once told me that he now felt prepared to play any male role ever written. That's impossible. And that person is also no longer an actor.

Although Meryl Streep can do any number of accents, she can't play a black nanny or an Oriental concubine or a fifteen-year-old girl. There's only so far that the most extraordinarily gifted actor can stretch and bend and change himself with the help of makeup and prosthetic devices and all the other movie magic that's at his disposal.

Rejection

JANE: We do not deal with telling an actor that he or she has not gotten a part. That's for his or her agent to impart. We tell the agent—and it's good for the agent to know the reason why. If it has come down to three people, and their client was not the one picked, it's good for the agent to know that their client was very special. The rejection has nothing to do with the actor on a personal level, but that's a very hard thing for an actor to perceive because he has personally been rejected.

JANET: An actor who keeps getting close, keeps getting callbacks, keeps being one of three but doesn't get the role—he or she is on another level already, and that's something to take pride in. They're *getting* that far, they're getting beyond that first call, obviously that actor has got something. Eventually they're going to click. If, however, after twenty years, an actor can never get beyond the first call, then maybe he should think about another career.

Becoming a Casting Director

JANET: The best way I know is to start working in a casting office. You start entry level—as a secretary, receptionist—and work your way up to an assistant.

JANE: Assistants who have worked with us over the years, as they type up a contract and fill in all the blank spaces, learn what all the requirements are. It's a slow process that's done sort of by osmosis. You have to learn the practicalities, the business aspect. SAG publishes a book that is full of legalese, but it's a reference.

JANET: You don't need to have the whole book memorized. You need to know the basics. You need to know about drops and pickups, things that if you screw up, it's going to cost the company money. A "pickup" refers to a circumstance where you hire an actor for three days and then three weeks later he works again for a week. The company doesn't have to carry him—in other words, pay him for that whole time. As long as there's ten days in between working sessions. And you have to know that you can't start someone on a weekly and drop him. If he's on weekly, then he's on salary until the end. You have to start him on a daily.

You have to know that if an actor travels to location—that travel time is work time, and you pay him the days he travels—so that if he arrives on the set and he doesn't work until four days later, you're paying him for being there.

JANE: Business aspects aside, most important of all, you've got to learn who the actors are and learn as much as you can about what they are capable of.

Dialect Coach

The Dialect Coach teaches actors and actresses how to speak convincingly in a dialect or with a foreign accent, working with them on sounds, intonation, speech patterns, and rhythms so that they may assume, as fully as possible, their role as required by the script.

Robert Easton

ROBERT EASTON, known as the "Henry Higgins of Hollywood," has taught actors Sir Laurence Olivier, Gregory Peck, Charlton Heston, Anthony Hopkins, Al Pacino, Sir John Gielgud, Robert De Niro, Robert Duvall, Bob Hoskins, Arnold Schwarzenegger, and Jeff Bridges and actresses Jane Fonda, Ann-Margret, Lily Tomlin, Jane Seymour, and Jacqueline Bisset—to mention a few—how to

speak in accents other than their own. Easton's fascination with
dialects led him to master hundreds of accents—from southern
Missouri to Dutch to Pakistani. His is an indispensable service in an
industry where a performer can be called upon overnight to become
another nationality or ethnic group. Easton has coached people in
person, by tape, and by long-distance phone across continents.
Moreover, he is a well-known character actor in his own right,
having played dialect roles in sixty-three movies and over a
thousand TV and radio shows.

In WORKING with actors, I use every teaching aid I can,
including color-coding the sounds, respelling, repetition drills, and
anecdotes. I can mark their scripts and put their dialogue on tape, but
the magic only happens when they cease to be actors trying to do a
dialect and start to give it flesh, blood, and innards, becoming the
people who talk that particular way because they were raised in a
certain environment at a particular time.

For example, in the 1930s during the Depression, with a Scots/
Irish background living a life of poverty way far up in the Smoky
Mountains—that happens to be the character Lloyd Bridges is now
preparing for on *Winter People*. Lloyd's inner metronome is very quick,
so we slowed it way down. I suggested that he emphasize by length-
ening the words—say "Strroooonnngg." You see, New Yorkers emphasize words by going *louder*. The English emphasize by going *higher*
in pitch. But these North Carolina mountaineers emphasize by length-
ening: "That boy is really meeeaaan," or she is "uuuuuggly."

My Latino clients, when using a compound phrase with a noun
and an adjective, tend to stress the noun: "The president lives in de
White *House*. We would stress "white" because we're interested in
what kind of a house he lives in. And a Spanish-speaking client will
say, "In my *country*," whereas we're interested in *which* country, so
we'll stress "my."

Most people feel that a "dialect" is what *other* people have. People
will come up to me and say, "Do you know the only place in the
United States that has no dialect?" They'll have picked one particular
place, like southeastern Idaho, and they're absolutely convinced that

there's no dialect in that area. Or clients will say, "I want you to teach me how to speak with absolutely no dialect." And I'll say, "Fine, keep your mouth shut." When people ask me what the difference is between a national language and a dialect, I always say, "A national language is the dialect that had the best army."

"Henry Higgins" American Style

For a while I was coaching my actor and actress friends for free. Then I realized that I had spent a lot of time and effort to learn how to do all of this, including my education in speech at the University of Texas and phonetics at London University and a huge investment in dialect books and records. My wife, June, and I talked it over, and we decided that it wouldn't be wrong to charge for teaching. It was obviously a service that was needed.

I started off in a very modest way with a little class at the Beverly Hills Playhouse in 1964. I would charge my students four dollars for a three-hour session. Many of those people are still very loyal, repeating clients. I do charge them a little more now. I think the record holder is John Saxon. I've taught him seventeen or eighteen different dialects over the years.

My coaching started as a sideline business. For many years I was able to combine it with acting. But gradually the curves crossed. The coaching took more and more of my time, and I started getting a great deal of overseas location work. I would get an offer for an acting role but had already committed myself on a coaching assignment. It got to the point where I'd be working for a director on a project coaching other actors and he'd say to me, "You remember when you used to be an actor?" So the myth kind of got around that I had retired from acting.

In the last ten years, I've been out of the United States more than I've been in because I've had long location assignments in Europe and Asia. So dialect coaching is what I'm known for now.

Besides a hundred or so *actual* dialects, I've had to literally create new ones. On *Flesh and Blood*, a Dutch-Spanish co-production with an international cast, I was asked to come up with a composite sound that took place in an unspecified medieval country. Rutger Hauer, who is Dutch, was in it, along with two top Australian actors—Tom Burlinson and Jack Thompson—and a whole bunch of Spanish, Dutch, Portuguese, English, and American actors. I was asked to standardize all the different accents that existed in the cast and make sure nobody sounded either American or Australian, since in medieval times neither of those continents had yet been discovered by Europeans. One very fine Spanish actor complained, "Thees ees cracy. I esspick pearfek English. I pronounce weed great pray-see-shone and claritee. I artikoly berry cayre-foolee. Nobody eber misunnerstance any war I say. For hawaii do I need to have thees man titch me?"

Breaking It Down

Sir Laurence Olivier is a great technician in terms of going for the finished product and working backward to achieve it. The first time I coached him, on *The Betsy*, he played this Michigan car magnate who was loosely based on a Henry Ford type. So I taught him the rural dialect of a small town in Michigan in the late 1800s.

We had a lot of time to talk between takes, and he asked me if I had always wanted to be a dialect coach. I said, "No, when I was younger, my great dream was to be an aeronautical engineer and design airplanes. And the whole time I was in grade school and high school, my strong subjects were mathematics. I used to get A double-plus in algebra, solid geometry, and trigonometry."

"Well," said Sir Laurence, "the way you analyze and break down these dialects is really the engineering part of you. You bring an analytical mathematical approach to it that most actors just sort of do by the seat of their pants."

You see, many actors are very good at picking up dialects by imitation. But there can be a terrific trap in that, if they assume that words that are in the same sound class with each other in one dialect will be in the same sound class with each other in all other dialects. For instance, the average American who has heard an English person saying "hahf pahst" with the broad "a" of "father" is apt to say, "Would you like some "lahmb?" which is wrong. It's "lamb," as in "pram." Or he may wrongly assume that the Englishman who says "pahspawt" will also say "pahssenguh."

Research

I have an enormous collection of nineteenth-century dialect plays, poems, and novels, including dialects from England, Scotland, Ireland, Wales, and America, in which the writers worked very hard to indicate the correct vowel and consonant changes. Even more important, they wrote with an understanding of the *grammar* and *vocabulary* of these dialects.

In this century, Eugene O'Neill continued that tradition. You read an O'Neill play, he's done his dialect homework. And I keep doing mine. If I'd just stopped with what I knew twenty years ago, I could teach the commoner dialects. But I feel compelled to keep learning new ones, refining what I know and finding exceptions to what I had thought were rules.

I compulsively listen to radio and television whenever there's anybody with an offbeat dialect. I tape them and make notes. The tapes and my handwritten notes now fill two enormous filing cabinets.

A godsend for me is the C-Span cable network showing the deliberations of Congress. Representatives are elected every two years from 435 different districts, and they're always identified as "So and so" from "Such and such," and quite often they'll mention their hometown. Another marvelous source is the Discovery Channel, which has all those great documentaries, so I have an opportunity to hear Australian aboriginal, Nepalese or Balinese, and so on.

Yesterday I had a morning session with a Croatian client. I have a lot of information on Yugoslavs, who are Serbians, Slovenians, and Macedonians, but not much on Croatians. So I made eleven pages of notes on her. Now somebody's going to want to sound Croatian sometime and I'll be ready to help them do it.

In my research, I employ a kind of Gestalt method. Instead of taking two months to research Romanian and then three months on Brazilian, followed by two months on South African, I use a scattergun approach. I record anybody off the radio or television who has any kind of dialect that I'm not familiar with, or where I detect a subtle variation in a dialect I already know and make notes on anybody I hear. In any given week, I'm taking in new information on maybe thirty to fifty different dialects. This keeps me from getting bored and burning out.

I'm not only interested in phonetics, dialects, and linguistics, but also am fascinated by folklore, anthropology, psychology, history, and geography. These studies help me to understand why dialects have developed in so many different directions.

Learning Dialect vs. Learning Language

The ability to learn dialects is not as related to the ability to learn a foreign language as one might suppose. I've had clients say to me, "I'm going to play the part of an immigrant from such-and-such a country. And I should be able to learn the accent very quickly because I already speak that language." And I find out that it's often no help whatsoever. The fact that they speak that language doesn't necessarily clue them in as to how a speaker of that language would speak English.

Some people I've taught very obscure dialects to, dialects they've never heard before—have an amazing aptitude. Again with singers, people assume it must be easy to teach singers because they have that wonderful ear. That's not necessarily the case, either—there are singers who are magnificent at hearing every subtlety involving music but cannot hear the music of spoken speech very well. Conversely, some of the people who have the most facility for picking up dialects cannot carry a tune in a bucket! I can't.

Although I don't speak any foreign language, I can create an authentic-sounding gibberish merely by using the appropriate sounds and intonation patterns of that particular language. I know all the *sounds* that Russian has that English doesn't have, all the sounds that Austrian and German have—this helped me to switch Arnold Schwarzenegger's accent from Austrian to Russian in *Red Heat*. In working with an Italian, I know he won't have certain English sounds, but he will have some sounds that are halfway between two English sounds. If you take the analogy of piano keys being English sounds— instead of playing either piano key, the Italian is going to play the crack. I can pretty much predict the problems an Italian will have with words like "beach," "peace," and "sheet."

Working with all these foreign clients is grist for the mill when I have to teach their accent to someone else. The information that I get on the difficulties they have, I analyze just like a chemist. I break their sounds down into constituent elements, then I synthesize those sounds and build it back up.

Teaching Dialect

I have had situations where I've had three people come to me who are all going to test for a starring part in the same film. They all bring the same test scene. And I've got to teach them the same six pages of dialogue. Each session is completely different because of the individual way they assimilate what I teach.

One of them may be extremely *ear*-minded and may be able to pick up an accent with almost tape-recorder fidelity. As does Lily Tomlin—who has a fantastic ear. Same thing with Jane Fonda when I coached her for *The Dollmaker*.

Now perhaps one of the other three cannot really hear the subtle sound differences. They may be very *eye*-minded. I'll go through their pages and *respell* everything for them. Or draw little pictures of the different mouth positions. Anything that's visual—writing down and saying, "This rhymes with that," "This is a pun for that," or, "We'll add or subtract this vowel or consonant." Charlton Heston has mastered half a dozen different dialects by my transliterating his script or respelling what the TelePrompTer says.

The third way people learn is *kinesthetic*. Many actors and actresses have been models or athletes or dancers, like Patrick Swayze and Jaclyn Smith. These clients have a great deal of awareness of the body. So I talk to them at length about the physical aspects of sound production. For example, most Americans round their lips on the long "ooh" sound. If I'm teaching Ulster dialect and saying the word "confusing," the lips should *grin*. So I'll say, "Don't round your lips, grin them."

Very occasionally, I'll get a client who knows the symbols of the international phonetic alphabet—that's rare. I used to teach it down at USC. That's a very scientific way of making notations on all these little subtle sounds—the ones that are the cracks between the piano keys. But usually I just use my own kind of simplified respelling.

I find that one of the best teaching tools I have is humor. When I was teaching at USC I had the first class in the morning—which none of the other teachers wanted. My students would come staggering in. They'd been up late the night before rehearsing or sewing costumes or building sets, and then they'd be geared up and go out afterward and maybe have a few drinks and do things they shouldn't do. They were feeling neither physically great nor mentally alert when they came into class. If I wanted to illustrate a dialect point, I would tell them a story—if it was a little bit on the bawdy side, so much the better because areas where people have a little bit of tension are the areas where people laugh.

Arnold Schwarzenegger

Many people see this Mr. Universe body and think, Oh well, he's developed his body to that extent so he can't have developed the mind, but he's an extremely intelligent man. Arnold is from a little farm community outside of Graz in Austria. When he used to go into Graz, the sophisticated worldly people in Graz would laugh at his country dialect. So he learned the Graz dialect. Then when he went to Vienna, the sophisticated worldly people in Vienna laughed because he had the dialect from Graz. So then he went to Munich, and the Bavarians laughed because he had this Austrian accent. "Then," he said, "I came over here and everybody laughed!"

One of the features of his Austrian dialect is that many words that we would start with *p* he starts with a *b*. I was coaching him prior to one of the Conan films. So the line was, "We are going into the village, looting and plundering." And Arnold kept saying, "We are going into de willich, looting and blundering." And I'd say, "No, Arnold, it isn't a *b*, it's a *p*. You're not going in blundering, you're going in *plundering*."

Now on *Red Heat*, he's playing a Russian policeman. And I'm teaching him all this complicated stuff about what the Russians call the "soft" or "palatalized" consonants. And he's doing very well, but there's a line, in a scene eventually cut from the film, where he finds a guy who's been shot and he grabs the guy by the wrist to verify whether the man's alive or not. And every time we work on it he feels the man's wrist and says, "He has no balls!" And I say, "No, Arnold, you're holding him by the wrist—he has no pulse!"

Scarface

Some clients want to learn just the words in the script and nothing else. But someone like Al Pacino, who works in a very improvisatory manner, wants to be able to depart from the text and tap-dance around the dialogue. He rarely reads the same lines twice in the same way. So he wanted to learn his Cuban dialect with that kind of freedom. It takes longer to second-guess what he might come up with, so for him, learning a dialect is literally like learning another language.

On *Scarface*, he was having difficulty with what are called the unaspirated *p*, *t*, and *k* sounds. In English, air comes out when we say those sounds at the beginning of syllables. Many languages, like those of China and India and the Cuban dialect, have both the aspirated sounds where air comes out and the unaspirated sounds where the air is muffled or blocked. Pacino was having trouble with those Cuban sounds where the air is blocked.

As luck would have it, we were sitting on the beach, back of his place in Malibu, when a couple of brown pelicans passed by. And I said in a Cuban accent, "Hey, mang, doce are p'elik'ans!" and he could imitate it perfectly, so he had the unaspirated *p* and *k* sounds. That came to be our refrain. If you've seen the film, there is a very offbeat scene where he's just stoned out of his mind in the bathtub and the television set is on and there is a shot of flamingos. Pacino stares at them and says, "Hey, mang, doce are p'elik'ans!" It was an inside joke for me.

Talent or Crew

Whether I'm considered a crew member or not usually has to do with who hires me. If the company or the producer pays me, then I'm considered part of the crew, and my position in the pecking order is in the same ballpark as the assistant director, the cameraman, or the art director. When I've been hired by a particular star and am paid by that star, I am there as part of the star's team. And I coach that star and only that star. If they are uncomfortable with their dialogue, particularly if they have script approval, which top stars do, we work out something more authentic in terms of words, phrasing, and grammar that helps them make the dialect believable.

Coaching Dialect

Actors vary enormously in how fast they can acquire an accent. Lily Tomlin—an incredibly fast study—appeared in this film with Bette Midler, *Big Business*, in which she played two roles. One of her roles required a West Virginia dialect, which I taught her in *one* 2-hour session. In her play, *The Search for Intelligent Life in the Universe*, I thought she was brilliant in every character she did. And yet she is such a perfectionist that she asked me to work with her, polishing her Brooklyn character, which I already thought she did a lot better than most people who think they do it well.

The few people I find difficult tend to be those who are not very experienced performers and those who have had a particular type of what passes for "method" training. Not the *real* method, because Stanislavsky was very much into helping people create different kinds of characters. He wrote one book called *An Actor Prepares* that deals with very basic, beginning acting exercises . . . telling you how to move inward, to internalize and identify with the character. Then he wrote two books that were intended for more advanced actors called *Building a Character* and *Creating a Role*. The two latter books deal with playing characters that are quite different from what you are. Stanislavsky talks about the "inner metronome" and changing inner rhythms—talking and moving differently from the way you normally talk and move. Many people stay fixated at that very basic level of "Let's internalize it" and "Let's convince myself that it's me." Those kinds of people are scared to death to play a part that's different from them. If they can't identify with it, they either won't do it or will try and change the characterization, saying to a director, "Like, uh, man—you know, like *I* wouldn't say that, man." A good director will say, "Well, I don't give a ____"—and you can fill in whatever blank you like— "*what* you would say, the *character* would say it. And if you're going to play this character, you damn well better say it that way."

The Love of Dialect and Teaching

For what I do, there really is *no* course that would prepare anybody. It's taken me forty-two years to learn how to do this. It really is a field that I pretty much, in the form that I do it in, have pioneered. We now have "The Henry Higgins of Hollywood, Incorporated." The corporation is me and June, and we are all the officers and the entire board of directors. And we hold our annual meeting in the shower!

There are a few other people who claim to be dialect coaches, but from what I have heard they don't do it the same way I do. In a couple of cases they are academics who have not been actors. If they are only academics and they haven't been performers, they can perhaps in a very dry way describe some of the phonetic and phonemic principles, but they can't put it in the form an actor can relate to.

There are other people who are actors, but they find it hard to explain their "seat of the pants" feel for dialect to other actors—they can't break it down systematically. Having been an actor, I understand the temperaments of all different kinds of performers who have had all different kinds of training—from excellent method actors like Al Pacino to technically trained actors like Sir Laurence Olivier and Sir John Gielgud to people who are themselves superb acting teachers like Nina Foch.

What keeps me continuing to teach dialect is that I experience an enormous vicarious pride when my clients do well—when they get nominated for an Oscar or an Emmy or a Golden Globe, and even when they just master a dialect to play a role more credibly. I feel blessed that I have gotten to know some of the most interesting people in the world and honored that they talk to me with amazing frankness. Sometimes if they're having problems on the set, they'll discuss these things with me, use me as a sounding board, and get to where they're feeling better about it. I have often been a confidant, or father-confessor, and have been told very confidential things. The nature of my work is fiduciary, based on faith, and I never reveal the things they tell me. They'll tell me personal problems, sometimes things that have bothered them since their childhood. I value the fact that they can confide in me and see me as friend as well as teacher.

Stunt Coordinator

The Stunt Coordinator interprets, organizes, and choreographs the action and stunts for a motion picture and hires stuntmen/women—the people who double for actors and actresses when it becomes too dangerous for the actual performer to accomplish a required physical feat. He works closely with the director, first assistant director, and camera crew. He is responsible for ensuring that all safety precautions are taken and that all stuntpersons are properly trained and equipped to handle the proposed stunt(s).

Kerry Rossall

KERRY ROSSALL was born in Burbank and grew up in the San Fernando Valley. While attending university in San Diego as an economics major, he spent his summers teaching surfing in Hawaii. Upon graduation, he went to Europe and continued surfing; when he returned to the United States he hitched back to California, where he was hired by Mammoth Mountain as a ski patrolman. He worked there for four years until he was accepted into the Naval

Aviation program (*An Officer and a Gentleman*–type school); he was immediately shipped to Pensacola, Florida, for initial Marine Corps boot camp, commissioning (ensign, U.S. Navy), and primary Flight School. He was completing the program when the Vietnam War ended, and with a consequent drastic reduction in the number of pilots the Navy would need, those in training were offered immediate release. He walked away with a substantial background in aeronautics. His previous training would prove fortuitous when he entered the film business under the tutelage of legendary stuntman Terry Leonard. He has performed stuntwork in *Apocalypse Now*, *The Wind and the Lion*, *1941*, *Blue Thunder*, *Cobra*, *Rambo III*, *The Abyss*, and *Downtown* to name only a few, and worked with such highly acclaimed directors as Francis Ford Coppola, John Milius, and Steven Spielberg.

T HE GENTLEMAN who got me started in the business was Terry Leonard, the legend. We met at Mammoth Mountain where I was working in a blizzard on the ski patrol. He had on a yellow Stuntman's Association parka and had no front teeth—got 'em knocked out coming down the hill. I asked him if he wanted a little gauze to stop the bleeding. He said, "No, it's my third set . . . I just wanna go skiing. . . ." So we spent the day skiing together and talking about his business.

Eventually Terry called me up to work in Spain on a movie called *The Wind and the Lion*. The director, John Milius, was a raging surfer from Malibu, so we hit it off right away. John's next script, *Apocalypse Now*, was to be directed by Francis Ford Coppola, and when Terry was hired as the stunt coordinator, he brought me aboard. I was about to spend the most unique six months of my life in the jungles ringing the South Philippine Sea.

Apocalypse Now

Initially I was only supposed to "double" one of the surfers in the scene where Duvall orders his men to surf a beach during an enemy bombardment. But the actors they hired were spending a little too much time quenching their thirst and visiting the homes of beautiful women and, it also turned out, didn't know how to surf quite as well as they claimed. Francis caught wind of this and ordered all of us to have a "surf-off" to see who could really ride. Well, let me tell you, talk about luck of the draw! I was in my element. Steve and I, the other double, were immediately outside, and these two "actors" (who had already been on location for six weeks) couldn't even get through the shore break, much less ride a wave.

Steve and I are laughing and looking back as we take off on a wave—he's a goofy-foot and I'm regular. It's a little peak and we've dropped down and are kind of fading back to where it's gonna snap, and we slam boards because we're looking down the line instead of at each other, and it's the damnedest thing you ever saw—we jumped into the air and . . . changed boards! We couldn't do it again in a hundred years if we tried! Francis and Grey Fredricson (the producer) just laughed and waved us in, fired the other two clowns, and gave us the parts! So that's how I got my start as a stuntman and an actor. I ended up working on that picture for six and a half months, involved in virtually every major action sequence from being blown out of the surf to jumping out of helicopters.

The Helicopter Explosion

Remember the helicopter attack Duvall leads on that small village with the Wagner music blaring over the loudspeakers? In the continuing battle after the initial airborne assault, Duvall orders one of First Air Cav's Hueys to touch down in the school courtyard and pick up the desperately wounded to transport them to the closest M.A.S.H. unit. Just as the chopper is lifting off, a Vietnamese woman throws a grenade past the door-gunner and it explodes in the belly of the chopper. There was me and three other guys in there. It was a mock-up of a Huey copter elevated to accommodate the charges. When I came out of the side door—we were on a count—everybody else was on oxygen and the helicopter was laced with gasoline.

It was a timing sequence where the helicopter was sitting on what we call "weak knees," which by design collapse with the slightest provocation in the direction of least resistance.

The other stuntmen were packing only two minutes of oxygen. If anything in their recognizable sphere of safety was malfunctioning, they could immediately show this by releasing the iridescent handkerchief each had in his hand. I would then relay this information simultaneously to the special effects team who, as planned, would directly cut [call off] the filming of the scene.

There was a sequence of three bombs—one major bomb to blow the weak knees out. Another to set the gasoline off. And finally a concussion bomb to blow the gasoline-ignited vapors outward in full consumption.

The filmic interpretation of this action in *Apocalypse Now* lasts only a few seconds, but seems well remembered by audiences. For Terry Leonard, Steve Boyum, Joe Finnegan, and myself, I'm sure the memory will last a lifetime.

The development, staging and execution of this stunt was complicated by several factors, including a minimal oxygen supply, virtually no vision or hearing possible, numerous intense explosions, and full envelopment in a gasoline fireball while riding a two-and-a-half-ton helicopter that plummets eight to ten feet to the ground. In developing this stunt we realized that communication with the effects team would be impossible unless one of us could at least hear, see, and move. I became the eyes and ears of my fellow stuntmen, who remained strapped in their seats in full burn suits with only two minutes of oxygen lashed to their chests.

The first time we tried it, we had a malfunction and we couldn't do it. There was a couple of hundred thousand dollars shot—with special effects and everything else. We had to cancel the stunt. Francis was a little anxious about the danger of it all and was seriously considering using dummies. Terry Leonard would hear none of it, protesting, "Francis, dummies look like . . . dummies. . . ."

We also had a runaway fire about two weeks before—during another explosive scene. Our fire suits and all our materials were in a certain area—and the fire burned up all four of our fire suits. That was kind of a bad omen!

Joe Finnegan had to fly back to the United States, have everything remade immediately, and bring it back for this shot. And it was now looking as if we might not get to do it. There are quite a few elements involved to have it all go perfectly—as it must.

That first bomb was to blow out the restraints on the weak knees, and the count was supposed to go "1—2—3—BOMB!" That was my cue to hurtle myself, like the proverbial sack of shit, some eight to nine feet to the cement deck, which I did with pleasure—to remain perched in the Huey doorway would have been unimaginable. The helicopter was laced with two- and three-gallon bags of gasoline. In fact, there was a gasoline bag hanging about two feet from my head on the left side and more in front of me. The count began, and the last I remember hearing was the "t" in the number "two." With a thunderous bang ringing in my head and the visual realization that I was airborne and about to attack the concrete face-first, I closed my eyes, but that had no effect upon my impact. It snapped my head straight back; and even hearing the internal sounds of my shoulder tearing itself apart was only secondary to the consequences of imminent contact with the Huey's massive rotor blade. (Because substantial rotor movement was necessary for the successful translation of this stunt to the audience, the rotor was designed with a small but powerful rocket at each end of the blade—supplying just over thirty seconds of continuous thrust and propelling the huge rotor into a more-than-believable rotation.) After the first explosion, the rotor moved so fast that when I started to exit, it took my feet out from underneath my push-off button and up-ended me. So I came down, and the first things I hit—instead of my toes, knees, hips, and elbows—were my forehead and right shoulder.

I heard that crack—kind of a strange sound—and I knew I had done some serious damage to the shoulder and taken a pretty good knock on the head. But I thought, Jeez, at least I'm still conscious.

At this point, I realized I was on fire. And I was supposed to get up and go back to the helicopter and go on with that. Turned out to be a hell of a shot!

It was covered by seven cameras, cut-in in such a way that it kept the pace, which is what Francis wanted. If you were doing that for a stunt show, you would have held for a lot longer. But it worked for the shot.

And the car going over the bridge that gets blown up as the Cong inside leap into the water? I was one of those guys, too. It was a timing shot where three of us went off one side and three off the other.

You have to be aware of where the camera is at all times. That becomes problematic when they sometimes have a number of cameras shooting simultaneously.

In revealing the size of the village we were attacking, we had coverage from boats in the bay, helicopters, and camouflaged cameras on land, as well. Several hundred extras, the U.S. stunt team, the U.S. Aerial stunt team headed by David Jones, the Filipino stunt team (thirty men), and a contingent of at least seven Filipino military Hueys were all strictly choreographed and coordinated for the scene.

148

As we're getting set for the fly-over, we look down at this village that we built just to destroy it for the film, and there are these people— local inhabitants—who have moved into one of the houses. They saw this nice new rice-paddy house and they moved in there and were sitting having lunch as we're getting ready to waste the whole village. It took so long to get the shot set up that nobody had noticed them moving in—an Asian family sitting in a house that's about to be toasted.

They were looking up at the copters as if they were at Universal Studios. Luckily, the assistant director had spotted them and averted what could have been some very bad news. The copters and jets had to land and refuel.

Remember when the Playboy bunnies bump and grind at Hau Phat and the soldiers go crazy during their performance? Well, Terry Leonard is the guy who grabs the skid of the copter as the girls are taking off and I'm the soldier that latches onto his leg, attempts to climb up his body to the chopper, only to have his pants tear away, dropping me into the drink with him shortly thereafter.

There are six major stunts in *Apocalypse Now*. Along with Terry Leonard, Joe Finnegan, and Steve Boyum, I was involved in five of them. There was not a better education than to be actively involved in the creation, design, and execution of the stunts in this epic under the guidance of people like A. D. Flowers, Joe Lombardi, Terry Leonard, and Francis Ford Coppola.

The Actors

Duvall and I played racquetball every night after work for just about six weeks—three-sided open air racquetball. And I tell you what, he's in some fine shape. He's an outstanding athlete. I took Bob out to teach him the rudiments of surfing, and on the first wave he got smashed in the head by the board. But he was willing to try anything. He'd never been exposed to riding waves, and he was supposed to know surfing jargon for his scenes. He picked up enough lingo to sound like he knows what he's talking about. After all, he gets paid to be an actor, not a surfer. My favorite bit was when he says, "I'll surf this goddamn beach . . ." He throws his hat down, rips his shirt off. "If I say this beach is safe, this beach is safe!"

I remember when he said the line that has become a classic—"I love the smell of napalm in the morning." It's something everybody remembers. I was sitting there just off-camera, just looking at him as he said perhaps an even more revealing line with that brooding, pouty look on his face, "Someday this war's gonna be over. . . ." There was something about that instant—you knew as they were shooting it that the moment would be lasting.

Coppola is unique. He lets you know *exactly* what he wants to see. And if it can be accommodated in a reasonable time frame, he'll give you free rein and allow you creative room to contribute things yourself as long as you don't overdo it and what you do is commensurate with the flow of the picture.

Cobra

I was the guy who drove the van in the underground parking lot into a solid cement wall in Stallone's picture, *Cobra*. That's what we call a "no-brainer" in the business. Hopefully, I wasn't too uniquely qualified.

I cracked my sternum, and the guy next to me broke his back.

I was in the van doubling for the actor. We had a preliminary shot where Brigitte Nielsen is up against the elevator door. We're the bad guys and we're racing around trying to kill her.

Terry Leonard was coordinating this. So he said "Bring the van down here, come out of the hole pretty hot, and then stop thirty feet away. This is Stallone's fiancée, and we've just got to be real careful here."

There was eight feet of carpet in front of the elevator. We have these nylon stocking-caps on. We come flying down to our mark—but the wires behind the dashboard, unknown to me, had fallen down and looped over my foot. I tried to pull off the gas, but I had to twist my foot free and was very late getting to my brake. I thought I was going to kill Brigitte Nielsen. People started diving out of the way.

I finally got my foot buried on the brake—still makes my heart pound to think about it. And I slide up to about five feet in front of her, which was *not* supposed to happen.

Terry Leonard was real nice about it. He leans into the window at this point and says, "Trying to make it a little bit exciting, aren't we?" I could barely talk, just, "Yeah, my foot here . . ."

It's helplessly terrifying when you think you can't get your foot off the gas and you have no place to go.

But we continued it from there, backed the van up. Now we're going to do the shot where she's already exited. The guard's still there and pointing his revolver directly at the van.

Now what is known as an articulating dummy is rigged in the real guard's place. By use of an overhead pulley and cable system our "guard" will have considerable lifelike movement just before I drive him through the closed elevator doors with the blunt front end of my van. I'm supposed to fly in and hit this thing at about twenty miles an hour.

I had the steering wheel in front of me, reinforced front, camera behind my head. They had a "suicide knob" on that wheel, and they didn't want to take it off. The suicide knob is a little handle grip, and I wanted that knob off, but I couldn't get it off. I had a guy next to me. We could have put a dummy in there—but at twenty miles an hour, we figured it was all right.

So I said, "Hang on . . . here we go." We took off at about thirty miles an hour. You rotate your thumbs and hands to the outside. At impact, when the wheel turned back, the knob caught my thumb. My thumb turned, pushed my shoulder back and opened up my five-points, and as my chest rebounded forward, my sternum cracked. We hit hard enough that the seat of the guy next to me collapsed and he cracked his vertebrae. I couldn't talk, and he couldn't walk!

As we hit the wall, I look out the side window and see the number-two van—which is used in case there's a problem. They were pushing it in. And by now I'm thinking, "I really don't want to do this again. That's just fine, thanks, guys, we'll see you again tomorrow."

What It Takes

It takes discipline and perseverance to educate oneself in a business that ranges from trial-and-error to computer-generated specifics. There was a day when a stuntman standing on a set reading a computer printout was regarded as revealing weakness. Not true anymore. The physical demands of this profession must be complemented with knowledge of the intellectual and business skills required in today's sophisticated international marketplace. Lacking this extra preparation, you risk being perceived as a simple commodity rather than a creative force. You can't do stair falls all your life!

Most of the guys that come into the business have good hand-eye skills, have been athletes. But they're thinking men, too. If every move isn't planned out just right with the special effects coordinator to meet the needs of the director and protect the life of the stuntman—well, you're just not going to last a whole long time.

Dealing with the Director

Safety is on everyone's mind, and if a director isn't as safety conscious as I'd like, I'll sit down with him and try to elicit what the problems are, and outline the potential risk involved. And if he can't understand that—and we talk with the first AD or the unit production manager or the producer, and we still can't come to an agreement—then I'll suggest that he find someone else. I would prefer to go for a walk, talk it over and give him the benefit of the doubt—maybe he just doesn't understand the stunt's ramifications.

Fear

When I find that I'm afraid before performing any stunt, it tells me that further preparation is necessary. Anyone who works with risk factors like this has to accommodate the possibility of danger.

There is no fear instinct at work. You're not thinking, "This is not going to work. I'm afraid." That train of thought is not going to get you through.

In flight school we lost four guys the first week—two in a midair collision and two more in a thunderstorm. Things like that happen. It comes with the territory.

When you are confronted with the loss of life, the reaction, besides the sense of personal loss, is, "Jesus, how could that happen?" What you want to know immediately is—"What led up to this?" As dreadful as it may be, evaluation and re-evaluation are the only answers.

Requirements

Even beyond the obvious required athleticism and hand-to-eye coordination (which can save your ass), there is always an element of luck that helps you to break into this line of work.

How does luck happen? The legendary Leo Durocher (Yankee ballplayer, manager, and author) once said, "Luck is the residue of desire."

Desire being a conscious impulse toward an object or experience that promises enjoyment or satisfaction in its attainment—that's what this job is about. It's a journey toward a destination "devoutly to be wished" for.

Your physical and mental skills will certainly be tested. But as excursions go, this is one I wouldn't miss.

I'm just kind of lucky, I guess.

Choreographer

The Choreographer is responsible to the director for creating the dance sequences in a motion picture. He or she must be aware of the requirements of the camera and provide the "coverage" necessary for the editor. The Choreographer also finds and trains any dance "doubles" (dancers who double for the principal actors and actresses, usually for reasons of technical expertise).

Jeffrey Hornaday

JEFFREY HORNADAY started working in Hollywood as a "gypsy" dancing in television, movies, and nightclubs while simultaneously studying with Lee Strasberg at the Actors Studio. Disillusioned with being a "mindless" body, he dropped out of the Hollywood scene to sell sunglasses. He was finally rescued by a friend who convinced him to assist her in choreographing *The Miss Piggy Special*. Soon after, he won the right to choreograph *Flashdance*, the hit movie that was responsible for his meteoric rise in the film/dance world. Since then he has choreographed the films *A Chorus Line* and *Streets of Fire*, Michael Jackson's *Captain Eo*, and several videos, including Stevie Nicks's *Stand Back*, *Say Say Say* with Michael Jackson and Paul McCartney. Recently he launched a directing career doing television specials, pilots, and *Madonna's World Tour* live in-concert series.

I REMEMBER going to see the movie *Cabaret* one day when I was fourteen or fifteen. It had an overwhelming influence on me. I went back and saw it seventeen times. I didn't know anything about dance, I didn't know anything about film, but I was very moved by the idea of a human story being told through the visceral elements of music and dance. The story was conveyed powerfully, with both music and dance being integrated, as opposed to the old musicals where people just broke out into song and dance arbitrarily. The connection for me was seeing narrative music and dance become the subconscious mind of the story.

Flashdance

Frankly, none of us knew what "flashdancing" was. It didn't exist. When I came to the project two weeks before principal photography, the director, Adrian Lyne, gave me the emotional framework—what he wanted to get out of the dance scenes and how they needed to fit the story.

Adrian worked on two levels. One was psychological and emotional, the second was sensory and visual.

For example, for the opening number he said, "I don't know what we're going to see here, but I know I would like the element of water in it." And he described that the dance had to be a reflection of this girl's spirit. This was her only outlet, this was the only place where she had a voice.

I could relate that in terms of improvisational dance, because I know what it feels like when you let yourself loose. I would improvise, just start to jam; that's when stuff comes out of you that isn't conceptual, isn't "in your head." Instead of approaching the choreography as something to be designed or staged, I spent about two weeks on my own in a dance studio with a video camera. And I would blast it as loud as I could. And I just jammed and jammed and jammed and videotaped it.

I would take the videotape home at night, study it, and find moments that looked absolutely spontaneous. And I used those moments to develop a language of choreography with the idea in mind that with the right dancer to execute it—like Marine Jahan—even though the picture was very stylized it would look like it was happening at the moment.

All the music was written up-front, which was great. There's a big danger in trying to shoot choreography and then write the music later. I know some movies in which that's been done and they have been successful, but for me it tends to feel like the dance is superimposed, that it didn't originate from that source of music. Choreographers are often perceived as dictators. That's how people are raised in dance, from the ballet tradition, which can be detrimental. My belief is that if you hire somebody who is a soloist, he's going to bring something to it as an actor would to a part. My focus is to try to get into a head space with the artists where they feel really free to be themselves or to be silly and to be daring enough to try something that they wouldn't try on their own. I try to nurture and guide them along so that things start to come out of them organically.

Marine is not only a brilliant technician, but she could take anything I threw at her. I was trying to keep an eye on her to make sure I wasn't messing with her internal rhythm. Because then suddenly it would stop being an experience and start to become a piece of choreography. It's a fine line, but you can feel it, and I believe an audience knows when they're seeing something that's built by a toy maker or something coming from a truly loose, free place. It was about keeping a clear eye on who she is and treating her as a person and an artist and not just a piece of meat.

The Strasberg method did affect me there, I must admit. For instance, there is interesting tantrumlike behavioral stuff on the videotape. Sometimes Marine would actually get upset—"why can't I just do this?"—and I would steal a moment from that outburst, videotape and choreograph it into the actual dance, and it would work.

Flashdance couldn't have been more perfect, almost a cliché kind of experience. None of us had a clue that we were going to be accepted, much less successful. And I'd never seen it with an audience until opening night in Westwood at the Village, which is this gigantic theater. People were reacting as if they were at a football game. They were screaming, cheering. And I was sitting there thinking, Holy shit, this is working!

I was twenty-five or twenty-six at the time. I had that pink glow— it had a "Camelot" feel to it. Doing something you love doing, having people respond to it, having your peers acknowledge you, and gaining a certain level of respect. It was the fix I needed in order to go forward with my life.

Dance Double

There's a great upside and there's also a great downside to the dance double. If you give the audience a point of "character"—in other words, you see Jennifer Beal's body dancing head to toe in one shot, and then in another shot you see the double, Marine, dancing head to toe—even if it's quick cutting and quick movements . . . it's like you can recognize somebody walking down the street with her back to you. You can feel the difference, your animal instinct knows that there's something going on.

So we nixed the point of comparison by using Jennifer only in close, tight shots and never ever seeing her body dance. That way you assume that the body dancing is hers because you never see a different body.

The upside to that is you're unlimited in terms of technique and choreography. The downside is you never connect the actress's face to the movements. Sometimes the medium or wide shot—how the person reacts facially as she's doing that move—has great impact.

MTV and Storytelling

MTV literally "hit" while we were in postproduction on *Flashdance*. We were using English music videos as prototypes for the kind of look we wanted. And at the same time there was the emergence of the health craze, aerobics. The exercise craze, *Flashdance*, and MTV were all reflecting a new self-conscious sexuality.

I think the benefit of music videos is that they provide a completely new avenue of work for young directors, choreographers, photographers, and editors. And there's great latitude in terms of experimentation. Rock and roll traditionally has been a pioneering influence, pushing the edge. Music videos reflect that visually with the counterpoint of new music.

It is so difficult for film choreographers to get experience. And it is completely different from stage choreography. I started thinking and learning about choreography as I was starting to direct video—this was even before *Flashdance*. As a result, the techniques of choreography were based on camera and editing, designing choreography with a "cutting scenario" in mind. Dance has a tendency to look like it's been shot in a box in most choreography that isn't designed for camera

156

up-front, that is staged for the proscenium. Video can provide a training ground, a place to get experience.

Something for young filmmakers to be aware of, for those who are beginning in video, is that ultimately a feature film or a narrative piece has a cumulative effect of story and character. Ultimately a film either lives or dies on the emotional involvement an audience has with the character in the story. And in MTV videos everything exists effectively as three-minute visual leaps. There's not an emphasis on character and story. The problem is that many people are having their visual inspiration come out of gratification of the "frame" and not the larger story context. It is equivalent to taking a Polaroid and trying to apply it to a two-hour story.

A Chorus Line

It's a different procedure and psychological tack when you are choreographing something for a soloist or something for an ensemble, as in many of the numbers in A Chorus Line.

Whereas Flashdance was an absolutely contemporary, modern piece in its day, Chorus Line came from an older, more traditional world—the world of musical theater. In a way, it didn't make artistic sense for me to try to do a reproduction or a straight transference from stage to film. Michael Bennett's assistant choreographer could do that. I told myself and the director that, even though we were working within the same musical context and with the same melodies and songs, in terms of the musical arrangement, staging, and choreography, I wanted to start completely from scratch.

I'll never forget it. I went to New York, and the rehearsal studio that we had on the second floor of this theater on Broadway was gigantic, with one large wall of windows. I remember walking into the rehearsal studio with my tape recorder and putting on the music to the Broadway show. And in this gigantic room by myself, I turned and looked out those second-story windows, and exactly across the street at eye level was the marquee for the Broadway show A Chorus Line. It had these runner lights saying, "A Chorus Line—the longest running show in history, Mike Bennett's brilliant production." I stood there looking at this thing almost in tears, and thought, What the fuck have I gotten myself into?

But the trick that worked for me, which got back to the Strasberg/ Stanislavsky method, was to isolate and focus my attention on very specific tasks and not get into "the big picture" initially. That gave me a sense of inspiration and excitement about the material and making each segment take on a life of its own.

Logistics

Flashdance only had one or two dancers doing a style of dance that they were familiar with and this contemporary music that I identified with.

In *Chorus Line*, I was going into a theatrical medium using 150 dancers. It wasn't just the creative process of staging the dances. I had to become, in a sense, the production manager and first assistant director because I was the only one who knew what it would take in terms of scheduling and budgeting and time to block, rehearse, stage, and shoot eleven dance sequences in three weeks with 150 people.

The choreography wasn't just about how it would look on the screen, it was about saying, "Okay, I need to break, because we can't hold 150 people and pay and carry them, I have to make 75 look like 450, I have to select. . . ." And we broke it down into five levels of dancers, good through bad levels of technique. I had to coordinate and schedule those people so they would only be used on certain shooting days and take into consideration the fact that many of them had to leave the set by six in order to do a Broadway show.

It was a massive logistical undertaking.

I had to be an adult and look at it before going into the project. And also I had to do it for specific personal reasons because, in terms of results, it was a no-win situation. If we did a brilliant movie, people would say, "What's the big deal, Bennett did it before." And if we did merely a good job, people would remember the Broadway show nostalgically—and it would be like a great book: the movie would never match your memory of what the book was.

We knew that going in. I think what people conceive of as controversy over the film came out of this show being folklore. It's part of the American folk movement and not to be tampered with. It wasn't a breakout conceptual approach to the piece, although there was quite a bit of controversy surrounding the making of the film. Ironically, for me, the film wasn't controversial enough. Had we approached it solely as a film unconnected with the Broadway show, it would have nullified the controversy and made it more of a *film* as opposed to a filmed show.

Choreographing in 3-D

When I worked on *Captain Eo* with Michael Jackson, I did a lot of homework; the approach I had used with Marine Jahan on *Flashdance* didn't quite work. It just wasn't happening like it did when I was jamming.

So we found a way through videotaping ourselves dancing *together*. I would then say, "Michael, come look at this, see when you did this? Do that here." The videotape became a translator.

The intention of the producer on *Captain Eo* was to try and bring together everybody who was tops in their field: Vittorio Storraro shot it, Francis Ford Coppola directed it, George Lucas produced it.

It presented a completely new set of problems because of the 3-D. You can't have anyone break a frame. If you're shooting me in frame and I stick my hand out at the lens at you, it looks like I'm going to hit you in the face. Three-D is unbelievably effective that way. But if my fist touches the top of the frame line and goes a little bit out of frame for a second, the 3-D illusion evaporates. Where sometimes it's very effective to have people come popping out of frame and to break frame lines with their arms and with legs kicking out of frame, you can't do that in this new context. In a sense, it's having to learn from scratch how to shoot dance.

Legacy of Fosse

I sometimes feel guilty confessing this, but the old musicals really don't do anything for me. For me, Fosse was the one. He was the filmmaker, the director, and part of his process, part of his storytelling, happened to be choreography.

We talk about Fosse leaving a legacy. I think he finally put that to rest with *Cabaret*. Audiences were seeing musical numbers and singing and dancing in an absolutely realistic context that didn't require a leap of imagination to be believed.

He is certainly my biggest influence. I am, of course, indebted to Gene Kelly and Fred Astaire. For example, there's a script I'm working on that uses dance in a more traditional manner, so I can't deny that whole chapter of dance history. But I can't imagine that innocent convention of the breakdown in the story for the song and dance operating in a present context. That's not to say we can't be inspired by the imagery and the finely crafted aspects of that kind of choreography.

But even as terrific a work as *West Side Story* is, for example, a young audience wouldn't swallow it—if it were made today.

Madonna Tour

Going back to a primitive level, man has been dancing and singing since the beginning of time. When it's done effectively and in a truthful way, it'll press that button and people will respond. When I directed Madonna's tour this year—65,000 people standing up on their chairs dancing and singing—a button was pressed there.

It's the first time I've choreographed a live show. We incorporated a production designer who's done opera and performance arts, and we used a new projection system that had never been used before.

It was as if we were building a Broadway stage every night. And there were these white reflective panels on receding three-dimensional planes. And with these super high-powered projectors, we would project photographed images onto the entire stage. I think there are only ten or twelve of these projectors in the United States. And because the screens were on different levels, you get an absolutely three-dimensional effect. We could turn the entire stage into different environments. Also because of a big profile star and tour, we had a perfect budget, we got to really experiment, it was a gas.

Toward a New Musical

Movies tend to become so departmentalized—the music department is separate from photography, photography is separate from choreography, choreography is separate from the music. Sometimes you can feel a lack of cohesiveness.

My dream is to take an artist—say, a composer, someone like Sting, or a conceptual thinker—and work in conjunction with them, so if you're devising a scene or a musical number, you can sit down with them at the piano and say, "This is where we want to go, we need the transition here, this element of the story we want to touch on in this number," so that it becomes a completely integrated musical.

That's what I would love to do one day—cross-fertilize departments to a greater degree. That's where all the work is headed.

Teacher

The Teacher instructs school-age children who are employed as actors in a film. In addition to teaching the required curriculum, she also serves as welfare worker by ensuring that the environment on the set is physically safe and morally suitable for minors and that appropriate rest and meals are furnished as delineated by state labor laws.

Adria Later

ADRIA LATER taught public school for five years but, after her divorce, suddenly felt "going out to a little school in the San Fernando Valley" was not what she wanted to do any longer. When numerous calls to the Board of Education for an application to teach children in motion pictures were received with "Sorry, there are no openings," Adria went down in person to speak to the man in charge. Impressed with her initiative, he gave her an application. She applied and some weeks later got a call to do one day's work on *The Bad News Bears* starring Walter Matthau. That one day turned into three months, and since then she has been working steadily as a teacher in the motion picture industry.

She has become Steven Spielberg's preferred instructor on the many films he has made using child actors and has now had twelve years of experience of working with children and babies on such films as *The Bad News Bears in Breaking Training, Mommy Dearest, Jaws 1987, Willie and Phil, The Hand, Harry and the Hendersons, Opening Night, Raiders of the Lost Ark, The Ewok Adventure,* and *E.T.* Most recently, she and another studio teacher, Judy Brown, have started a business called Baby Wranglers of Hollywood and, with the new surge of interest in using babies in film, hope to offer their skills to production companies.

THERE ARE several facets to the job—it is not strictly being a teacher. I received a letter which read, "Thank you for being a mother, a friend, a guardian, a psychologist." And that's true.

In terms of how I teach—every child will be different. Because the children bring their own books from their particular school and I carry on with that curriculum. When we go on location, I try to stay in touch on a weekly basis with the "home" school.

In Seattle, working with Josh Rudoy on *Harry and the Hendersons*, I graded all his papers, clipped them, and stuck them in an envelope and sent them by pouch to Los Angeles, and they were taken to his school. That way the teacher could call the office and let me know if he was keeping up with his class. In the Bahamas, I graded all the papers and enclosed them with a letter saying, "This is what I've been doing, this is how many pages I'm doing a day in math, and this is what we are doing in reading. . . . If you want me to go faster or slower, whatever, call the office at Universal and they will telex me." And then I got a notification saying, "You are doing just fine. Just move along as scheduled."

A School Day

Children, by law, should have at least three hours of schooling a day on the set. I often have only twenty-minute increments to work with, which doesn't seem like much. And it isn't, if you are pulling three children into the classroom. By the time you get them all set up and they pull their papers out, maybe you don't get so much done. But if you are working one on one, you can sit down and go through one-half page in a math book in twenty minutes. You can go through a spelling list or do an oral test on words. You can't do intense studying. I'll say, "You have to read *Oliver Twist* for the book report. Read a little of that." Twenty minutes isn't enough to get into algebra, although that depends on the kid.

Three hours doesn't seem like a school day, but when you think what happens in a school day by the time thirty or forty kids are out from recess and in from recess, and they have music and art and P.E. and lunch and school messages and taking attendance—there is a lot of extra time taken in the classroom that you don't take in the studios.

You have to use psychology and be flexible. I don't think you can separate yourself and say, "I'm the teacher"—you have to get into the child's head and empathize with what he's going through. Particularly if he is preparing for a difficult scene.

When they are still off the ceiling from the wild scene they just did running around and popping balloons at a birthday party, that's not the time to give them a math test. That's the time to have a spelling bee.

E.T.

On *E.T.* there were ten children. All the other teachers with more seniority than I had didn't want to do a picture with that many children. So I got the job. The first week I made a list of all the subjects my kids were taking. I looked at it, and I had forty-five subjects. And the children were all different ages. Because of this, the producers allowed me to have an additional studio teacher on the film.

Drew Barrymore was beginning first grade. She was a nonreader, just beginning to get into her education. I think E.T. was alive to her, E.T. was real. For the scene where E.T. was dying, Steven brought Drew in and started talking about E.T. dying, and the camera was all set to go. And as he talked, the tears started to roll out of her eyes and down her face. Steven never said, "Action," never said, "Roll 'em." He just made some slight indication with one hand to the camera crew and continued talking to Drew—and she cried, she was so sad that E.T. was dying, the tears just kept rolling and the cameras started rolling. There was no rehearsal or blocking. Steven managed to capture that moment because he was so connected with his cameramen. And with Drew.

Lucky Number Seven

Another film I worked on with Steven was *Indiana Jones and the Temple of Doom.* They had an extensive casting search to find a little Chinese boy—in Hong Kong, Hawaii, and all the major cities in the United States: San Francisco, Texas, Chicago, and New York. They couldn't find anyone.

Somebody suggested that they might find someone right in Chinatown in Los Angeles. Forget casting calls and child actors. They held a little casting call in this school in Chinatown. Ke told me later that his teacher told him to try out for the audition. He went home and told his mother he wanted to try out for a film. There are nine children in his family—and he is number seven. Lucky number seven. The seventh child in a Chinese family is a lucky child. His mother said, "You'll never get it. Forget it."

Apparently at the interview there were thirty or forty kids lined up, and Ke walked to the front of the line and said, "I want to be first." He read his lines. I later asked Kathleen Kennedy, Steven's producer, "You were looking at kids from all over the world. How did you feel when you saw Ke?" And she said, "I called Steven that night and said, 'I found him!' I knew that he was just terrific."

Ke's family is ethnic Chinese from Vietnam. He is one of the boat people. They had only been in America for four years at the time he was chosen to do the film. No one in the family spoke English. He went to a school in Chinatown. English was spoken in the classroom, but all the kids were Chinese and spoke Chinese at lunch and on the playground. So his English was very broken. I found him to be an avid learner, very bright. And he had such a thirst to learn English.

He was in the sixth grade—twelve years old. So we had to cover math, spelling, and reading. He was wonderful in math and moved on so quickly that last year when he went back to seventh grade he pulled almost straight A's. The film was a tremendously beneficial experience educationally. Working five months—one on one—all that individual attention. His English improved remarkably because everyone on the set spoke English. He wanted to learn new words every day and then use them. For example, we studied the word *noble*. And I explained to him that "noble" meant "very fine, very good, very grand." He went up to Harrison Ford the next day and said, "Harrison, you are a very noble actor."

He loved Harrison Ford. And Harrison was wonderful with him. Ke got confused when they were shooting out of sequence. They would ask him to respond and do something that maybe was happening at the end of the film but that they were shooting the first day. But Harrison always took the time to pull Ke aside and explain what was happening. Harrison was very patient and would break everything down for Ke.

Steven Spielberg asks for me on his California-based pictures now. The first time I worked with Steven was on a movie called *1941*. I was sent out on the job for two weeks, which became eight weeks. I had three little boys. We had a lot of night shooting down at the beach. I would always stand by with their jackets and make them hot chocolate and just be there for them. And Steven, although he never said anything at the time, observed everything that was going on around him. At the end of the movie he came up to me, gave me a big hug, and said, "If I ever do anything with children, you are going to be there."

Steven has just seen me work and knows that it is one less thing he has to worry about. When I'm on the set, every time I've ever been with him, the children are very happy. And they learn all of their subjects, and when they go back to school they're ahead. He knows that is an area he never has to be concerned with. He knows that if he is not shooting anything in particular at the time, he doesn't have to turn to his AD and say, "Go get the teacher and tell her to take the kids now."

The way I work is, I stay in touch with the AD and say, "Hey, it looks like they are going to be a while setting up lights, so why don't I grab the kids and get twenty minutes of schooling now." I take it upon myself. So Steven was familiar with the way I work, and he wanted to have that continuity and have me on his films. He does that, by the way, with most of his crew. He has not just singled out the teacher.

I had a direct line to Steven and felt free to talk to him if there was something pertaining to the children. Or if they were tired or cranky or had been up late, I would say, "They're a little tense today." He always understood. His rapport with the children in his films is exceptional.

Other directors I've worked with are so focused on what they are doing that they really only like you to deal with their assistant director.

"Sorry, Teach"

I find that people get a little lax in their language every once in a while, but they'll turn around and say, "Sorry, teach." They watch themselves. Because they are working with children, and they know that it's inappropriate to be using that language in front of a minor.

I think of it as being like the police officer on a freeway. When a police officer is driving behind you, you and everyone around you are probably going fifty-five MPH because of the presence of the officer in your rearview mirror. And when he is not around, you speed up to sixty-five. And I'm not saying that if the teacher wasn't there everybody would be breaking the law, but maybe if there were no teacher there, the person might get a little tense or tired and forget he hasn't given this kid a break in two hours. Not that he would intentionally do something, I just think our presence there is a reminder.

Filming as Education

Unlike television, where a child can be working year round on a series, film requires a few months of a child's time. So they can go back to "normal" life. The three months away from school is not detrimental as long as they are keeping up with their lessons. The experience they get working in an adult world, dealing one on one with adults, is part of adult orientation.

And it's especially educational when they film out of town. On *Harry and the Hendersons*, which was filmed in Seattle, Josh was eleven years old and had never been away before. On days we didn't shoot, I took him to all the museums in town, we went on a ferry boat to another island offshore. We went all over Seattle and the underground city. He documented the entire trip in a scrapbook, took pictures of everybody in the crew. Wrote things underneath the pictures. By the time we wrapped, he had a fabulous book.

It is a very enriching experience for kids to be in a film. And children who work in film are, for the most part, very bright. If you were to test all of the kids in the film industry, you would find that they had very high IQ's.

I find children who aren't in film tend to be shy. But children who work in film are very outgoing and friendly, very charismatic, which is probably due to the nature of show business. They are so alive, so energetic and full of excitement. And they have to be a quick study to act.

I've never encountered a temperamental or "studio" brat, as people might expect. As in any classroom situation, if two children are chatting, I'll say, "Settle down now, we've got thirty minutes in here. As soon as you finish your math, begin reading that story and try to answer the questions." As I would if I were in a classroom teaching thirty kids.

When a picture ends, I feel a sense of loss. The children are like my sons or daughters. You not only teach them, but you become very close to them. I see myself as a teacher, friend, confidante.

Cause for Concern

I have a concern about a law that says a guardian or studio teacher/welfare worker is no longer required on the set for children who are between sixteen and eighteen, on a nonschool day, which covers vacations and weekends.

A child in the state of California is still a minor until eighteen. It is courting temptation, when a film goes on location, to leave a sixteen-year-old boy or girl in a hotel room alone without a parent or a welfare worker. And I can only speak for what I think my son would do. If they said to him, "Matt have you ridden a horse?" he'd say, "Yeah, I've ridden a horse."

"We want to do a close-up on your face, Matt. I mean we have a stunt guy to do it, but we really need you to do it."

Knowing most sixteen-year-old boys and sixteen-year-old girls, if a director asked them to do something, said, "I really need you for the shot, I'd prefer not using the stuntperson," they would try to do it— whether it was to drive a car fast or to jump a horse or to maybe work a couple of hours later.

I feel that children could be put in a hazardous situation or even an uncomfortable, pressured situation on a film set—I mean who, even an adult, wants to say no to a director?—without the intervention of a parent, guardian, or welfare worker.

I am really surprised that the government and the state of California opted for that one. Especially after the *Twilight Zone* incident. There was no welfare worker.

I feel that if they'd shot it at four o'clock in the afternoon and there had been a welfare worker, the welfare worker would have said, "Hey, you are using explosives in the water with the helicopters over-head. You cannot do this shot with the kids." And it wouldn't have happened.

In most cases, I think producers will want us there for their own protection. They don't want lawsuits if anything should happen. But as far as changing the law as it reads now, I think there is going to have to be an accident. There is going to have to be a sixteen-year-old girl who comes back from location pregnant or something that is going to throw it into the newspapers. They are not going to listen to us. Sometimes they don't pay enough attention to teachers and advocates of child protection in the business.

The Future

I've changed a lot since my days teaching in a San Fernando Valley classroom. I'm working with assistant directors and have discussions with people over three feet tall! Over the years you learn to figure out the teaching/film business—"My God, they have eight scenes planned for this kid today!"—and learn to filter the absolutely necessary from the expendable.

When I did *Bad News Bears in Breaking Training*, I was really working very hard with the AD's, helping to schedule and working with the kids and coordinating with the mothers. Leonard Goldberg, who was the producer, asked me if I had ever thought about leaving teaching and getting into assistant directorship. He said, "I would really like to sponsor you. I think you are wasted here." And at the time I'm thinking, I've only been in the business a couple of years. I'm a single parent.

Matthew was only five or six years old, and I knew the kinds of hours AD's work—fifteen-, sixteen-hour days. Teachers basically are on an eight-hour day, and I can come home at the end of an evening and be there for my child. So I said to him, "I'm flattered that you would consider me, but I just can't envision myself doing that because of the hours."

I also discussed it with the AD on *E.T.* And he said, "Don't leave if you're happy where you are. You have no idea how your personal life will be affected. If your son is home sick, you don't get to call up and say, 'I've got a five-year-old sick in bed. He is throwing up. I'm going to stay home today.' It really is a commitment, and don't ever make the move unless you are ready to give your life to it."

But now looking ahead—Matt is sixteen and two years away from going to college, I have thought about changing. I might need more money. And I'll have more time. I've thought about publicity since I loved the press tours so much. Or associate producing since I'm a good coordinator.

Advice

When I came into the business I was on an emergency list of eleven teachers. There were forty teachers in the union divided into three lists—meaning all of list one would have to be working before list two, and all of list two before list three.

Now there are eighty-five teachers. Up until about six months ago (late 1986) we had forty-five teachers in the union and forty on the emergency list. They have just done away with the emergency list altogether, and we are all one union. So we have eighty-five teachers in the union, on a rotating list. And then there are nonunion teachers—with the increase in nonunion films, they are taking away work from us too.

The industry just doesn't need that many people. In a busy time of year—say, from September to November—we are all working overtime every day. From January until July or August, I would say that more than half of us are out of work.

So as far as looking at this and saying, "What a terrific job and what a wonderful industry. I think I'll break into it," I would advise against it. I would not start out now because I don't think I could make a living. Since I've got twelve years of contacts within the industry, and families to help me, and many films, television shows, and commercials under my belt, I think that I am going to stay busy. But there are a lot of teachers on that list who are not going to work.

As far as someone new coming in, no contacts . . . this is really not the place to be. It is overloaded. Also, the trend now seems to be the "brat" pack—you know, the sixteen-, seventeen-, eighteen-year-olds, and it's really twenty- and twenty-one-year-olds playing teenagers— so that cuts down on the number of children working in films, which of course directly affects how many teachers will be working.

Animal Trainer

The Animal Trainer handles and directs animals, domesticated or wild, for film and is charged with their training, feeding, grooming, and transportation. He or she is also responsible for ensuring that American Humane Association (AHA) rules are respected while the animal(s) are under his care during the course of the production.

Clint Rowe

Growing up in Tucson, Arizona, CLINT ROWE used to go looking for muskrats and deer and remembers being grounded for catching rattlesnakes. When he was fourteen he worked for free cleaning cages for Jungle Jim and his Wild Animals, a gypsy carnival that performed at shopping centers, introducing youngsters to cougars, elk, bear, and "animals you don't usually see in the suburbs." Clint joined Jungle Jim on Disney's *Wild Kingdom* television series in Alaska, working with a grizzly bear and some wolves. This led to a five-year stint at Disney doing the *World of Color* series and more experience with a wide variety of wild animals including bears, raccoons, cougars, tigers, and lions.

It was *Down and Out in Beverly Hills* that brought fame to Clint through "Mike the dog," who broke the Lassie and Rin-Tin-Tin prototypes by playing an anorexic, yet endearing, member of a neurotic Beverly Hills household. Clint's expertise with other animals, wild and domesticated, is apparent in such films as *Natty Gann* and *The Thing*.

THE FIRST thing you have to establish is a relationship of trust. Without that you can have an animal work, but it's just horrible, it is just not anything.

And the next thing you've got to find out is what motivates them.

It's not just love. I think every dog loves his owner. He has to learn to come to me for a reward and that the reward is good. You try to have him gravitate toward anything that's good. You take everything in steps with these guys—you can't just go in and show them a script or say, "Look, you've got to sit and beg here."

They have to learn to learn, and the only way they're going to learn through a volition of their own is if they anticipate that it's a good thing to do instead of a bad thing.

Find out what he likes, food or praise or a ball. You have to give him what he wants before he's going to give you what you want. It's a two-way street. You're the leader in that relationship during training, but when you finally get him to the set it's a fifty-fifty deal, and you're no more than he and he's no more than you.

I've had Mike for quite a few years. With any animal, it takes a long time to do the training for a film. You can obedience train a dog in a few weeks, but it's going to take a year to a year and a half of training before he's really ready to go into a comprehensive film part. He has to understand everything that you're asking. Once that's done, once all your basics are there, then you can do a film with him. If you don't, when you get on a set he's going to be confused and anxious, and no personality will come out. The key in training is preserving his character and allowing his personality to grow.

If you don't have proper preparation, you don't have a good working animal. You have to take him to every environment that you can think of and expose him to everything and make sure that he feels good about it.

Behaviors

You can say what he learns are tricks, but they're really behaviors. There are about 110 basic responses that you can build on. With Mike we've combined those and they add up to perhaps five hundred behaviors.

Your standards are "stay," "sit," "down," "come," "fetch," "speak"—because they've got to bark for screen—and "back up." Without those basics you can't combine. You put as many basics on as possible, through incremental steps and repetition to the point where he doesn't have to think about what he does. Like driving a car for humans: eventually it's subconscious.

An example of combining would be where in *Down and Out in Beverly Hills*, Mike had to toss a food dish. There's about nine different behaviors in that, combined into one. It's "sit and stay, look, speak, fetch it, hold it, toss it, hold it, drop it, speak." And then you can go on because after he speaks he's got to stay, so that's eleven, and he's got to look again, so there's twelve.

I stand wherever they want him to look—I'm at the angle that is usually behind the camera or behind an actor or off to the side. In that case, I was behind the psychiatrist, against the wall.

Diet

Diet's extremely important. You have to look at your dog as an individual and say, "What does he seem to function best on?" Mike seems to do real well on vitamins C and B, brewer's yeast, cod liver oil, and vitamin E. When he works, I want a steady energy level from him all day. I've experimented with feeding him once a day, twice a day, a large meal in the morning, a small one at night . . . What's worked best for Mike is this: I fill a crock pot with brown rice, carrots, potatoes, peas, corn, and all sorts of vegetables, and he'll eat that in the morning before he goes to work. Then I give him broiled chicken and turkey throughout the day for rewards, so there's a lot of protein going into him.

Resistance versus Resentment

When you go on set with your animal, you think of his future. Everything that he does leads toward the next minute, the next hour, the next day. If he gets upset or anxious about anything, it's going to transfer onto that future. When negative stimuli become part of that future, you've built a resistance in him to you, to the environment. That can become resentment.

Resistance is just a little bit of a mistrust. And you can slide by on it. It's taking him a little farther than he understands. If I push you, you're going to resist. That's natural. If I keep pushing you, you're going to resent it. And that builds and builds, and then I have to push you harder and harder. Every creature has an inborn desire to rebel against something that is wrong, something they don't understand.

You don't intentionally want them to resist you. Sometimes, in ignorance, you've gone into a situation where you've betrayed their trust in you. For every uncalled-for negative, you're going to spend a thousand positives to get back their trust. Because we're human we do make mistakes. In the work, I might say, "Mike, let's do it," over and over again and he's tired or he's got a minor infection or is unsure of his environment, and I'm not reading it. He can't tell me what I did wrong. In situations where he has not performed well, it's often taken me days to figure out what I did wrong. At that point you hope it's not too late, and you go back and re-create the situation as closely as possible—and make it good.

The problem is you can never duplicate it exactly. When you cross into resentment, you have a problem. Resentment is never forgiven by an animal, and you may as well retire him.

I was accused of being conservative on one show. What I said was, "I think he can do it and I'm pretty sure he'll have that in five days," but I was not going to say, "Oh, yeah, no problem." I *am* protective of what my animal is capable of. Because who knows, Friday he may be sick. And *he* is the first priority—not them, not their film.

I have only had situations where an animal will not perform with animals other than my own. With my own animals, I've never held up the company. If I know that it's going to take more time, I'll let them know ahead of time. I've worked with animals in the past that aren't my own, but I will not do that anymore.

First of all, unless you've spent enough time, you don't have a relationship and he's not tuned in to who you are. Second, often they just don't have the training that's necessary. Without that relationship and without the training, you can't accomplish what you can with your own.

It's a unique training situation. It's not like the circus. The circus is a set routine that the animals do day after day, year after year. They click in at the same time every day. But a film animal has to be highly adaptable, go into a new set, a new environment, new people, new lights, new temperature changes, new atmospheric changes, maybe the director's uptight that day, maybe your animal just didn't get enough rest the night before. These are variables you have to be aware of.

Performance

The relationship with your animal never becomes as deep as when you're actually working. That's when it is at its highest point, because you're both so in tune. When you're working you have a real tight bond with the animal, there's nothing I've ever experienced that can come close. I know he's an animal and doesn't relate as humans do, but animals are sentient beings who operate from a world of feeling. There is an awareness and energy there that's electric. It becomes completely a two-way street.

Dogs aren't like us, they're not saying, "Okay, we're up for twelve hours here and we're going to work." They sleep a lot; it's unnatural for them to come in and always be on. So you have to conserve their energy *and* their emotional attitude.

When he doesn't perform well, there's usually just three reasons: he doesn't feel good, he's tired, or he doesn't understand. You can never say, "That dumb animal," you always have to say, "What is the problem, what am I doing wrong, is there something wrong in the environment, does he not feel good today, is he tired?"

If he isn't performing well, hopefully you have a good rapport with the director and he's understanding. If I feel the director doesn't have an affinity for my animal, I won't work for him. Unfortunately I've learned that through years of experience. When I have worked for someone who doesn't care, it is always a mistake on my part because I cannot function with him.

Some directors I've worked with were afraid. Their self-esteem was threatened—they were going to get labeled as "the guy that did that dog film" instead of some epic.

I would say the majority of actors have been great, they'll help you all the way. And it's hard for them because they're concentrating on everything else. I've seen actors threatened by a dog. If an actor has a block against working with animals, it makes my job more difficult.

Often if they're sitting on a couch next to him, they will pet him, because it's a natural thing to do. But he's got to cue at a certain time, and if they're petting at that point, he won't cue because that's his reward. So you have to say, "Look, just put your hand there, but don't pet him." Then you either get the actors who say, "Oh, okay!" and pull their hand away in fright as if they did something very wrong— and I have to assure him them it's all right and to relax. Or you get the ones who can't stop petting. Then I have to tell them to approach Mike like a prop. With a cigarette and a lighter on the table, they have to pick up the cigarette, light it at a certain line; that's how they have to approach him. That makes it easier for them.

I won't put Mike in when the director is blocking the scene because there's always myriad adjustments. Let's say Mike's going to come through a door with an actor. They come through the door, stop at the counter, and go to a chair, and the actor sits down. That's how they block it. But then as they're near their last little bit, the director decides to change *which* chair the actor will sit in.

If you prep the dog to go to the first chair, it's really hard now to ask him to change and adjust to the second chair. You want to make sure that the actors are exact. You watch a good actor, he'll do the same thing every time. They're amazing, they'll stop almost in the same spot, they'll put their hand in the same place.

An actor who is unpredictable is really hard for me to work with. None of them are completely unpredictable, but some are a little sloppy. . . .

Conserving Energy

Mike's going to do three good takes on most scenes. After that, his performance is going to drop a little bit. You keep your fingers crossed that everything is together in the first three takes.

Some scenes, sure, you're going to need seventeen takes for him to, say, hit a button just right, or a certain look might take six takes. But if you go over into five to ten takes consistently, your animal's energy level is going to wane. And if you're doing ten to fifteen takes on every scene, your dog's not going to make it.

To conserve his energy, when he's through with a setup, he's off set. I take him to the trailer or my truck and try to have him rest. I want him in a quiet environment without a lot of stimulus and noise.

He builds up such anticipation to go on the set . . . he loves to work. You can open the trailer door and he'll walk to the stage without you and go to work. You can't let him do that because I'm always afraid something's going to fall on him. But he knows exactly where everybody is and he'll just go there and wait. "Yo, Mike's here, where's Clint?"

A Turning Point

There was one film project that completely changed my attitude about working with animals in film. It was working with wild animals in another country.

Other people had turned down the job, said it was impossible. I didn't believe anything was impossible. They hired me to go over, capture these wild animals, and train them for a horror film. When I got there a local trapper had been hired to trap these animals. He had caged a number of them together in a little box, and they were fighting each other. I said, "You can't do this."

So that started the battles, which escalated. They weren't being fed properly. The people were allotted money to buy food, but how much food was really bought? Do you understand what I mean? It was all going into their pockets.

I found out I didn't have much say. I realized that the first thing I had to do was get them out of there. I had to battle over the types of cages I wanted built for them. Finally I got the cages built. I fought for every single thing, and what it would come down to in every fight was, I'd say, "Well then, I'm going home," and then I'd get what I wanted.

They were supposed to give me eight solid weeks. I never had that. I had to get them to walk, run, come in groups. I didn't understand the species at the time. We put up chicken-wire fences and then put a native every ten feet around that fence, because they're scared of people.

The biggest enlightenment came when we brought in one big male that none of the others had ever seen, and he never touched them and they were all scared to death of him. That's when I realized it's attitude, it's how you communicate nonverbally with them. From then on, I was in charge. I could walk in with them, move them. I never hit them, you never have to hit them. It's all threats. And if one wouldn't back down, I would net him. They basically dominate each other. In a fight, the biggest thing is to hold one down, and a net is the same type of thing.

We had a big truck and a ramp that came down to feed them, and I'd walk in the truck and yell, "Outside, outside." They'd all run out and then I'd come down the ramp, and as long as I stood on that ramp, they wouldn't come back in. I could just turn my body three quarters and they'd all move.

I was able to teach the conditional response. Taught them to go to a buzzer for food. They understood after a while, but it was so stressful on them and they're beautiful creatures. After a while you just think, What the hell am I doing here? You have a certain pride in saying, "Jeez, I got thirty-six working together, they're running together and moving together," but in looking back, it was ethically and biologically horrible.

Intimidation is one of their behavioral modes, but that's within their own social structure. When you put them in a different environment, they're thinking, There's a human being and I'm scared of him and I'm being pushed into this. Human beings should not superimpose their social structure on animals.

Setting Standards

When I came home I was broke. It was a hard time, but it helped me make a lot of decisions about what I was doing, taking responsibility and saying, "I caused this. I can blame them for making my job difficult, but in my first week there I sensed it."

I had about ten animals—dogs and some birds. I gave away all my dogs except Mike and his backup, Dave, and Jed, and said to myself, If I can't make it with these animals, I'm in the wrong business.

And from then on I didn't really work as the system normally works. They expect a trainer to train any animal. I wouldn't do that anymore. I gave myself two years. If I couldn't make it in that time period, I was going to sell everything I had and do something else.

When the two-year period was up, it didn't look good because *Natty Gann* had just been released, and while Jed got critical acclaim, there was no work forthcoming, no phone calls.

Down and Out in Beverly Hills was due out in February, and January was the end of my two years, so I was depressed.

Fortunately, *Down and Out* popped.

Success and Neurosis

Stardom or success does not lead to neurosis in an animal, unless it leads to one for the trainer. In *Down and Out in Beverly Hills*, that was a realistic portrayal—even as it was comedic and outrageous. You watch dogs, they really react to what the people around them do. There are some very neurotic little animals. The dog "Matisse" that Mike played was just a reflection of the people around him.

The Future

I'd love to do documentaries on animals and their relationship to people, rather than continue on and do film after film.

I have a very good friend, Doug, who has a beautiful 1,200-pound bear. And Doug said, "What the hell do I ever get? I get a bear ripping someone's head off and carrying the body into the brush." It can be very limiting. If I can get a character that is interesting for my animal, then it's worth it.

In *Down and Out*, Paul once said, "Let's have him eat something here," and I said, "Well, we can't, can we, because he's anorexic," and he said, "That's right, thanks." Simple little thing like that, but it is keeping him in a form of character.

When a new project was brought to me—it's a very violent film with lots of dog fights—I said, "I won't do dog fights." They didn't like that, of course.

So I called the American Humane Society and said, "Do you support me?" and they said, "Well, our guidelines are a little hazy in that area." And I said, "I am against muzzled fights. We are trainers, and it's our job to train animals to create an illusion for the filmmaker, an illusion of reality. Not the reality itself."

Because of that, we had a meeting with some other trainers who are active in the business, and the issue of animal fights and sedation of animals was brought up in determining new guidelines.

But I think you have to go by your own standards no matter what anybody thinks, whatever the group thinks. The public and producers need to be educated about animals. All of us, myself included, need to contribute more to animal behaviorism through what we do, because we deal in a specialized, unique field.

Animal trainers in the film industry need to raise their guidelines higher than anybody else because first, we're in the forum. If something happens, we are going to get the publicity. We have a great deal of influence because our animals appear on-screen. And second, if the guidelines aren't high, you have no protection against unqualified trainers.

Advice

If you want to get into this business as a trainer, I would advise getting your own animals, working your own animals.

In terms of the medium, an animal trainer has to understand camera angles and to know if a shot is feasible for your animal. You should understand editing and how a director works.

Go out and meet trainers. You have to ask yourself, "What kind of service can I give to this show or to this industry?" You can't look at what they're going to give you. Make yourself valuable. Make yourself knowledgeable. And the more your animal knows, the better he's going to work and the easier it is for both of you.

And be willing to turn some things down if it's not right for your animal—or for you.

6
THE LOOK

Everything you see on-screen—background buildings and scenery, the makeup, hair and costumes worn by performers, the items handled or moved about by the actors during the making of a motion picture—all contribute to the "look" of the movie.

The people in this chapter are responsible for making the conscious choices that provide an overall visual impression for the audience.

Production Designer

The Production Designer is charged with creating the visual design of the film. He or she works closely with the director to determine how he sees the film, and by choice of colors, textures, and materials determines the overall "look" and contributes to the emotional tone of the film. The Production Designer supervises the search for locations, designs the sets, oversees the drawing up of blueprints and the building and dressing of sets, and coordinates the various departments that contribute to the artistic design of the film and the execution of those designs—namely construction, set design and decoration, props, costumes, hair, and makeup.

Polly Platt

POLLY PLATT grew up as an "army brat" in Europe, wanting to be a painter. Exposure to the theater inspired her to pursue scenic design. At the time, women were discouraged from pursuing this male-dominated profession, so Polly graduated with a degree in costume design from Carnegie Tech. She went to Arizona with some of her colleagues to pioneer a repertory theater company, a venture that ended in tragedy when her first husband was killed in an automobile accident. Eventually she returned to New York, where she found theatrical work and met Peter Bogdanovich. They discovered a mutual fascination for film, fell in love, collaborated on free-lance writing assignments, and got married. Together, they came out to Hollywood, where Roger Corman put them to work on his low-budget pictures—Peter writing and directing; Polly producing, co-writing, scouting locations, and editing. After collaborating on two successful studio pictures (*Paper Moon* and *What's Up, Doc?*), during which time their daughters Antonia and Alexandra were born, Polly and Peter separated. Polly went on to a successful career as a production designer on such films as *A Star Is Born*, *Bad News Bears*, *Terms of Endearment* (for which she received an Oscar nomination), and *The Witches of Eastwick*. She also wrote *Pretty Baby* for Louis Malle and executive produced the widely acclaimed *Broadcast News*.

WHEN I was about twelve, I had artistic leanings. I wanted to be a painter. I drew well—that was my talent.

My mother took me to a small summer stock theater outside of Boston. I had been to the theater and always believed what I saw on-stage. I believed the actors were *real* people. But at this particular play, I think it was *Arms and the Man*, during the act break I went out behind the barn and saw all the actors in their costumes in the dark with the light streaming out from the theater—an extraordinary sight. They were all smoking cigarettes and talking, not acting at all the way they had been on the stage. I suddenly realized there were people who did this as a job. I decided that I could do the scenery since I could draw.

In the late fifties and early sixties a bunch of us went out to Tuscon. That was the first time I saw American Indian work everywhere—Papago baskets, Navajo rugs. I had seen a lot of Holly-wood movies where the Indians wore feathers and war paint, and I thought, This real stuff is beautiful, why don't they show this?

Then I started looking at John Ford's movies—*Rio Bravo, Fort Apache*—all these films about the American Indian-U.S. Cavalry wars. I thought his production design was authentic. But in truth, the U.S. Cavalry in the 1870s Southwest were not perfectly dressed—the army didn't have the money. Ford ignored the history there and had them all in perfect uniforms. A director makes a decision. And if he wants to stretch reality, as De Mille or Josef von Sternberg did, then that becomes a reflection of his style. Joe von Sternberg once said about *The Scarlet Empress*, "I don't have to go to Russia, I *am* Russia!"

Maybe the current stress on authenticity began in the late sixties. Somehow, after the Eisenhower years, the McCarthy era, Vietnam, and the murder of our president, we began to feel we were not being told the *truth*. And now the things coming out about Kennedy, the president we had all admired—maybe he wasn't the man we thought he was.

I think that the search for what was truly "real" started just about then.

The Job

Your first responsibility as a production designer is to find out what the director is doing—what kind of picture he is trying to make.

A director is like a novelist in that if you read all of his novels, you start finding out that there's a body of work that represents the artist: his interests, his themes.

I try to find out what his vision is. You have to sit with him, and this is where the skill comes in—you need to be able to draw from him. And it's terribly difficult in films because you go from film to film and you don't know the director very well.

Why does he want to make this story? How does he *see* it in his mind's eye? Is he a romantic, a cynic? What is he *doing*?

You want the film to have a cohesion artistically and locations that *mean* something in terms of what we're trying to say in the story.

You wouldn't ordinarily shoot a fairy tale in a slum. Find out what the director wants, and if he's not thought about it, make him think about it.

Paper Moon

The next thing is to be able to get his confidence in you up to the point where you will be listened to and your ideas will be used. Because if you're a good and talented production designer, you can greatly influence the way the film looks.

For example, *Paper Moon* was written to be shot in Georgia. And I said to Peter, "Georgia is a beautiful state, it's very green and foresty, but I think it should be shot in Kansas where it's flat and barren. Another thought is, let's not do the 'depression' they're experiencing, but rather show these two little people constantly alone against this vast Kansas sky, emphasizing their isolation and helplessness."

When we began preproduction, I had a picture of my father sitting in a paper moon in that era, and Peter fell in love with it, so that became the title of the movie.

Tatum O'Neal was my suggestion. I took one look at her and said, "Boy, if I were a casting director, I would put this kid in films." She had this low scratchy voice and was very advanced for an eight-year-old girl. She would look you up and down and say things like "You sure have a good body. . . ." She was really a fascinating girl. I used to call her "Whiskey" because of her whiskey voice. Peter wanted to cast Ryan O'Neal as her father, which turned out to be a great idea.

That was the last picture we worked on together.

Design Budget

The budget—that's the enemy. If you get a reputation for going over budget, people will not hire you. So you must work within the budget, and you must be clever with it.

Maybe a million dollars is allocated for actual cost of sets and design staff salaries. It depends on how many sets and locations you have. Basically, you know you're going to have to pay a production designer at least two or three months preproduction, maybe three months of shooting schedule, an art director assisting me who is getting more than scale, property master, and set decorator.

So the more you know about this, the better you understand why pictures cost so much money. It's like the budget of the military. We're all so horrified at how much money we spend on defense—and I'm not defending the defense budget, but an enormous amount of the budget is salaries for officers and soldiers and sailors and WACS and so on.

Often the men who give us the money to make the films are not aware of the significance of the production designer. It's like, if you make tomato soup—a lot of those guys who sell the soup don't know how tomatoes are grown, they're into selling or packaging or putting a label on it.

If you're really smart, you get in there and *you* hire the property master because everything the actors touch is a prop and you want to make sure that it's right for the character or the movie visually.

Of course, you hire your art director, an assistant—someone close to you who will help you, and you hire your own set decorator. If the director has a set decorator he thinks is good, you don't oppose that. But it's even in my contract that I hire my own set decorator.

If there's a costume designer involved, you do your best to hire someone very capable. I want control over these things. The film's characters should be identified by colors and what they wear. It is essential that you have a relationship between what a character is playing and how he or she dresses and what his or her house or office looks like.

You check out how the production manager has scheduled scenes to coordinate with locations. He's responsible for watching that you stay on budget. So the production designer and production manager are in an embattled position, but it serves them both to work *with* each other.

You also work with the cinematographer, check with him about the colors you're using, especially if you're using white. Cameramen have a very hard time with white because it's difficult to balance the light.

Planning

I don't sketch anymore. Now you're supposed to hire an illustrator and tell him what to do. In fact, schedules have become so short that you spend most of your time looking for locations and building sets. You almost skip that step—it's almost redundant. It's a dying art. What's become big is going back to an older style of filmmaking:

storyboarding. It's helpful, even if you don't stick to it, to keep the theme in your head.

If I can't figure out how to design the set, something's amiss with the scene. It's not that the writing is bad, but if I'm having problems, then I start thinking, Well, maybe it should be set in a different location. . . .

I hang around the set all the time, watch what's going on. Things have a tendency to change, and I want to be in tune with that.

I make sure that I get to know the actors. I discuss the set with them—what their house would be like, for example—and sometimes they have much better ideas than I do. You don't want to give them an environment they can't handle.

Problems

Mostly you go to the producer with your problems.

Hopefully, the producer trusts his director, and the director is king. When that doesn't happen, they become adversaries. And you can get caught in the middle. It takes skillful negotiating in critical, powerful situations. That's why many crew members have a tendency to disappear. It's too dangerous, you can get ground up in the powers rolling around. Grist for the mill.

You have to be a warrior, and sometimes I think winning the real battle is overcoming the coward in you. My own demons are the hardest. It's just horrible when you're confronted with something and you think, I just can't do it. We all go through that. When the breakthrough comes, your subconscious mind is working on it—you've just got to let it through.

For *Targets*, my first film, I designed a set that was going to be inside a sound stage. I did my own drafting; I drew it knowing I had this huge sound stage. I had been used to designing for a small proscenium theater, and it never occurred to me to measure the sound stage because it was so big.

We prebuilt the walls, and as we were putting up the set the construction coordinator came up and said, "Did you measure the stage?" And I said, "No," and he said, "Well, we're at the end of the hall and the bedroom's not going to fit."

I had designed the set too big to fit the stage!

We were doing long dolly shots because this was about a murderer and we wanted to hold suspense by following him around the house—

through the kitchen, dining room, hall, and bedroom—all in one take. What I ended up having to do was take out sections of each wall, and it cost a lot of money.

Since I was also the producer, I did not get fired as production designer!

Another stumbling block in production design is coordinating various opinions while still holding on to your concept of the entire film. Taking the director's point of view, my point of view, the script, the actors' points of view, and trying to pull it all together to achieve "nirvana."

You must have an overall concept that every set, every costume, and every location refers to. How do you pull it all together?

And *time*. Often a director is so busy he doesn't get a chance to look at everything, and what an embarrassment for the designer to have an entire crew—120 people at a location at six o'clock in the morning—watching when the director walks up and says, "I don't like it."

It's happened. I've worked with directors who won't go and look at locations. He'll say, "Show me the pictures." He doesn't have the time, and maybe subconsciously he doesn't want to have to make those decisions.

The Set as a Character

I think architectural training is not necessary for production design because it is not about building houses or whatever—it is about *character*. It's about knowledge of people and how they live. What would this kind of person choose as curtain material, where would this story take place?

For instance, *The Thief Who Came to Dinner* with Ryan O'Neal and Jackie Bisset is about a computer expert who sees so much theft going on about him that he decides to become a thief himself.

It was originally set in Chicago, and I said to the director, "You know, I really don't like people who go into people's houses and steal their jewelry. We're supposed to be on this guy's side, so let's take it out of Chicago where everybody has pearls that were their mother's and the watch that belonged to their father and those things that we feel so bad about losing. Let's take it to a city like Houston where everything is new, replaceable, insurance covers it all—or Hollywood, where you can just change the initials on the ashtrays, you do the new shag rug when you move into somebody else's house."

So we moved it to Houston, and I tried to make everything very modern and replaceable so that we wouldn't hate this character for being a thief. Also, because it was about acquiring money, I made it a game for myself to use a lot of green in the sets and costumes.

On Surviving

From production designers to set decorators, script supervisors, camera operators, you name it—you'll find they do their work, do as they're told, keep their heads down, and stay out of the way.

You may have good ideas, but if you get a reputation for being a big-mouth busybody who is always making suggestions, you may find yourself having a hard time getting work.

On *Terms of Endearment*, I showed Jim Brooks (the director) a dining room where Jack Nicholson, who was playing an astronaut, was to serve dinner to Shirley MacLaine. It was a masculine house, and I put all his memorabilia up on the walls of the dining room.

Jim was very uncomfortable, asking me questions: "Where's she going to sit when she leaves the table?" or "Where's he going to make his exit?" He kept fussing, didn't say, "I hate it," but was generally uneasy in the room. So I said, "How about we shoot it in the kitchen?"

The truth is I had been to visit the astronaut, Cernan, in Houston. He lived in a small apartment and had all his memorabilia in this kitchen. He had saved the spaghetti dinner that he took up on a space mission. He had the glove, the spoon, the knife, and the fork that he had taken up to the moon—all in the kitchen. "Sometimes," he joked with me, "if I really want to impress somebody, I'll let the person eat with the spoon that I used on the moon. . . ."

I told Jim about that, and he got so excited about it. And the kitchen was where we shot it. People have commented to me how brilliant that was, but basically it was a collaboration. Jim doesn't like one room; "How about the kitchen?"; he's dubious, so I tell him about Cernan; he thinks about it and ultimately chooses that idea.

The point is, there was this production assistant who kept saying, "Come on, he would never put all this stuff in the kitchen." Finally I took him aside and said, "When you have my job you can say whatever you want, but if you don't want me to throw you off the set, shut up."

That's just an example of how anyone from director to production assistant can say, "I think this is shitty," and all of a sudden the whole thing turns to sand and falls through your fingers. You really have to be stable. And *then* go home and drink.

You've got to get tough. But by the same token, charm and beauty and tact help a lot. If you're on the crew and you're not diplomatic and savvy, you may have a hard time surviving in this industry. Even if you are in special effects or something that requires raw, pure skill and talent, you still have to be wise politically.

With any job in the movies, you have to cultivate the ability to read other people's moods and recognize their needs. You can learn these social skills. I used to be much more truculent and difficult in the early years. It was terribly important for me to be right. I was really a bulldog. And you have to be, or your work ends up a mishmash.

On Academy Award Recognition

Are the Academy Awards a motivating factor? No. Although, wow, when you get nominated, you'd sure like to have it happen again! The guys who nominate you are your peers—it's a no-kidding, huge, knockout thrill.

When *Terms of Endearment* began to be such a big hit, I thought everyone was going to get nominated, but not me—because we had no money for the sets, and I thought the work was practically invisible.

I wanted to be nominated for *The Last Picture Show* and *Paper Moon* because I thought I deserved it on those two. But on *Terms*, I was surprised. I thought it was just the same job I'd always done, only not so big, just tiny stuff. But I wanted it—oh, my God, I wanted it so bad. I wanted it right up to the very end. Yet when I didn't win, I was depressed, but not bitter.

Losing. Driving home alone, in this big limousine, I knew that if I had the Oscar in my lap, I would *not* be alone in that limousine.

I had lost to *Fanny and Alexander*, which was a very impressive film. And maybe it's better to drive home alone, no Oscar, and learn that "success has many fathers, but failure is an orphan."

On Being a Woman in the Industry

For a long time I was extremely defensive, saying, "I'm an artist first. My sex is immaterial. . . ."

It's fascinating how personal perception can get distorted. Early on, I felt I wasn't getting jobs because I was a woman, and I became defensive about it.

Now I feel my womanliness is an advantage and helps me as an artist—although, in my opinion, it is hard to be a sane woman and mother and still work artistically in this industry, which more and more is becoming a *business* and is controlled by men.

Over the years, with the children, I realized that biological destiny, I guess that's what you'd call it, has definitely affected my career. I have a feeling that what makes each of us valuable—and that means men, women, and children of both sexes—is what we have to offer individually.

What I have to offer has to do with the fact that I am a woman and also an artist. So I bring a certain ethic—artistic and practical, a quality that is intertwined with being a woman and an artist—to whatever I do. It's inescapable.

I am not a feminist, nor the opposite. I try hard not to think about such personal politics. But I do have problems asking women to do things for me like getting coffee. The thing about being a woman is that it is so endemic for us to be servants, or rather to take care of things and people, that it feels very strange to change that role.

And there aren't many in positions of power to look to as role models who don't operate autocratically, who do not walk on the set with the "Okay, where's my apple, or cigar, where's my drugs?" attitude. It is possible to be a director without being a bastard, although it's sometimes a great attribute to be incredibly thick-skinned.

I had lunch with a friend, a very successful woman executive in films. Beautiful, bright, honest, makes plenty of money, and is very powerful. I'm forty-five, she's thirty-five—she told me, "The only thing I envy you is your children."

For me to say my children have held me back is ridiculous, but it has made it harder. And I have been tempted to think that without my children I would have been king of the world.

So being a woman, I think, has not so much to do with "who do you sleep with" or what heartbreaks and what affairs, nonaffairs, or marriages you've had, but with "Are you able to do what, biologically, is part of your life?"

Every woman I know well, in spite of the incredible agony they go through with children, would say, "Have them. Do it."

You really have to grow up. *You* may not grow up until *they're* fifteen, but the journey is rich and there are places that are forever closed to you if you haven't had children. Raising children is my greatest trial—the fire, the tortures of hell, because I didn't understand how to do it. I'm so successful in my work, and people pay me for my opinion, and my children will not listen to me about *anything!* You can feel so helpless.

Advice

People ask me, "How did you get into production design?" or, "How did you get so far?" and I always laughingly say, "I slept my way to the top! Of course, he was my husband!" It used to get a lot of laughs. We did it together.

You can go to school: UCLA, USC, Carnegie Mellon, NYU film school, and you can get trained, but I recommend, as groundwork, studies in theater and fine arts. I don't care if you've earned a degree, but *read* history. History and literature are essential.

If you want to be a production designer, study to be a director and approach film as an art for interpretation. You should take some drafting, not so that you can do it, but so you can read the blueprints. You need to be able to read and draw plans, sketch ideas, write, understand a little math, though my math is rotten.

Although you don't have to know fine details like what a cabriole leg is, you really should know styles and periods of furniture. Over the years I've picked up a lot. You need to be able to communicate to your set decorator what you want, such as "I think she should have a Queen Anne chair in her bedroom. . . ."

To know the great playwrights of the theater and to love drama or the dance is wonderful because then you understand that a set is a place where the action happens. Often people with heavily architectural backgrounds don't understand that.

Production design does not often overwhelm the story. But you do see production design that does not help a particular film. A film that I was quite impressed with, *Sophie's Choice*, allowed the house to dominate the story. And there's a scene when they're all on the roof of the house and it looks like they're going to fall right off. It made me feel terribly uncomfortable—that should not have been happening at that moment.

I have tremendous respect for the audience. I don't care if they're swamp people or from New York, city or country. People are sensitive, they see everything. Especially in a film, they seem to become more alert, more than in real life.

I think film is the great American art form. That's why I get very depressed when I see a film that I don't think is good. It diminishes all of us.

Giving it all up and staying home would be a disservice to the children. I'm already too locked into my daughters, I love them too much. They worry about me if I'm at home without a date, or a job. You've got to let your kids go their way, keep off their backs.

I don't think I dared to admit to myself that I wanted *success*; I wanted an interesting life. Wanted to *get it* right. Where some people go wrong is that they're so determined that they must *be* right that they lose their sense of reality.

I know people who say "I've seen life and I know the way it should be." If you think you know all the answers, then you close those essential pores, or those parts of your brain that are helping you to grow. You mustn't close yourself off to pain either. Personal pain, your children's, your husband's, your friend's.

And be humble, then learn to unlearn. To become experienced and believe you know it all is to lose spontaneity.

Looking back, there is only one thing I would have done differently. I think I would have conducted my personal life with as much strength and attention to ethics and reality as in my work.

I wish I had had the *personal* sense of my own worth, to treat myself with the kind of decency that I treated the projects I worked on. But it's never too late, is it?

Set Designer

The Set Designer is responsible for the execution of detailed "plan and elevation" drawings of the sets and construction elements within the set to be built for a motion picture. He or she drafts blueprints from descriptions or drawings provided by the production designer and thereafter oversees the construction and any modification of those sets. The Set Designer also works closely with the director, cinematographer, and special effects department to determine how portions of the set are to be used and photographed.

David Klassen

DAVID KLASSEN picked up drafting and drawing from his architect father and, upon graduating from high school, got a job as an apprentice in Universal's blueprinting department. He worked his way up through the various classifications (at the time there were six stages), attaining the "senior lead" position, which qualified him to supervise and delegate set-designing duties as well as doing the hands-on work. David has set-designed over thirty-five films, including *The Blues Brothers, Three Amigos, Beverly Hills Cop II, The Toy, The River, Running Scared, Cobra, Blade Runner, 2010,* and *Vibes.* He is currently pursuing a career in production design.

THE SET designer executes the production designer's ideas. And, for the most part, the production designer is the one to get hold of you for a job.

The production designer or art director will give me rough sketches of what he wants for a set—it could be anything from a rough thumbnail sketch to a very elaborate rendering that either he or the production illustrator has done. He will rely on me to put all the detail work into it.

The drawings are similar to architectural drawings. We draw plans, elevations, sections and details that the prop makers can build from.

The production designer, from reading the script, will have determined the period—whether it's Colonial or Greek revival, Victorian, present day, or futuristic—but he will rely on the set designer to put in all the moldings, details, the windows, the appliqué, the staff work, and the mantels over fireplaces, etc.

What the Camera Sees

I have been a photographer, and that is a definite plus in determining how lighting and composition affect the sets and what the camera is actually going to see.

Dollar for dollar, what you're building you want to see on the screen. You always want to be in touch with *what the camera is seeing*, to figure out exactly how much you have to build. It's senseless to build something that's going to cost a substantial amount of money and not even see it in the film.

A production designer or set designer has got to look at the set as if he's directing it for the action and see what is taking place in the background, what camera angle he's going to take. Since I've been starting to move into art direction, I'm becoming more conscious of what the camera sees and how the action is going to be played, and I will often make suggestions.

Blade Runner

I would say *Blade Runner* was one of the most difficult pictures I've done. The challenge resided in its being a period film with a "twist." Although it took place in the future, it had a forties theme to it. We had a long preproduction period. The production designer had been on the film one year before cameras rolled. And I'd been on the picture for about eight months.

It was an extensive amount of drawing, everything from vehicles to back-lot streets, which at that time, I believe, cost in the neighborhood of three million dollars.

Ridley Scott, the director of the picture, had been an art director at one time, in England. He was a perfectionist and was in tight with the production designer on all of the design work. Working with a director who has been an art director himself, you are under quite a bit of scrutiny. That was a great advantage because Ridley had the design insight but delegated the work to the production designer and his art department. With some former art directors who become directors, their design background can be counterproductive because they don't realize they have to let go of the artistic execution at some point.

Set Design Problems

Many directors, especially visual ones like Peter Hyams and Ridley Scott, want to have a set that'll give them a tremendous amount of depth of field. You've got to create depth because film does not pick it up—it's two-dimensional. For example, one way you can create depth is to have consecutive archways or openings seen from one room into the next room and the next.

I've had to cut a set right in half and add twenty feet to the center of it. You'll have extremes like that. Or, they might have you just make a doorway bigger. Or if they want to track, do a dolly shot down a corridor that's looking into every room, and your hallway is not wide enough, you might have to make that wider.

The set designer also has to stay in touch with the special effects art director because when you have a special effect—for example, an explosion—it usually involves the set.

Something all set designers have to adapt to is disappointment when our work ends up on the editing room floor because of time or because they just never shot it. And that's going to happen. The director could change his mind. He might come in and see a different portion of the set that he'd rather shoot—instead of, say, the stairwell, he might want to hold all the action right in the dining room or out in the foyer. So you want to make sure you've got all the set they need, but you don't want to overbuild.

Advice

You've got to have a flair for illustrative drawing and *drafting*. Your drawing technique should be good because your drawings are your living. You have to have an architectural drawing background.

An extensive knowledge of the history of architecture is enormously helpful. Knowing the different historical periods, knowing detail in architecture. A lot of set designers don't know it, they have to research it, which we all do at some point or another, but the more you know, the better you're going to be and the more work you're going to get.

A set designer is called on not only to do basic four-wall sets, but to design cars, planes, helicopters, military vehicles, futuristic vehicles. And often engineering concepts are used, for instance, in automobile design.

We design everything from crossbows to horse-drawn carriages to spaceships.

Set Decorator

The Set Decorator works closely with the production designer to achieve the visual look of the film. To do this he or she decorates with furniture, drapes, textures, carpeting, personalized memorabilia, paintings, and so on. The Set Decorator supervises the set dressing crew, consisting of a lead man and swing gang, and calls on various crafts for their expertise, namely furniture refinishers and painters, drapery and upholstery personnel, greensmen, electricians, and the like.

Marvin March

MARVIN MARCH graduated from the Yale School of Drama and began working as a carpenter on Broadway with an eye toward lighting design, but he got "sidetracked" into set decoration for the theater and, eventually, for film. After working on Francis Ford Coppola's *You're a Big Boy Now*, he flew out to Hollywood for a "thirty-day vacation." As it turned out, he started to work on *Star Trek* and "never went home again." He has concentrated on set decorating for films since 1967 and is a four-time Oscar nominee for his work on *The Sunshine Boys*, *The Turning Point*, *California Suite*, and *Annie*. Among his many other credits are *The Group*, *Summer of '42*, *Ghostbusters*, *Flashdance*, *The Golden Child*, *Peggy Sue Got Married*, *Lethal Weapon*, and *Presidio*.

WHEN THE set decorator goes to work on a set, the wall color, wallpaper, paneling, and floor treatment have already been installed by the production designer. Predicated on meetings with the director and production designer, the set decorator designs and plans what he will dress into the sets.

Props versus Set Decoration

"Props" pertain primarily to those elements used by the actors in a film—an attaché case, a fountain pen, the food he eats—and to the stage items such as bath towels for swimming, "fall" pads for stunts, and small kitchen utensils. Some items like telephones, TV sets, or pots in the kitchen will be chosen by the set decorator because they are part of the decor.

Say a man is walking in an alley and it's barren. We may "dress in" a ladder, paint buckets, and garbage cans. That is set dressing. But if the man uses that ladder and climbs up to the second-story window, that ladder is now a working prop.

Set decorators also work on exterior sets—street lamps, windows, street markets, and the like.

Preparation

The demands of the script usually determine "prep" time. The first priority is to become familiar with the requirements of the script. The second is what artistic and physical changes have been made by the production designer and director. And the third priority is to discuss the concept of design with both of them.

It's my responsibility to be sure there is sufficient time to execute the work, that there is sufficient stock available—whether it's fabric, restaurant chairs, or thirty-five desks for the news office in *Fletch*.

It is also my responsibility to keep the cameraman (director of photography) happy. I once did a twelve-foot by sixteen-foot living room with ten table lamps because the cameraman wanted to see a light source wherever he pointed the camera. This is also part of set decorating. The more involved and experienced decorators can anticipate and prepare for unannounced problems.

On one film the production designer, Dale Hennesy, and I showed the director, Woody Allen, a set prepared for filming the next morning. Woody looked, smiled, and said, "You know, I thought about this set, and I don't think my jokes can play in it. I'm going to need something else." With Woody, there's no finger pointing. He just said, "I don't think this will work." He discussed the problem with Dale, asked how long it would take to change and what he could film in the meantime. Luckily another set was ready, and he finished there until the changes were made.

You don't know the reasons—sometimes it's realistic, sometimes whimsical. Personalities. There are times when a director will come in, he's not prepared, and he'll look for a problem that's going to take two hours. Those two hours will give him the time to do his home-work.

Set Decorating Crew

By union definition, I am a white-collar worker and not allowed to carry, move, or fix any item pertaining to set dressing. I am allowed to research, search out, and make arrangements for purchase, rental, or loan of any item I need.

The lead man is my right hand, and he carries out and executes whatever I need done. He'll be responsible for bringing my choices onto the stage, getting them positioned and hung, and returning them at the appropriate time.

I like to choose my own lead man, be assured the chemistry is right, that his values are compatible and his objectives similar to mine. He, in turn, has a crew who reports to him, and I like to have input on whom he hires.

Painters are part of the construction crew but will do the necessary work for me. In the studios there is usually a refinishing department geared to the decorator's needs. I also work closely with the studio fixture department. For instance, I'll walk onto a set and say, "We need wall sconces here, and there we need an overhead fixture." If the department doesn't have the proper selection, I will buy or rent else-where for the crew to hang and hook up as required.

Drapery works in a similar way. After a discussion of corridor treatments or reupholstery, I have to be sure that there is sufficient yardage and an appropriate design. In a movie like *Ghostbusters*, when the arms of a monster spring out of an armchair, the problem becomes more complicated.

The Sunshine Boys

I've made a reputation on "character sets" filled with detail. One morning just before rehearsal, I mentioned to Herbert Ross, the di-rector, that I thought the set was pretty well complete. He answered, "Marvin, you're not halfway there yet. This man has lived here for thirty-five to forty years, and there's a lifetime of detail and clutter to see." My jaw dropped because there was so much already. My crew and I spent the next three days raiding and seizing whatever we could from our own homes, the Salvation Army, and whatever other sources we could tap. We came back on Saturday to position all our bounty. I'll never forget the moment when I walked onto the set with a handful of new things, looked around, and could not find a place to put them down. It dawned on me: "The set is dressed!"

Working with the camera, everything is bigger and fuller than life, but it comes off, people believe it. They say, "It looks just like my aunt's place," or, "I grew up in a kitchen just like that one!"

The most exciting moment is usually just before the shooting company arrives. You always work up to the last minute. Suddenly you look around and the set's done. It's the only time to see everything together and to be assured it feels right. That's a moment that belongs to me. Pride of ownership. It's fleeting because soon the shooting crew comes in, walls will be knocked down, and half the furniture is taken away as sixty or more crew members go about their business.

I'll tell you, though, I love anything that has character and detail and involves research. I didn't think I'd get a kick out of doing a fifties movie, but I loved doing *Peggy Sue Got Married*, a Francis Ford Coppola film starring Kathleen Turner. It's a flashback. She's graduating from high school in 1960. I lived this time and didn't appreciate the detail then.

I have a collection of books, my pride and joy. I also count on libraries. On a given project, we often buy additional books on specialized subjects. Walking back through history, that's moviemaking.

On the *Summer of '42*, I drove up to Fort Bragg in Mendocino with my wife and infant son to work on location. We rented a garage apartment overlooking a pine grove and saw frost in the middle of July—a charming time. We had a minimal budget. There was an interior of a cottage that Jennifer O'Neill rented for the summer. There was a harbor where the ferry boat docked, a small-town drugstore, and a few other sets.

I was young. In my ignorance and bliss, I said I would find my decorations locally. When I started to look, everything was sparse. I searched all over the place to find things. I was getting one of this and one of that, and my "finds" were starting to dictate the design of the picture rather than the other way around.

We had our collection of things in a corner of an improvised stage in a Veterans of Foreign Wars auditorium. The production manager walked in and said, "Listen, I'm going to bring the director [Robert Mulligan] over this afternoon to look at the props and decorations." I said, "You can't do that—they're all in a pile, they're not even cleaned yet."

And, of course, the director came. He was skeptical, saying, "How're you going to use this? What is that for?" Finally I said, "Look Bob, you're scheduled to rehearse tomorrow at nine o'clock; I'll get as much roughed in by then as I can. We'll see where we're at."

In the morning he and the actors trooped in. I waited until rehearsal started and then disappeared. After rehearsal I returned and asked, "Bob, do you need anything changed?" He said he needed something over there on the post, a can opener, I think, but that was it. There was never any problem after that. The point is, you "sell" a design—a whole look—individual items unto themselves are meaningless.

Many of the decorators come up through the studio ranks. Some worked as commercial or residential decorators in the real world. The more experience and training you have, the more you have to offer. There is no set course. People hire you because they gain confidence in you. I got started because a production designer, Albert Brenner, believed I could be a decorator.

Design Challenges

Decorating has many aspects. Sometimes the challenge is to fill kitchen cabinets and make them look real; sometimes to make the garage look like it belongs to your uncle, the inventor and repairman; sometimes you have to give a character a home, a life, and a personality you never find written into the script; and sometimes it's a bigger-than-life set.

In *Ghostbusters*, remember what went on in Sigourney Weaver's kitchen? She had a one-bedroom apartment, and the kitchen had to be the size of a hotel lobby to accommodate the "action." We had huge areas of space, and in our business that's not okay. The camera becomes uncomfortable and complains. What's wanted are pictures, details, and furniture.

I live in that kind of world—it's a challenge to make that room or that set look right for the camera, the director, and the audience. It's not work for the artist who likes to live and work in an attic. People have to share. And you need recognition and appreciation. You can't work by yourself. You ask, Whose job is this? Whose job is that? Well, it's everybody's job. Making a movie is everybody's job.

Property Master

The Property Master is responsible for preparing the prop breakdown and budget and for selecting, positioning, and maintaining all props. Props are items that are carried or handled by the actors, including weapons and ammunition, tools, money, toys, games, sporting equipment, food and drink, office and household supplies, and so forth. The Property Master, unlike the set decorator, physically positions the props on the set or on the actor.

Emily Ferry

EMILY FERRY grew up in the worlds of theater, art, and literature—her father a playwright, her mother a member of the archival staff at the Metropolitan Museum of Art, the family business a bookstore. She also watched movies whenever she had the chance. She recalls being so powerfully affected by the film *Women in Love* that she wanted to be a part of creating such images. As a teenager she met her first husband, a property master, and dropped out of college to work on props with him. When she decided to go out on her own, she started doing commercials, an easier arena to break into for a woman because "you gave her toys and makeup and rice casserole commercials." She got her first union break on the film *Uncle Joe Shannon*, which led to an invitation by the producers to co-master *Raging Bull*. Two years later she got a chance to work with the cinematographer of *Women in Love*, Billy Williams, when she served as property master on *On Golden Pond*. She has since worked as the property master on such films as *The Right Stuff, True Confessions, Against All Odds, Creator, Sweet Dreams, Black Widow, Little Nikita,* and *The Two Jakes*.

THE NATURE of what I do requires that I be there when the filming actually takes place. A set decorator prepares a set and then goes on to prepare the next set. So he or she is not there when the filming takes place. I have my own concept of what the film is going to look like and how the actors are going to read the lines, and I want to watch what happens. Movies have their own life. They start off as little babies. You think you know what they're going to be like when they're old men, but they become something completely different. If I wasn't on the set the whole time, I couldn't be part of the growing process.

Props

One way to describe a prop, though it's not comprehensive, is to say that it's anything, other than the actors, that moves. A bologna sandwich, a dog, automobiles, briefcases, sunglasses, and pens are typical things that move.

The walls and the floors, the structure and concept, of a set would be the production designer's. The furniture, drapes, and kitchen appliances would be done by the decorator, and then the things that moved within the room would be props. For instance, if there's a tea set and it's just going to sit there and look beautiful, then the decorator would get it. But if somebody picks up one of the cups and throws it across the room, it becomes a prop and the property master is in charge. Of course I work closely with the set decorator; it would be ridiculous for me to introduce a Georgian tea set into a modern house.

Reading for Props

I can skim a script in an hour to know what the prop situation is going to be. I read all the Agatha Christie mysteries when I was a child and got to the point where I could pick the ten sentences in a mystery that gave away the clue. Reading a script for props is like that. The problem areas leap out of the pages at you—lines like Raymond Chandler's "a tarantula on a slice of angel food."

You then have a preliminary conversation with the director, the production designer, and the producer to discuss the artistic and financial concerns. This discussion provides necessary input for the next step, which is breaking the script down into categories, such as printing, food props, props that are going to be particularly difficult (you want to start on those right away), props you can't do anything about until you talk to other department heads, and so on—briefcases full of lists of props categories.

You always have at least one person working with you—an assistant property master. I like to think of them more as partners than as assistants because they are indispensable in carrying out the logistics of acquiring and handling the props.

If it's a particularly complex or large show or is shooting in different cities at various times, you would have one or several persons in addition. You might call in extra help for a particularly ghastly day, like on *Raging Bull* when we were doing the boxing scenes with hundreds and hundreds of extras. We needed people working throughout the stadium to be able to make it all happen. One person was dealing with boxing gloves and mouthpieces; somebody else was dealing out flashbulbs to fifty still cameramen. And not only were we giving them to the "photographers on-screen," we used a great many for visual effects—on the lightboards, which were set up beside the camera to give the impression of the old B-2 flashbulbs. So the prop master, electricians, and effects people all worked that out together.

Preproduction

I like to have as much time as possible before shooting starts. Some things are perishable and can't be gotten until the last minute, but there *will* be so many last-minute changes that to add things you knew you had to get but didn't is asking for trouble.

If there is any way to get a double on something, I do. Sometimes decisions will be made to use a one of a kind of something—for instance, an antique watch. You've shown lots of watches to the actor and the director, and they pick this one watch. I always want to say, "Are you sure you want to do this?" It's an incredible pressure. Things do get broken no matter how careful everybody is. It's very scary to enter into a situation with only one of anything. If I have no choice, I'm extra cautious and I lay awake at night wondering if the prop is truck safe.

The preproduction discussions I have with the director and the production designer are the basis for choices I'll be making throughout production. Often I'll make a decision that seems to come from nowhere but actually comes from something buried in my subconscious that I didn't even remember I'd heard once six months previously in a meeting. That's one reason I like to work my own sets.

Guns and Other Weapons

I'm very careful about weapons, both keeping track of them and storing them. Guns and knives are like magnets, they attract attention. The minute you bring a gun or an animal on the set, people come out of the woodwork and, because of that, they're dangerous. You keep weapons out of sight, unloaded, and under lock. If you're going to deal with fully automatic weapons, you need a special license. During preproduction, you'll want to take care of that paperwork.

Changing Roles

In the silents, property masters started out as gag "writers" because films were completely visual. Charlie Chaplin, Buster Keaton . . . it was important that it be immediately obvious what they were doing. Those comedies were funny because of physical things—a banana peel that someone slipped on, a suitcase that kept falling over, a bicycle whose tires wouldn't turn. That was our role—taking care of those funny things as well as, often, creating the scenes around them.

As the industry changed, our role changed. We don't write gags anymore. And nowadays prop masters become involved in many legal situations. What product is cleared? Where will we not get into trouble about this or that? If I'm going to get something for use in a film, it's my responsibility to see that there isn't a backlash. If you don't clear it yourself, you at least have to alert the legal department. That was something that never existed in the years of the generic label, where you never saw a brand name, nor was it something that we addressed as property masters until recently.

Production

Once a picture is shooting, I stay with the director on the set as much as is humanly possible. I like to work intimately with the actors, make sure everything needed is there and that there are no mismatch problems (seeing to it that a glass left half-full in one shot remains half-full in the next, for example). So during production my time is at a premium. I find myself making phone calls at lunch and doing things on the way home at night because it's the only way to get them done without having to leave the set. And I feel a terrible anxiety when I do leave the set, as if something will occur in my absence that I'm not a part of or that something awful might happen. I hate to be surprised in dailies. I want to see what I contributed to the scene as opposed to "Oh, is that what they did?"

Working with Actors

A piece of film is like a layer cake—there are the things immediately up front that you see, then there are things a little behind, and some things even farther behind that. I think the audience picks up subliminally on the entire image. Things that appear to be unimportant, or off in the distance, people really are seeing, and it contributes to the cumulative effect.

The other thing to remember is how much props help the actors. I feel that an actor should be able to live in a set as though it were his own place. If he wants to open a drawer and take something out, it won't be yesterday's call sheets. Therefore the background pieces are important if for no other reason than to make the actor feel at home.

Actors who come from the theater expect to do everything themselves. If they're moving a briefcase from the closet to the bed, they take the briefcase back to the closet themselves for the next take. It shows an awareness of props, and you can usually pick the New Yorkers from the West Coasters that way, too. It's rewarding to see an actor, slowly, over a couple of days or weeks of shooting, learn that he can trust you, believe you're taking care of him, and know that you're there to make it easier for him to act—that the prop will be there for him.

When an actor comes to you to discuss "Will I have a wallet or a money clip?" or "What kind of sunglasses will I have?" that's when you have an opportunity to create a character with props—even to the extent of picking things that won't necessarily show. Obviously, if there's a point in the script where an actor uses a pen over and over again, you want to make sure that he has a pen that he loves and a whole bunch of identical backup pens. Then take it one step further and say, "If he's using a pen all the time, do you think he'd have a pad in his pocket?" or, "Would he ever take his wallet out and write something on the back of a business card?" I try to anticipate what might happen so that if six weeks into shooting the director suddenly says, "Well, why don't you pull out your wallet and pay for a soda here," you don't have to panic and think, We never picked a wallet.

Breakaway Props

If you're going to jab an actor with a gun butt, you can't use a real gun because you would break his jaw. So you make a rubber gun that looks like the real thing. Or if the script calls for an actor to get hit over the head with a chair, you've got to have a chair that will break and not hurt the actor, so you'll have a chair made of balsa wood to match the dining set. Bottles used to be made out of candy glass, but now they're made out of a resin material.

Rich Fortune Cookies and Rotted Eggrolls

Food is considered a prop, whether or not it is actually eaten by the actors. In *True Confessions*, Bob Chartoff, one of the producers, had the idea that money given under the table as payoff to a policeman from the proprietor of a Chinese restaurant should be hidden inside fortune cookies. I found a man in Chinatown who was willing to encase five-dollar bills inside fortune cookies. So I got fifty new five-dollar bills from the bank, went back, and gave them to my fortune cookie maker. He said, "Okay, come back tomorrow and I'll have the cookies ready for you." I said, "Wait a minute—when I get those cookies, how do I know that the money's in there?" And he said, "You'll just have to trust me."

We got the cookies and they looked perfect, but we ended up not shooting the scene that way. So I put them in a paper bag and locked them up in the prop box because you never know when they might decided to shoot the scene anyway. At the end of the show, I thought, I guess I'll turn the cookies in as money. But I couldn't bear to break them up because it was such a great gag—somebody should have a dinner party or a benefit with them. So I went to the accountant with my petty cash account and the cookies. She said, "These are fortune cookies." I assured her, "Yeah, but there's a lot of money inside them." She said, "How do I know the money's there?" And I said, "You'll just have to trust me." To this day I don't know what happened to those cookies or if the money's still in them.

A prop that would appear so simple in that movie turned out to be one of the headaches. Toward the end of the movie, Tom Spellacy [the detective] finds a food container with rotten eggrolls inside, and ants are crawling all over them. Earlier on in the movie, there's a line: "The last thing she ate was eggrolls," and the girl is now dead. So I bought the old-fashioned heavy Cantonese eggrolls that were popular in the forties (not the new thin-skinned Thai eggrolls that are so hip nowadays), very carefully cut them up the way they used to, diagonally, in three pieces, and stuck them in a little plastic dish—exposed— on top of my file box in the prop truck. I left them for two weeks to get really disgusting. I would check them every day. Two days before we shot, they were looking as moldy and rotten as I could hope for. But the night before they worked, a janitor came into the truck to clean up and threw them out!

Walter, The Trout

Usually the property master gets the animals, unless it's a special deal involving a particular animal and trainer. One of the animals it was my mission to procure was Walter, the trout, in *On Golden Pond*. In the script, Walter was originally a bass. During preproduction I mentioned getting a bass to the man who would be getting boats for the film, and he said, "You can't put bass into that lake." Apparently it would destroy the ecological balance because the bass would eat everything else. So I had to go back to the director, Mark Rydell, and tell him, "You know Walter, the bass? He just became Walter the something else." We talked about it and ended up picking trout.

They wanted a huge trout, so I started talking to the Fish and Game Commission, which had about six very large fish in their weirs— big enough to be Walter, who was supposed to be ten pounds. The problem with trout that big is that they immediately go to the bottom of the lake where it's darker and colder. It was summer, so the surface water was warm. And it was important to Mark that the trout look very much alive. We ended up putting men in scuba gear in the lake who would hook the fish through its mouth without hurting it, then release it at the last minute when Henry Fonda tugged on his line. To protect the fish, as soon as we thought they might be getting a little wilted, we would let them go or put them back into cold water and take them back to their weirs—which meant each fish could only do a very few takes. You can see in the movie that the fish is big and squirming and very much alive, but it takes that much setting up to pull off a "prop" like that.

Period Films

Period films are absolutely rife with pitfalls. For instance, if you're doing a fifties movie and you want an actor to do the trick men used to do when they had their T-shirt sleeves rolled up and their cigarettes tucked under the sleeves—striking the match against the matchbook with one hand—it's hard to do that with a modern matchbook. Matches now strike on the back since strike-on-the-front matches became illegal.

True Confessions was one of my most challenging films because it was a period picture that had to do with the world of the Catholic church in the 1940s. In the sixties the Catholic church went through a complete turnaround, and it was very hard to get information on what liturgical items looked like before then. I ended up getting a missal stand and a censer from a church in Chicago because we just couldn't find the right items on the West Coast.

The Dolls

In *On Golden Pond* Katharine Hepburn has a childhood doll, Elmer, which sits on the fireplace. It was a great responsibility to come up with a doll that could be *Katharine Hepburn's* doll, and it had to be a boy doll because there was a scene with Hank being jealous of the doll. There are very few boy dolls. I went to doll shows and doll auctions and did all sorts of research in doll books. We looked at hundreds of dolls, and nothing was right. By then we had arrived in New Hampshire and were getting closer and closer to shooting the scene, and I was thinking, I'm going to slit my wrists. Finally the production designer, Stephen Grimes, said, "All right, we're going to have to make this doll." So I found a modern Gepetto, a woodcarver named Michael Langton, who made ventriloquist dummies, and he made me a doll. I took it in to Kate and Mark Rydell, and Kate looked at it and said, "You know, that's not half-bad"—which from Kate was sweet praise indeed.

In *Sweet Dreams*, there is a doll that Patsy Cline brings home to her children. She never makes it home because she dies in a plane crash with the doll. We again went through hundreds of dolls, and finally the director and I found one we liked. I locked the doll in the trunk of my car, and on the road I stopped at a Goodwill store to buy some antique luggage. When I came out my car had been broken into and the doll was gone. I just stood on the street corner crying. I knew that whoever had the doll or whoever's child was enjoying the doll had no idea what that doll meant to me. I would have paid $500 to have it back. It was the only one of its kind, and I had to go in and tell the director, "You're not going to believe what happened. . . ."

Getting Credit

The main prop challenge in *Creator* was the concept of "Lucy," the deceased wife of the character Peter O'Toole plays—the cells for Lucy and the containers that Lucy was in. We went to a real cryogenics place and got actual liquid nitrogen containers. When one of the reviews of *Creator* said that the liquid nitrogen container looked like a fire extinguisher, I was quite hurt and wanted to write to let him know it was the real thing!

A more serious gripe . . . there's a Property Master's Standing Committee that has written letters to the Academy of Motion Picture Arts and Sciences asking them to consider us for the Oscars. We have received polite replies, but no action. It is incomprehensible to me that property masters are not considered along with the rest of the art department.

Sometimes a prop is worth several dialogue scenes. There is an example of this in *The Right Stuff*. In the scene at Holloman Air Force Base where the astronauts are in training, the director, Phil Kaufman, wanted to show what enormous stress these astronauts were under. Phil and I talked about the "hand reflex needle"—a device that would have horrific implications but still be believable. In this test, one of the astronauts would put his hand down on a table, this huge needle would go into it, and the hand would start to twitch uncontrollably and take on a life of its own. I found an inventor, Len Kuras, and together we came up with a design. When the needle appears in close-up, there is an audible groan and a great in-take of breath that spreads across the theater. "Oh, my God," people say. That three-second image powerfully evokes what's taken me so many words to describe to you.

Advice

There is no formal training program at the moment. There needs to be a more accessible way to get new blood. The way you learn is by working with another prop master and by living, looking, and paying attention to what's around you. You may learn everything there is about medical props if you're doing a medical show, then you never have to hook up an IV for the rest of your career. You're constantly making mistakes, picking up the pieces, saying, "I'll never do that again," and moving on.

You have to get familiar with the Yellow Pages, learn to give "good phone" and be resourceful in acquiring strange items—like the horse condoms I got for *Sweet Dreams*, which they didn't end up using—but it was on the prop list. It was going to be a gift to one of the characters at a bachelor party the night before the wedding. So not only did it have to be a horse condom, it had to be a *period* horse condom. I'll never forget the look on the accountant's face when I turned in the bill: "You spent fifty dollars on *what?*"

The reason I got into property was that I love films. I dropped out of college because I desperately wanted to be making movies. For some people, the right thing might be to go to one of the many fine film schools and get a degree in film. Sometimes people get into the business to be one thing and end up going in another direction. For someone of a different temperament, being a property master might be too obscure an area. I love props because they are a way of physically contributing to cinematic images.

There's a prop master story that's been around so long, it's probably apocryphal. It's about a property master, years ago, doing a western out in the parched desert, the middle of nowhere. The director came to him and said, "I want fresh flowers for a graveyard scene." The prop master grabbed a driver, drove to the nearest train station, waited for the *Sunset Limited*, ran into the dining car, pulled out all the roses from the bud vases on the tables, and took them back to the director. That is what we all aspire to—the ability to think on our feet and get the "impossible" accomplished.

Lead Man/Swing Gang

The Lead Man assists the set decorator in locating, acquiring, and arranging for the transportation, loading, unloading, care, and positioning of all items of set dressing. He is responsible to the set decorator for breaking down the script for set dressing items, for preparing and filing the necessary paperwork in connection with the rental and purchase of these items, and for staying within the set dressing budget. He supervises the swing gang or set dressing crew, who physically dress and strike the set, and coordinates with the construction, paint, drapery, upholstery, lighting, grip, and prop departments in the accomplishment of the various stages of set dressing.

Paul Meyerberg

PAUL MEYERBERG has been a lead man for ten years. After a varied life studying biomedical electronics and working as a production assistant, recording engineer, film distributor, and assistant director, set dressing finally proved to be, in his own words, the "path of least resistance." His many credits include *Ghostbusters*, *Flashdance*, *Fletch*, *Crossroads*, *Quicksilver*, *Two of a Kind*, and *Nuts*.

THE JOB of set dressing is to have the set ready when the company arrives to film. When the camera rolls, our job essentially ends. The set now belongs to the prop master. When they finish shooting and walk out, it becomes our set again, and we undress it and return the stuff or save it.

Gang Bosses and Dog Houses

The lead man "leads" the crew around. Originally they were called "gang bosses." I think there's still language like that in the contract. It sounds like the chain gang, which has negative connotations; that's probably why they changed it. They used to have a "dog house," which had the swing gang and the gang bosses in it.

And the decorator went and did what he had to do, and when he decided he needed his crew, he would come in and say, "You are my gang boss and you four are my men." The gang boss was really nothing more than a grunt who was half a step ahead of everybody else.

Today the position has evolved into something very different, and I know a lot of decorators might cringe at this, but it's almost an assistant decorator. A good lead will do the logistics and paperwork, make sure the truck has the right furniture, pick up the right furniture, and deliver and return it unbroken and in good condition. The lead person will have already discussed with the decorator what he wants and will be able to virtually dress the set, subject to the decorator then coming in and approving it or asking for relatively minor changes.

Just that rough dressing could take an hour, maybe four hours, so that can be a lot of time saved for a decorator. The burden of responsibility is a gray area, and it depends on the decorator. Some decorators like to do a lot beyond what I consider to be the domain of their work.

Some have bigger egos and don't want to do that, some don't have the ego but are workaholics. One decorator might walk in, pick two pieces of furniture, and let you do the rest. Another decorator might walk in and pick not only every stick of furniture, but every hand prop, book, picture, and every other morsel that goes into that set.

The first thing I want to do is list what is set dressing in the script. "He walked over to the bed," and you highlight *bed*. He looks at the picture of his mother on the wall, and you highlight *picture of mother*, so you know there are certain things that you have to have.

There is a gray area in between working props and set dressing. The actor when he lights the cigarette with the cigarette lighter is very clear cut. "He walks in, and he throws the sofa across the room"—the sofa is a working prop, but in all likelihood the set decorator is going to get the sofa.

You have a meal. They pass the dishes around. The dishes are theoretically a working prop; most set decorators will get the dishes and the silverware and all the other related things. The prop master will have the food.

Communication

If you're lucky, you're out with the production designer, the location scout, the set decorator, and the director among others, and they're discussing sets and saying what sorts of things they want to do and how they want to do it.

Then the decorator will sit down and discuss with the lead, give him or her an idea of what he wants. The more communication between the decorator and the lead, the better. You're not approaching it from the point of view of "covering," although you hear the line "I saved his ass" quite a bit. It happens that the decorator will forget or overlook something, and we will have it there. But rather from the point of view of feedback and suggestions, if the lead man arrives at the set an hour before the decorator with the furniture, he will take the initiative. The lead man won't sit around with a crew of three or four swing gang drapery, carpet, and green people, and two drivers—and do nothing.

Theoretically, I'm in charge of the swing gang. But other departments will come to the lead person in the absence of the decorator. You have a working relationship with construction, paint, gaffers, and grips.

The essence of the relationship between the decorator and the lead is to have a communication that's safe, clear, and caring. Your responsibilities tend to be different. The decorator is supposed to be more artistic, and you're supposed to be more nuts and bolts, but you work together. And without each other, you don't survive. As important as the job of set decorator is, he cannot operate without a crew.

Support the Decorator

The decorator is responsible for coming in on budget. If you can do something for $65 instead of $100, you do it for $65, and you're being supportive of the decorator.

The position of the lead person is to be supportive of the decorator. And supportive is the full range from emotion to actual physical things being there. This should work in reverse as well, the decorator trusting and supporting the lead.

Once you get beyond the prop houses, there are people who will rent. There is the furniture store, the antique store, the lamp store. There are literally thousands of people who can be a source of set dressing materials.

Buying or Renting

Buying or renting depends on what it is, how long you need it for, and what you're going to do with it. If you're going to have a five-thousand-dollar sofa in a set that you're in for three hours and that's it, you rent it because your rental is going to be a fraction of the price of buying it.

If you have a sofa that's in a fight sequence, and the guy takes his knife out and stabs another person, ripping into the back of the sofa, you know you're going to buy it. Buy it wholesale, buy the cheapest you can within the realm of what you need for the visuals, and also figure that you have to have cushions to replace the ones when you do second, third, and fourth takes, and so forth.

Acquiring Experience

You start working as a set dresser. That experience is absolutely necessary. I've seen leads and I've seen decorators who have never gone through the ranks, and it can be a difficult experience.

I did swing gang. The people who have not done it tend not to understand. The lead person who will say, "Let's try the piano on the other side of the room," has never picked up that piano. Or the lead who sends a truck out to First Street, then to 100th Street, and after that back to First Street has never ridden around in a five-ton truck being bounced all over the place and doesn't understand when the guy comes back pissed off and disgruntled.

Where I get unhappy is when a decorator says, "No, I want to do it; no, I don't want you to do that," and it becomes very "Oh, let's do the paperwork, pick up the pieces, and bring them back and pack the truck, and now what do you want me to do?" which is mundane and stifling.

The best experiences are with good, creative decorators who do their jobs, who know what to pick, and are open to creativity from other people—not only the lead, but anybody involved.

The best part is when the set decorator says, "Now we need to prop the room," meaning with hand props and little chatchkes. I'll hop into the station wagon or the crew cab, and we're on location and I visit eighteen antique stores or thrift shops or whatever they happen to be, come back with all of the stuff, put it in the set, and hear him say, "Wonderful."

Costume Designer

The Costume Designer is responsible for researching and designing the costumes and accompanying accessories (shoes, hats, stockings, jewelry, and the like) for the actors and actresses in a motion picture production. He or she works closely with the production designer in determining the appropriate period, styles, fabrics, and colors, consults with the cinematographer to determine requirements for colors and textures, and coordinates with hair and makeup to assure that they complement the costumes. As head of the wardrobe department, the Costume Designer oversees the making, fitting, acquisition, and rental of all the wardrobe items and is responsible for the work of the cutters, fitters, and key and set costumers.

Rosanna Norton

As a child, ROSANNA NORTON designed clothes for her favorite comic book character, "Katie Keen." She started working life designing ready-to-wear fashions, but when her then husband, Bill Norton, got his first directing job, *Cisco Pike*, she switched from the "rag biz" to the "movie biz." She has been designing costumes for movies ever since, and her work has appeared in such films as *Ruthless People, Nothing in Common, Innerspace, Carrie, The Stunt Man, Cisco Pike, Airplane, Airplane II,* and *Tron,* for which she received an Academy Award nomination.

I NEVER studied costume design. It's being taught in funny ways. For stage I understand it; for movies it's a different thing. I feel there are things that *can* be taught. But I think it's an artistic kind of work, and you have to have the ability. You can be trained to sketch, but in the movies we are doing nowadays the costumes need to reflect reality, especially if it's a contemporary movie.

To be able to make the actors look right and to represent that reality does not necessarily involve what we think of as costume design in the traditional sense of the sketches and the seamstresses all working up in the wardrobe department—not that classic image we have of Edith Head working furiously on the back lot of the studio. That's not to say we *don't* work furiously. We do.

You need to be a good psychologist and work well with actors. Clothing is such an intimate, personal thing. The work involves pleasing yourself, the actors, the director, the producers, and the art director—and making clothes that allow the actors to perform. If the actors don't feel happy and comfortable with their wardrobe, you're in trouble. You can't have them feeling grotesque, unless that specifically is the idea.

You have to meet and talk with the actors and the director, see what you can bring to them, what can make them look good, simple things like when the clothes are not flattering.

I try very hard to avoid having the costumes overwhelm the subject matter. And one reason actors are known as temperamental is that they are gun-shy of that. I definitely think there are certain garments that should never appear on the screen. You never want to put your leading lady in a down vest—she'll look like a baked potato.

So much of my business is compromise. I have to compromise between my idea of what would work and what the director wants and then what the actor wants.

You have a vision, if you're strong, of what the actor should be wearing, and maybe you're right—but it's *their* clothes. They're the ones who have to appear on the screen. You have to find clothing that works well in every way, and so much of that is in the mind of the actor and the director. So it's not just a matter of having an abstract idea and drawing a sketch.

Those sketches that we see from the early motion picture days are so stylized that you can't really get an impression. We're not seeing so much of that anymore—where the actress, no matter how heavy she was, would be a pencil and they'd use the ten to one ratio on the head-to-body size, which is for fashion illustration.

I never really sketch until I have a *bod!* Only if it's an extreme character—say, a clown—I'll sketch. I did this picture called *Get Crazy*, which had all these rock-and-roll acts and punks and all different kinds of styles. We didn't get the cast until very late on that show, so I sketched beforehand. And the background people, the extras, can be cast to fit your designs. But as far as the stars of the show are concerned, you pretty much have to wait until they're cast.

Design in Costuming

I work most closely with the director and the people under me, the tailors and the costumers. However, I must say that very often shows do not have costume designers, just costumers. Things have changed in the business. In the old days the movies always had a costume designer; it was just understood.

Nowadays they're not always needed because much of it is shopping. Things are just purchased. That's a good deal of my work, and I believe that is a part of design—selecting things. You make a design decision in that selection. And the costumers have their own union, are very capable designers, and make artistic choices. I am in the Costume Designers Guild, but there's also Local 705, which is the wardrobe costumers union.

It's a very nebulous area, in terms of who does the "designing." It used to be there was "the designer," and the designer did the gowns for the leading ladies and, for the most part, clothes for the leading men. And the others were done by the costumers. And the costumers, of course, got powerful and got good at it—which is as it should be—and there was also less and less need to have gowns.

I went to a meeting of my guild, and we were told, "Everyone needs to bring in a sketch of some gowns, we're going to have a show." I had to rack my brain: "What gown did I do?" I did a gown in *Carrie* that got blood all over it! You don't get to do gowns anymore. When you look at old movies, you see the actress, no matter what's going on, wearing something fancy, and it's all designed and carefully done—and it's not real. But it wasn't meant to be real.

Now, very often, you're trying to portray reality. So the job of the costumer—which is to be in charge of continuity, to see that the costumes match and do the shopping—has gained importance.

I have a staff of people working under me who are the costumers and the tailors. Those are the people I'm dealing with every day. And the director and sometimes the producer. And I'm talking to the casting people every day, asking, "Where's the actor, where's the actress? When are we going to get the cast?" You always want your actors right away, and sometimes you get them, but rarely. Usually the casting goes on longer than you want, and you have to wait before you can do most of your work.

If it's a modern show, you go shopping. You work out of some costume house usually, Western Costumes or one of the studios who has a stock. It would be crazy for me to have costumes of my own because you never know what you're going to need. Sometimes I think, Gee, I really should have some police uniforms, and then I'll never get another show with police in it. Though there are some things you'll always need, like a waiter's uniform.

We are responsible for accessories, which gets a little gray—in the area of props. Things like luggage and jewelry. I always do my own jewelry because that's part of the design.

Color is very important, and that's where you work with the production designer and the set designers. You have to be very careful with color because in film certain colors will tend to dominate. And of course, you want to flatter the complexion of the actors and actresses.

Incorporating Hair and Makeup

With period, you do the research. And styles are very strict. When you see a woman, having worn rollers all day, show up with this bouffant hairdo—very out of date—that's period, and it's funny. So period makeup and hair will look funny to our eye, and the actors are supposed to be heroic or beautiful—you don't want them to look funny.

If you look at movies made in the fifties with the uplifted bosom and the merry widows, those have nothing to do with the period that the movie was supposed to be portraying. That was a fifties look with a slight nod to the period.

But if you're trying to do something that looks really authentic, it can be a problem because no one wants to look weird. For instance, on one movie, in all the research I did, they wore really strange-looking hairdos—braids over their cheeks and ears. Nobody wanted to hide their face like that, so while I could be very authentic in costuming, the hair was a compromise that had to be made.

The Birth of a Costume

Let's trace the birth of a costume. You've got the script, the actress is cast—now I'm out trying to find the costume that she's going to wear when she first meets "the man."

I have an idea in mind, and the director says, "Well, I like this place that my wife shops at because they have a good look, and this character would wear something from there." I go there and maybe I don't find anything, and then I send the costumers out all over town.

They come back with a bunch of stuff, and I look at it. I choose the ones that I like, and they take back everything else. I take it to the director, and then we see we can't find anything we like, so we decide, Okay, I'm going to make something.

Then I'm happy! I make two or three sketches so he can have a choice, and then I show the director and the actress the sketches, and maybe they'll agree to one, with some modifications. But in the back of the director's mind, he's thinking, Boy, that little suit my wife has . . . So I'll have my "baby" in the workroom and we'll have a fitting, and the director will come in and say, "Wait a minute. No, I don't think she'd be that dressed up," and then it's back to shopping on Rodeo Drive.

No Mystique in Clothes

We don't have a mystique in costume, which causes us difficulty. In the camera department, if they say, "We need a lens," everyone takes their word for it because they really don't know what that lens is. But in costume, clothes are a common article, so people don't want to spend money. It's just clothes, it's just people and today and T-shirts, what's the difference?

But the costume is on the screen. It's got to look right. So it's tough because the movie company's often reluctant to put money into this area. Clothes are such a common thing, and everybody has tastes in clothes. It's too ordinary. It's just not allowed the mystique that other aspects of moviemaking have. People say, "My wife wears great clothes. She always looks great. She wants to get into the business. Let's make her a costume designer." And that happens. I'm not complaining because they do wash out. And if they do make it, that's fine. But it really is more than just being able to shop wisely.

Challenges

The normal, contemporary dramas—say, an *Ordinary People*— are almost more of a challenge than the full-blown period pieces because you're studying personalities and taking a very close look at people. You don't get to have flights of fantasy, but it's interesting in that life imitates art, and you're giving an intimate glimpse of people. You want to reflect that in the clothes.

Sometimes the hardest movie can be where it all takes place in one day. The audience is going to have to look at the same damn costume for the whole movie. That can be harder than coming up with twenty changes. If one of those changes is not great, you can live. But if you have to sit and watch this one costume for the entire movie, it had better be good.

I don't like to think about the clothes getting dirt on them. At lunch, one of the actresses was walking out to the park. I had put her in high heels and white linen pants, and I didn't have a double—we usually have doubles just in case. She's walking to the table, teetering along, and she's got this bowl of soup on her tray and the wind comes up and blows the soup out of the bowl and onto her chair, and I come running over to stop her from sitting down. Designing for movies—everything is big. Boy, can you see it on the screen! I've done a little television, and on television you can't see it, but on the big screen that chili on the shirt shows.

I'll tell you my worst nightmare. I'm on top of this huge haystack of clothes and there are hundreds of naked extras converging on the haystack, and I'm looking at my feet and trying to pull out pants and they're screaming out their sizes and I'm digging and trying to throw the clothes down to them.

You really live with it. You just have to be ready no matter what it takes. I know that I have a certain amount of time—say, two weeks—but I don't know how I'm going to make it all happen. It's a lot of pressure.

Advice

You've got to know garments. You have to know physiology, how to flatter the body. You have to know about garment construction, tailoring, and color. Some people don't think you need to—they just do the sketches, pick out the clothes. But I am interested in the whole process. I physically sew many things.

I think clothes are very evocative of our feelings. My idea of heaven would be to do a huge extravaganza where every single stitch is custom-made. Some really fantastic, futuristic, no-budget-limitations extravaganza—for Fellini, maybe!

Women are very much discriminated against in all aspects of the business. And it's a miracle that we're not discriminated against in this one area. It's one of the very few jobs in movies (other than acting) where women are generally "in" in the creative aspect. There are a lot of smart, ambitious women who want an outlet. So it's the one area where we do have women and have always had women. There really is no discrimination. Clothes—that's women's business!

As far as how people got into costume design for film . . . some have been costumers, some were sketch artists, some of the older ones were able to start out when the studios used to have in-house designers. And it helps to have connections!

I think a lot of my work is being able to think fast and make enough compromises to please the most people with the least injury. It's a group art. You're not designing for an ideal as you would in haute couture. And so much is in the spots, the laundry, and other stuff like that. People have this vision of someone in a room glamorously sketching. You should see me around the lot with my old sneakers on and sweat pouring off my forehead. You have to have good feet!

Key Costumer

The Key Costumer is responsible to the costume designer for the selection, acquisition, rental, and care of all wardrobe items. He or she prepares a costume breakdown and, in consultation with the costume designer and production manager, a wardrobe budget. Thereafter, the Key Costumer is charged with fitting the actors, setting up relationships with clothing stores and wardrobe houses for the required items, and keeping inventory of all clothing. He or she sees to it that all clothing is properly tailored, cleaned, or treated and that any alterations are executed. Working closely with the costume designer, the Key Costumer selects items of clothing and hires the set costumers. In the absence of a costume designer, the Key Costumer is deemed head of the wardrobe department and is responsible to the production designer and director of photography for the design and photographic acceptability of all costume items.

Jim Tyson

JIM TYSON started out at Disneyland sewing the tails on the Three Little Pigs costumes. His first film industry–related job was at the largest wardrobe house in Hollywood, Western Costume, hanging up dry cleaning. From there he graduated to "cleaning off horseshit" from boots and eventually to sizing clothes and routing stock (organizing the clothes by size and putting them away), finally establishing himself as a costumer with a flare for military shows. Since 1974 he has been a free-lance costumer, working on numerous films, including *The Right Stuff*, *Top Gun*, *Cannery Row*, *The Natural*, *Jumpin' Jack Flash*, *St. Elmo's Fire*, *Body Double*, *Fletch*, *Predator*, *Beverly Hills Cop II*, and *Rain Man*.

ONE OF the finest experiences I had was working with Laurence Olivier as his personal costumer on *The Betsy* and on *The Jazz Singer*.

I always referred to Olivier as "the Big O." There's a great basketball player called Oscar Robertson, and since I consider Olivier a great actor, it seemed an appropriate title.

I'd say, "The Big O is dressed now," over the walkie-talkie to the assistant directors, and they would shake, saying, "What's the matter with you, Tyson? His title is *Lord* Olivier." But Olivier assured me that "Lord" was one of those four-letter words and he didn't want it used around him. "Call me Larry, dear boy," he'd say.

One hot and humid night, Olivier had to wear a tuxedo and makeup on his hands to make him look many years younger. He would try to button his shirt, getting makeup all over it, and I'd have to get the makeup man in and say, "Shit, can't you powder this stuff down more, it's getting all over him." Well, makeup problems fixed, we finally got him dressed, and damn, he looked good.

After the tuxedo scene, he had to do a love scene with an actress. Changing into his pajamas for the scene, he says to me, "Jim, dear boy, you've got to find me some toilet water." I said, "What the hell is toilet water?" He said, "I'm going to sweat and start to smell during this love scene. I think you Yanks call it cologne." So I said, "Okay, Sir Laurence, I'll find something."

It was about three in the morning. We were shooting in the mansion where they had shot *The Great Gatsby*, and we could only shoot at night because it was a museum during the day. I ran around asking everyone, but nobody had any cologne. Finally a woman working as an extra had a Binaca-size sprayer of Jean Naté. I ran it back to Olivier and said, "Sir Laurence, it's a woman's cologne, Jean Naté, but it's the best I can do." He looked at it disappointedly and said, "Well, dammit, she hasn't any tits anyway. . . ."

Although he's the ultimate gentleman, he has a great sense of humor.

Every couple of weeks he used to give me fifty dollars because I worked hard for him. I was making good money on the movie and tried to refuse him. But he'd say, "Dear boy, I insist, go out and find yourself a bird." I didn't know what he was talking about, but a friend told me later, "He's giving you money to go out and have a drink with a girl. . . ."

One day on *The Betsy*, we had been working about fourteen hours, he turned to me and said, "My dear boy, it's only the third damn day on this movie and it feels like the fifth month in the desert on *Lawrence of Arabia.*" The heat on the East Coast in summer was unbearable.

Later, as we were walking back to his trailer ("the cabana," as he called it) a woman of about seventy-five darted out of the bushes with an autograph book. In a heavy East Coast accent, she said, "Oh, Mr. Olivier, Mr. Olivier, I would love to have your autograph. I saw *Wuthering Heights* a hundred times and I loved you in it." Olivier was wearing his tux and looked very dapper. Exhausted as he was, he took the time to sign her book. The woman, grateful for the autograph, said, "I do thank you, Sir . . . Lord . . . or how should I address you?" He gazed down at her and said, "You, my dear, may call me Heathcliff."

Initial Preparation and Budgeting

If a picture is facilitated with a costume designer, the costume designer will hire the key costumer. Otherwise the costumer will be hired by either the director or the production manager.

The designer hired me on the movies *The Natural, Body Double, St. Elmo's Fire,* and *Jumpin' Jack Flash.* You build a rapport with certain designers who like to work with you and vice versa.

When the costume designer has broken down the script for his or her purposes, he or she will then give it to the key costumer, who will, in turn, break it down scene by scene—interior or exterior, day or night.

The costumer will then determine how many changes the lead actor or actress has in the film and how many costumes will be required for the principal cast, bit parts, and extras in the film, enabling him to figure out the costume budget. The costume budget must be able to accommodate any unforeseen changes in the script that would require additional wardrobe.

If you are doing a movie with a lot of action, it is sometimes necessary to have many identical costumes for the lead. There are times when you might have two separate units working the same day, and you'll need identical wardrobes for the actor, the stunt double, the stand-in, the photo double, and even the squibs (bullet hits). Having the identical costumes makes it possible to photograph all of these in the same day. I had a friend who gave me good advice—he said, "Go to the production meetings, listen to what they want, but when it comes to wardrobe do it the way you think it should be done, because you are the expert."

You can be certain that if they say they are *not* going to need a double outfit, nine times out of ten they will turn around and say, "Wardrobe, where's the double costume for Mr. Hoffman? We have just rewritten this scene to include a fight and will be using a stunt double." I always make it a policy to double outfits on lead actors in any movie, unless I'm absolutely sure the situation doesn't warrant it. Because if the costume you need doesn't happen to come back from the dry cleaners' overnight service, they may not be able to shoot that day. How much does that cost the studio? A lot. And certainly more than a double outfit.

I like to have as much of the movie prepared as possible prior to shooting, even though it's always the same story from production: "We're not going to need that wardrobe until the end of the schedule." Then they change the schedule and you have to come up with that wardrobe somehow. Whether it is needed the first day or the last, I would rather be prepared and look like a hero than be unprepared and look like a fool.

The Breakdown "Bible"

We work mostly out of trailers or forty-foot trucks, depending on the number of costumes needed on the movie. The trucks and trailers are equipped with built-in racks on which the clothes are hung, in preparation for use in the movie. The costumes are arranged by the actor's name and the character being portrayed, such as "Clark Gable—Rhett Butler." They are further broken down by scenes, as in "Interior Mansion, scene 1 to 6, black frock coat with velvet buttons." After the costume has been used in a scene, it is tagged with the appropriate scene number and character's name and is stored in the designated area of the truck or trailer. Should the costume be scheduled for use in a later scene, it would be retagged, stating the additional scene number.

Immediately following shooting of a scene, a record of the costumes worn and how they were worn (buttoned or unbuttoned and so forth) is recorded in a master log book, known to us as "the Bible."

The key costumer does most of the administration. Once the costumes have been designed, he or she chooses the people to work with the actors. The key costumer does not normally work with an actor on the set but does the initial fittings for the lead actors and actresses and then turns the costumes over to the set costumer.

Our set costumers are on the set early in the morning, hanging the clothes in the actors' and actresses' dressing rooms. They are the ones who deal with the actors and actresses during the day's shooting. They key costumer is, in turn, preparing for the following day's work, fitting actors and actresses who have not yet been fitted. Once the show is set up, the key costumer usually checks in on the set first thing in the morning and again at night. The set costumer stays on the set all the time, which frees the key costumer to shop with the designer or prepare for the next day.

Maintenance is also the key costumer's responsibility. He or she sets up contracts with the dry cleaners and ensures that the costumes are cleaned and cared for.

The Set Costumer

The set costumer and key costumer must work closely together at all times. It is the set costumer's responsibility to keep the key costumer informed of any changes that may be happening on the set. For instance, a scene previously scheduled with ten policemen now requires thirty. The set costumer would immediately contact the key costumer and say, "Hey, Jim, we need thirty cops tomorrow." The key costumer would not know of this change because he is not normally on the set but is taking care of other responsibilities.

The biggest responsibility of the set costumer is wardrobe continuity. Movies are rarely shot in continuity, so a set costumer must have complete and accurate notes on every costume detail. Robert Wagner may be wearing a white dinner jacket for the interior and exterior restaurant scenes. The interior filming may be done on a restaurant-dressed stage at the studio, while the exterior shot may be done six weeks later at a different location. Every detail of Mr. Wagner's costume must be the same in both scenes, if the script denotes it.

Incorrect notes or failure to take notes at all times may cause mismatches and could result in a scene having to be reshot.

I personally make a much better key costumer than set costumer. As a set costumer I hated taking those goddamn notes! I have always seen the key costumer's role as backing up the set costumer and making certain that he or she has all the costumes needed to make the set run smoothly.

The epitome of aggravation for the key costumer is having fifteen costume changes for your lead actor and actress, three of them needing duplicates—and this just happens in the middle of the Christmas shopping rush when you are out of petty cash. (It is easier to get the firstborn child of the producer than it is to obtain enough petty cash from the studio). You cannot charge anything because the studio is late in payment of their outstanding account—or else your name is not on the "approved shopping list." It is 9:00 P.M. and the store is about to close, the clothes need massive alterations and have to be ready on the set at six the next morning. And the final straw—you, of course, wanting to be responsible, have to use your own goddamn credit card!

Studio Service

The system used by some of the major department stores to facilitate the studios is a nice convenience for the key costumer. He reports to a special service area and is issued a big "dog tag," authorizing him to shop until he drops, selecting as many clothes as he likes. After all selections are made, the costumer takes the clothes to the service area, where a memo is written, giving a forty-eight-hour grace period for the costumes to be taken out for approval. A purchase order is written for the costumes kept, and all others are returned within the forty-eight-hour grace period.

The only problem with the system is having to return $10,000 worth of clothes and having to say, "Sorry, none of them worked."

The Right Stuff

I interviewed with Phil Kaufman for the position of wardrobe supervisor on *The Right Stuff*. His main concern was the portrayal of the character Chuck Yeager, and he asked me how I saw him. I said, "He's like Gary Cooper—strong, silent type. Doesn't say a whole hell of a lot—'Yup,' 'nope.' " He said, "I agree. You're hired."

The biggest problem I had in doing the costumes for *The Right Stuff* was re-creating authentic Mercury space suits. I even went so far as to call the Smithsonian Institution, who flatly said, "No." I finally made a contact at the Houston Space Center. This contact agreed, after a little Hollywood bribery consisting of a few autographed pictures, T-shirts, ashtrays, and cigarette lighters from Tinseltown, to loan me one of Gus Grissom's original space suits.

The budget-conscious producers wanted to make one space suit and switch it around on all seven guys. I said, "Gentlemen, you've got to be kidding. If you don't have those seven guys in seven space suits, you don't have a fucking movie. Every magazine, every publicity hound, is going to want to see these guys in a group—wearing seven space suits, not one. If we're going to be realistic, we should make seven space suits or forget it. Furthermore, none of these guys are the same size." It wasn't the producers' fault. There are very few people who would understand what it takes to costume an epic movie like *The Right Stuff*.

After finally getting the go-ahead to reproduce the space suits, I said to myself, Okay, Tyson, if these suits aren't believable, they're going to laugh you right out of the theater. The suits for the astronauts in the original space program were by the B. F. Goodrich Tire Company. I contacted them and was told that everyone who had worked on the space suits twenty-three years before was either retired or dead. And since the script for *The Right Stuff* was not officially sanctioned by NASA, information was hard to get from them as well.

In researching the original space program, I stumbled upon a picture of the astronauts training in navy high-altitude pressure suits and realized that many of the components appeared to be similar to those in the space suits. Further research led me to a contact in New Jersey who had seven of the old navy pressure suits, complete with helmets. I bought them. I then asked an aeronautical engineer for advice on transforming the navy pressure suits into Mercury space suits. He said, "It will never work." Well, if you've seen the movie, you've seen the suits. One of the great shots in *The Right Stuff* has the seven astronauts walking down a corridor, gleaming like seven silver knights. I think it's probably my proudest moment.

After the release of *The Right Stuff*, people asked me why I didn't take the next step and try to become a designer. That's not where my talents lie. Although I can be creative, I'm more the administrative type. I like dealing with the production managers, being responsible for the budget, hiring the costume crew, and handling all phases of administration. The designer and the key costumer should complement each other. We need them to get the creative end going, and they need us for the administrative end.

Costuming nowadays is a young up-and-coming person's business. The producers and the directors who are coming up are in their mid-twenties, early thirties. They want a new look. They feel that the older costumers do not relate to their generation, and they don't talk the same language when it comes to clothes. So the costumers in their fifties and sixties, even with all their experience and ability, are finding it difficult to get work. Besides, how many years can you work sixteen hours a day, with a minimum amount of help? They just don't give you fifteen, twenty people to do shows anymore like in the old days. I went to New Zealand as the sole costumer. Try lugging one hundred hampers in rain and snow by yourself . . . it's damn hard work!

Advice

Forget going to college if you plan on becoming a key costumer. Your efforts would be better spent working in one of the costume houses in Hollywood. Working in a costume house will serve you in much the same manner as an apprenticeship in one of the trades. Here you learn the business from the ground up. You may have to clean the horseshit off boots, just like many key costumers before you. You learn the basics—patterns, fabric selection, dyeing, and so on. But you also learn essential things like how to organize and fit one hundred extras in period costumes, how to know when police and military uniforms are correct for the time and place in a period picture, knowing how much stock is available for costumes of the 1920s and 1930s, how to handle an actor or actress who is in a shit mood, has ten costume changes, and doesn't want to try on clothes, how to help a stylist or designer, in a subtle way, who can't decide which outfit to choose. These are a few things that might give you an edge. Although in this crazy business, don't count on it.

Once when I was interviewing for a job, I explained to the guy who didn't have a clue, "Let me tell you what it's all about. It's eight at night, where you got some twenty-nine-year-old producer, the lead actress, the director, and the production manager together hashing it out in one room. The producer and production manager are telling me, 'Don't spend any money on the actress because I'm telling you it's not in the budget.' The director's saying, 'I want something fabulous from Neiman-Marcus.' The producer's arguing with the director: 'I think it should come from Bullock's or Hollie's Harp.' The actress is saying, 'I won't wear red.' And the director's saying, 'Red would be divine.' You've got to put this all together—while you're worrying about whether you have credit at the store and if you can get there by 9:00 P.M., fit her in the morning, make the alterations, in addition to ten changes, and it has to look perfect. And that's where it lies."

Top Gun

There is nothing more satisfying than helping to establish a costume look, such as in the movie *Top Gun*, with the fighter pilot helmets looking sharp, leather jackets with the great-looking patches . . . and Tom Cruise. Guys still come into Western Costume saying, "Hey, do you have a flight suit from *Top Gun*? I want to look like Tom Cruise." Cruise was concerned about how he looked in the flight suit and said to me, "You know, these uniforms, I look short in them." I told Tom, "You're never going to be a 42 long, kid. But you've got charisma, and there's nothing like a man in uniform. You can't miss."

Tom Cruise is going to go on to do hundreds of pictures, but, coming from a military costumer, I don't think he'll ever look better.

Makeup Artist

The Makeup Artist is charged with the application of "street" and "character" makeup on the actors, actresses, and extras on a motion picture production. He or she consults closely with the director and with the actors and actresses, if available, for their input on the evolution of the characters and with the production designer, costume designer, and cinematographer for their input on colors and textures and to ensure photographic acceptability. As head of the makeup department, the Makeup Artist is responsible for preparing a makeup schedule and for supervising and/or coordinating with other members of the makeup department, including assistants, body makeup artists, special effects makeup, and hair stylists.

Ben Nye, Jr.

BEN NYE, JR., was "raised at Twentieth Century-Fox," where his father was head of the makeup department. He used to roam the back lot, which was "a magical place—castles, South Sea Islands, barns with three hundred antique cars in them." He watched his father work on Tyrone Power, Monty Woolley, Ann Sothern, and Bette Davis, among others. As a young man he embarked upon a set designing career but received a call from his father during a production boom to work as a journeyman makeup artist. His father trained him in five lunch periods, and since then Ben has established himself as a top-flight makeup man in his own right on such pictures as *Marathon Man; Sorcerer; Heaven's Gate; Blood Brothers; Cutter's Way; Sgt. Pepper's Lonely Hearts Club Band; Chilly Scenes of Winter; The Muppet Movie; Desert Bloom; Terms of Endearment; The Witches of Eastwick; Spaceballs; Planes, Trains & Automobiles;* and *Big Country.*

I SEE the actors first thing in the morning before anyone else does. It's an intimate relationship.

There are actors who are so thorough in their preparation, who are so into the character they're creating, they're that way throughout shooting. And there are actors who rely completely on my expertise and input to co-create the character.

I think my job is to support them all. There is a certain vulnerability there, but I don't know if that vulnerability is as great or as mysterious as people would like to think. Most of these people really have it pretty much together when they come into the makeup chair in the morning.

Some actors want to add certain things through superstition or habit. And it's not my business to override that. It is my business to make sure that it fits into the character, to see that it's technically done in a subtle way, and to let them express themselves. I'm not a dictator. It's *their* face. I do have to be in control, but I believe I'm still in control if I'm collaborating.

The most thorough preparation by an actor that I've seen was Dustin Hoffman's daily process on *Marathon Man*. During the filming of the torture sequence, Dustin would lie in a tub of ice and water each morning until his body trembled and appeared white—symptoms of a person in shock, which was exactly what his character was going through. In the concluding scene, after Dustin's character had been tortured, escaped, eluded Laurence Olivier's henchmen, and was finally confronting the Olivier character, to give the appearance of complete exhaustion, Dustin would alternate chinning himself on a bar and sitting in a sauna, both of which he assembled on stage. All of this physical preparation complemented Fern Buchner's makeup perfectly.

One place where there can be trouble is when actors want to take themselves out of character to make their appearance more in line with what they want the public to see. I think they have their identities a little mixed up there. You have to be very subtle in those situations. Sometimes you win and sometimes you don't. You get an actor with a lot of power and it's just tough shit. And they don't really care whether the movie would suffer because their character is incomplete or not. They are more interested in looking like who they think they are as a celebrity.

Tools of the Trade

You have a box of tools that are your old friends. Brushes, curling irons for hair, special little brushes for eyebrows, and techniques you have developed over time. Then you have other boxes of supplies for doing fashion makeup, old-age makeup, appliances, hair work. And another case that just has prepared hair or mustaches that are dressed or undressed. These are what you work with in applying both "street" or normal, everyday makeup and "character" makeup, which is more specialized, to convey aging, weather, physical exertion, racial origin, robot or humanoid creations, and so on.

I'm usually hired after the production designer and the costume designer and I work with a hair stylist who will have all the complementary techniques.

There's usually some indication that the screenwriter gives in the character description. That will clue me in to what kind of makeup is needed. Along with that, I'll get input from key people—that is, the director, producer, costume designer, and cinematographer, as well as the actors and actresses.

In *Marathon Man*, Roy Scheider starts out as this slick, undercover CIA double agent, a mercenary guy who's put through a lot of torment by the Olivier character and is eventually stabbed to death by him. You map out the day-by-day evolution of the character. The makeup evolves with the character and what happens to him, how he interacts with other characters, what social-economic background he comes from, what magazines he reads, what he eats, and so forth.

I'll have one assistant throughout the picture, and then on days when we have crowds, doubles, I'll take on extra help and use body makeup artists if required. Body makeup artists, incidentally, by union dictum, must be of the same sex as the person(s) to whom they are applying makeup.

When I did *Heaven's Gate* there were mornings where I had twelve makeup artists assisting me. We were staying in Coeur d'Alene, Idaho, during the Casper, Wyoming, sequences. We'd get up about two in the morning, drive for forty-five minutes to a high school gymnasium in Wallace, Idaho. Several streets had been turned into Casper, Wyoming, circa 1850.

We were making up 1,200 people, regular cast and extras. After preparing for fifteen minutes, the extras would start filing through. There were about five different classes, each with their own appearance created with makeup and wardrobe: the lowest class of immigrant just arriving on the top of passenger cars covered with soot; immigrants recently arrived and trying to make a start for themselves; mercenaries a slight step up; landowners; and the nouveau riche. I had spent many evenings with Mr. Cimino looking at photos from the period and discussing how I would convey the look of the people of that period through makeup.

The longest I've ever been on a movie was a year on William Friedkin's *Sorcerer*, which was based on the original *Wages of Fear*. We went to Paris; Jerusalem; Elizabeth, New Jersey; New York; Santo Domingo, R. D.; Farmington, New Mexico; and Tustapec, Mexico. There was a very large cast, and I was working virtually alone. Mr. Friedkin had assembled an international cast of unusual and interesting faces, which was a big help to me. To be able to get the work done each day, I designed the makeup to require a minimum of application time. Creating the human physical damage inflicted by oil well explosions and terrorist shootings consumed most of my time. My greatest challenge on this project was maintaining continuity of the deterioration of Roy Scheider's character as the company moved around the world.

On *The Witches of Eastwick*, I met with Jack Nicholson, who as a rule doesn't like to wear makeup. He finds makeup acceptable when it really has something to do with the character visually. Jack's makeup evolved as it went along. I think the only thing we really talked about in the first meeting was that he would have a ponytail, and that we might do something else with his hair to make him look devilish, twisted into horns or something. Nothing was terribly defined.

It evolved daily into Phantom of the Opera proportions. The director, George Miller, continued to ask for more . . . painting Jack white with blood in his eyes and under his eyes all these shadows—purples, blues, and greens. Every imaginable color was on his face, his hair all teased up, and sweaty and slimy, and frothing at the mouth, painting his tongue black. This evolved from no makeup at all.

We worked backward on the chicken feathers scene where the women put a hex on him near the end of the picture. We knew there were going to be certain things that happened to Jack—being dragged along the ground, having the feathers from the pillows get plastered all over him, having his hand go in the ice cream, vomiting in church. Before we did any of those things, we had to actually run them through our mind's eye and figure out what they would look like as a composite. We ended up gluing little feathers for days and days. And of course we never shot in sequence.

And we knew that the women all had to have this transition from before and after the Devil (Jack Nicholson's character) had his influence on them. The criteria was to be very subtle in the beginning. Susan Sarandon's visual evolution was the most dramatic. The design involved taking her from "plain Jane" to megaglamour with a blueprint of fine touches, including foundation color, glamour highlights, shadows, eye makeup, lip color, and Bill Fletcher's exquisite wigs. And you put these ingredients with changes in costume, and what the audience sees is magic. The other two women's characters, Cher and Michelle Pfeiffer, evolved through the same process.

Making Choices

Satisfaction for me resides in when I pull something off, when something works. When you stretch yourself a bit and you see your work on the screen and you feel, God, it works.

On any number of films, I could have made a choice to devote myself to a star. I could have only done Jack Nicholson in *Witches*. I'm starting my fourth picture with John Candy, and after the first one I could have done only John. But if I create a position where I do only one makeup for months, I get stale. I'm not a motor-home potato. I don't hang around. I prefer to design the makeups, do a bunch of people, get myself involved.

My frustrations have to do with budget and time limitations. And directors who don't have much artistic insight into the characters' appearance. I've had some directors, when I have suggested little things that might add a touch visually, a little texture to a scene, say, "Ah, no, forget it."

My goal is to work with directors who have made films that I admire and who have a point of view socially *that enlightens us about ourselves*. In terms of my choices, I'd rather work on a story that is about Man as opposed to some violent, technological, mechanical thing where I could maybe win an Academy Award. A *Terms of Endearment* as opposed to an *Alien*.

Advice

My suggestion would be, first, to take a beginning class on makeup in college. There are a number of good books on makeup. Try to get involved in some theater. Look at a movie and say, "How was that done?"

There's an all-day test to get into the union, mostly practical, and a small written examination, which is important. There are so many facets to being a makeup artist—old age, hair, dressing beards, how to put a beard on, how to put a bald cap on, how to do beauty makeup, how to use lifts, how to put on appliances, how to do special effects gunshots, bruises, cuts. You are tested by a select group of makeup artists.

I would like to see the craft maintained at a very high level. That is not happening. It's getting diluted. There are so many increments of the craft that unless you spend a good deal of time practicing them all, you can't be a good all-around makeup artist.

I had the benefit of apprenticing with skilled, trained artists and being able to call upon my father. And, in my early days, working on people like Danny Kaye and Red Skelton, who came from vaudeville and knew how to apply their own makeup for characters they had worked up over the years, forced me to come up to their standards in terms of the quality of my work.

I think the people we have coming in today are talented, they're fine people. There's just nobody to teach them. The makeup artists who have left the business for any number of reasons have taken with them so much knowledge. The system doesn't exist to pass it down anymore. We need an apprenticeship program. Who's going to finance it? The studios used to. The bottom-line question is: In ten years, if makeup artists aren't taught to be complete makeup artists, what do the producers think they're going to get? They will expect what they envision to be executed. Who's going to do it?

I think it's a "you scratch my back, I'll scratch your back" process. Do they want highly talented people in a very sophisticated business? And we all know that the profits are there to support a training program, even though the studios say they're hurting and they want to give us less. All they're doing is killing the talent pool just to increase their profits a tiny bit.

Hair Stylist

The Hair Stylist styles and, if required, cuts, colors, and washes the hair and wigs of all actors and actresses in a motion picture production. His or her responsibilities include researching the appropriate period and styles, providing the hair dressing supplies, selecting and dressing the wigs, toupees, switches, and falls, styling and thereafter touching up, combing, spraying, and generally maintaining the hairstyles between takes. The Hair Stylist works closely with his or her assistant(s) and the makeup artist and consults with the production designer, costume designer, and cinematographer to determine their requirements with regard to hair.

Lynda Gurasich

Upon graduating from beauty school, LYNDA GURASICH filled out an application with the hair stylists union. Two years later she got a call from Warner Brothers to stand by as an "auxiliary," allowing her to work once all other union stylists were busy. It took another three years before she "had enough days" to qualify her for the rigorous two-day union entrance examination. Since passing the test and being admitted as a "lowly group three" over twenty years ago, she has become a respected and much-sought-after motion picture hair stylist working on such films as *What's Up, Doc?*, *All the President's Men*, *The Best Little Whorehouse in Texas*, *Silverado*, *Poltergeist*, *Coming Home*, *The Witches of Eastwick*, *Dick Tracy*, and *The Autobiography of Miss Jane Pittman*, for which she won an Emmy.

I CARRY an assortment of combs and brushes, a hair dryer, and mousse. These days it is mousse. It used to be something else. It changes with the times. Always hairspray and always curling irons, and if I have a show, my own show where I know I'm going to be iron curling, I take the old-fashioned stove and all of the different irons.

The stove is a little metal box with a hole in it, and you have different-size irons and you plug the box in and then you heat your iron—it allows you to control the heat. If it is an electric iron, it gets to a certain temperature whether you like it or not; and some hair is too fragile for that temperature, other hair is so heavy that it isn't enough heat.

I do take along electric rollers as well, although the last two shows I haven't because electric rollers are "out" now supposedly. What's "in" now is iron curling and a lot of scrunching and moussing.

I always carry cans of brown and black hairspray just in case they rush in and say, "We need to double the actor, and we're going to use George the driver," and we need to make George look like the actor. So you get your colored hairspray and try and match him up colorwise and then shape the hair around his head somehow, without cutting it, to resemble the actor's head.

I always have shampoo if it is my show, and most trailers now have shampoo bowls, and I do occasionally wash hair.

Of Wigs and Hair

I own an assortment of wigs left over from other shows that I use if there are extras and it's a period thing. But if a principal is going to wear a wig in a film, the wig is made for her ahead of time and you work with that.

Some actresses consistently use wigs—like Dolly Parton, whom I worked with on *The Best Little Whorehouse in Texas*. There was a lot of iron curling—all on wigs, none of it is ever done on Dolly's real hair. Cher prefers wearing wigs for films so she doesn't have to worry about her own hair. She can go in and have the wig fitted. It is set later so she can go on home. She feels comfortable working that way. Other people hate wearing wigs and would do anything not to have to.

The Job

Before I start a show, I go to the beauty supply house and buy what I know I'm going to need for the film and then bill the company for those supplies. If it is going to be way out of the question or there is something the actress wants, you'll want to apprise the company of it. They don't want any surprises.

When I'm first called up, I ask to see the script. The older I get, the more I want to see what I'm going to be doing. I've turned down pictures because I thought they were tasteless.

Then the difficult part—going in to talk about money. They all want to pay you scale. So you have to negotiate for over scale and tell them what you made on the last picture, and naturally if a star has requested you, you have a little more leverage. If you don't have that leverage, you know that if you turn it down or don't do it, there is always somebody else waiting to do it.

You hate to be taken advantage of. Some people are wonderful negotiators and can negotiate with a smile, keep it on a friendly basis. And others are a little cutthroat, and then you resent having to work for them even if you do come to terms. You just have to be tough. And then there are favorites—actor, actresses, producers, directors you're fond of—whom you want to work with, so maybe you do it for a few dollars less.

Once I accept a job, I make notes on the hair from my reading of the script. In the script of *The Witches of Eastwick*, for instance, it is mentioned that Susan's character, Jane, is transformed after she sleeps with the Devil and that she just blossoms. Her hair was all of a sudden prettier somehow. Now it didn't say anything about a color change; that came later with discussions. It was my idea and George Miller's to brighten and redden her hair. But at the time I read the script, I just made a note that there was going to be some sort of a hair change. Often these decisions are changed back and forth fifty times before you actually shoot it.

You just have to get a ball park. You have to make a note of when it is raining in the script or how much night work there is. And if you are doing a picture in Hawaii, you know that nobody's hair is going to stay curly because it is going to rain all the time.

In terms of when I have to be on the set, there is a ruling that we have an eighteen-minute setup time. In other words, if the actress's call is at seven o'clock, we come in at 6:42. It's enough time to plug things in and let them heat up and set everything out.

The setup in a trailer—to use *The Witches of Eastwick* as an example—was six stations for two makeup men and three hair stylists. Usually the makeup trailer ends up being the place where everyone loves to be because it is very friendly and that's where the music is and that's where everybody sits and gossips.

Hairstyling for films is using the quickest procedures. There is not enough time to wash, wet set, and put someone under the dryer, hence the irons, hot rollers, and hair dryers. There is not a lot of permanent hair dyeing or bleaching on the set, but temporary coloring is quite common. Rinses and color sprays are used quite often to fit the needs of the day.

Getting Jobs

I am actually hired by the production manager, who usually makes the ultimate call and hires me. But I get the jobs either through the actor or actress who requests me or through a producer or director. And if nobody has a preference, a production manager may remember that I did a good job and suggest me.

When I am not working, my name is on a list with the union and often they will call with a job offer.

Personality

The most important thing with makeup and hair is personality. You have to make the actor feel at ease and happy in the morning. I try to see that someone brings coffee or tea. You have to feel them out and be sensitive enough to know whether they like to talk in the morning or don't and would rather study. You want to start their day off well. You have to become immediate friends. That is just part of the job.

I usually see the principal actors and actresses before shooting starts. The film I am doing now is Lawrence Kasdan's *Accidental Tourist*. He tested several women for the lead role, and I met the women who tested when I did their hair for the test. And when Mr. Kasdan made his choice for the lead actress, he then had a meeting with us both to discuss hair.

It doesn't always happen that way. A lot of directors can't be bothered, so what I usually do is ask for the actress's phone number. Very often they ask for mine before that because they are very interested in their hair. It just behooves me to make contact ahead of time so that I'm not standing there with egg on my face the first day of shooting because they want something exotic that I hadn't planned on.

Controlling Hair

Often the actress will think she is doing me a favor or herself a favor and she'll go home and put conditioner on her hair and the next day her hair is soft and lifeless and you can't do anything with it. You can't make it match the way it was the day before, and it is just miserable. So a few years ago, three other motion picture hair stylists and I went into business. We made our own shampoo and conditioner and hairspray. We thought maybe if we had our own products, we could give them out to our actresses at the beginning of the show and say, "Just use this."

For research on period pictures, I have several books at home that I have collected over the years on hairstyles, period hairstyles. And the Time/Life series of books "This Fabulous Century" documenting life from the 1800s to the present is enormously helpful in looking at real people as opposed to fashion models.

I did a period picture in 1978 back when Afros were really in. The picture took place a little before the turn of the century. And, of course, in those days there weren't Afros. We shot it in the South, with hundreds of extras, and every extra had an Afro. And there was one hair dresser, and what do you do with a situation like that?

Nobody would go for any permanent straightening because they were a flash in the pan, they were a two-day player or an extra. So I got black stocking caps and just put them on everybody because they were in the distance so you couldn't tell. At least it got the Afros down. You have to try to anticipate those kinds of things ahead of time and realize you're going to have to take five hundred black stocking caps down to Mississippi.

Black hair requires different treatment from Caucasian hair. I did a lot of hot combing, which is using that same little heater, sticking a metal comb in there to heat up, applying lots of oil to the hair, then straightening it with this hot comb. I couldn't do permanent straightening because it is time-consuming and tricky. Even the principals wouldn't want to do permanent straightening because black hair is very fragile and tends to break off easily.

To age black hair you usually just add crepe wool, which is a crimped wool that you use as a stuffer for rats and things like that. And you can take a few of those and just put them in black hair.

For Caucasian hair you generally use "hair white," which is not a very good product, but it is about the best we have. It looks like they went *whoosh* with talcum powder if it's badly done. It is a liquid that you try to brush in. In the old days the film wasn't as fast, so you could see every little tiny hair in detail. Nowadays film is so much faster that all of it is blurred out, so any fine, intricate work that you do won't be picked up.

There is no Academy Award for hair, though there is for makeup. I think hair should receive a special award, both in film and in television. I don't feel that you have to have a category every year and submit names whether they are deserving or not. Some years there are no specifically wonderful hairstyles, so an award shouldn't be given, but then other years there are—and, in those years, hair should be recognized.

Advice

Hair stylists are still mostly women because there used to be a law that only women could be hair stylists and only men could be makeup artists. But about ten years ago that was judged unconstitutional. It's changing very slowly—there are more men getting into the hair area. But it is still predominantly women.

I have let people come in and watch me on a show or on commercials where there isn't that crucial a rapport with the actors. You have to clear it with a lot of people first. They have to sit quietly and save their questions for later.

As far as breaking into the motion picture hair business, there was one man who wanted to get in as a hair stylist, and he did it the most clever way. First of all, you have to be a licensed hair stylist in order to get into the film business. He was, and he would read the trades. The trades would publish who was working on location where. This was local locations; it would say the television show *Moonlighting* was working on a local location in downtown Los Angeles. So he would call the studio and find out the address where they were shooting and find out the name of the hair stylist, whether he knew them or not, and drive to downtown Los Angeles and walk up to the hair stylist and say, "Hi, my name is so-and-so, and I know your work, and would it be all right if I just observed you?" Well, that appeals to your ego, of course. And so you say, "All right." Then he'd ask all the right questions and then ask if he could come and watch you one day next week, and you say, "Of course." And he did this every day with different hair stylists and different companies. He was very polite and unobtrusive. At the end of about a month, there must have been about twenty hair stylists who knew his name. And the next time they worked and had to hire another hair stylist, if there was nobody left on the union list, they would call this guy. And he must have gotten his days in within a year. You have to get 120 days within an eighteen-month period in order to get into the union.

Working with the Crew

On the set, the second assistant director is my liaison with the rest of the goings-on. And he runs into the trailer every five minutes saying, "How much longer?" Or, "Can I get anyone coffee?" Or he'll send a production assistant in to ask that. Or he'll say, "The camera is getting close."

On a period picture, the production designer or costume designer feels responsible for the whole look of the picture. And some of them feel that includes hair. In *The Best Little Whorehouse in Texas*, the costume designer and the production designer had these ideas about color and ornaments in the hair. Theodora Van Runkle, the costume designer, would show me her sketches and say, "I feel that all of the hair on the whores should be up for this particular scene." Or, "I had envisioned Dolly's hair to be all over on one side." If it really doesn't go against my particular thing I had in mind, I'm more than happy to say, "Fine, I'll do it on the side." I don't think egos should get too involved. They always are, but you have to try and be reasonable.

But I have the best time with the actresses. In *The Witches of Eastwick*, Susan Sarandon, Michelle Pfeiffer, and Cher were great fun to be with. We had the best time. We would all read *People* magazine aloud in the makeup trailer and then just hoot over the stories.

I do get very attached to the films and the people I work with. Working in films is like the 4-H Club. You get this little pig and you nurture it and feed it and train it and clean it and wash it, and then you take it to the county fair and you win the blue ribbon and it goes to the butcher shop. So each picture is my little pig. . . .

7
THE ARTISTS

Before the cameras start to roll, artists are employed to conceptualize the images to be captured on film. The illusion of realistic backgrounds and landscapes must be created. Camera angles, selected tones and shades of color, framing and sequence of images—all these are premeditated.

The imagination of the men in this chapter transforms the written word into pictures and canvases.

Production Illustrator

The Production Illustrator provides sketches, paintings, and storyboards for any of the principal individuals or departments that may require them. He or she must be skilled in "thumbnailing" (rough conceptual sketching) as well as detailed rendering and painting and should be familiar with shot description, continuity and cutting, composition, camera angle perspectives, and special effects. The Production Illustrator's skills are most frequently called upon by the director in preplanning shooting angles, camera movement, intercutting and editing possibilities, continuity requirements, and the staging of action sequences and by the production designer in visualizing sets, locations, and period. His or her storyboarding abilities may also be used by the producer to present or sell a script or concept, by the production manager to plan the shooting schedule, by the cinematographer in creating a shooting breakdown, or by special and visual effects to plan the physical and optical effects.

Ed Verreaux

ED VERREAUX graduated from the San Francisco Art Institute and started drawing underground comics in the Bay Area in the early 1970s. He has charted a varied course in Los Angeles from driving a school bus to animating commercials and feature films to conceptual illustration and design. His many credits include *Empire of the Sun, The Blues Brothers, Star Trek—The Motion Picture, The Color Purple, Mad Max Beyond Thunderdome, Indiana Jones and the Temple of Doom, Poltergeist, E.T., Raiders of the Lost Ark,* and *Scrooged.*

ONE OF the key functions a production illustrator provides is storyboarding. Storyboards are drawings or photographs that illustrate the progression of shots in a film sequence. The illustrator's responsibility is to lay out a sequence of well-designed shots that serve the needs and ideas of the screenplay and support the mood, style, and intention of the director—economical storytelling with strong continuity.

Splash

As an example of how a production illustrator can help a producer, I worked with Ron Howard and Brian Grazer on *Splash* when they were developing it. At the time, they didn't really know very much about special effects, and they hired me and Mitch Susskind, who was the visual effects coordinator on *E.T.*

I worked on visuals for about a month, and Mitch worked on different approaches to the effects. We were exploring whether it would be feasible to shoot underwater and, if so, out in the ocean, in the Bahamas, in Lake Michigan, in a tank, in a pool, or if it would be most feasible to have people on wires in front of a blue screen. I was developing an undersea world and storyboarding a couple of sequences. These visualizations of specific scenes and sequences helped to sell the project to the powers-that-be.

There's one sequence I storyboarded that they did actually use, where the Tom Hanks character is down at the beach and he falls in the water and his boat's going around and around, and he's drowning. And all of a sudden the mermaid pulls him out and he's on the beach and the boat's still going around in a circle and he doesn't know how he got there and he looks out to sea and then he looks back, but he doesn't see the tail of the mermaid flip on the surface before going down.

Working with Spielberg

As an example of how a director might use production illustration, Steven Spielberg, when he sits down with you, usually does little thumbnails of his own, which you then flesh out. You're really a translator, you fill it all in.

One of the reasons I get along with him so well is that I can pick up what he's saying right away and I've got a good memory, so I don't lose sight of the things he throws at me over the course of the week or two that it may take to complete the two hundred drawings. I keep all the little bits that he wants in my head and make notes as we go along. He is very specific. He knows what he wants almost immediately. In essence, you're being a wrist and a hand for him so that he can then take the drawings and show them to the special effects people, the optical people, the stunt people, and say: "This is what I want. In this shot the car is coming at you, in this the camera pans with the car, and we see it as it hits the plane, it blows up." Or: "Indiana Jones slides down the mine shaft, and then you cut to a close-up." In short, it's a visual comic book of the parts of the script that he chooses to storyboard.

Storyboarding is useful for special effects shots, explosions, planes flying through hangars, things like that; also opticals, any time you do special effects that involve blue screen, wire shots, front projection, rear projection, any time actors have to stay on a certain side of the stage or a certain side of the camera because you're going to be matting in something on the other side. It's a communication device.

They're very important, at times, for communicating with the editor. When he's cutting, it's helpful if he can flip through a story-board book and realize, "Oh, in this scene the director wanted this." Or when you get a young director, somebody who doesn't have much experience, the producer may want you to help him get his thoughts in order.

Working with the art director or the production designer, an illustrator can often come up with ideas of his own, one picture being worth a thousand words.

Or with the set designer . . . I've been working on *Scrooged.* And we've just got another set designer on the show who's going to actually be doing the set, but I've already designed a lot of details. It's Santa's workshop at the North Pole. I've already come up with bits, so I'll say, "Let's see if we can incorporate this in here, maybe these will just be little plant-on bits."

Imagination is essential. I think that for anybody to be really good at production illustrating, you've got to be imaginative.

You should be a fair hand at drawing and painting, but you don't have to be a great renderer because there isn't time. This work is not going into the Louvre. You may only have an hour or two to come up with something because there's a production meeting this afternoon and the production designer just had a great idea.

Raiders of the Lost Ark

Talking about beautifully rendered versus expeditiously rendered—*Raiders* came about because I got a call from this guy I had worked with on *Star Trek,* and he said, "Lucasfilm, Inc., is getting ready to do this thing called *Raiders of the Lost Ark.* It's a Steven Spielberg film, and the guy you should talk to is Frank Marshall. Here's the phone number. I was just over there, but I don't think I'm going to get the job."

I called them up and got an interview with Frank Marshall. And I didn't get the job—not right away. Somebody else did. He didn't work out, and they called me back about a month later and said, "We'd like you to come in and meet Steven."

Thumbnails

Steven gave me three little thumbnail sketches from a chase scene to do. One was Indiana Jones being knocked through the window of the truck, one was him hanging on to the front bumper looking over his shoulder, and one was him riding a horse along by the truck and then jumping off the horse and all these guys were shooting at him. So I went home—this was a Friday—and I really busted my ass, stayed up all weekend doing this thing, and came back in Monday and gave it to Steven, and he said, "You've got the job."

Steven liked my work, and I'm kind of surprised because I go back and look at some of it, and from a technical drawing standpoint, it's pretty weak.

When the film came out, they did a huge media blitz. There was an article in *Time* and in *Newsweek*, and there was a three-paneled insert—one of Steven's, a little rough sketch, and then one of my drawings next to it of Harrison shooting a gun at the camera in the bar fight, and then a cut piece of film from that scene.

This friend of mine told me that one of the best older illustrators who is a legend in his own time had seen my illustration in *Time*. Guy didn't know me from Adam and he said, "Look at the kind of guys they're letting in the union now." I actually went and talked to this other illustrator, and he said, "Maybe I was a bit rough on you," and I said, "Well, not really because I have to admit, I've got a lot to learn in terms of drawing ability."

But there's a level at which you become too precious, and time is of the essence. It's a strange balance. It's important to be fast, but you've also got to be legible and clear, and you've got to be able to give it some life and some beauty and some vision, so that whoever's going to look at it will say, "Yeah, wow, wouldn't it be great if we could do that." You want to try to make your drawings inspirational.

There's a level of precision that you want with special effects. If you want to show a series of cars doing gags and roll-overs, you want to be as precise as you can so that the effects guys and stunt coordinators can look at it and say, "Well, nah, we can't do this."

The vaguer you are, the easier it is to cause miscommunication.

The Goal

If we do our jobs right, we can help the company prepare, we can help the art department prepare, we can help the director prepare, and save a lot of money at the other end because the production designer and the director are in sync with each other and there aren't as many surprises.

E.T.

Originally, *E.T.* was conceived as a horror film.

What happened was, the summer of 1981 I was working in town doing a bunch of concept sketches for John and Bo Derek for *Tarzan, The Ape Man* when I got a call from Spielberg's office: "We need to have some storyboards done really quickly because we're trying to budget this next film that Steven's doing. The guy who's going to do the special effects can't budget without knowing the exact shots." So I went over to this guy's shop and spent three weeks storyboarding from the script.

The original story was about this farm or ranch family that lives out in the middle of Wyoming, and they're beset by five aliens. They were these semibirdlike characters who start off real small and get bigger and bigger till finally there's one who's six feet tall who hypnotizes cattle and guts them. It was a weird and scary thing.

I did the storyboards and sent them off and didn't hear from Steven for a couple of months. Then in the autumn I got a call from Kathleen Kennedy, Steven Spielberg's producer, who said, "We're over at MGM and Steven's totally revamped the whole idea. Could you come over and work with us on this project?"

So I went over, and Steven was talking to Carlo Rambaldi, the designer of E.T. And Steven introduced me to Carlo. There were all these books of photographs of faces—old people, children, infants—and they explained to me roughly the concept of the story. I worked with Carlo for about two months. After each week of drawing, we'd go back and see Steven and pin everything up on the wall. The process was in the vein of, "Well, I like the eyes, but I don't like the mouth." Whenever you're trying to do something that's never been done before, the first thing you do is strip away everything. At one point I was racking my brains thinking, God, this looks like stuff I've seen before. How can I break out of this? And I found myself thinking about this comic book I'd seen as a kid. It was about alien invaders, and I remembered one frame where there were weird heart-shaped spaceships that looked like big faces floating down from Mars.

It seemed such a contradiction because they were very happy, "have a nice day"–type faces, and yet they were supposed to be aliens invading earth. And that's possibly where E.T.'s head shape came from. In the final analysis, the concept for the physical appearance of E.T. came from us all. It was an evolutionary process—Steven, Carlo, me, and George Lucas and Kathy Kennedy, Mrs. Rambaldi . . . whoever was in the room had their ideas.

Carlo began to sculpt, and we had three basic head shapes. They were all, more or less, that E.T. shape, but they had different forms. I've got hundreds of those sketches in my portfolio.

It evolved over about six months. At one point Steven and I sat down and made a list of all the motions that we thought E.T. should have. And I did a series of animation model sheets of the different poses, delineating what he was supposed to be able to do because he was, after all, a machine. And you have to define what the machine does before you build it.

Steven had homed in on this infant–old man image—and the voice . . . I remember at one point Steven saying, "What do you think E.T. ought to sound like?" and I suggested, "Oh, you know, kind of like Mickey Mouse, a high voice." And Steven said, "No, I think he ought to have a deep voice," and he actually said, "Elliott," in that throaty E.T. voice. And I thought, Boy, that's kind of strange. . . .

That's an example of Steven's style. It seems so effortless the way he comes up with things that you think, Oh, hell, I could do that. But the point is, *he* is the one who *does* do it. And when it's done, it seems so simple, so obvious, and nobody else has been able to do it.

Mad Max Beyond Thunderdome

Mad Max Beyond Thunderdome has got to be the most memorable experience because I was in Australia for a year working with an Australian crew. They're very open. Not that Australians are more open than Americans necessarily, but in some ways their film industry is. It's more "Hey, everybody pitch in, let's make the movie."

Here in the United States, because of the unions, there's a compartmentalization, which is there to protect people's jobs but in some ways makes the process stifling. As an artist I'm interested in creating and being a part of teams that create interesting and amazing visuals, things that inspire people and move people. You want to be able to get in there and do it, and when you're in a very organized and compartmentalized system, it's much more difficult than when you're in an open system.

They have this saying in Australia: "No worries, mate, she'll be right." In fact, George Miller, the director, even warned me about that the first week I was down there. He said, "You have to watch out because we tend to procrastinate—there's a real mañana syndrome."

We didn't have a script for the end of the movie, we had a rough outline, so every night I would get him in my room with the writer and two directors, and I would say, "Okay now, we've got to figure out what happens next in the story. What happens when Ironbar-Bassie jumps off the train? What's going to happen? Come on, you guys!"

And we had these wonderful conversations—all the doors open because of the heat. And the sun is setting and it's just the most harsh, most beautiful place in the world. We'd be looking out and somebody would start telling a story about when they were in France in 1942, and two hours would pass and we hadn't dealt with the ending at all. It was so wonderful . . . and so frustrating at the same time.

Advice

There are people who give courses on production illustration. Find out what classes are being taught at the various schools. Seek out art directors. You have to start somewhere—go meet people, write letters to whoever's in charge of ILM (Industrial Light and Magic). Find a production designer you like whose movies you like; write a letter to Steven Spielberg.

In terms of technique, you should have a good grounding in figure drawing and perspective. You should understand perspective fairly well, because you need to know how to lay out a set and put figures in it. You would want to have a portfolio that would show that you can do storyboards and continuities, that you can sketch, that you can do some painting, that you understand architecture. You should certainly watch a lot of films and see how they are staged, see how cameras move, see how things are cut together, get a sense of pacing in terms of shots.

Staying Hungry

When I came down here, there were two things I wanted to do. I wanted to do children's books because I love Maurice Sendak's work and thought, What a great way to make a living. That was an offshoot of the cartooning and the etching I'd done. And I wanted to make animated cartoons; I ultimately had wanted to direct and write and produce my own, more along the lines of underground cartoons. I never saw myself doing a feature film like at Walt Disney. I saw myself as a filmmaker/craftsman working in my garage.

In the sense that I'm always going to be an artist—I paint at home on the weekends and I draw, I always have, always do cartoons, do my own Christmas cards—that hasn't changed.

The exigencies of money and getting along and getting married have entered the picture. But I guess there's still some of that garage craftsman in me.

Ultimately I want to do production design, barring becoming a garage craftsman, of course. But it's not the usual transition to make in this business. Historically the transition into production design is made from set design rather than from production illustration. It's easy to get typecast. And everybody's in that boat. The production designer on this project I'm doing now wants to direct. I want to be an art director. When does it stop? It probably never does, and in some ways that's good. It means that the fires are still cooking. You're still excited and you're hungry to do good work.

Matte Painter

The Matte Painter designs and paints the backgrounds for matte shots. Matte shots use specially designed masks with one or more specified areas cut out so that when placed on a camera or printer lens, the areas not masked are exposed. These shots are used in special effects for combining separate images onto one piece of film or in shooting live action against a prephotographed background. The Matte Painter's skill is comparable with that of a landscape painter in that he or she creates background landscapes to be shot on film whenever real backgrounds are deemed too difficult or too expensive to shoot or, as in the case of fantastic and science fiction films, do not actually exist. The Matte Painter consults with the director, production designer, and cinematographer in creating a painting whose photographic realization best serves the needs of the film.

Albert Whitlock

ALBERT WHITLOCK, great-grandson of the man who invented the "safety match" and grandson of a London interior decorator, started working in the British film industry as a go-fer in 1929. He studied lettering and scenic painting on his off hours, becoming known for his titles and matte work on such classics as the Somerset Maugham film adaptations of *Trio*, *Quartet*, and *Encore*. During World War II he became involved in matte painting, which eventually led him to America to further practice this craft. Today Albert Whitlock is considered by many to be the godfather of matte painting. His paintings having appeared in approximately five hundred films, including *The Milagro Beanfield War*, *The Sting*, *Marnie*, *Torn Curtain*, *Frenzy*, *Topaz*, *Ship of Fools*, and *Missing*. He has designed and executed the matte paintings for all of Alfred Hitchcock's later movies (beginning with *The Birds*) and won Academy Awards for *The Hindenburg* and *Earthquake*. Currently he lives in Santa Barbara and spends his time painting and enjoying a quiet life with his wife, June. Occasionally he comes down to Los Angeles to advise on features and to lend a guiding hand to the younger generation of matte painters, including his son, Mark, who works at Illusion Arts in Van Nuys, California.

MATTE IS a French word that allegedly means "masking out." You matte out, mask out, and put something else in its place.

Matte painting started fairly early in the 1930s. Years ago film used to wobble around and flicker. It wouldn't have been possible to do matte shots any earlier because there would have been jiggling between the two exposures. With Bell and Howell cameras and with the tightening of tolerances in the perforation of film, it got to the point where it was possible to expose film once and then expose it again—with a painting—and not get movement.

Coming to the United States

I had always thought of coming to Hollywood—it was Mecca to people working in England or anywhere in Europe. Hollywood was the Mecca of filmmaking, no question.

I thought, Well, if I could just get to San Francisco, there's certain to be some sort of movie activity. But in fact there wasn't, as I was to find out. Now I had a big decision. I had two boys, eight and four, and a reluctant wife. I had to drag her screaming and kicking from Windsor, where we lived. I was approaching my fortieth year. It was a very difficult decision to make. I was too old to go over, strike out on my own, and *then* send for them. I mean, a younger man might have, but then there's always the danger of the "Dear John" letter.

So I took them all with me. And it was a tough thing to do. It wasn't an easy time, with the Eisenhower years and a recession on here. I didn't find anything in San Francisco. But I had done title work for Disney's British pictures. *The Sword and the Rose*, in fact, got a special commendation from Walt. So I wrote to Disney's studio, tried to make a connection. It was immediately negative.

So my wife and I were in bed. The kids were screaming and hollering. And we had actually been putting clothes the day before into our suitcases to go back to England. And this is just like a movie— there was a knock at the door. It was a telegram from Western Union saying, "Would you like a job at Disney? We've got an urgent thing for you to do if you're interested." And they were even thoughtful enough to send the fare, which I didn't have!

At Disney I did the titles for *20,000 Leagues under the Sea* and eventually got into the matte painting end there with Peter Ellenshaw. No question he's the man I owe the most to. He was the doyen of matte painting.

Hooking up with Hitch

I was full of ideas and couldn't get them implemented at Disney. So I broke away, free-lanced for a while, and ended up at Universal— and actually put into practice a lot of the ideas that had been accruing in my mind.

Making things move within the painted picture, if I have any claim to fame at all, is my contribution. Moving clouds and water effects within the painted area, so instead of it just being the painting, very inanimate and often a detriment to the scene, it brought interest to the background. Hitchcock was very taken. I had first met him in England when I was on *The 39 Steps* and the original *Man Who Knew Too Much* as a go-fer at Shepherd's Bush.

Hitchcock caught up with me through Bob Boyle, the art director on *The Birds*. I got very close to Hitch. He loved matte paintings. He even used them rather gratuitously at times. He had a matte painting in every movie he worked on after *The Birds*, regardless of whether he really needed it or not.

The Hindenburg

I eventually got an agent with the success of *Earthquake* and *The Hindenburg*. One year my name was even in lights on a huge billboard on Broadway in New York, for *The Wiz*.

The ship, the *Hindenburg*, was the star of the picture. The actual ship didn't exist at the time the movie was being made. And it was nine hundred feet long when it did exist. So it was kind of a job getting that on film. They built a twenty-five-foot miniature, but it was only used once. We photographed it for stills—see, it never moved very much; it was such a ponderous thing. In five feet of film it barely moved anyway, even when it was at speed. So it was possible to do a lot of it with stills that were painted over and some pure paintings. We made it look dimensional by having a white module the same shape that would fit it in another exposure and pass shadow effects over it to look like cloud shadows, which would give it a three-dimensional look.

It was all done with paintings—entirely. Seventy-four paintings.

The Sting

There were only two paintings in *The Sting*, but they were very telling. One was a broad scene of Chicago in the early thirties that was shot on the pier at Santa Monica. And then we shot a scene on the back lot of a train coming along the El, which I did with a miniature inside the painted area for the scene where Robert Redford, in his sleazy boarding house room, is awakened by the noise of the train going by.

I bought an Italian miniature train that was very close to the elevated train of the times. We stop-motioned it for the scene. I was able to establish the high-rise buildings of Chicago in the 1930s with the dawn light on them by shooting in the ambient light of evening when there was no direct sunlight on the set so that the people moving down below were in shadow. I designed and shot that myself. An old master of mine in school—and I'm going back sixty years—used to say, "A problem well stated is a problem half-solved." This goes for the shooting of the live part of a matte shot.

Designing the Matte

When somebody shoots film, brings it to you, and then asks you to superimpose a painting—without your design input—it can become a problem. Some moviemakers say to matte painters, "Here, put a painting on this." It's not the ideal way to go.

The ideal way to go is what Disney did. There was an ideal time, as there is with everything. The golden age for matte painting was the Disney era between 1954 and 1961, when I was there. Not that I was the top man, but it was perfect because you had the total confidence of the man who mattered—Walt Disney himself—and a great interest on his part. And then my work with Hitchcock. Hitch would say, "Whatever you say, Al." And he let me design it totally. . . . Designing is going out and setting up the scene. It's now done by everybody else. And it's wrong. I only get involved in things where I can design it myself.

The obvious thing is to leave it up to people like me. But today you get situations where they're in a hole. Their film doesn't make sense, and they come to you and think that if you do a painting for them, it will geographically explain something. Audiences are not interested in geography. They're interested in people. The incidental background builds the atmosphere for a picture, but it isn't the movie.

On *The Birds*, Hitch said to me, "I don't need scenics, Al." And what he was saying was, "A girl's driving a car. And we see a setting sun on the horizon, but the principal thing is the *girl is driving the car.*"

I once mentioned the words *establishing shot* to Hitch, and he looked at me quite balefully. I don't think it was in his vocabulary. If you go to Paris, you don't try to consciously get the Eiffel Tower in the background. But if you're *not* making the film in Paris, then you feel obliged to do it. It's wrong thinking. Chances are nothing is happening in the shot, so when the editor comes to it he says, "Do we need this?" Well, if it's a good movie, obviously they don't. If it's a bad movie, they might stick it in anyway.

Matte painting should serve a film, if that painting is absolutely required. If it's an image that can't be acquired in any other way, that is the time for the matte painting. There's nothing like the real thing. But for instance, on *Frenzy* Hitchcock needed a prison scene. And he wanted to see the whole cell block, but we couldn't get into a prison in England. The Irish Republican Army prisoners were hopping over the wall like rabbits at the time, and security was dreadful. So they wouldn't let us in. I had to mock up a scene that was 90 percent painting.

After that Hitch said that he would give me a lifetime contract— "*My* life, Al. Not yours," is what he said. So that gave me tremendous leverage.

Hitch

My association with Hitch extends on and off over forty-five years. Hitchcock was a study. He always knew what he wanted, and he always told you why. When people talk about him being "the master," they're so right. His timing in coming into the industry was perfect.

Hitchcock was just sufficiently into the silent era to realize that it was a *visual* art. And when sound came in, he realized that the thing that could destroy movies would be sound. Which it did and still does today. I mean, how many times have you seen two heads against a row of books? You don't need that. That's a radio play, isn't it?

Hitchcock established characters visually. The old dragon whom Joan Fontaine was the companion to in *Rebecca* was an irascible, nasty old woman, and her invective was horrible. But what said more about her than when, in her rage, she ground her cigarette in the mushy remains of her breakfast? That did more for her character than any spoken lines could have—a visual thing.

About the character, Mrs. Danvers, Hitch asked me once, "What made her sinister?" And I said, "Well, I don't know." He said, "I never let her make an entrance. She was always there." The camera would turn around, and there she would be—hovering like a vulture. She never came through a door. Again, a simple visual. But it created an unmistakable impression.

I directed a few scenes in *Torn Curtain*. "You can do this, Al. You don't need me," Hitch said. Then, of course, there'd be Paul Newman saying, "Where's Hitch?" And I'd say, "Well, he's left that to me, you know." And Paul would be very upset.

But I didn't want to be just another director, doing something that somebody else didn't want to do, which is the way most of them start. Directing is another world. You're in a rat race to begin with. Even Hitch, although it was part of his psyche to be so, was never entirely free. He always feared authority, even middle-level authority. He always felt that he was a victim. As I say, that was part of his psyche.

The Challenge of Realism

As a craft, it has changed—it was bound to happen. Movies so fundamentally changed that while there's still a great need for matte painting, it's an entirely different requirement. Romantic films were very much the vogue for up to half of my career. The western, for instance, was a very romantic genre. I worked with John Wayne for years on and off; he and I were in one another's pockets when I was working with him down in Mexico on the Batjack movies. John Wayne was fascinated by mattes, by what I could do. But they don't make westerns anymore, except as novelties.

This is the age of "realism," and I do like that challenge, although I sometimes deplore the fact that the movie industry got stuck in a kind of Victorian attitude of "realism at all costs." Films like *Missing* . . . People would say, "But this is a docudrama!" We painted crowds in that where they couldn't get them, and that excites me—to make people believe the crowd is real. The crowd in the stadium was all painted—just a few real people to back up Jack Lemmon, but the rest were painted.

A futuristic piece isn't half as difficult. The audience is suspending their credibility anyway. So, if it doesn't look real, you can say, "Well, it *isn't* real."

Advice

Matte painting is an interesting craft. But it's *craft*. Not an "art." To use mathematicians' language, it's a beautiful equation. The fact that you can get a little bit of paint and, with film, create an incredible scene—don't you think that's quite a beautiful equation?

You've got to be more than just interested in doing this. You've got to be fascinated by it. As I was and still am. You must be impelled to do this—not be able to stop yourself. And have a strong ego to get into it or, for that matter, any sphere of endeavor. Everybody's looking for ego reinforcement; they really are. I don't give a damn—the most modest person who takes the trouble to want to do anything has an ego.

And matte painters should have more skills than just matte painting. I knew how to do models and miniatures, titles.

I say there's no art involved, but when you read about artists and the thing that drives them, you realize that you do have to have a really strong incentive. You have to have a passion.

Constable, the English painter, had a passion for painting. He wrote things about England to his wife, who was an invalid and couldn't always be with him, that really hit home to me: "The sound of water escaping mill dams, willows, old brickwork—I love these things."

If you see Constable paintings—*The Hay Wain*. When Delacroix looked at it he was astounded. There's a feeling that the rain has just finished. "Dews, breezes, bloom, and freshness," he talked about—he walked into the country with tremendous humility. How can anybody with the kind of feeling and the kind of drive to say, "I want to catch this on canvas"—how could he fail?

He wasn't that great a technician. If you look at *The Cornfield*, for instance, it's absolutely fraught with the most dreadful faults—you know, a roadway with a boy drinking from a brook, the brook up here and the roadway down here. Everybody knows that water finds the lowest level. The brook should have been down here and the road up here. And if the boy had stood up, he would have been three times taller than the sheep that are in the lane. But you look at it and it is astounding—you can *feel* the heat of the sun on the cornfield. A thousand photographs don't have the soul of England that this painting has. It makes my flesh creep.

This is the passion that we're talking about.

And to some degree you've got to have this kind of drive. I do feel I have that.

Inspiration

A year and a half ago I went to Amsterdam to Rembrandt's house and saw his etchings and paintings. I'm standing in the room and thinking, here's where he painted. I was overcome.

The Dutch painters—Ruisdael and all the landscape painters. Matte painting definitely has affinities with landscape painting, in that you see it from a distance. And where I brought something into matte painting, though I got most of it from Peter Ellenshaw, is when you do the very first rough-in, it isn't precise individual objects that you're interested in, it's the effect—the impression, not a detailed rendering.

Impression

A matte shot stays on the screen for five seconds maximum. So in that five seconds you have to create quite an impression. The abstract, the design, has to be right because it imposes itself on the audience. You can't expect the audience to search for things. When it comes on, the time of the day and the effect is much more important than the objects in there. Even if it's a very complicated architectural thing.

Practicing with Emotion

Practice. Practice. And when you're painting, it's an emotional experience. The emotion imparts itself to the painting. If you look at some very highly rendered paintings or another matte painter whose name you won't print, his work is totally unemotional. It's well rendered; you can't complain about that. But when you look at it, it's dead—it just looks back at you. It doesn't breathe.

June, my wife, would call me up on Saturday, when I had to go in on weekends. It'd get to be four o'clock, and she'd say, "Are you coming home to dinner?" I'd say, "I'll be there in half an hour." Two hours later she's calling up and saying, "I'm cooking dinner." I'd say, "I'll be right there." But there would be this thing—if I don't do it now while I'm thinking about it, it will escape me. So there you are—and my God, it's ten o'clock. Unless you're involved in that way, you're not going to do anything that's worth a damn.

The fact that a matte is only fleetingly seen on-screen doesn't bother me. It serves a purpose. I said to Hitch once, "All this work, all this effort, Hitch—for just a cut." He said, "A film is made of cuts, Al. That's all it is. A close-up is just a cut. What that cut does is what counts."

8
THE MOVERS

During the shooting of a movie, people and vehicles and equipment must be located, placed under contract, and moved around by certain key crew members.

The Assistant Directors often guide the movement of seas of people.

The Transportation Coordinator rounds up and maintains a fleet of vehicles to be used both in front of and behind the camera.

The Construction Coordinator provides and transports men, supplies, and equipment to create entire towns that miraculously spring up overnight for the sole purpose of being shot by a camera for only a few days or weeks.

The Location Manager finds shooting sites that already exist.

The Caterer lays out food feasts for hundreds of crew members and actors within very short periods of time.

The Wrangler handles livestock, moving herds of horses or stampeding cattle across the camera's horizon.

The Production Coordinator oversees the movements of all these people, acting as go-between for the production manager and crew members.

Without the people in this chapter, nothing on a movie set would move at all.

Production Coordinator

The Production Coordinator assists the production manager in the execution of his tasks. He or she is responsible for setting up and organizing the production office, relaying information between the production office and the set, filing the production paperwork, and prioritizing information for expeditious handling by the production manager.

Lisa Cook

LISA COOK began working in Hollywood selling popcorn at the now torn-down Pan-Pacific Theater. Her first production job was crafts service, "the doughnuts and coffee routine," on a low-budget picture called *Bloody Birthday*. Since then she has been the production coordinator on numerous low-budget features, including *Nightmare on Elm Street*, *Nightflyers*, *The Wraith*, and *Hamburger . . . The Motion Picture*.

THE PRODUCER is above the line, the crew is below the line, the coordinator *is* the line. He or she is there to help the production manager get everything done.

In preproduction you're breaking down the script, incorporating revisions, helping to keep everyone else up to date on the changes in scheduling. The art department often needs a lot of help at this time because they're scattered all over the place. They're building in one place, dressing someplace else. You're trying to get promotional material. You need to know how actors become signatory of SAG, how to look at day player contracts—this huge envelope comes across your desk every morning.

You're setting up the office 50 percent of the time. Very rarely do you walk in and everything is just there. I've even had to find the office, deal with the real estate agents, get it furnished. When I did *The Slayer* we had a tiny office and they gave me about two hundred dollars to furnish it—typewriter, furniture, everything. I said "okay" quite blithely and did it. All the furniture was from the Salvation Army.

Once you start shooting, there's all the paperwork that is generated—the call sheet, which you have to get to the people who can't get it on the set. The production report comes in the day after; it should really be checked over—it's all numbers, a record of what actors were there, what hours they worked, how much film was shot. And that has to be distributed to the right people, usually the producers, the bondsmen, the investors, all of whom want to see it because it's the log of how things are going. There are all the camera reports and the notes from the script supervisor, which you have to get to the editors. And scheduling dailies.

Things tend to calm down once you've been doing it long enough. You get a pattern going. You spend maybe an hour and a half in the morning doing all the paperwork and then kind of wing the day-to-day problems. Especially if the crew is out on location, there's constant communication with the office for things they need—money or something needs to be run out there or "I can't reach this actress, I'm a mile from the phone so please keep trying her"—that kind of thing.

Each production manager is different, each one has his or her own style. Some want to be involved in every aspect of things; with others the less they know, the better. You establish what to filter, and you don't bother the production manager with a lot of mundane details, unless it's information he needs to act upon.

The production manager will give me all the information, and once you learn what kinds of things this person forgets and needs to be reminded of, you learn what it is you have to do. We remind each other; there's a lot of checks and balances.

Requirements

The job requires that you be very organized and good on the phone, and that you cultivate a great memory for small details.

There's no course you can take to learn this. You can't learn anything really about the film business in a classroom. So much of it is dynamics that cannot be duplicated under any other situation except when thousands of dollars are at stake and you're under the gun.

A person's success as a production coordinator has a lot to do with the ability to deal with stress—rolling with things, being flexible. I imagine there are certain kinds of role-playing games you could do that would help you find out if you're that kind of person. But I think you just have to do it and find out for yourself. I've seen people flip out because they just weren't built for it.

You need to be able to deal with information being thrown at you and people making tons of demands on you all the time. It's problem-solving on a moment-to-moment basis—finding out the most expeditious way to solve those problems.

Also, it has to do with how you get along with people because the production coordinator is pretty much the representative of the production. You're the person everyone comes to—the one answering the phone, the one they go to for help. It's a troubleshooting position; you're at people's beck and call. Your job is to coordinate their needs with getting the picture made.

Women's Work

I've never worked with a male coordinator. I'm sure there are good ones, as there are good male script supervisors, but I have yet to work with one.

Women are more detail-oriented and diplomatic in ways men aren't. Women's roles are changing so crazily. It used to be they didn't have to be part of the rat race. It's not always optional these days—women do have to work in many cases.

Women bring in a balance because most production managers are men—the yin and the yang. I also think women adapt better to this particular job. Men don't like being in a subservient position. And that's basically what it is, answering phones and bringing people coffee. It doesn't rub me the wrong way because I'm not treated like a dingbat. It's a learned trait, knowing how to serve people and put them at ease.

Moving on to Production Manager

I'm thinking ahead; I don't want to be a production coordinator forever. One of the most educational experiences I had was on the last show. The production manager let me production manage two days of pickups, and there's nothing like doing it yourself. I felt, No problem, I can handle it, it can't be that different. Well, when it's on your head and you're not turning to someone and saying, "Well, what are you going to do about this now?" the buck stops here, I lost a lot of sleep.

No doubt about it, he did me a great emotional service by letting me do that—dealing with the key grip screaming at you for overtime. . . . There's just no experience like that. Everybody's pal is the coordinator ("What a gal!"), and now you're "management."

It was scary. Part of me was saying, "It's not for me, I'll just be a coordinator until I decide what I'm doing," and there was another part of me saying, "You have to do it, it's a stretch and you're going to go through a lot of pain and anxiety, but that's what it's all about." I've gotten very comfortable being a production coordinator. There's really nothing new they can spring on me at this point, but I don't want to be a production biddy all my life.

I would hope—I'm twenty-eight now—that by the time I'm thirty-five I would have a reputation as a production manager, possibly a line producer. I think that's a healthy time frame. I used to read *People* magazine when they had a section on "up-and-coming kids" between the ages of eighteen and twenty-three, and I realized, with horror, that I was too old to be an up-and-coming—I was over the hill!

Everyone has his own pace, and I've relaxed about it. Things have worked out. I've worked hard, earned it, none of it was dropped in my lap.

When I make that transition, I'm going to have to let go of my personal feelings for people and deal with them as a "boss": "No, you can't have this," or "You're being unreasonable," firing people and haggling over rates. I'm dreading that. But you can't take the criticism and disputes personally. They're dealing with you in their work persona, and you're dealing with them in yours. They're not challenging you, they're challenging your decision. These are people you will drink beer with and everything will be fine.

On the other hand, as a woman I don't want to become hardened. There's the production biddy, and then there's the production "hag"— Bette Davis sitting there in a dark suit: "She's tough, man!" I still wonder if men are alienated by women in power positions. I wonder if grips don't go out with female AD's because they're "higher up" in the hierarchy.

The Set Romance

The nature of the industry is so temporary. Everything is "just for this show"—"It's only a movie," and "We're building a town—it'll be gone tomorrow." It's a hedonistic culture: live today; you might die tonight, so don't worry about IRAs and what you're going to be doing when you're fifty.

One of the biggest pitfalls is the set romance. There's nothing more thrilling than falling madly in love with the boom operator. Then you come out of it and realize you really didn't have anything in common except the picture.

Sets are very romantic places. There's camaraderie, flirting. You're in your own little world, and it's a very family thing. It has always amazed me how you can go on location with a crew and there are people who are married and are obviously having location romances with someone.

There's this code of silence no one would ever think of betraying, which I guess is respectable in one way—minding your own business. There's an understanding that on a movie you can do pretty much what you want. The picture gets "wrapped," and your relationships can get "wrapped."

A friend of mine, an AD, was involved with this woman, got her on the show as the extras coordinator. Next thing you know she's having an affair with the set carpenter. Sounds funny. But there's nothing worse than seeing your "person" flirting or getting involved with someone else. It's right in your face. And you're working under great stress. You have a real emotional tie to these people. There are people I've worked on a terrible show with, and when I bump into them at a party or something, it's like running into your brother or sister because you've been through this trauma together.

There are certainly things more meaningful in life than to have done a picture together, but things get skewed. That's another thing that has come to me with experience and maturity—learning to enjoy it for what it is. Don't make it into something it's not.

I always feel melancholy when a picture wraps. The seasoned pros who've done it enough say, "Ah, just another show, see ya next time." It's true, especially in the nonunion world—it's small and self-contained. I try to brace myself for when a picture is over, try to plan something to take up the time because you get fond of the people you're with. They're like school chums—somebody you've seen all fourth grade, and now it's summer.

I used to feel that working on features was like diving. You'd dive into this pool. I didn't have to deal with my life, especially when I was on location. "I'm working, I can't think about that right now. I'm out of town, I'll call you when I get back." Then you come out of it and take this deep breath. You can run away from yourself very efficiently—it's "gotta go, too hip . . . working, gotta run."

There's not much time for putting it all together. So when you're not working it focuses all that soul-searching into a very short span.

Hollywood Dreams

When I came out here, my fantasies of Hollywood were based on a complete misconception of what filmmaking really was. I thought, Just another bunch of people, all working, having a great time, but bigger—the student film mentality of "We're all making this creative work of art." And, of course, you get out here and it's like Detroit—a big industry.

I'd thought about directing. The last few months in school, I worked on a student film, and as student films go—you do everything, slate, light meter—the film had lots of dolly moves and dramatic effects.

The reality of Hollywood filmmaking is quite different. The job of directing is a complete mystery to me. If somebody held a gun to my head, I could probably do passingly well, but it's amazing to me that a director can think so abstractly. It seems a cross between being a master carpenter and understanding, "writing one note a day for a symphony." You've got to be able to think of the whole thing and do it inch by inch.

I remember Norman Mailer likened it to the army, a traveling circus, and a bunch of musicians all mixed in one. And it is, but there's a very definite structure, a definite hierarchy, and you have to learn how it works. It's not just a bunch of people making movies, it's a crew, like on a ship or in the army. There's a very definite order to the way things get done. I love a good system, so I just adapted to that right away. If you put four people on a desert island and tell them to make a movie, they'd still eventually end up breaking it down the same way. There are logical reasons why the jobs end up the way they do.

Los Angeles is definitely a company town, and if you like film, there's nothing like living in a town that focuses on your job all the time. And it's living on the brink. You're right on the ocean, in the midst of the entertainment industry, which is highly publicized all over the country. I feel I'm right in the middle of an incredibly stimulating, sometimes overstimulating, industry, but I can't imagine living anywhere else. I read about people wanting to chuck it all, move to New Mexico, open a bookstore. I don't think I'll ever reach that point. I'm enjoying what I'm doing too much.

I'm a big L.A. booster. Everyone says it's so devoid of culture, so ugly, and so on. I spend a lot of time going through the paper, clipping out events I want to go to, looking into organizations—I've turned into this PTA-type woman! I don't actively participate in the New York versus Los Angeles debate. New York is not Los Angeles, and Los Angeles is not New York.

Not Working

The worst time was when there was a general lull in the industry, which was in January of 1982, I think. There was a period of about two months. You find out that it's not how you manage when you're working, it's how you can get by when you're not working. That's when you really call upon your resources to pull you through.

It's great at first. And through hard experience, I've learned to pace my cash flow to where I'm not flat broke when the job ends, but it's such a dramatic shift. It can be a little unnerving. This postpartum depression sets in. You've been working full-tilt-boogey for months, and you wake up the morning after it's over—it's like a dream, suddenly nothing to do.

Remaining Anchored

I can't imagine just happening into this business. For me, it was such a cherished dream to get a job. There are those who come into it through their family—their dad was a painter for sets, that kind of thing. There are people who came from other walks of life; there are those who have been in the industry and left. It's an industry that destroys a lot of people.

I'm grateful that I am firmly anchored as a personality. Drugs are a part of this environment. I think the popularity of cocaine has to do with the fact that the business is based on having a good time, and this makes you feel even better, gives you energy, keeps you awake to make you feel better that much longer. Many people are emotionally at odds with themselves; they're negating the traditional values. And this business is so untraditional. You get support for *not* being very cerebral or introspective or sane. Those kinds of people, "they're boring, they're just chugging away."

But they are the ones who are going to survive.

Advice

Do whatever they give you to do very well, and eventually someone will notice. If it means doing craft service, even though you don't want to make a career of it—if you have the right attitude and are obviously bright, you'll get the reputation "he [or she] did craft services really well—table was always neat, always had enough, never any complaints from the crew, had hot coffee all night during night shooting," and they're not saying you make great coffee, but that you were there, never had to be reminded, you were given a task and you did it.

There was a film professor who gave me great advice: "Get your English degree because that's going to serve you no matter what you end up doing, especially in Hollywood because it's such a vacuum. If you never crack a book again, at least you've learned something. If you want to make a career in features, go to Hollywood right away and get going. Don't go to New York or Chicago. You can work for ten years somewhere else and become a real big fish in a small pond. When you finally get out to Los Angeles, you go right back to ground zero. They don't care."

Summing it Up

There's no substitute for loving your work, and your work never lets you down. Every day I'm just so thankful that I'm successful in an industry and in a job that I love. Whenever I get self-pitying—"my life is such a bust"—I think, God, I'd go crazy if I had to do something I hated. I know people outside this industry who are terribly unhappy in their jobs. No matter what, I've always had the satisfaction of my job.

And then, personally, there's no substitute for doing things that are in your best interest. That scares me sometimes when I think I'm teetering on the edge of being so alone, being so single-minded about getting what I want, or making my job so satisfying that I have nothing else.

I think things will work out the way I want them to. I may feel kind of at loose ends at the moment, but if I can just put the same kind of faith and energy that I put into my career into my personal life, I'd be all set. You have to rely on yourself, you can't look to other people. They will always let you down because they're only human. You really have to build a strong sense of self.

There's just nowhere to hide on a film crew. If you're bad, everybody knows it. I knew someone who was working for the government, and they told him he was working too fast and to slow down!

In film, you're constantly being challenged and constantly evaluating what kind of person you are because it's so keyed in with your job. You're always pushing yourself one step further.

Postscript: *Since this interview, Lisa has gone on to production manage the features* Two Idiots in Hollywood, Loon, *and* Tremors. *She also production-managed a comedy special for HBO and served as production associate on* Major League.

Construction Coordinator

The Construction Coordinator schedules, coordinates, and supervises the construction of the sets on a motion picture production. He or she prepares a set construction budget in accordance with the blueprints, if existent, commissioned by the production designer and drawn up by the set designer, hires the key construction crew, and follows up on all aspects of construction including preparing and approving orders for materials and equipment, filing receipts, maintaining a log, issuing memos in connection with any changes in construction plans, and acting as liaison between the production designer and the production manager on all construction matters.

George Stokes

GEORGE STOKES started out as an actor in the motion picture business at age fifteen, did six features and a couple of series, and decided to retire at the ripe old age of eighteen. After he got out of the army in 1965, he gave the motion picture business a try again, this time as a carpenter. From there he quickly moved up the ranks, becoming first a foreman and then a coordinator. George has been in charge of construction on over sixty features including *The*

Deer Hunter, Young Frankenstein, The Planet of the Apes, Capricorn One, Tom Horn, Two Jakes, The Slugger's Wife, About Last Night, The Golden Child, and *Baby Boom.* His is a motion picture family—wife, Stanzie, is a casting director, and son George Stokes, Jr., also works construction.

I'M THERE to give the production designer the looks he wants. But I've got to keep within a budget and satisfy the money people.

When I'm going through a budget with a production designer, it's my job to pick his brain. If there's no prints, for example, and he says, "All I want is a couple walls of paint," and I don't question him further and just put in a budget of $2,500, next thing you know the prints come down and I've got the Taj Mahal—for $25,000.

Approved Overage

Now I have to go to the money guys. They'll either say, "Go ahead, we'll get the extra money"—that's known as an approved overage—or, "You can't have it." Then everybody gathers in one room to hash it out. If the director is adamant, wants it, and the production designer agrees, then it's up to the producer either to do without that shot or to give them the money to do it.

A room will initially be budgeted for a certain amount. Later on, when the designer has picked out the room he wants on a scout or has actually had it built, we'll find out it's going to take five hundred extras to fill the room up, which is too much. So it's "Let's cut the room in half." Somebody's got to pay to cut that room in half. Now the construction budget's been bumped a couple thousand dollars.

Shooting "Practical" or Building

That's why one of the first things I do, after I've seen the locations—local and distant—if there aren't any prints, is sit down with the production designer and ask him, "Are you going to shoot practical?"

"Practical" means shooting what exists, what doesn't have to be built. After we do that, *then* I'll sit down and make a budget.

Even when I've done that, you'll get one of those situations where they decide to shoot everything practical, as on *Baby Boom*

"We'll build just one room—$75,000. We'll build a real small apartment—$85,000. We'll shoot the vet's office and everything else practical." I did the budget on it but ended up needing to ask for another $400,000 because they decided to build more, after we were already into production.

On *The Slugger's Wife*, we went on location with a budget of $300,000. We were going to shoot mostly practical—only build a baseball diamond and a small house, and then build the interiors on-stage.

We get down there and the producer says, "Let's not shoot this hospital, let's build a hospital." Then we "find out" baseball players make a lot of money, so now the little house is a big house. So the budget doubled, went from $300,000 to $600,000.

The Crew

My crew consists of my three foremen—a construction foreman, a labor foreman, and a paint foreman. This is the nucleus.

I'll look at my budget and schedule and see I have ten days to build this restaurant—I'll need a hundred guys. The foreman has a list of people whom he uses. So I'll leave it up to all three of my foremen to do the hiring and firing.

I don't care if it's a guy driving a stake in the floor—everybody likes to feel that what they do is important. So I spend a lot of time making sure that my crew knows they're valued. And it comes back to you. You make them happy, they give you good work. If they're unhappy, they'll lay down on you a little bit and the job is going to end up costing you more.

I have a strong ego. I've had to learn to let somebody else's ego outshine mine. Take pride in what I do, but the director and production designer are the ones who are going to get credit for the look. When they come in and want changes, I know as soon as I turn around to my foremen, I'm going to hear a lot of bitching. But I know what the guy's up against. I'll try to give the production designer what he wants—make him happy—and turn around and make my men happy, too.

Having Backup—Writing Memos

I learned a long time ago not to do things unless the powers-that-be say yes. If you have a headstrong production designer, which is most of the good ones, they say, "I *want* this." All I say is, "Yes, you got it." *Then* I go to the powers-that-be and say, "I need the money."

On one picture we had a production manager who said, "Yeah, go ahead," every time. Every time he said that, I would write him a memo saying, "As per our conversation, I'm going to build this and it's going to cost X number of dollars, which will be added to my budget."

This is extremely important. Otherwise you can get saddled with the blame for spending too much. You have to have backup proving expenditures were authorized. In a situation like that, if you can, bypass the production manager and write memos to the producer— send the production manager a copy of the memo, but deal with the producer directly. If you don't have a strong producer, it just makes everything that much tougher.

I also get production designers who don't want to be bothered by you. I'm up against a schedule, and I've got to have questions answered in order to do my job. So it's a tough line to walk—you can be crucified by either side.

Materials

You can't really stock up too much beforehand; that would be a waste. What if the director decides not to do it a certain way? Then I've got all this extra paint and materials. So I get materials *when* I need it.

There are a multitude of lumber yards, paint stores, and hardware stores that cater to the studios. I can usually get something within an hour's notice. If I have to, I'll send the trucks out to get it. So I'm working with the transportation captain, and I've got to have trucks and drivers available to me.

Of course, staples like two-by-fours or nails I can't run out of when I've got a construction crew working because production will come to a dead stop.

Servicing the Company

My job involves not only getting the sets built in time to be shot, but also servicing the company while we're shooting. What I mean by "servicing" is "Tomorrow morning, can we have this wall out of here?" or "Can we add another four feet to this sidewalk?" Getting things ready for the next day—making sure the shooting goes smoothly. So overnight we'll get guys in and do whatever it takes.

Working with the Production Designer

There aren't many production designers who can visualize exactly what they want; it's all up here [in the brain]. But when it gets down to the building, it all gets short-circuited.

So it's "This is what I want." I build it. And then it's "No. Let's change this." Often it has to do with painting—getting the color they feel they want. When I did *I Ought to Be in Pictures*, we painted a house, but the director said that wasn't exactly what he wanted. Not that the painters were bad. He just decided it wasn't quite right.

There are also changes that you have to make because the director and production designer have differences. Production designer says, "I visualized this," and the director says, "No, I wanted it bigger," or, "I want the bedroom off here."

I don't hassle production designers with money problems. I keep them informed of what it is costing because their reputation is also on the line if they spend too much. If a production designer gets a reputation for being very expensive—one who will use real tiles instead of foam or who designs very expensive, elaborate moldings—people aren't going to want to hire him.

You can't approach a production designer, or really any creative person, saying, "No, you cannot have that." They'll come right back with, "I *want* that." Give him alternatives. He wants crystal doorknobs for all the rooms in his set. I'll just say, "I can get these doorknobs, but they're $75 apiece. Or I can get glass ones that look just like them for $2.50. Or you could go with brass knobs with engraving, that will fit into this look, for $10 apiece."

You don't want to back 'em into a corner. You try to make decisions yourself. One particular designer, when I first did the budget with him, said, "We're going to paint this set." Now that's cheaper than wallpaper. But he got into some real exotic paints. We're talking four to five processes—so in the end it would have been cheaper to wallpaper. Next time I budget a set for him, I'll add an extra 25 percent, to give him that option instead of going to him later and saying, "I don't have the money to do this set." It's good if a production designer and construction coordinator make several pictures together because you begin to think alike.

Research

I'm working on a picture right now, *Couch Trip*, directed by Michael Ritchie. The hospital in the script was built in the fifties. The windows that were put in throughout the hospital don't exist—I've got to have them manufactured. Bear in mind, all we're going to do is photograph them, so the windows don't have to work, they just have to look like windows. There are books I use and some very good research people in this town who can get you pictures. If I can find a picture of what I need, I can manufacture it.

Lillian Michaelson over at Zoetrope has a great research library. So if I need to build a padded cell, I'll call her up and say, "Give me everything you have on padded cells." Next thing I know, a whole box comes over with a stack of pictures of padded cells from every period.

Then and Now

Years ago they wouldn't even bring someone like me on until the prints were all done. You'd have four or five months of prep time to build the sets. Now it's last minute—we build sets off of drawings on napkins in restaurants or verbalize it.

Even when you do get the time—I had about four or five good months of prep on this last picture [*The Golden Child*]—you can get into night shifts on construction work because major construction jobs—interiors of temples, a twenty-foot-high Buddha, an airplane interior—were being filmed at the beginning of the shoot.

There used to be a very rigorous test to become a coordinator; in fact, there were tests for everything—special effects, prop makers, even carpenters. The Producers Association finally stopped them because they were afraid of lawsuits, afraid somebody would say, "You failed me because I'm black," or "because I wear glasses."

Now you just put in your thirty days and pay your money to get in. There's coordinators coming from the prop makers department, special effects. It's hurting the studios because it doesn't work. There was a guy, a painter, who became a coordinator because he was the friend of a production manager who became head of production at a studio.

This painter was sent out on location, given the title of construction coordinator. When they came back, they told the union that he had coordinated from this date to this date. He got his card. And the first picture he did after that, they went overbudget, had to bring in another coordinator to bail him out, which held up production.

Staying Honest

There are bad coordinators, and I'll bad-mouth 'em every chance I get. I hope it gets back to them. It's very easy to rip off a production. It's possible to make phony lumber bills, build tracts of houses with the money stolen from shows. They often get away with it because they're in cahoots with the powers-that-be or kicking back some money to them. I see it happen.

Every day I do a production cost report in which I record meticulously what I spend on material, what I spend on labor. All my bills are up to date; anybody wants to check my records, they're there.

That's because I've been in the situation where a production manager had gotten ripped off very badly by a coordinator. I found out *how* badly. That coordinator had subcontracted work and equipment out—a job would actually cost $2,500 and he'd charge $5,000 and pocket the difference.

The production manager really didn't trust me. I had to prove to him I was living in his back pocket, let him know everything I was going to do before I did it. This is why I hate bad coordinators because if a production manager or production designer has had a bad experience, I've got to go in there and start from scratch and earn their trust.

Casualties of the "Deal"

It's not making the movie anymore, it's making the deal. The movie is a secondary by-product. They don't want to spend it below the line. They spend it above the line. It's, "Let's spend $12 million on this star and that star and get everybody on the Phil Donahue show."

And the unions are out to destroy themselves. In another five years it's going to be tough for the below-the-liners. They're not going to be able to make as good a living as they're making now. Salaries will drop. Time between jobs will get longer. And they'll cut back on the below-the-line—get people for six dollars an hour as opposed to seventeen dollars an hour, go nonunion.

The major studios are doing it just as much as the independents are. They're shipping people out of town and shooting nonunion movies. It's getting more and more prevalent.

Advice

Start somewhere and don't be afraid to ask questions. I've helped, I'd say, half a dozen people to become coordinators. I have no fear of competition. Ask me how I estimate sets. Ask me how to read prints. There's no way to learn except to do it and ask questions.

First Assistant Director

The First Assistant Director is the director's right hand in the organization of the set. He or she is responsible for maintaining order and discipline on the set, keeping the production moving to meet its scheduling goals, establishing the crew and shooting calls, and overseeing the selection and management of the extras. The First Assistant Director's duties include preparing the production board (an accurate, up-to-the-minute shooting schedule), establishing with the director the number and types of extras required, blocking the extras (positioning and choreographing extras' movement for a take) upon occasion and if required by the director, and generally seeing to it that the directives of the director are carried out. He or she is the liaison between the director and the production manager and is assisted by the second assistant director.

David Sosna

DAVID SOSNA grew up in Chicago, "watching television and wanting to direct movies and reading *Variety* while other kids were watching baseball." His first job in film was as a driver delivering film to the lab for a local producer of industrial films. While there, he met a California editor who offhandedly suggested David give him a call should he ever get to Los Angeles. David flew to Los Angeles the next week and managed to get a job in Hollywood "winding 16-mm commercial-release prints onto little red reels." He eventually got an assistant editor union card, but when he discovered it would be seven years before he'd be allowed to actually cut film, he decided to pursue other avenues. While serving as an operations clerk (or "lot rat") at the Burbank Studios, he took the highly competitive Directors Guild of America training program test, getting the highest score that year. As a politically naive DGA trainee, he got fired from his first assignment on a motion picture and thought his life in the motion picture business was over. Fortunately, the director of the DGA program went to bat for him and he continued to work steadily, accumulating the four hundred days necessary to graduate to second assistant director and eventually becoming a first assistant director on numerous motion pictures with top-flight directors, including Walter Hill (*48 Hrs.*, *The Warriors*) and John Landis (*Trading Places*, *The Blues Brothers*).

THE PRIMARY responsibility is to help the director realize his vision while keeping the show moving forward efficiently. To do that, the director's got to have what he needs to make the shot. Things have to progress in an efficient and timely fashion.

I'm like an executive officer on a ship. The director is the captain who decides where the ship is going to go and what battles we'll engage in. I get it there. This is about knowing the street—a big part of the job:

A director and I were in a Baltimore restaurant one night. I could see the restaurant was "mobbed up," "connected," from the guys in the room, the owner's style. They were wise guys. So we walk outside; now I've been in a lot of American cities, and if the neighborhood is connected, it's spotless. Pregnant women walk around alone, nobody's afraid. This is why the Mafia started.

So I said, "Come on, let's go downtown. They got a strip place called the Block. Let's see what it's about." We walk through this alley, and we cross the line into the non-Mob neighborhood, the ghetto. Here come two big black kids up the street. The director turns to me and says, "We're going to die. We're going to die right here in this alley. . . ."

I look at the kids and I say, "We're not going to die. Nothing's gonna happen," because somehow I knew they wouldn't mess with us so close to occupied territory, and besides, we both looked Italian.

They walked by us and it was fine.

Now I don't know how I knew that, a middle-class Jewish kid, but I did; and that's real important: sensing what's going to happen, knowing the street.

Discovering the Gift

Four hundred days as a trainee, then I became a second, got really good at it, and became one of the big feature guys with a specialty in working large crowds. I discovered that, for whatever reason, I have this bizarre gift: I can run a crowd of five hundred hard cases, and they all do what I say, and the director likes it. It's managing people, in large numbers, usually. You could get an MBA who's trained to manage people and he wouldn't know how to do this; he wouldn't have this weird skill.

I did a movie called *Rollercoaster*, which worked pretty well because it looks like a working amusement park. And that's the illusion you go for—unstaged reality. The parks were closed, of course. All those people were hired extras propped by us, given balloons, doughnuts, dolls, babies, baby carriages, newspapers, and anything that looked right.

I would tell the crowd that people with birthdays from January through April, one-third of them, should go over to the merry-go-round and walk to the roller coaster. I'd split and distribute the rest of the crowd and make a few jokes, bad ones, mostly, so they'd relax, and then just start them walking. I knew where the camera was looking and what the density of the crowd had been in previous shots. This way I was able to give each shot a realistic-looking background. Everybody liked it, and I started with this big crowd reputation. Even so, when it was time for me to move up, I said, "Oh, jeez, I'll never be able to become a first, it's too scary."

The Warriors

The first feature I did as a first assistant was *The Warriors*. I had met Walter Hill, who wanted to hire me for a show in Los Angeles. That show fell through, and he got a picture in New York. I said, "Let me do that show." Paramount told me I couldn't, that an L.A. first would get torn up by the New York streets.

So they go to New York without me and I'm at Universal on the back lot doing an episode of *The Hulk* when I get a phone call: they'd been shooting for a week and the New York first had made some tactical errors. He used some ethnic slurs in a minority neighborhood. People went crazy. Bottles started coming over the buildings onto the crew, and the studio wanted to fire the guy.

They called me and asked if I would come and do it. I said, "Of course." It was my big break.

Now I get to New York and haven't even seen the script—no prep, nothing. A limo meets me at Kennedy with a script and a stack of production reports showing what's been shot. I started working on the way to the city. I cross off those scenes in the script, read it, and show up for work.

Everybody on the production says, "Thank you for coming, we're glad you're here, and by the way, we think the crew's out to get you."

On my first day on the set it was clear that the company had no leadership—another big part of the job. The guy I was replacing wasn't organized. The company was getting a slow start each day and not getting very much work done. In spite of this, the crew still had a real hostility toward West Coast people. I was a West Coast guy replacing their East Coast pal. It wasn't pretty.

The First Shot

My first shot with the company included a fire under a subway track, a crowd, a bus, and a fire truck. The fire engine comes around the corner and brings us to a bus. Our hero gets on, and it drives off. Simple shot. Vehicles start showing up, and I'm looking around and saying "hello" a lot and generally being ignored. This is my first show as a first and I'm a little nervous anyway. The trucks are different, the guys are different, everybody told me I'd fail—the whole nine yards.

I ignore all that stuff and go deal with the firemen, the subway guy, the bus guy, and get things ready to go. So now I'm ready and I go to the director and tell him, "Walter, we're all set." He looks at his watch, gives me a look, and says, "Okay. Show me." It was much earlier than they had started before and he was surprised, to say the least. I show him everything's ready and he says, "Now when you send the fire engine, make sure you roll the camera first!" I fell over! "Walter, what've you been dealing with here?"

Anyway, things went fine, and I got Walter's trust. Everybody else was still cool and aloof. The other first AD was pretty unhappy. He'd been hanging around to take over when the L.A. guy fell on his ass.

Mob Scene

The next week on *Warriors*, we had a big riot to do. Now on a riot shot you have to be very clever with the choreography, or they'll all bang into each other and it'll be a disaster. And you have to know camera and how to stage it so it looks like they are crashing and falling. This was an especially tricky sequence because the kids had to be in formation, then break on cue and run like hell in twenty different directions.

In addition, you also have to be forceful enough to make the crowd want to do what they're told. You can't just lay it out and pray. These were a thousand kids, all Harlem hard cases: the kind that motivate teachers to quit teaching. So the whole proposition didn't look promising. The teamsters were taking bets on how long I'd last— you know, how many minutes before I got pulled into the crowd and laid out cold.

But it's like being a lion tamer sometimes—you can't let them smell any fear. So I used an old AD trick I'd heard about: I told the crowd to be quiet for a sound check and that it was a firing offense if anyone talked before I said to. There was, of course, no sound check. I waited a while until they got bored and things started to fall apart while I looked for the two biggest, meanest-looking kids in the crowd and waited until they started talking and screwing around.

As soon as these two did, I landed on them. "People! When I tell you I want it quiet, *it will be fucking quiet!!*" The place fell silent immediately; even the crew stopped talking. "You two! Come over here." They sauntered over, very tough and very ready to tangle. I got close to them, in their faces as far as everyone else could see, and told them that if they walked out the gate without saying a word or smiling, I'd pay them for the night, give them a bonus, and they could go home early without doing any work. They agreed and left like altar boys.

As far as the crowd was concerned, I was the single toughest human being living and they weren't about to mess with me. The crew, who read about these kids in the paper every day, thought that this was pretty amazing, and they started to turn around and work with me after that. I had gained their respect now because they had never seen anybody do that before, especially with kids like these.

Understanding the Picture

I usually get hired right at the beginning. The first thing I'll do is read the script through just to "get" the movie we're making. Then I'll break the show down. I start by numbering the scenes and clarifying the scene headings in the script. This converts the studio script, the versions the actors and director read when they signed on to do the project, into a shooting script—something the crew can use to make the picture.

The studio script might say "Joe's Face." I'll change it to:

INT. JOE'S BEDROOM—NIGHT—(RAIN)
CLOSE ON JOE'S FACE.

This way the art department builds all the correct sets, the effects department rigs the correct window for rain, camera lights the scene correctly for night and not day by mistake, and so on.

Next, I'll read the script again to determine the logistics. I'll count the speaking parts, extras, cars, stunts, effects. Then I write in all these details on breakdown pages. There's a breakdown page for each sequence [the series of shots required for a scene or a logical group of scenes].

At the same time I make a list of questions I'll take to the director. "Do you want the shot this way? Do you want a point of view here? Is this going to be an insert?" I get a rough idea of all the requirements. I'll ask about his coverage, the shots he'll need for the sequence. I'll ask if he'll see street traffic out the window in a location interior. Then we'll decide together whether or not I'll hire extras with cars to keep the traffic consistent, shot to shot, or if I can use what's out there.

For example, suppose the script calls for a ninja warrior to come swinging through the window with an Uzi. Right away, this is a stuntman. I have to hire him, or more likely, the stunt gaffer will.

I have to get a breakaway window from special effects, get the location department to get permission to take the real glass out and put the breakaway in. They'll tell me how fast I have to replace it. Is a stand-by glass truck and five glaziers required?

The director will show me and the crew on a location survey where the ninja goes after he comes through the glass. Is there room for him? Do we have to unbolt tables and move them? Is an air bag required? Does he fire the Uzi?

If he fires the Uzi, does he hit the wall? Do we have to squib it? Squibs are bullet hits, small explosives set off by the effects man during the shot. Do we have to put in fake wall facings so that we can be ready for take two? How fast can we reload the glass for take two? Do the shots hit people? If they do, are they blood hits? Do we add little bags of blood and sew them into the wardrobe so when the bullet hit goes off, the clothes tear and some red stuff shows up? If so, that takes more time for take two, and I'll schedule accordingly.

Falling Doubles

Sometimes it's not just making sure you have what you need, but also seeing a solution to a time/money problem and working it out with the director.

Say there's a scene where a guy gets shot and falls out of a window ten stories up. . . .

On the ground are one hundred police, thirty picture-cars, and a crowd of five hundred—all period, 1920s wardrobe. There are also searchlights, machine guns, and other period props. This is expensive rental equipment and requires many additional crew people, men's and women's wardrobe, makeup and hair, props, effects, transportation, and so on. A lot of time and money. So I'll ask the director, Does he plan to pan the stunt double down to the crowd, or will the double drop out of frame above the crowd?

That one decision changes the requirements that I need for the stunt shot considerably. If the director will stop the shot before the double comes down to the crowd, then I can schedule things that day so we do the stunt while the crowd's being made up. Perhaps I'll release the crowd early so that we can send them and a lot of additional crew personnel home without overtime, finishing the day on a smaller shot, like the one-man stunt. Either way, the sooner the question is asked, the sooner I can find the optimum way to schedule the day and provide all the departments with the necessary information quickly. I need to know the show as well as the director so that when he turns to me and says, "Let's blow up the bridge," I'll be ready with what he needs. This close relationship is why the job is called assistant director.

Organizing the Schedule

After all this, I'll take each breakdown page and put it in script order. I'll read them all, as I would the script, to double-check and make sure I haven't messed something up. Now I start to organize the shooting schedule. I'll put the pages into groups of sets—all the exterior Joe's Place, then exterior saloon, and so on. I try to make the most efficient schedule I can and still not hurt the movie.

An example of hurting the movie would be doing the last scene, the hero's death scene, as the first shot in the schedule. This puts tremendous pressure on the actor, who's doing heavy work in front of strangers in an environment in which he's not yet secure. Another way would be to schedule, inflexibly, all the interiors in one set together in a complex interpersonal drama. It may make sense logistically to stay in the same room for four days rather than move back and forth several times. However, if the nature of the relationships change, and the director feels that the picture would be better served by giving the actors a chance to grow in their parts, then this traditional production department approach would be the wrong thing to do.

Now I'll show the schedule to the director and fix any problems he has with it. Then on to the producer and production manager to solve their concerns. When everybody is happy, the schedule is locked and I print copies to distribute. The production manager will use it to finalize his budget—how many days will the water truck work at so much a day, that sort of thing.

Now we can start shooting the picture. That's how you make a schedule.

Identifying Problems

The art director certainly knows how to build a set better than I, but has he forgotten anything or not heard the director clearly? Has he remembered a facing, a matching window from an exterior, a backing, a return, whatever? These are questions that the director, probably preoccupied with story and casting, wouldn't think to ask. I'm there to make sure that ground is covered.

Size Up

Part of the job is finding out about someone very fast, reading them correctly the first time. On the street, a man comes charging up to the camera. Have I hurt his house? Is he in need of some kind of emergency help? Is he a local resident and I've made him sore because I've blocked his driveway or made too much noise? You get good at it quickly, or you get hurt by it.

One time, on *The Blues Brothers*, we were on an unfinished freeway bridge in Milwaukee, the one that the Bluesmobile does a back flip on. Our location person had talked to the wrong guy. The right guy hadn't been informed. He was a middle-level bureaucrat named Jack with a heavy Jewish accent. He was sore and wasn't going to let us use the bridge.

Now there weren't a lot of unfinished freeway bridges close to Chicago. This guy's anger had to be figured out and turned around. There just was no satisfactory way to get the sequence without this location.

I saw that this wasn't about money. He was just angry at being ignored.

As everyone was walking away, I said, "Yussel. Where can I get some kosher pastrami?" Yussel is Yiddish for Jack. His face lit up, and we started talking on a more personal level. We were two Jews in a city where there weren't all that many. After a bit, I told him I was sorry we had made a mistake and talked to the wrong guy. I assured him it was an accident and no one meant any disrespect.

He gave us the bridge, and I got a pretty good sandwich that night.

Motivating, Managing, and Deciding

Sometimes you have to motivate by being tough, by pushing a little. I'll see somebody being hesitant. They're afraid they'll get in trouble for doing something without permission. I'll give them permission and force them into moving forward, if that's what it takes.

Sometimes two departments argue, and I have to decide. Effects needs to park its truck in a spot props wants to be in, so I have to make the decision.

Sometimes delegating is the answer. You tell people what you want and get the hell out of the way so they can do it. You give people the room to excel, get involved, and make a contribution. The failure of American management to do this, I might add in a case where no one's asked me, to motivate by passing on responsibility and authority to lower levels in the chain, is part of our country's failures in the workplace.

That's the nice thing about pictures: you can try things and experiment. Senior production management isn't concerned, as long as the work gets done and no one is hurt or abused. We don't have a lot of people standing around telling you how it was done twenty years ago, so if you want to, you're free to try new things.

It's a little like they say in that book *The One-Minute Manager:* Give people goals and objectives, and congratulate them when they meet them; provide constructive advice when they don't.

Crazy Making

What you have to deal with can make you crazy sometimes. Hollywood can collect some bad people: people who lie, cheat, and betray. There aren't that many, but even a few are too many.

After that comes incompetents—people who can't do the work, know they can't do the work, and still present themselves as capable practitioners, regardless of how badly they will screw things up for all the rest of us who are busting our ass.

After that comes the argumentative, pain-in-the-ass, irritable types. I suppose everybody has problems and that's just life in the big city.

Then there are systems that haven't changed in too long. Studios make you use lousy water trucks because they're still on the books as a capital asset and they want the depreciation. It looks good for the accountants, but a bad water truck can kill you in the much greater costs of actual production. That's American management again.

Or you have second-rate craftsmen because a studio won't pay the going rate. Or there'll be another bean counter who loses sight of the project, the good movie we're trying to put into the theaters, the one that will bring millions of dollars into the company if it works. This guy will try to save nickels, forcing us to lose thousands on the set. That'll change your digestive habits in a quick hurry.

Way, way down the line comes the things you can't control: rain, airplanes, sick actors, whatever. Those are acts of God. You get someone started on the problem, if someone can, and put your feet up and relax till it gets fixed.

The Toll

People outside the business have no concept of how hard this work is. Preproduction days are usually ten or eleven hours. Production days, days when you're shooting the picture, are twelve plus driving, plus dailies. The work alternates between backbreaking tedium with little margin for error and spectacular, complicated, and demanding logistical challenges realized in an air of uncertainty and bravura temperament. We get put to bed wet, as the wranglers say. If you don't think you'll love it, go on to something else.

The Meaning of Power

The job's not about power; it's about authority and responsibility. Power is someone else's view of the authority you need to make things happen, unencumbered. It's having the ability to keep noncontributing people, regardless of rank, out of the way.

The job itself is satisfying when done well, for me, at any rate. If you think it's satisfying because you're giving orders, then you're approaching it wrong. You're in it for the wrong reason. You're not getting the director's vision realized: you're getting your ego stroked.

The job is to get the director's vision realized as efficiently and pleasantly as possible without hurting the picture.

Advice

If you really want a career in production because you like it and it suits you, then stick at it. Just keep doing it and don't let them grind you down.

Send letters. Work for people. Sweep up. Do whatever you can do and they'll let you do. Never give them any rest. For about three years you'll be in despair. You'll think you'll never get in, and then one day you'll be where you want to be.

If you give up the first time somebody tells you to get lost, then they've beaten you and you should find something else. The world rewards people who are aggressive and tenacious. You have to be willing to stand up in front of a room full of people and tell them what to do and what you expect and what you will tolerate. You need to be able to know what the hell you are talking about. When you don't, they'll know and the game'll be up. This is a job where experience and whiskers count.

Perceptions

Assistant directors spend a great deal of time dealing with clear-cut logical issues. For the most part we don't deal with subtleties, nuance, creative, nondeterministic issues. We don't have long discussions with executives, writers, or actors.

As a result, there is the erroneous perception that assistant directors can't direct, can't handle creative issues. This notion ignores assistant directors who are unique, who are intelligent or have a personal point of view. If you've got a point of view, then you can bring something to the party. We certainly have the requisite technical understanding.

What this all means is that you have to stop being an assistant director to move forward. The problem is, once you learn how it works, people will pay lots of money to keep you where you are. They need you and want you there. They, of course, see their needs as more important than your own.

Next

I've done a few pictures now, and it's time to move on. It's a noble profession that offers the satisfaction of a hard job done well, certainly.

But I'm writing a screenplay now and have three very powerful treatments besides. I'll direct one of them soon and go on from there. I got into this because I love movies—always have. Now it's time for me to make some of my own.

Second Assistant Director

The Second Assistant Director operates as "the legs" of the directorial category. He or she is responsible to the first assistant director for preparing and distributing the daily paperwork—the call sheet, the production report, and the actors' time sheets—and for issuing, collecting, and correctly accounting for the extras' payment vouchers. He or she sees to it that the cast and crew is in the right place at the right time; maintains a log of the events of each shooting day; selects, positions, and directs the movement of the

extras (also known as "blocking"); and carries out the directives of
the first assistant director.

Victoria Rhodes

VICTORIA RHODES graduated with a film degree from USC.
Unable to secure a position in the film industry, she took a job
teaching algebra to junior high school students, which she claims
"is very good training for handling a film crew." While teaching,
she registered for both the Directors Guild and the Camera Assistant
trainee programs, passed both examinations, and chose to go with
the DGA program. She quit her job to launch into the long-awaited
film career just in time for a Screen Actors Guild strike that shut
down production in Hollywood. Returning to teaching, she waited
for her first break, which finally did happen when she became the
DGA trainee on *Whose Life Is It Anyway?*, then *Blade Runner*.
Since then she has been second assistant director on *The Color
Purple*, *Three Amigos*, *Dragnet* (1987), *Extremities*, *Johnny Be
Good*, *Kansas*, *Blue City*, *Quicksilver*, and *Streets of Fire*, among
many others.

THE "CALL SHEET" is usually about legal size. I write everything on it, and at the end of the day I take that out as my Bible—
with notes on the order of "Camera broke down, 11:52, 20-minute
delay"—and transfer that information to the production report.

Before you wrap, you have to give call sheets out to everybody for
the next day's work, which will tell everyone what time to be there the
next day, what your sequence is . . . Actors, stand-ins who are extras
but considered part of the crew, all the crew, director, cameramen,
everybody gets one.

I'm there way before crew call. The only people who arrive at the
same time I do are the drivers and set dressers. And the drivers stay late
because they always have last-minute runs. We're the first and last
people on the set.

I have to make sure that makeup and hair and wardrobe is all set
up before the actors get there. Then as the actors start walking in,

saying, "Where do I go?" I've got to be there to tell them, "Okay, this is where your dressing room is, this is where makeup is, let me get you some breakfast, you'll be first up."

Fantastic actors will say, "Great, let me put my stuff in my room, I'll be right into makeup." Wonderful actors will sit in their rooms until you get them, and really bad actors will not even be there, you'll have to track them down.

The second AD is primarily responsible for the extras on the set during shooting. But at the beginning of the day you're responsible for everybody who has to be on the set.

The extras will come in after your actors. And it's all supposed to time out so that the crew will come in maybe seven, seven-thirty. They will get a rehearsal where they figure out what they have to do. What I hate is when they want to rehearse with the actors, because I have to take the actors out of the process—makeup or hair or wardrobe—bring them out to rehearse and then get them back into the process.

It's split-second timing. This person is going to be with the makeup guy for fifteen minutes and then will have to get out of the chair because I have to put another person in that chair.

You've got to be on top of it. On my call sheet, which I keep in my pocket, I put a slash mark through their number—each actor has a character number. Then I make it into an X when they're ready to go in front of the camera. I don't write down, "They've been to makeup and they haven't been to hair." That's three different things they have to do before they come in front of the camera. I can't make that many notes. It's too cumbersome to keep taking out your pen and pencil.

I've got to keep prodding some of them. Some people hate to be up in the morning, and they're bitches. Some don't care, they're here to work; some people think that you should come and clean their house, basically have no regard for the second AD.

When the first AD comes in after all this, I let him or her know the status: "This person is ready, this person is almost ready, this person has not arrived yet, we have called, he is late."

You get all the actors in the first scene ready, get them to the set, they have a rehearsal, and then you have about ten minutes to block the background, hopefully. And the extras should have been walked past wardrobe by this time. Usually they never see makeup and hair unless it's a special deal or a period piece. They do their own makeup, they do their own hair, and they usually have their own wardrobe.

Say there's a St. Patrick's Day ball scene. Green is your dominant color. Not everybody has to be in green, but I have to look through the camera to make sure it looks predominantly green, see what the side-lines are, so I know where to hide people—know what's on-camera, what's off-camera. Maybe the scene's a minute, I might like somebody to enter halfway into the scene, so I'd like them to be waiting right off-camera to walk right onto the screen. I have to make sure there's no equipment in the way, no bags, no purses or anything.

And then I start blocking it so that it looks a) busy, b) casual, or c) manic.

Moving Extras

Moving the extras around is the only creative thing that I get to do. It's the only thing I do that gets on-camera. So at this point in my life, I'm very conscientious about expressing my ideas. The only time I wouldn't handle the extras is in a specific situation—the director might want the waitress to walk up and offer an actor a drink at such and such a point. The first AD might take over that one cross because it's important, they want to cue that one particular person as opposed to me, who's cueing thirty, fifty, or a hundred people.

Your extras crowd will differ. I just finished shooting a nonunion show in Texas, where a hundred people in five seconds would clump into this one moving mass instead of spreading out and mingling, which was what the scene called for. It was a party scene. If you didn't give them specific direction, they just stood there, which was under-standable. They had never done this before.

If you're in Hollywood, they're going to be more conscious of where the camera is, and they'll move around with less work on my part. With a large crowd of extras, I'll pair people up or put them in groups of three and four and give them all specific counts, like "Start moving after the count of ten."

And if it's a smaller scene, maybe thirty people, I'll give them stories: "You two were together, you're having a fight about this, and you really hate it that he does this and he really hates it that you do this," and really get them out there because extras tend to be passive. They're used to being the movement in the background, and I don't want that. I want them to look real.

The director sometimes gets upset, he says, "Listen, they're the crowd, they're not the actors," and that's right, but I found that the more experienced the director is, the more he likes it. It gives the film more life, more vitality.

As soon as the director says, "Cut, print, new deal," I'm preparing the actors for the next shot, and I go back to herding them into makeup.

And bear in mind, six hours after somebody gets to work, they have to eat. If I bring an actor in seven hours before we're going to break for lunch, I have to give them breakfast. If I don't know that, then I can be incurring $25 meal penalties per person every half hour.

Then I have to know that this guy is not going to be needed in this next scene, I can break him early, or I can break these twelve people early to lunch and then they can come back earlier, so that when we come back and turn on the lights, they will already have been touched up through makeup and ready to go.

Production Report

I have to have an understanding of the contracts. If they say, "Hey, we cannot finish this actor in six days," I have to go through my paperwork and look up their deal. How much is it going to cost us for them to go over a day, is it better for us to go into overtime to finish this actor today or to just come back tomorrow?

At the end of the day, the script supervisor will give you a script report that notes when we started, the first shot, time and duration of lunch, the first shot after lunch, time we wrapped, the pages we took credit for, the seconds and minutes we took credit for, the scene number we finished on.

I have to go through and make sure that in their haste to leave they didn't add up seventy seconds on something instead of a minute and ten; that they didn't count a scene as having credit taken, when it was only partially completed, like "71 part" means there's another part we have to film before we can take credit for that scene.

And at any point somebody can ask you things like "The musicians we brought in, did they ever play, or did they just pretend to play?" because they get more money for the amount of time that they're actually playing than if they're pretending to play. I have to know when they actually started playing and when they finished and record, "They played for half an hour."

I do all that at night on the production report. Then the next day, after I come in, as soon as the crew comes in, I say, "Tomorrow we're going to be outside doing a night shot," and the grips will say, "We'll need two Condors to put the lights up," and electric will say, "We need three more electricians," so that I can put that information on it.

In the office, the production manager is the head. On the set, it's the director. And sometimes the two don't see eye to eye. So I have to figure, "Where am I sitting at the moment?"

I talk to the production manager directly. The first AD stays on the set all the time, so I'm the only one who can really leave the set. I'm the one to go to the production manager and say, "Listen, I talked to electrical and they said we need three more electricians for tomorrow night's work," and he'll say, "Well, do they need to come in right away to prerig, or can they come in later on?"

And I'll go back and say, "Can they come in later on?" Run back and forth.

Toward the end of the day, I fill in the rest of the call sheet, have it photocopied, take one, give my first AD one, and hide the rest. I don't give them to the actors until the actors sign out. I've got to be at the door, know whom I gave them to and whom I didn't.

The actors' times are more likely to change than the crew call. If they get a call sheet at five, and then I give them a completely new one when they wrap, most likely they will lose the second one and come in at the wrong time and be mad about it.

Some actors are mentally only thirteen years old, and when you say, "It's time for you to go home," they run out the door. I've had to literally stand between them and the door and say, "Yo, this is your call sheet," or run out and put it on their cars if I know where their cars are. Or put the call sheet in three different places—in their briefcase, their trailer, and in their hand.

Then I start thinking, it's the end of the day, whom are we not going to need? Because why have people sit around? Maybe if we're only doing two actors, some of the makeup and hair people can go home.

I start dismissing people. I say, "Okay, what shots do we have left?" and they say, "We're going to see this way and we're going to see that way." So I say, "Everybody on this side of the room for extras I can dismiss."

At the end of the day, after signing out the actors, I collect the vouchers of the extras, which has what time they started, what time they had lunch, how long it was, what time they finished. If they brought something that was extra—an evening gown or a skateboard or their own car, whatever—that's extra money. I record all of that on the production report.

I have to get the script supervisor's report, the camera reports for how much film we put in the camera, how much film we printed, how much film was a take but we didn't like it, how much was waste, and keep a running total of all that. Ask sound how many sound rolls we did and keep a total of that. It all goes on the production report.

And then, after that it's the unusual: "So-and-so drove a nail through their hand and went to the doctor." Or we had an elephant today with four trainers; we had minors, so we had a welfare worker.

You are in charge of the production file, you keep a whole set of these production reports at home or in your office or on the set.

I give copies of the production report to a driver, who will take it and put it on the desk of the production coordinator, or if I am close, I will do it. But it has to go into the office that day. And the production coordinator will then get the production report to the people who need to see it, like the producer and the director. The director doesn't want it, usually.

The production manager does want it, and then executives, so they can see how you're doing, how many pages . . . and ask, "How could you work twelve hours and only get six-eighths of a page?" And you say, "Yeah, but in six-eighths of a page the Indians come over the hill and kill Custer."

Or if we're behind schedule and over budget, then you keep track: "Okay, officially we are one day behind," or "We're two days behind," or "We're half a day ahead." And then what day of the production we're up to. "This is the twentieth day of forty-six days."

The Color Purple

It was really hard—long hours, lots of stuff happening all the time. But we had a great cast. Even if they weren't working, they would come out to the set, be there for the other members—Danny Glover and Rae Dawn Chong and Adolph Caesar.

There wasn't any tension among the crew members (the crew was about half black), the tension was with some of the people in North Carolina. My good friend was Whoopi's stand-in. And we started hanging out with the electricians, most of whom were white. So we would go out to a restaurant, and people would whisper, "My God. You see that black girl with a white man?"

And the guys would just eat it up. They would turn and say, "Well, I'm going to have an orange juice, honey, what would you like?" and I'd say, "Well, I don't know," and the people'd just stare, slack-jawed.

Here they expected Steven Spielberg, and this black guy [the first assistant director] and this black girl seemed to be running the crew. And they're saying, "How can that be? I don't understand."

Not only are you using their houses, but you're using them as extras. And I'm telling them what to do, and they have to listen to me.

We were doing a scene in the town where Sophia has just punched out the mayor. Oprah Winfrey's just decked the mayor. I placed a circle of white townsfolks around her, yelling and screaming. Then I put all of the black people standing back a bit and told them, "There's an invisible wall, you cannot go further, you cannot go help her, you just have to watch."

Then I went back to the first white group who were all in a circle and said, "You're really mad, she has knocked out the mayor of your town, and who does she think she is?" and a guy kind of raised his hand and dropped it and raised it again, and he said, "Excuse me, but would it be appropriate to say racial things?"

It was like he knew better than to start screaming out "Nigger!" when I was standing right there.

I'm sure that in his lifetime he's never had to ask permission. He would have just said it. But the way he did it—it was like he respected my position, he knew what I was asking for, but he didn't want to take that extra step without running it by me.

It made me feel good that he would have the courtesy to ask instead of just doing it. And then when he got the permission, he said, "We can say . . ." and I said, "Don't go overboard," and he said, "Oh, no, I understand, I understand."

Woman on the Set

You get mad, even if it's somebody like a boss, like the director. I'm a firm believer that as long as everyone can walk, then they can go to the catering truck and get their own lunch. And one day at lunch the director on this show's just standing there, looking around. And he says, "Well, I'm going to talk over this scene, somebody should get me some lunch."

And I just turned and looked at him, because I was the only one close to him. And I said, "I beg your pardon?" And he says, "Well, I don't want to stand in that long line."

And I said, "Sir, we have kept the extras back until the crew gets in the line, so if you go now, you will not have to wait."

I was not about to go and get him lunch, because as far as I know, I wasn't wearing an apron, and he was not paying me for that.

He's a first-time director who was in the industry in another capacity, so he thinks he really knows what's going on. Only in my mind I see someone who has never taken into account simple facts of set life and shooting—the sun's going down, or it's starting to rain, and we have to get in the next shot, those second-to-second decisions that have to be made.

So there were plenty of times when I had a lot more experience than he did.

It's hard to get over the ego and the fragility of first-time directors. They're out to prove that they can do it and that they're in charge. They don't have the security to say, "Look, I know you're doing your job," and be open to suggestions.

Training to be authoritative can hold you in good stead. There aren't too many women assistant directors. If you put your foot down for anything, you immediately become a bitch. If you are a guy and you put your foot down, then you're just being strong. It's an automatic thing.

Something I discovered in teaching—when a male teacher yells, he has this baritone voice that rumbles through the room.

When a woman yells, it's this soprano, and she sounds like she's losing her mind. "Ahhhhhh [screams], I said sit down!!"

So I lower my voice when I yell. I don't have a high voice anyway, but I have a very strong voice, and when I'm yelling, "Rolling," or, "Be quiet!" or something, I will lower my voice so that I will sound authoritative instead of crazy.

Goals

I really want to direct. I have great stories I want to get across. And what I'd like to do is make my statement in the casting.

For example, in Walter Hill's *Streets of Fire*, Amy Madigan's part was originally written for a Hispanic man. And then she came in and read for the part, and they changed the name but didn't change the part. It was great because she's tough, she's not a sap. They didn't suddenly give her doilies to be making or say, "Now it's a girl, so maybe she should be cooking."

And in *Alien*—there was supposed to be seven guys. And then they made two of them women and didn't change the dialogue and had one of the women survive to the end, which was really unusual for a movie. Usually she would be the first thing to go, right? She should walk up and say, "Oh, a monster, oh! . . ." and then die.

Or in *An Officer and a Gentleman* with Lou Gossett, Jr.'s part. The character was actually conceived as a white man and became a black, and that worked beautifully.

Progress

The natural progression is trainee or PA to second AD, first AD, production manager, producer. So it's going to be harder, but not impossible, for me to go to director. I'm supposed to tell them, "Let's release these twenty extras because they're costing us too much money," or, "You can't have that light because you can do it cheaper with these other lights." So it's more in the vein of producing.

And when it comes to being an assistant director, I have such a knowledge of my craft and getting the production work done that it's never questioned, "Why don't you hire a second AD in Texas instead of one from Los Angeles?" They'll hire me.

It's been good for me to learn a position of authority to 90 percent of the crew. And it's given me the confidence to know I can do it and to watch other people's mistakes.

Authority is important in directing. In Japan it's a natural progression from assistant director to director because they want you to have that background, so that you can just walk in and say, "I know what I need." Then you can let loose with that creative part of you that was confined to doing the extras.

Transportation Coordinator

The Transportation Coordinator is responsible for the selection, functioning, and maintenance of all vehicles used in a motion picture. He or she determines the number and types of vehicles needed to transport cast, crew, and equipment and finds and acquires all picture cars (cars that will be shot on film). The Transportation Coordinator hires the transportation captain(s), hires or oversees the hiring of the drivers, assigns vehicles and routes, and sees to it that all vehicles are properly equipped, operationally safe, fueled, and ready to roll.

Dan Marrow

DAN MARROW was working as a manufacturer's rep when his brother, a teamster, showed Dan a paycheck. Comparing it with his own, Dan decided to turn in all his suits and learn how to drive trucks. He started driving for Paramount Studios, eventually becoming a transportation co-captain with his brother on *Flashdance*. Since then Dan has been placed in charge of transportation on such films as *Terms of Endearment, Explorers, Ferris Bueller's Day Off, Top Gun, Some Kind of Wonderful, She's Having a Baby, Planes, Trains, & Automobiles*, and *Big Business*, among many others.

THE TRANSPORTATION coordinator interacts with every department, from the guy who sweeps up the floor to the producers and the directors and the stars, and he has to get along with everybody. You don't move up the ladder just because you know how to drive trucks.

What to Look for in a Driver

You're looking for someone who is conscientious, punctual, and who, no matter what he's driving, takes good care of his equipment and makes sure it's always in good running order. Though he doesn't need to be a mechanic, he should be familiar with automobile repair. There are a lot of vehicles that might need work.

You want to avoid breakdowns and anticipate problems because any time you hold up the company, it costs a lot. If a car breaks down or has a flat, it doesn't matter whose fault it is. It's holding up the company.

Normally, on a big production, they're going to spend maybe $80,000 a day. So if you blow an hour because the camera truck broke down on the way to location, you're talking some big bucks. Or even if a driver is late picking up the star—that's fifteen minutes that costs dollars and cents, not to mention ill will generated in the star.

A coordinator wants his drivers to be like his shadow. Anytime I need a driver, all I have to do is turn around and one's standing right behind me, and I say, "Go move that truck," "Go take care of that picture car," or, "Quick, he needs a ride to go shopping." They've got to be right there and ready to move at a moment's notice.

You want guys who can think for themselves and who'll cover everything when you are not on the set because you're out taking care of something else.

And when you're out shooting exterior locations, it's important that you always have teamsters by the camera, because the camera crew may need to turn the camera, and trucks are going to be in the way and have to be moved.

Hierarchy

The transportation coordinator answers to the production manager and the producer. Below him is the captain, who serves as the coordinator's assistant. Then when you're on a major lot, you also have to hire a captain from the seniority drivers. For instance, on this show [Disney's *Big Business*], I didn't hire my own outside captain. I hired somebody from Disney who has seniority to be my captain.

There are occasions on shows, if it's a big show with a lot of picture cars or two or three units, when you might have two captains or a captain and a picture car captain—the picture car captain would exclusively assist you in handling picture cars while your other captain runs the set for you.

Picture Cars

A picture car is any vehicle that actually appears on-screen in the picture.

In *Big Business*, for instance, the opening scene is a period shot. It's supposed to be 1948 in West Virginia in the Appalachians, and these two couples are going to the same hospital to have babies, and one is rich and one is poor. So the rich people are in a 1947 Cadillac limousine, and the poor folk are in a 1937 International pickup truck.

And then you've got the background cars that are on the street and drive by for two seconds. You don't even know what they are, but they still have to be in the right period with the right look.

Normally you rent them from the studio or from guys out there who own old cars, unusual cars, and do a lot of business renting not only to movies, but for commercials or print ads.

Number of Drivers

If you're shooting on a sound stage, you only need a few drivers to run errands, pick up equipment, pick up the cleaning in the morning, deliver the film at night.

During the day, wardrobe has runs, everybody's got little messenger runs, so you've got maybe three to six guys driving around in station wagons and little minivans or pickup trucks.

Throughout the show, you'll have a couple of guys who work with the set dressers, one of them usually driving a truck to haul the furniture and heavier items and another driver in a station wagon or pickup truck to take the set decorator shopping.

You also will have at least one truck for your construction crew because they're either building a set or tearing it down or going out on some location to paint.

Driving crews can be as small as eight to ten guys on-stage or as large as twenty to thirty on distant locations between the local drivers you hire there and the drivers you hire in Los Angeles.

Planes, Trains & Automobiles

On *Planes, Trains & Automobiles* we were traveling all across the country—we went to Buffalo, New York City, Chicago, St. Louis, the second unit went to Cleveland for a few days; we were all over the place. At one point I had, between the Los Angeles drivers, Chicago teamsters, and Buffalo teamsters, over forty drivers.

It's a comedy starring John Candy and Steve Martin, about these two guys who are trying to travel home for Thanksgiving and their plane gets sent to another airport because O'Hare's snowed in.

We were supposed to be in Chicago for three weeks and then come back, but we wound up being out of town for three months. There were last-minute changes all the time, we were chasing the weather, looking for snowy highways. Chicago had an unusually warm winter, the snow melted before they could get their filming in. We sent a scouting party out to Buffalo—"Yeah, there's good snow here. . . ." We get to Buffalo, the snow starts melting, so we moved to Batavia, thirty miles east of Buffalo.

That was the biggest challenge—moving a company of sixty to eighty people and all of the equipment and going into different jurisdictions, working with different unions, and hiring different drivers.

When you hire through local chapters of a union, every area has its own jurisdiction. They've got their own qualified drivers, but they don't always understand how the movie business works because they're used to delivering milk, so it takes quite a bit of training to break them in.

The hardest thing about going out of town is locating properly equipped vehicles because there are specific types of equipment that movie crews use.

You don't get them just a pickup truck. They need a crew cab, which is a one-ton pickup with two rows of seats, two sets of doors, and a lumber rack on it, and you go to St. Louis and it's hard to find them. Or you need motor homes for your stars and, of course, the picture cars.

We had this one car that Martin and Candy supposedly get in St. Louis—a rental car that they crash and it catches fire—so I had six of the same car in various stages of disrepair. Two beauty cars were in perfect shape. They looked like they had just come off the rental yard. Then there were two cars that were involved in the stunt; the car's going the wrong way down the highway and two semis sort of shave the sides off the car. And then I had two burned-up cars for after the car catches fire and burns up.

In the script, the car always runs. So I had six matching cars and kept them running and looking right, moving them around the country. And then I had rental car buses, twenty-year-old Greyhound buses, more picture cars, and on and on, very difficult, and they all had to be acquired under a great deal of time pressure.

Types of Vehicles Used

I'm in charge of all vehicles. The honeywagons, the trucks, cars, station wagons, vans.

If a shooting company is going out of town, a coordinator will generally go there weeks in advance to locate equipment, to meet with the unions, and to hire drivers and locate picture cars. Sometimes it's cheaper to find things locally than it is to ship them all the way from Los Angeles.

Among the vehicles we always need:

The Camera Truck. Generally, a five-ton truck that has a box that's about twenty-four to twenty-six feet long. It's completely shelved on the inside to carry all the camera cases. It doesn't just haul things, crew members actually *work* inside the truck.

It's got a dark room that has a light inside, usually a twelve-volt light and a 110 light because you'll normally plug the truck into an outside electrical. If you're in the middle of nowhere, you have twelve-volt lights that work off batteries. And a fan. Sound equipment also goes on-board.

The Production Van. A semitractor and trailer, this one is shelved to carry all the lights and grip equipment and lumber, and it's towed by a tractor that normally has two 750-amp AC/DC generators to provide electricity.

The Wardrobe Trailer. Either a twenty-six- to twenty-eight-foot trailer towed behind a pickup truck or a big semitrailer. It's always doubled-racked for clothing. It'll have an ironing board and irons, and sometimes they have washing machines and dryers inside.

The Makeup Trailer. This one has counters, mirrors, makeup lights, hot and cold running water, a basin to wash hair, and space for the makeup and hair people to store all their curling irons, hair dryers, and other articles. Usually the trailer will come with its own generator to provide the electricity to run all this.

The Prop Truck. Houses all the props and special effects, the stand-by painter's box, the craft services guy's trash cans and brooms. It almost always has a Coca-Cola cooler to keep sodas and candy bars and gum and things for the crew.

Then you've got the Motor Homes and Dressing Trailers for your big movie stars.

On this picture [*Big Business*] we've got two very big stars, Bette Midler and Lily Tomlin. They have what are called "fifth-wheel" trailers—huge trailers towed by pickup trucks containing a full kitchen, queen-size bed to lie down on, a living room, TV, VCR, and a makeup area.

Bette does all her own makeup and hair in her trailer, as opposed to Lily, who has her makeup done in the makeup trailer. But Lily still needs her own trailer to eat her lunch in and to rest between shots or take meetings, work on scenes, and the like.

There is also the honeywagon, usually a long truck with a long trailer that has seven or eight rooms with bathrooms and air conditioners.

The big stars normally aren't in the honeywagon because they've got their own motor home or fifth-wheel trailer, but everybody else goes into the honeywagon, so you've got a teamster on that and he cleans the johns all day.

Finally, you've got messenger cars, normally station wagons, full-size, or fifteen-passenger maxivans, which can double to shuttle the crew from a parking lot that is two miles down the road from the shooting site.

Breakdown

In preproduction I will get my script and I'll break it down for picture cars—background cars, cars involved in stunts, and cars used by the principal players.

In *Ferris Bueller's Day Off*, for instance, the mother had her car, the father had his, Ferris's sister had hers, you know, everybody had a car. You go over all that with the director and the production designer: "Well, what kind of car would this person drive?" and "Yeah, she's got the family wagon and he's got the nice sporty car," and so on.

You also deal with the production manager on making the best deals: Do you want to rent the car for two weeks because we only need it for two weeks in the middle of the schedule? Is it going to work in the first week, in the fifth week, in the last week? Do we need to make a rental deal for the run of the picture? If we need it for the whole picture, is it cheaper to buy the car and then sell it when the show's over rather than paying for rental?

On *Planes, Trains & Automobiles*, I bought eight or nine cars, six of them being the same cars. I spent maybe $25,000 just in parts for these cars.

They have a set schedule for every single day of the shoot, and I know in advance what is going to work where—"Day 48, Friday, interior limousine," for instance.

Workaholism

It's very difficult to make the kind of money that we make anywhere else. And it's the kind of business that allows you to take time off if you want to. You could work like the devil for nine months a year and make enough money to live the next three or six months without having to worry about your income.

So most guys don't work year round. Now, I'm sort of a workaholic, and I've been working year round for years now, but that's with the idea that I'm not going to be in this business forever. I'm hoping by the time I'm forty-five that I've made enough money, I'll do one show a year, work four months a year, and maybe branch off into something else.

I want to retire and play golf. Too many times you hear about guys who work in this business for years and years, and they finally retire at sixty-two, and six months later they die.

I don't want that to happen to me.

The job ages you prematurely, especially if you're successful and get caught up in working the hours and doing show after show. You finish a show and you're beat, but somebody calls up and says, "Come work for me for another six months and make good money," and it's hard to say no because you never know. You say no one time and they may never come back and offer you another job.

Location Manager

The Location Manager researches, scouts, and selects the locations for a motion picture production. He or she prepares a location breakdown, sets up relationships with the film commissions, fire, police, state, and highway authorities, and arranges for necessary licenses, road permits, security, and site rentals. During preproduction, the Location Manager works closely

301

with the production designer and the director to determine the type of locale they are seeking and thereafter with the transportation captain and assistant directors to ensure that filming takes place safely and legally. He or she is also responsible for properly "closing out" a location—namely, ensuring that any inconvenienced parties have been compensated and that relations with the state, police and highway authorities, film and housing commissions, and the general population are intact.

Ron Quigley

RON QUIGLEY won an assistantship at Screen Gems (now Columbia Pictures) while studying theater arts at UCLA in the mid-1960s and, after graduation, was offered a job there, which he couldn't accept because of the draft. After 3½ years in the Supply Corps of the U.S. Navy, he hotfooted it back to Los Angeles and found employment with a "far-flung division of Columbia called Audience Studies." Not satisfied, he sent his résumé out to thirty or forty heads of film companies and landed a prime job as an assistant to the president of a film company, but unfortunately the company folded after he'd been there 2½ years. Ron had been sitting out of the business for a year, surviving on $25,000 he had won on a game show, when he got a call from a friend who had become an independent producer. He needed an assistant. Ron came on as location manager—the only blank left on the budget form. Among other tasks, he was assigned the job of driving the art director—who hated to drive—around Los Angeles to scout locations. When this art director was replaced, Ron was the only one who knew what the locations were. He stopped being the overall assistant to the producer and wound up "up to my ears in locations," not really knowing what a location manager did. He learned *fast* and has since been location manager on numerous films, including *Black Sunday, The Brink's Job, The Formula, Pennies from Heaven, Big Business,* and *Big Shots.*

I T STARTS, as John Huston might have said, with the script. You get the script, and having read it once or twice, you sit down with the producer, director, and production designer.

The location manager is getting direction from the other side of the table—the producer, director, production designer. "The character is such that he wouldn't have a high-tech house," or, "He would live in a suburban, middle-class house"—they're trading ideas back and forth.

The location manager will say, "I think we can find that look in Oregon," or, "That's a style you'll find in Florida."

You do a lot of research. Plus, the best location managers have been around. I've driven across country probably ten times and have a very good visual memory for landscapes and locales. I've run into some people who could drive through the Grand Canyon and remember what was on the radio but not have any recollection of what the Grand Canyon looked like.

I have folders and boxes of pictures, travel brochures, and . . . thank God for film commissions. My favorite is Arizona, they do it all for you. You don't have to ask them questions like "What does it take to get a road permit in this part of the state?" or "Can I film on the interstate?" They volunteer the information because they know what's involved in making a movie. In some states you almost have to drag the information out of them.

You make a list of locations you need to find that makes sense to you. The step after that is to try to find the places, and in that sense the location manager is working very much in the production designer's area.

I take pictures. I tend to shoot like crazy, possibly twenty or thirty rolls of thirty-six exposure film on an initial scout. On *Pennies from Heaven*, I had 150 rolls of film taken.

When you're inexperienced, you tend to take your direction from the wrong people. I've had the situation where the producer was telling me the character should live in a Spanish house, red tile and white walls and the whole thing. And I went out for four days and came back with stacks of pictures of Spanish houses.

The director wanted Early American. And it is very unnerving when you come back with your pictures and they start going through and throwing things out, particularly when the photos you show them first are the ones you think are going to be the best.

In *The Formula*, George C. Scott is a cop investigating a couple of murders, and Marlon Brando is an oil magnate. In the script, the two giants meet for the first time in a Texas-style oil field with the derricks and the pumps going. You're at ground level and there's a lot of geometric forms with the open work of the derricks casting shadows.

I took the director and producer, who was also the writer, and showed them an oil field in Long Beach with all the derricks. It was just as described in the writing. They were overjoyed because they hadn't known that kind of thing existed in Los Angeles.

And I did something that I rarely do, because generally if you've sold something, you leave well enough alone and say, "This will be it, now I'll go and find the next location."

I said, "You know, this is really great, but there's another place that's a totally different concept, way off the wall; it's not dirty, it's clean." And it's a place I've always loved. Up north of Los Angeles on a hill, there's a single oil pump, the rocking horse–type thing.

I took them up there and it was a gorgeous day and this thing just sits up on top of the hill. They flipped over it, to the point where they rewrote the script, for which they needed approval from Marlon Brando. And Brando, looking at all of this land, threw in a statement about abuse of land.

That's probably the most creativity that a location manager can hope for. To say that creatively I came up with something that wasn't in anybody else's mind and it worked perfectly—that, I think, is the most satisfying thing that you could ever hope for.

Indecision

There are people in the film business, in positions of power, who find it difficult to make decisions. They'll say, "Well, I'm not sure."

You show them a place as written and they say, "Well, maybe that's not it." Meanwhile . . . mentally your clock is ticking because you know that it's the nature of the film business that they're not going to keep the cameras from rolling until all of the locations are set. The cameras are going to roll on the first of the month, and come hell or high water, you'd better have all of the locations. In your mind, you're thinking, I don't have that time, and nobody's going to give me time.

What happens, too, is—say, in the script they're walking down a city street and go into an old-style dry cleaners in the middle of the city. And you find the perfect place, here's a city street, there's the dry cleaners and a deli over there that they just came out of in the script. And the director looks and says, "Gee, yeah, but maybe they go to a gas station instead."

There comes a point where you realize life is too short. Early on in one's career, you try to please everybody. And the only way to do that is by working lots of weekends on your own.

Later on, you get to the point where if you have done everything right, and have found something that works, and it is somebody else's indecision that's creating the problem, don't hesitate to say, "I don't think that exists, I think this is it."

I remember we were scouting in Chicago on *Pennies from Heaven*. And I had been there for probably three or four weeks because there's a small town called Galena, Illinois, that hasn't changed much in at least fifty years, a great little town. And we were doing a 1930s period film, so this was going to work. Plus we had a lot of Chicago to do, and at that time we were planning to do a great deal on real locations. I had covered the area pretty well. The production group— which was Herb Ross, the director, and the two producers and the production manager and the production designer—all come into town, and we get into a van and start driving around Chicago.

Now Herbert knew Chicago very well but hadn't been back in years, and what had happened in the interim, in the name of urban renewal, was the bulldozing of a lot of areas. You would drive through, and instead of an abandoned building, it was now a half square block of vacant area. Herbert kept looking and saying, "It reminds me of pictures of Berlin. This isn't the Chicago that I know."

This went on all day. We get back to the hotel and get out of the van. As we step out onto the sidewalk, Herbert turns to me and says, "How well do you know New York City?" And I said to Herb, "I grew up there, but . . ." He said, "I think we'll have to shoot parts of Brooklyn and have them work for Chicago in the script." And the mouths all fell open, because everything had been aimed toward Chicago.

I was thinking, My God, if I now have to get on a plane and fly to New York and scout and try to make all of this work in Brooklyn, it's going to take me forever. I *was* on that picture forever.

Luckily we went to dinner, and one after another of the people got Herbert's ear, and by the end of the evening it was, "Well, let's go out again, we can probably make this work."

The Perfect Location

I don't think the perfect location exists. You may think you've found the "perfect" location, but if that location isn't easy to get to, doesn't have a lot of room for the trucks, isn't near something else . . . then it's not a good location. If you can park and it's near everything that you have to shoot, it's not going to be the perfect look.

There are two lines I hear with some regularity. The production designer might say one of these to you: "I'll never make another movie without you." Of course, the transportation captain hated the inconvenience you caused him. Or if you and the transportation captain have a good rapport, he understands what the problems are. Then the departments—the grips give him a hassle because they had to load and unload a pickup truck twice.

That other line is, "Who picked this location?" You get the grief. You can't be sensitive. And you can't be obstinate because a lot of the job is PR. When the neighbor across the street, or the road inspector, whoever, doesn't like you—comes out threatening all kinds of things—you're the one who has to calm them down.

Once in a while you have to dole out the money. I just had a situation where the guy was going to have us shut down, and it turned out legally he had the right to and literally was looking for $500. So we paid him off.

Road inspectors are notorious; I don't know why, must be something that they learn in road inspector school for saying, "I'm going to shut you down."

For a location manager, that phrase just sends chills up your back, because if the company gets shut down because of a location problem, it costs a fortune. So it's up to the location manager to find out what the problem is with the road inspector. They want you to know that they're the boss. Although they don't put the road in, it's always—and I have heard this expression all over the country—"It's my road."

Symbiosis

Once for MGM I was asked to find a place where they could build a fort because there are no existing closed-wall forts without going to somewhere in east Texas, where they didn't want to go.

I spent two weeks north of Phoenix parking my car and walking over hills to find an area where you didn't see the road, didn't see any power lines, didn't see houses, and it was 114 degrees. And I was saying, "What am I doing? Why aren't I taking a vacation? Why am I out here in the middle of nowhere doing this?" And, being a kid who grew up in New York, "How do I make sure that I can find my way back to the car so that they don't, a week from now, find a pile of bones out in the desert?"

What we ended up doing was going to old Tucson and doing up their Mexican square like a fort. It still exists. There was a semien-closed area with a Spanish church you've probably seen on the air a million times because people are always shooting at old Tucson. It was built for a picture back in the 1940s, and it's still one of the best streets around. So we just built up the walls some more, it cost probably $250,000, and we put a gate on one end.

Then the show fell apart at the last minute, and I went to people at old Tucson and said, "Well, they pulled the plug and we're all going home, so you can have the fort." They said, "Not so fast. We're not sure we need a fort." I said, "But you now have the only enclosed fort other than east Texas," and they said, "Well, we've been doing very well with a Mexican square, we may want you to just tear the whole thing down," which would have cost us another $75,000.

"Or," they said, "you can finish off the back side," which we were never going to see and therefore was never built and was wide open. So we thought about that and we finished off the back side for about $30,000—chicken wire and the whole thing—and it is still there, and I'm sure that they've rented it a million times, as a fort.

It's a perfect case of a symbiosis that works, and that's the way it should be. That's the whole nature of location managing. It's that everybody should make some money at it. I use somebody's business and he gets a rental fee and I get a place that I couldn't afford to build.

It doesn't always work out that well. I've had cases where people will say, "Gee, because you were on the street and my business is right down the street, nobody came because you were there, and I rented you half of my parking lot and I lost a whole bunch of money." I had paid a hot-dog vendor a couple of hundred dollars. And I found out later that with the sight-seers, this guy went through his entire stock in one day because he didn't have enough for all the people who were standing watching us make the movie.

Budget

For the most part you make up your own budget, you tell them how much it's going to cost. They may then, if they think you're way out of line, ask you to trim your budget. But a lot of the costs are not flexible; you want a Bel Air mansion, you're going to pay $5,000 a day for it. You don't get $500 Bel Air mansions.

Closing Out

On a feature, the ideal is to do all your locations first. Do your out-of-town stuff first. Then come into town and shoot local locations, then go on-stage. Now, once the company gets on-stage, the location manager's job is pretty much over. At that point you get some wrap time to clean up the details. You make sure that everyone's been paid who was supposed to be paid, that the files are in order, so if someone wants to go out six months from now and do some retakes, there is an accurate file and they don't have to come searching you out.

Another large aspect is that we represent the film business. And I don't care whether you're in Los Angeles or Santa Fe, New Mexico, wherever. People tend to lump "the business" all together. I've always wanted to leave an area knowing that the next guy can shoot after me. Purely in terms of self-interest, you may have to come back for retakes. God forbid that you can't get back into the same place because you've left someone angry or unsatisfied. You can pay the person off, but if they say, "That damn film company, I don't care that the guy gave me $500. He blocked my driveway and the trash collector couldn't get in today and my wife was all over me," then that doesn't help.

Of course, there are some people you can never satisfy. I've had to finally say to someone, "There's nothing I can do about it, and legally I'm within my rights, and sorry." But you try not to have that happen too often.

Prospects

There are a couple of ways to go from location managing. It can be a great stepping-stone. You can get the on-set experience and work in to becoming a second assistant director, get a DGA card, and then work up to first AD to production manager.

The other way to go is to work your way into producing. The idea is you get close to a producer or a director, but more likely a producer, and possibly get a job on a future project as an associate producer. People will negotiate that, saying, "I'll be your location manager, but I also want to do more, so call me location manager/associate producer."

If You Can Sell Bibles Door to Door . . .

The best thing that can be said about a location manager is, "He can get whatever you need." And I think if you come across as having an uneven or sour disposition, people won't believe that you can. Being a good salesman helps. I worked my way through college for a while selling Bibles door to door. And I figured if I could sell Bibles door to door, I could do anything.

The person who tends to become very emotional would not be a good location manager. And there are location managers I wouldn't want to spend more time than I had to with, but they are also the kind of people who portray a very serene exterior—and go home and kick the dog and probably scream at other location managers.

Early on in my career, I found myself getting caught up in the panic of "Everything has to be done now," and during shooting there's nothing that comes up for a location manager that is not "I need an immediate response." I kept scurrying around until I finally realized 90 percent of the time when somebody says, "I need this right away," if you don't run and do it, and you wait for the second time—when they really need it—you're better off. Half the time you run off, you neglect something else, and by the time you get back with whatever it is, "Oh, well, no, we've decided to do it some other way."

I also realized that when I was letting myself get a little hyper, I was driving other people to get even more hyper, and that wasn't helping anything. Since then I try to keep a very calm demeanor on the set.

I know two location managers who have exactly the kind of patience the job requires. They are former priests.

Caterer

The Caterer is responsible to the producer and the production manager for providing all the meals for the cast and crew on a motion picture production. He or she is charged with preparing diverse foods of high quality, delivering the food in a timely fashion and at the convenience of the film company's shooting schedule, keeping food costs within the budgetary constraints of the picture, and following union guidelines for preparation and cleanliness. The catering crew works closely with the second assistant director to determine when the company will break for meals and with the transportation coordinator to determine how and when the catering truck will be accommodated at each site.

Steve Michaelson

STEVE MICHAELSON never wanted to be a caterer. His first job at twelve years old was washing pots and pans for his father, who founded Michaelson Food Service in 1958 and instituted the fully equipped catering truck now used in the film industry (previously it had been box lunches or thermoses brought out to location), building his company up from two trucks to twenty. When Steve Michaelson, Sr., died, Steve had a master's degree in public health and was in a doctoral program in preventive medicine, but he felt he owed it to the memory of his father to try to maintain the success and uphold the reputation of the family business. He took a leave of absence from his studies. And, discovering that he loved the motion picture catering business, he never returned. Today Michaelson Food Service, Inc., is one of the most successful catering companies in Hollywood and has serviced many motion pictures, including *The Blues Brothers, The Bounty, The Sicilian, The Morning After, S.O.B., On Golden Pond, Witness, Scarface, Taps, All the Right Moves, The Mosquito Coast, Melvin and Howard, Moon over Parador,* and *Rain Man.*

T HE PRODUCTION company is concerned with two things— one, the quality of the food and an appropriate menu so that there's no grievance, and two, feeding them fast because they've only got half an hour for lunch. So we have to feed any size crew for no more than ten minutes. If you've got fifty people or a thousand people, they still have to be fed in no more than ten minutes. And we can do that, it all depends on the type of menu we have and how many serving lines we got; that's the whole key. If they have a thousand people, I'll have eight to ten serving lines so that only eighty people are going through each line, and I can feed everybody in ten minutes.

The "Chuckwagons"

We have two types of trucks that are equipped for all the food storage and preparation: the step van, which is the older style, and the kitchen trailer, which is pulled by a tractor.

Each one of these trucks has three full ovens, a big grill top, about eight to twelve burners, and a fifty-gallon coffee maker—except in England, where they have boilers so you can have 120 gallons of hot water because they drink a lot of tea.

We have full refrigeration—freezers, dry storage space, hand wash area, and sinks. In the step van, which is a twenty-six-foot box trailer, there are tables and chairs and room for some of the dry goods. In the forty-foot kitchen trailer, which is pulled by a tractor, we have a compartment for the tables and chairs. It's a more comprehensive, self-contained unit.

We take along everything when we go out to a location. We provide the seating, the utensils, the food, the umbrellas, everything, so we can pick up and go to the middle of the Mohave Desert.

Getting a Bid

I have a general manager who handles the everyday nuts and bolts of our business, like the trucks breaking down and checking on distant locations. I have an executive chef who does all the buying. That frees me up to be a PR man.

I have a list of all the heads of production of the major studios, which I go through every single week, calling to find out what's coming up.

The minute a show starts up nowadays, you get the driver captain saying he wants this caterer, you get the cameraman and his crew wanting another caterer, you get the director wanting a different caterer. So if I don't put in a bid immediately and we're not one of those that have been requested, we're never even going to have a chance.

There's two different ways of offering a bid. The first way and the most traditional: I'll give them a price that includes breakfast and lunch for between ten and twelve dollars per head. If they want dinner, it's extra. Labor's also extra, and if it's a union show, they have to pay teamster union wages for the cook and the helper. In order to be competitive, I'll throw in snacks in the morning and in the afternoon for no extra charge, or I'll do their wrap party for nothing.

Now on distant locations in the United States, it works the same way except for the fact that you have a couple of other components—the drive to the location, housing, and per diem. The driver's getting paid, plus he turns in his food bills and his hotel bills to the production company, then when he arrives on a distant location he's housed and given per diem or daily cash allowance for the entire time he's on the show.

A lot of local caterers have sprung up in some of the key spots, like Dallas, Chicago, and Miami. Where they used to call and say, "Steve, we want you in Chicago," we now have to compete with a local caterer. They're much cheaper because they don't have to pay housing and per diem. Housing and per diem amounts to $100 per person, cash. If it's a big enough show, I'll say, "I'll waive the housing and per diem." And instead of going to the Hilton Hotel, where it's $65 per night for a hotel room, I'll get an apartment for $800 a month and put both the cook and helper in it. I have to find ways to be competitive or I'm not going to get the show.

The other way of billing is called "cost plus." We don't do that in the United States, we do that in foreign locations, like when we were in Jamaica doing a show for Disney called *Cocktail*.

The price of food is very volatile in Jamaica, meaning that one week a piece of meat might cost three dollars a pound, next week it's six dollars. Sometimes there's customs duties, which are crazy. So we can't give them a per-head price. Instead, I'll charge "cost plus"—the "cost" of food plus a service charge or truck rental or both. All the bills for the raw food will be sent to Walt Disney Studios, and I'll charge them $2,000 a week as a service charge.

A Day in the Life

On a typical show, we get the call at four in the afternoon that they're going to want 120 lunches at twelve tomorrow and be on location for breakfast at six-thirty. That goes back to our executive chef, who now looks at his book of menus and says, "Gee, what have I got in my walk-in? I've got prime ribs, some fresh salmon, and some chickens and turkey." So he decides, "Let's give them a whole Thanksgiving-type meal tomorrow—turkey, stuffing, gravy, and let's give them a vegetarian lasagne and some fresh salmon." He writes that menu. Then he also starts writing up some salads—a cucumber salad, some herring and sour cream, a shrimp salad, a tuna salad, green salad, and also Jell-O, cottage cheese, and potato salad. We have ten salads and two desserts every day.

We have a night crew that comes in. They start at four in the afternoon and work till midnight. Our night chef is Ming; he's from China. Ming will look at this menu, and he'll take out the raw turkey, the raw fish, and whatever, put it on a cart that is labeled with the name of the film. That night he'll prepare a fresh cucumber salad, a fresh artichoke salad. And there will be two or three people to help him. Or if we're going to make tuna, the tuna's made fresh the next morning, so Ming'll put cans of tuna and all the fixings out, and when our morning guy comes in, he makes the tuna salad fresh. Ming'll also put heads of lettuce, cucumbers, and everything for a green salad, or spinach leaves, or whatever it is, so that the next morning the guy can do the chopping.

Everything's set so when the guy comes in the next morning he has everything on that cart that he needs to serve that crew. He then does his preliminary preparation, loads the truck, and goes out to location.

On any given show, it's two servers up to the first 140 people to be served. If it's over 140, we'll set up a second serving line.

On one feature, *Taps*, which was a military show set in Valley Forge, Pennsylvania, we were feeding 1,500 people a day in less than half an hour. We had all those cadets, and of course, we had use of the cadets too to help us.

Then on *All the Right Moves* in Johnstown, Pennsylvania, we fed 1,000 people hot meals and 12,000 people in the football stands—hot dogs, soup, and coffee and drinks—for a week. We had to have a thousand gallons of hot water every day, because we had to make soup, coffee, and tea. You have to be resourceful; you come into a town, and where do you get a thousand gallons of hot water, *now*? We ended up using this huge water cauldron that would hold thousands of gallons of water, which we found at the volunteer fire department. And we used the Johnstown Volunteer Fire Department to help distribute food throughout the stadium. We had seventy-five people who were wrapping hot dogs, making soup and coffee. These are the types of things you run into on distant locations.

Cooks and Drivers

We hire in different ways. Some of our very best guys have come up through the ranks from dishwasher to helper. They watched on out-of-town locations how you buy, how you plan menus, and how you cook certain items, and they became good enough so that they're now cooks.

We've also gotten some tremendous people through advertisements. Motion picture catering is a desirable area for cooks to get into. A chef in a restaurant doesn't make as much as our guys do. A chef in the union can make anywhere from $30,000 up per year, and up to $75,000 if they're on location a lot, with all the overtime. No restaurant in Los Angeles will pay that kind of money.

When we put an ad in, usually for a couple of weeks, we'll get fifty to a hundred responses. Over the phone, I can weed out half of them. I'll say, "We need a guy who's had five to ten years of cooking experience. Tell me what you've done."

"Oh, I worked in a Denny's."

"No, I'm sorry, that ain't going to do it."

Of those people, I'll invite maybe thirty or forty to come for interviews, and of those thirty or forty we're only looking for two. So we have the pick, and we can choose several guys who are exactly what we're looking for—completely qualified as chefs, but without prejudice as far as how they think it should be done. Hiring guys who've worked for other catering companies can sometimes be more trouble than it's worth because they have preconceived ideas of how motion picture catering works.

All cooks have to be members of the teamsters union. So we often get calls from guys looking for a way to get into the teamsters and thinking that by being a cook that's an "in." But that's not the way we do it. We hire qualified chefs. If they can cut it in the kitchen, we then think about hiring them and getting them in the union.

On Location

On location, we have purveyors in the major cities, relationships we have developed over the years—in Miami, Chicago, Dallas, Philadelphia, Fort Smith, Arkansas, Toronto.

The first time we go to a new location, either I or my general manager goes to that town, finds purveyors, and establishes our credit with them, because we don't want to pay cash, we want them to bill us in Los Angeles.

Once they've checked out our credit rating, called other people whom we use around the country to see if we pay on time, they give us credit, and if it works out well for the show, the next time we come back to that town we use them again.

When we go into a distant location, the first thing I want to do is use the hotel kitchen where we're staying. If the production company is going to have eighty rooms in this hotel for the crew, the location manager many times says to the guy who's running the hotel, "Help out the caterer. They'll prepare all the food on the truck, but could you give them refrigerator storage space and let them wash pots and pans in your kitchen?" They'll usually say yes.

But then they get all their rooms rented and we get down there, and it's, "Oh, no, you can't. We don't want you to interfere with *our* food." So then we have to go to plan B, which might be, "Let's go to a purveyor's place, store all of our food in his refrigerators, and get all of our stuff washed there."

If that doesn't work, then we rent a forty-foot refrigerated trailer, plug it in at the pier in Chicago, for instance, and while we're out at work during the day, the meat guy and produce guy will deliver and leave the bills inside the refrigerator truck. Then we'll go to a Mexican restaurant and have them wash our pots and pans for $20 a day.

You just have to kind of swing with the punches of whatever town or country you're in.

When we did *Melvin and Howard*, nobody would touch us with a ten-foot pole because all the restaurants wanted to do the catering. They all got together and said, "Let's not help this guy," so our guy had to go to one of those fifty-cent car washes and spray-clean all the pots and pans.

On *The Mosquito Coast*, we sent a guy down to Belize in Central America to set it up. And he got produce from a Mennonite farm—

chicken, turkeys, ducks, and fresh produce. And he found a slaughterhouse for fresh meat, where the meat could be hung and aged.

On *The Bounty*, we were on Morara, Tahiti, which is a little
island next to the main island, Papeete, and every day we had one
person who flew to the main island to bring meat back from Papeete
since Morara had fresh fruit and vegetables but no meat.

Advice

You have to be extremely flexible. When you have a social catering company or restaurant, you have portion control and cost control. You know that your food cost is 27 percent and each portion
weighs this amount and costs you this.

Forget it with us, because you have a crew that is heterogeneous.
There are drivers, craft service people, cameramen, grips, electricians,
wardrobe, makeup, stars, directors, producers. Some of them are used
to eating gourmet food, some of them are used to having a tuna
sandwich, some of them are used to eating a lot, some people just eat
salads.

And that also means that you can't portion control, because you'll
get a grip who'll want a big steak or several slices of prime rib. And
you'll get a wardrobe woman who'll just have a salad.

You can't worry or be upset when a guy wants seconds. When
they say they're going to have 100 meals, you better be ready for 125
every day, every single day, because there's always people and appetites
they're forgetting.

Then, if they say be ready at twelve for lunch, it could be anywhere between eleven-thirty and one-thirty when they finally eat, so
you have to know how to handle your food properly so that you don't
undercook it or overcook it, and that takes experience and constant
communication with the second AD.

Also moving. We may serve breakfast in one location and move
two different times until lunch in another, which will mean picking up
all your tables and chairs and reloading them. This is where on distant
locations they would always take us and not a local caterer. Invariably
the producer would come into a town, El Paso, Texas, or wherever,
and there'd be a big restaurateur, a friend of the film commissioner,
and he'll bring the producer to his restaurant, serve him a beautiful
meal, and say, "I'm going to feed your crew like this." Then the
producer would say, "Sure, we'll use you." But after the second day

when his food wasn't ready in time and the crew was complaining, we'd get the call to go.

If you want to start a motion picture catering company, my advice would be to go to work for one of the major catering companies first. There's a guy here who has a very fancy, very high-class restaurant, who used to wine and dine all the big producers, and they'd come in and say, "Oh, your food is wonderful, if only I could get this on location." He fell for it, went out and paid a lot of money for trucks, and went out of business. It's just not the same thing.

In a restaurant you get a certain clientele who come because they appreciate your food, and of course, everything's cooked to order so it's very good, but when you get out there and you've got a bunch of guys who would never come to your kind of restaurant and you serve beef Wellington, they'll say, "I don't want this garbage, I want *real* food." You can't take that personally.

You have to understand, you're not there to please any portion of the crew, you're there to please all of them. And if that means having vegetarian food for some people, low-salt food for other people, Reuben sandwiches—you give them all of that.

Wrangler

The Wrangler is responsible to the director for selecting and handling those animals considered "livestock" (horses, burros, mules, cows, goats, sheep, and hogs) to be filmed in a motion picture production. He purchases, rents, or provides the animals and arranges for their transportation, care, and feeding. He also supplies all the equipment and "rolling stock" (wagons, and so forth) required. He works closely with the director on the selection and performance of the animals and with the actors, actresses, and stunt people in handling, mounting, riding, and dismounting the animals. As caretaker of these animals, he must see to it that no ASPCA rule is violated, that the animals obtain adequate care, food, and rest, and that the required ratio of Wranglers to animals is respected.

Rudy Ugland

In 1957 RUDY UGLAND, son of a horse trader, started sweeping stables for the man who supplied horses for such motion picture epics as *Ben Hur*. Since then he has wrangled some of the biggest westerns, including *Heaven's Gate, Bite the Bullet, How the West Was Won, The Undefeated, Comes a Horseman,* and *Wild Horses of Valdez*. His most recent credits include *The Sicilian*, directed by Michael Cimino, and *Old Gringo*. When he's not wrangling on a picture, Rudy and his wife, Polly, live and work on his stable of sixty horses and fifty longhorn cattle in Saugus, California. On weekends they rodeo to let off steam.

EVERY ACTOR or actress who goes in to talk to a producer or director about doing a western, every single one of them was born on a farm or a ranch. So you know that when they say they were born on a farm, that they can ride, you know they're lying right there 'cause there's not a whole lot of farmers who ever rode a horse.

But still, you're dealing with a different breed of people when you're talking about actors. I'm amazed how fast they can learn because they want to, they have that ego—they want to look good. I don't care if you have two days to teach them, you could at least teach them to get into a shot and get out of a shot.

Now the hard stuff, you know, running or doing any stunts. That's what doubles are for. Doubles are all SAG [Screen Actors Guild], not wranglers. We don't do anything in front of the camera. We take the horses to the set, saddle them, bridle them, bring them back, but we don't get on them.

Jack Nicholson can't ride in a wheelbarrow, but when they say, "Action," he's as good a horseman as there is in the world. Marlon Brando, people like that, they're not horse people, but they're such great actors, they've learned to transform themselves into that image, and they can actually physically do those things on horseback.

And it's our responsibility to fit the actor with the proper animal. Being able to read an animal well enough to know if he's going to stand in front of that camera without moving for an hour, and then break and run down this mountain. If this actor or actress is going to be able to handle it. We have to fit that particular animal for the situation in the script and for the actor or stuntman riding it.

Picture Horses

You have to teach horses to stand and be patient for the picture business. If you're working on a ranch or you're showing horses, you ride 'em for maybe an hour, just conditioning. Then you'd take 'em to a horse show, ride 'em around for half an hour in the show ring, and then they're finished.

A picture horse, when he goes out to work that morning, he's going to leave at five in the morning, he might not be back until eight that night. A lot of it's standing around. But he has to learn to be patient, to stand, not dig holes, not fidget, not fuss on the set.

There's a lot of horses that can't tolerate it because they just don't have it in their nervous system to settle like that. Some people don't. And if you don't, you're not meant for this business, because you have to learn to settle. You work such long hours, you can't go at a hyper pace, fourteen, fifteen, sixteen hours, it's impossible.

Breeding these animals—I can just about look at a horse in the morning when I go to work and tell you how that horse is going to act that day. And it's something that I didn't learn overnight. I didn't learn it in a week, two weeks, or a year. But I sure as hell learned it when I got away on location, just taking these horses that were hand-picked for this business and going to New York or going to Spain or Italy. I've got to find these horses in a matter of a week. Oh, believe me, you'll pay attention.

Going into Business

You just work thirty days and then you become a group 3 wrangler, which is part of the teamsters. The name "Teamsters" comes from years and years ago when they did all the road construction, you belonged to that union because you drove teams. Now it's all drivers, we're just a small group in the teamsters in Local 399.

I started with one old rope horse and just kept buying horses over the years, buying equipment, saddles, and harnesses.

I've probably done the biggest western I know that's been done in the last twenty years—*Heaven's Gate* with Michael Cimino. What I admire so much about Michael, he gives you your job. He gives you the freedom to do it the right way. He wants the right look. He doesn't want a 1980-model saddle on a horse in a picture that's taking place in 1890.

Most people wouldn't know the difference. But out there in this country of ours, there's millions of horse people, and they realize it, and they are my judges.

We make good money. But I want to tell you, I'd rather take less money and have somebody say, "Boy, that horse and that equipment really look great." That to me is saying, "Here, you just won an Academy Award." That's my drug.

Wrangling a Picture

Usually you get your jobs through word of mouth, it's reputation. After I meet the director and get the job, I'll read the script, then go back and kick it back and forth with the director: "This is the way I see it, Mr. Cimino. John Wayne, he should be riding a big nice horse, a little on the flashy side. And this older guy here, he'd be riding maybe a calmer-acting horse, a horse that's not as flashy, not as eye-catching. Now the girl, she's riding this horse here that at one point has to fall down—we'll find ourselves a falling horse."

For every principal horse, you've got to have two or three, in case something happens—in case that horse gets a bellyache or comes up lame. You can't say, "Well, listen, I can't come in because old Sapphire doesn't feel like working today."

You try to get them to look like each other, and if they don't, you paint them, you dye them, you spray them.

If we're going on location, I'll bring, say, eight principal horses and eight doubles from here. Now I might need sixty other horses, but they're just in the background. I can't afford to bring all those horses and men from here. I can pick up local horses at a third of the price and use local men.

On *How the West Was Won*, we went to Rapid City, South Dakota. We didn't have any horses from Hollywood, we had all local horses. There were five wranglers, including myself.

I helped gather all the buffalo for the stampede. All the Indian scenes. Then from there we went to Orago, Colorado, and got into the wagon train part of it. And that's where I got my knowledge of driving eight-horse and six-horse hitches, big hitches.

I can remember one time we were driving off a mountain, we got snowed out. I was driving eight mules, and I was so cold that my gloves froze so that I couldn't move my hands up the lines. Now that's cold, icicles hanging off the horses' tails!

On Location

This is a good job, and I just don't know what else I would do. I would hate to think that I had to work every single day, because what I did this morning was not work, when I got up at six and went out and messed with these horses.

It's kind of a nomad's life. I spend more of my time away from home than I do at home. But I enjoy the travel, meeting the people, the challenges. Here's an old horse-trading kid, I've been all over the world in this business, spent summers in Hawaii working. People pay to go to these places. I've done four or five pictures in Spain. The toughest place I've ever been, workwise, is Sicily on *The Sicilian*. I was over there for seven months. There's no horses over there, just mules.

Took two trips to Spain to videotape horses. And when I came back to Palermo, Mike Cimino and I sat down and went through all the videos of the horses and picked out the twenty we liked best and shipped those over to Sicily.

I had forty head that were already over there in Sicily for background, but boy, they were rough. They don't ride those mules, just farm them, walk around with them.

Didn't have a translator. The first thing I learned was the colors. And "Hurry up," and "What time you want them there?"

I'm not going back there in a million years. Sicily has seen the last of this old rutabaga.

And then I've been in Death Valley in July and August on pictures where the heat is so bad you can't even touch the ground. Fortunately the horses will get really mellow in the hot, hot weather. They are harder to handle in the cold.

If a horse can't settle, you usually have to get another one because you don't have time. There's only been two or three times when I've had a horse completely blow up with me, where I was afraid of endangering the horse or another person. And I've always switched animals before that's happened. You can tell, you can read them.

Grooming for Westerns

Horses nowadays—you boot 'em up, trim their four tops, put bridle passes on them, clean their ears out. Back in 1890, 1870, they didn't have clippers and those guys weren't taking the time, because that animal was a work animal, he wasn't a toy like you have in your backyard today.

You'd settle this West with those animals. And they didn't really care if they were pretty just as long as they got them to that next destination. So I try to keep my horses looking like horses in the old days. I groom them, brush them, feed them, and I feed *good*.

But I don't cut the hair under their chins. In cold weather I like to see that long hair, I like to see that hair on their legs.

Now when we go to work on a picture job, I call the union and ask, "Who you got on the books?" I have guys that I prefer who know my animals and come up here the days they're not working. Those guys'll get the first calls. They're paid through the studio, but they use my horses.

Now one man can wrangle five "ND" horses, nondescript animals. They're just five horses that can be tied in the background. One wrangler can wrangle a team or a four-horse hitch. Two men to a six-horse hitch. One man can wrangle a cast horse and a double—for your actor, for a John Wayne or a Robert Mitchum. Or one man can wrangle two cast horses.

We do cattle, too. It'll take three men with the first twenty-five head, but every twenty-five after that you usually add another man.

Every once in a while we get a big cattle job. I did a picture with Jane Fonda and Jimmy Caan called *Comes a Horseman* that I had about nine hundred head on.

Training Stunt Horses

Basically in the last ten years, all I've been doing is supervising. Every once in a while I'll take a job with a friend or I'll go with a particular actor or with a particular stunt horse.

I've always been a half-frustrated stuntman, always taken pride in my horsemanship and being able to teach a horse to do different things. I think that right now I've got the best falling horse that's ever been in this picture business. When you go on a job with him, you know he's going to fall, it's going to be spectacular, and no one's going to get hurt.

He's an ex-racehorse that's not too tall, probably a thousand-pound horse, real normal in the body, but he's kind of got a long neck to him. And he's a brave horse. Two years ago I started him from the ground making him lie on his shoulder and fall over. And I worked with him for about a year, never did hurt him, just made him have that confidence that he can do it, and now he does it as many times as you want.

All you have to do is pull his head around and he falls down. And you can run with him and do the same thing. You just have to have your spots prepared, a lot of sand, a lot of soft spots, because I don't want to hurt him. If you hurt him one time, then he's going to quit falling.

The reason I'm not a professional fighter is that I don't like to get hit and because it hurts. It's the same way with this horse: if you hurt him, he's not going to want to do it. And he doesn't have to do it because he's a hell of a lot bigger than I am.

You have to have a bucking horse around this picture business, but he's a certain kind of animal. Nowadays in rodeos, they put them in a chute, you saddle them in a chute, you get on them in a chute, you turn them out. When we go on a picture job you're not going to have a chute there, so that horse is going to have to be able to be where you can put a saddle on him, let the man get on him, and then start bucking.

If you were going to stampede a hundred head of horses, I would have one corral, point A, feed them and water them. Then I'd take them to point B, hold them in another corral, open it up, shoo them out, and they'd run back to point A, where they get fed and watered.

That animal will perform for you if he's treated right. You can go out and take a look at any of my horses, they're fat, they're slick, they're healthy.

It's just like an athlete, when he's in shape and he's healthy, he can endure a lot. If you're weak and sick, and not getting the proper food, you can become awful miserable. And a horse can be the same way.

The hardest part is keeping them ready. Because I might get a call here today and they'll say, "Monday we need twenty head." Those horses all have to be in condition to do that day's work.

Saying "No"

The director will say, "Okay, listen, we're going to put the camera right here. Are those horses going to be able to come up over this hill? How fast? And can Jane Fonda do it?"

That's for me to say. If it's not safe [slaps hands], I'll tell the director that fast. I'm not bashful. If I had an inkling that you couldn't do something, that you might get hurt . . . how in God's name am I going to take somebody's two-million-dollar picture and say, "Well, maybe she could do it, maybe he could do it." When I tell you you can do it, there ain't no maybes in it, you're going to do it.

If you can't . . . that's the magic of movies. There's always that tight shot of the actor and that double on the big master.

It's easier to say "Yes" than it is to say "Sorry." In this business, they want you to say yes to everything. And I've seen what can happen, seen how you could hurt somebody or break a piece of equipment.

I've worked for the biggest hard-nosed directors in this business, and I love them. I mean that. Richard Brooks on *Bite the Bullet*, he's a hard man to work for, a demanding man. He wants perfection. Don't come to work if you're not prepared, and he doesn't want excuses, because they give you time to prepare these things. But I like working for a man who knows what he wants. What is hard is when you have to keep doing it over and over 'cause the guy doesn't know what he wants.

Frustrations

There's tons of frustration, like production managers who'll only let you have ten horses when you need twenty out there.

It's the arguing and fighting, and it's come to the point where, "Hey listen, apparently you know my job better than I do, so why don't you go out there and you do it?" Or, "You stick right with me when I say, 'That horse can't run any more, he's had enough,' and the director asks me where the double is. You jump right up and tell him you didn't want to bring in another horse because it was going to cost you fifty-five more dollars a day."

I don't want to take out twenty head if I'm just going to use ten just because I want to get those other ten on pay. Everything I take out, boy, I want it to be on that screen. I'm going to be honest with you. That's why I've kept the reputation that I have. I don't take kickbacks, I don't give kickbacks. I'll make the best deal for the company that I can possibly make, but I'm not going to turn around and screw a guy out of feeding his horse every day. I'm not going to go out there and tell him, "Hey listen, I'm going to use your horse and you'll be real proud of him because he's in this movie." I'm going to pay him.

On Wrangling for Movies

You have to want to do it bad. When I first started in this business, there was tons of work. Now the work's not plentiful, they're not doing many westerns. It's hard to make a living for a young guy who's got a family. Because you're going to have some starve-out periods. You're going to go four, five, six months without a day's work.

You've got to learn how to handle the money. Working six months and making that big money, that's a hell of a living. But you've got a tendency, the more you make, the more you spend, and then you say, "What the hell did I do with all that money?"

Plus you have so damn much to learn. You have to learn about teams, harnesses, saddles, you have to be a historian. You have to know what kinds of wagons they had in the mountain country, what kind they had in the desert, did they ride A-forks, did they ride those big Mother Hubbard saddles, all the Indian bridles, the gear that goes on them.

Just to get into the union is hard because there's just not that much work. I'd say thirty years ago there were three hundred wranglers. I'd say there's thirty right now. Not all of them are working.

If I had a son, would I advise him to get into the wranglers? I wouldn't. I'd say get in the camera department, get in the prop department.

Most wranglers have side jobs. They shoe horses or take some horses in to ride and train for other people. They'll trade horses, they'll just do anything to subsidize.

Respect

I'll never let actors or directors or producers get to know me. I won't carry on, I won't socialize with them.

They have to have the same amount of respect for you that you do for them. I'm not a great educated man as far as using words. I'm big, I'm as kind a person as there is in the world, but not everybody knows that. When a director or actor asks me a question, I give 'em the shortest, quickest, most truthful answer. "Yes," "no," is usually best. Don't give them any "maybes," don't give them any explanation. That's it, walk away.

And look them right in the eye when you give it to them. You'll be surprised how much respect you can gain. Cowboys have always had the reputation of being about half-wild, half-crazy. Might well take a hold of you and punch you in the nose. I'd just as soon keep it that way.

9
THE CAMERA

The camera captures images with light.

In this chapter, those who operate the lights and manipulate the camera to capture the images reveal how they do what they do.

It is technically demanding, and artistically challenging, for the Director of Photography, aided by his Camera Operator, Gaffer, and Grips, to shoot the scenes of a movie as the director would have them shot.

Key Grip

The Key Grip is responsible to the director of photography and gaffer for providing and placing all diffusion, for facilitating or actuating camera movement (dolly, crane, and boom operations), and for moving, erecting, and striking scaffolding. He or she also works closely with the gaffer in the selection and placement of reflectors, dolly track, and backings. As head of the grip crew, the Key Grip supervises transporting, rigging, placing, operating, moving, lifting, carrying, and striking of all grip equipment and accessories, as well as sometimes assisting other departments in handling and moving their equipment and materials.

Tom Ramsey

TOM RAMSEY took a television technician correspondence course from Colorado, got out to California on the G.I. Bill, and started working on nonunion films in various capacities. He finally got into the union as a grip on *Remember My Name*, an IATSE picture (International Alliance of Theatrical and Stage Employees), and has been a grip now for twenty-eight years. His many credits include *Easy Rider, Sweet Dreams, Creator, Ferris Bueller's Day Off, Pretty in Pink, Heart Like a Wheel, Where the Buffalo Roam, Melvin and Howard, Swamp Thing, Border Line, Swing Shift, Sweethearts Dance,* and *The Milagro Beanfield War.*

THE HEAD of the grips is the key grip or first company grip. He's the chief, the foreman. Then you have your second company grip, or best boy grip, who is my assistant. He takes care of the equipment, brings on extra men, orders supplies, and does prerigging. Then you have your dolly grip, whose job it is to handle the dollies and the cranes.

There are your hammers, called that because they all carry hammers. They're additional grips. Depending on the size of the show and the budget, you have as many as five or six.

Then you have your rigging grips, who hang platforms over the sets to hang lights on. The platforms are called "beds" or "greens." They also hang painted backings—anything from the New York skyline to the desert—and "translites," which is a backing that gives the illusion of being outdoors.

Breakdown

In the script, there'll be scenes described as day or night, interior or exterior, and then sometimes they put in things like "Dolly into close-up." So we mark where the dolly shots are going to be, where the night work is, where they think they're going to have a crane shot.

I have my own little breakdown. I have location and survey sheets, one for interior and one for exterior. And I'll note, on an interior shot, for instance, whether it's day or night, what kind of floor in that particular room, what kind of ceiling, how high it is, where the access is to the elevator if we're in a building, if we're going to have to get the windows or put a correction on the windows, or if we're going to have to hang some backings, or some blacks, or if we have to "tent in" a front porch for a day-for-night scene, or if we need extra men and equipment for night shooting.

The director of photography is my boss. Every time we do a setup, the actors are brought in and the DP, director, gaffer, and key grip are on the set. They rehearse. The director works out all the blocking, the actors do their lines, we all watch. After the director and DP put their heads together, lighting starts. The gaffers put a key light here, put some fill here, add the back lights, run some patterns on the wall, and the electricians or lamp operators start putting up their units.

Then we, the grips, begin to paint. We top all lights as needed, shadowing the light down on the walls, cutting the direct light out of the camera lens. We put shelves under the lights to cut the excess heat off a hot floor, desk, table, and so on.

We put what we call scrims or nets on the bottom, top, or sides of the lights, which reduces the intensity of the light. If a lady is sitting at the table and she has a white blouse on, there's a little too much contrast or too much heat, we bring a net right up on her shoulders, cutting the intensity down on the blouse, leaving her face in full light.

Easy Rider

I did *Easy Rider* years ago before I got into the union. They gave us a script, the old purple mimeo from the hand-crank mimeo machine, with no cover, and we looked at it, and it was all campfires, roads, and these two guys on motorcycles.

We had one 5-ton grip truck, which had grip and electric. We had one generator, two of those old Cortez mobile homes, a station wagon for sound, a station wagon for camera, and a convertible (our camera car). And I had my 1965 crew-cab pickup truck with a shell on it with the motorcycle mounts that we put cameras on to shoot along the side of the road. There were only about eighteen of us, and we were just a big family.

And we took off. We went up to Malibu and shot the commune scene because they wouldn't let us shoot in the real one in New Mexico. And then we went up by Panamint City, which is this side of

Death Valley. We'd be doing traveling shots. Peter Fonda and Dennis Hopper, the directors, would be on the motorcycles in front and behind of what would be the convertible with a camera in it, and behind that was the rest of the company and all the trucks and station wagons. I learned to stay a little bit in back of Dennis because he'd just throw on his brakes and say, "Let's shoot here."

We'd set up a shot, shoot, get back on the motorcycles, and away we go. We went through Kingman, Arizona, continued on to Flagstaff on Indian Road, up to Farmington and Taos, New Mexico, and down into Las Vegas, New Mexico, and on south. From there, clear down to Louisiana, Baton Rouge, Lafayette, Morgan City. On a highway, we'd point the camera down, shoot the white lines going this way and then shoot them going that way, and then we'd go across the bridge and shoot this way and then down and up both ways. It was crazy. Then we'd do the campfires wherever they'd stop. It was campfires and roads and campfires and roads. We had a ball because they just turned us loose. "Okay, be at Farmington, call is seven o'clock. Here's your hotel. . . ."

It was about ten weeks, we covered about six thousand miles. We had an advance location manager who would go ahead of us and make arrangements, you know, in all the places we were going to be. We ate some good food down south. No caterer. We just ate wherever we were.

Sweet Dreams

On *Sweet Dreams*, the story of Patsy Cline, the country singer, we had an English director by the name of Karel Reisz. He's such a gentleman. We loved him dearly. He wanted to know what kind of dolly track I was going to use and how much we were going to carry. We chatted about equipment, which is kind of unusual. He never missed a lick but always gave us time, understood our logistics very well.

Directors are primarily interested in directing actors and usually leave all the lighting and composition up to the DP. When they know a little bit about lighting or a little bit about how a crane works, it really helps. That feedback is great.

I'm a two-stepper. And they had a stand-in for Jessica Lange on *Sweet Dreams*. We were sitting in Moose Lodge in Martinsburg, West Virginia, waiting to do a shot where Patsy Cline/Jessica was going to perform before she got really big. They had a little dance floor, so I just grabbed the stand-in and started two-stepping with her. So we're two-stepping, spinning around and going all over the floor, and the music stops, and the stand-in says, "Okay, let's get ready for the take." I walked off, and just about that time Jessica came off the stage and said, "Oh, was that you two-stepping back there?" And I said, "Yeah, it was. I hope you don't mind." She said, "No, that was great. I love to see it."

Jessica's very outgoing. Nobody puts anything over on her. Serious business lady. But she's pleasant. People say, "Jessica Lange, you gotta watch out." I said, "Watch out for what?"

The first day in Martinsburg, I drove by a flower shop. I don't know what struck my mind—might have been sipping the cooking sherry—and I thought, Why don't I just send some flowers to Jessica. So I called the florist and ordered yellow roses. He said, "What do you want to say on the card?" I said, "Let's see: To Ms. Jessica, good luck, from the grip and electric crews." I think it kind of broke the ice. She was even more open after that, we had more fun.

I had a little rubber frog that I always carry in my pocket, and right before the breakfast scene I said to Karel, "Do you think we need a giggle about now?" And he said, "Tom, what have you got in mind?" I said, "How about I take this little frog and put it in the cereal, and I just let the head stick out?" So we got the rehearsal all set up. Jessica came in and she's looking around and seeing where she has to sit, and Karel was talking to her and he's trying hard to keep from cracking up. He said, "I want you to sit down and do the cereal."

And she looked down at the cereal. And saw the frog. And said, "What's that in my cereal bowl?" Then Dotty Pearl, her makeup lady, took a spoon and poked in it and kind of got it up and said, "Oh, it's a rubber frog," and Jessica said, "I wonder who did that?" And looked right at me. She knew I'd done it. And we laughed and laughed and laughed.

Location

I've done mostly location work. Sound stages get boring. You have to park and you have to use the commissary or bring your lunch and you have to punch out—nothing wrong with it, just more regimented.

On *The Milagro Beanfield War*, we shot for eighteen weeks, all in the Sante Fe area, mostly in Truchas, New Mexico. We had some weather problems. It snowed early, then it would rain, and it washed the beanfield away. It's a true story about a water rights fight between the big rich politicians who took it away from the poor Mexicans who were trying to raise beans and make a living. It's a whole racial thing between Hispanics and the developers who wanted their lands to put these big companies on.

It was a "grip" show, which means there was a lot of outside lighting with reflective surfaces with big Griffolyns, and we laid a lot of dolly track. When there's exteriors there's more work for us because we use more equipment outside and much heavier dolly track and more of it usually.

Night work's also a little more difficult because, besides the toll on your body, you're working in the dark and trying to get things set up before it gets too dark. Sometimes you lose equipment.

Learning Grip

All the equipment manufacturers have catalogs. And I'd advise anybody who wanted to learn grip to go to all the equipment houses and get all the catalogs, go to the grip section, and memorize the name of every piece of grip equipment so you know it by sight.

And when you get a chance to visit a set, come by and see what we're doing, stay in the corner, watch, be quiet, and make a list of questions. And at lunch, ask me questions and I'll tell you. Or if I've got a break after work, I'll show you how a C-stand works. A C-stand is a "century stand." It's a stand that holds our flags for shadowing. Or I'll show you how to use a bounce card, which is a white surface that we put up for the electricians to put a light in front of it. It bounces light back into the set. We have to know something about lights—the size of the units for the lights and which direction the light's gonna go and how we can get the most out of our bounce cards so we can shade and diffuse.

Dollies and Cranes

The dolly is a platform on which the camera is placed. It has a hydraulic arm that lowers and raises, and it has wheels that have capabilities of going sideways. You have to get a feel for the dolly, learn to work that arm up and down, slow or flat, learn to hit a mark just right when you move the dolly and work the arm at the same time. You have to wrestle with it.

Then there's cranes, the big Titan cranes, which you have to become familiar with.

Equipment Package

I have my own equipment. I have quite a large feature package. All the dolly tracks, camera melts, all the flags, all the diffusion from eighteen-by-twenty-four inches up to twenty-by-twenty feet. All the ladders and scaffolding, dollies, a lot of rigging gear, clamps, and little gadgets for hanging lights, for putting up flags.

It makes me a little extra money. I had to make a choice about twenty years ago whether I'd keep the little bit of stuff I had and add to it or get rid of it all and just rent from somebody else. I decided to keep the stuff I had, and I just kept on buying and buying and getting more sophisticated.

The equipment is a complete package deal, and then there might be extra, seldom used things—maybe a day here or there, we carry them on the truck and charge them as used. It's been worthwhile.

In terms of advising others to do this, it depends how deep they want to get into it. I know a lot of grips who just have their own workbox, which is a big box on wheels that carries all their special little adapters, hangers, and brackets for all their rigging. You could never rent that stuff because we make it ourselves.

Other guys have bought ten-ton trucks and put a package on it. Still other guys, like me, have a storage area, a shop, a drill press, and a bench grinding as well as all the tools. When a company rents a production van, which is a big forty-foot unit with two generators on the tractor, they just back it up and we load it up.

Suppliers on the Set

The grips are great suppliers. "Can I have a roll of gaffer's tape?" Sure. "You got some sash cord?" Or we'll be asked, "Could you make me a little shelf in the makeup room so I can set my case on it?" We always have plywood, so we put it up.

Most of the guys have a tool belt, and they will carry a hammer and a little pouch with screwdrivers, pliers, side cutters, tape measure, and a nail pouch with different kinds of nails in it. And the bigger tools like saws will be in a box close by.

In the old days when I was doing nonunion pictures, I could see the headaches that the propman had. I used to do a little boom work—it was just okay. I was good at it, but I didn't want to pursue it. Then I used to help the electricians, but I didn't like hot lights and wrapping heavy cable. But I loved the dolly and crane work. And I don't think I ever wanted to get away from it after I started doing it.

I'll be staying in grips—it's been good to me.

Gaffer

The Gaffer, or Key Electrician, is responsible to the director of photography for all lighting setups and procedures on a film production. He or she works closely with the director of photography and the key grip in the selection, placement, and desired level and balance of the lighting on a set or location. As head of the electrical department, the gaffer is also responsible for preparing a list of all electrical equipment required, supervising the loading, transportation, rigging, operation, and striking of all lighting equipment, and ensuring safe working conditions for his or her crew as specified by the building safety code, fire laws, and union guidelines.

Steve Mathis

STEVE MATHIS came out to California from Oklahoma on the invitation of a friend, arrived on a Friday, and started work as a "grunt" the following Monday on a nonunion picture. After a week's work with no pay, the director of photography convinced the production manager to hire him. Steve continued to work with this same director of photography, Dean Cundey, for the next three years. When Mr. Cundey did his first union film, *Escape from New York,* he managed to get Steve hired, claiming to the lighting local that Steve was the only one who knew how to operate a dimmer Mr. Cundey had invented, the "computerized light modulator." Steve was able to work for union minimum wages as the "modulator operator." He has worked his way up the lighting ranks from lamp operator to gaffer on such pictures as *Escape from New York, Halloween, Halloween II, The Fog, Weekend Warriors,* and *Back to the Future.*

THE DIRECTOR and the director of photography (DP) decide how they want to shoot a scene. After watching the rehearsal on a scene, the director of photography, the gaffer, and the key grip get together and decide how to light it. The gaffer then turns to the best boy, who's also been paying attention, hopefully, and together they figure out the best way to position the lights in order to accomplish the look.

The gaffer, best boy, and lamp operators—that's the chain of command from top to bottom—are responsible for all the lights and the electricity.

It's hard to figure out where the word *gaffer* really came from. In Old English, the gaffer was the foreman or "overman" of a gang of reapers. And I am overman, if you will, of the lighting team. If you call the lighting union, they'll tell you it's because we work in the "gaffs," or beams above the stages, setting up lights. It's also a fishing term—there is a long pole with a hook on it—and we do sometimes have to use extensions to set up lights. Take your pick. It's the common usage word for our position, although "chief lighting technician," which is the way the union categorizes us, apparently is supposed to convey more authority.

The best boy is second in command—my right-hand guy who conveys the plan to the lamp operators—actually the real foreman of the team. It's another of those titles whose origin has been lost, though the obvious explanation is he's my "best" man—without him I couldn't get anything done. And in the grip department, the second in command is also known as the best boy grip.

Lights

With lighting, you have to create something out of nothing with equipment that weighs a ton.

There are different kinds of lights—a key light, a fill light, a back light. When the light's up to key, that's basically the brightest light you want for your picture. For instance, in a restaurant you're not really keyed by anything because it's just a soft overall ambience.

I learned about lighting by doing. I have a hard time sometimes— a DP will want me to give specific technical reasons for choosing certain kinds of lights. Once the director of photography on a picture I was gaffing on called me up and said, "I hear you want to use a Sunburst 12K instead of an LTM. How come?" Both the Sunburst 12K and LTM are big blue lights used to simulate daylight. I said, "It's lighter. I don't want my guys to be carrying around such a heavy light." And he said, "Well, how many amps and what voltage is it?" I couldn't tell him. It's a big light, and if it works, it works. He felt that I should know the numbers of the voltage and so on. And maybe I should . . . but my knowledge is what I learned on the set and what *looks* good. The best way to learn to be a gaffer is to go work on a set as an electrician. You'll set lights up, you'll focus them on people, you'll put diffusion in front of them, and if you pay attention in every show, you'll learn a lot.

If you're working for me or someone like me, I'll tell you what the lights are. I'll say, "Go put a junior, which is two-thousand-watt light, over here and take it up pretty high and put some 216 [diffusion] on it." If you don't know what the junior looks like, if I have time, I'll go get it, and if I don't have the time, I'll send someone else with you and tell you to watch.

Each DP has a certain style and goes for a certain look that will indicate what types of lights he uses. I try to get a sense of what the cameraman feels looks good. Often DP's who've done mostly TV use hard light, which means there's no diffusion.

Diffusion is tracing paper or white soft material—like shower curtain material—which is used in front of the lights to soften the look. You can go to an equipment house like Film Trucks or Cine Pro and look through books that have swatches of different materials for diffusion. There are about twenty different kinds of material with different textures.

The thicker it is, the softer the light—but it also takes away the light. So if you need a high level of light, you have to take that into consideration. You'll have to use a bigger light if you want really thick diffusion.

Setting Up

Usually you have prep time before the show starts, and you can walk the new guys through most of the prerigging. It's not a hard job, assuming you can physically lift cable. You have to pay attention, anticipate what's coming. Once you get the lighting set up, you can't lie down and take a nap because things always change—even during the shot, something may happen and you have to adapt to it.

You get an idea from talking to the DP, from reading the script, and from seeing the locations of how much equipment you'll need, like "two arcs, four 10-K's." A "K" is a thousand-watt light, so a 10-K is a ten-thousand-watt light. That'd be a hundred times brighter than a hundred-watt light bulb. So you work up a rough equipment list. Then you go to an equipment house—say, Sequoia or Film Trucks—and you get bids: "Here's what we want, how much will you charge for it?"

There are definite technical things you need to know—the different sizes of cable, for instance. One cable will carry a certain number of amps. If you're going to use lots of lights in a building, you'll have to run the appropriate-size cable to the set.

On most shows, unless they're really low budget, you go out on a scout before shooting. After looking at a location, you'll know it's going to take extra time to hang the lights up out of the way or to run cable because you're going to have to park the trucks a quarter mile down the road. You work all that out before. You get an idea of how much cable you'll need, what size lights you'll need.

On a location shoot, you'd better have a good idea of what you're going to use. On *Radioactive Dreams*, we were in a warehouse in the City of Industry for two weeks. It was a six-hundred-foot-long set built inside this warehouse, and it had neon lights, strobe lights, and rock-and-roll lights—a really weird, complicated set. I had to have enough equipment to do that. So I figured out how much and had it delivered to the set and had guys prerig it before we started shooting.

Prerigging means to lay cable everywhere we think we might need lights, put the lights up on the scissor lifts. Some scissor lifts can go up to fifty feet. You can get a Condor, which is a cherry picker—and I don't like to use them because they are not as safe—which will go up eighty or ninety feet. I've been up seventy-eight feet with an arc as a lamp operator. Scares you—you're way up there in this bucket.

Even with thorough prerigging, when shooting actually is about to start, it's not always quite what you'd envisioned. You change what you can. But lots of times you just have to live with it. If it's a small scene and you realize you've put the light in the wrong place, you can move it because you're dealing with two or three people in a small room or something. But if you've got generators and cables, you're limited.

Budget

Before they even start hiring anybody, they'll have budgeted all the departments—at least on bigger shows—they've decided this is how much they're going to spend on equipment, the gaffer's salary, the best boy's salary, the lamp operator's salary, and we'll spend so much extra on night exteriors when you need additional guys and equipment that we aren't carrying "in the package."

You have to sit down with the production manager and work with him. If you're Vilmos Zsigmond, I suppose you can say, "This is what I'm going to do." But I have to be somewhat accommodating. If I want to use four 12-K's, I may have to give up something else. I just did a show at Warner Brothers, gave 'em an equipment list, and they flipped out: "Way too much, we can't afford it." So I had to go through and take out stuff that I might have wanted but could live without in order to get the things that were absolutely essential.

It's important for the gaffer to stand up for his guys. On nonunion films, for some reason, the gaffer, the key grip, and the first assistant cameraman end up having to be the spokesmen, in effect, for the whole crew. You're fighting for your guys, but by extension you're fighting for the whole crew.

Union shows are all delineated, how much you get paid for regular hours, how much for overtime. But on nonunion shows you're at the mercy of the deal you make. If I had a dollar for every time I've gone through this routine—"We don't have the money to pay over-time, but we're only going to work twelve-hour days." And then I say, "Well, okay, then let's go ahead and make an overtime deal. Double time after twelve. If you're only going to work twelve hours a day, it won't cost you a penny." Then they say, "I can't do that." And I say, "Why not? You're admitting if you can't do that, that you expect to work longer hours."

I won't do the film if they don't pay overtime. Even if it's token overtime. I just don't want to work fourteen hours without the proper compensation. Because when the movie comes out, I'm not going to see any of that money. I mean Debra Hill, the producer of *Halloween*, is a millionaire—and deservedly so. But when we went on to do *The Fog*, I told them we were not going to do it for a flat. And although we didn't get a straight overtime deal on *The Fog*, they were fair to us.

I don't like to use a big crew without good reason, but then again I don't want to beat my guys up, either. So you have to strike a balance. You have to have the confidence of the production manager and everybody else that you're not trying to screw them, because there is a tendency to get as many guys as you can. Our union encourages that—not in so many words, but they want as many people to be hired as possible.

You really can't do a picture with less than two lamp operators. I've done it with less than two, on *Halloween*, but that's rough. On *Back to the Future*, we had a basic crew of three—a gaffer, two best boys—and many lamp operators. If you do a union picture on a studio lot, they make you hire the studio best boy, and he's in charge of keeping track of the studio's equipment. Then you have your own best boy, because a gaffer wants to have someone he feels comfortable with.

If we're running behind and I'm out of guys, I'll physically handle equipment. You try not to as the gaffer because if you're off running cable and setting the lights, you're missing what it looks like from the camera. You've got to keep an eye out on what's happening so you can prevent any problems.

Magic Hour

You can learn a great deal about good lighting doing commercials and videos. They spend money deliberately to make their product look good. But you don't have to move very fast on commercials, which will kill you in film. On commercials they take a lot of time to make it look perfect. They'll spend a million dollars on an ad campaign, a series of thirty-second commercials.

On a car commercial, they may go to Sedona, Arizona, or Death Valley, depending on the look they want. They work from four in the morning to eight in the morning for the early morning sunrise, and from four in the afternoon till eight in the evening. Because when the sun is directly overhead it's ugly—it's flat, and you get shadows—so you try to work at *magic* hour. Actually magic hour is only about thirty minutes on any given day—when the sun's going down and after it's set when you still have enough light to shoot by.

Obviously in TV you can't wait for magic hour. You may be able to get a shot or two in then, but you've got to get so many pages covered a day—you can't wait for perfect light. Now on a movie like *Days of Heaven*, they shot mostly at magic hour; they had the money to do that. It was a conscious decision to make that look part of the film. But on most movies, you don't have that luxury.

The Scissor Lift

I try to work with directors of photography I like and respect. Occasionally, you need the bread or you find out later after you've accepted a job that you're not exactly wild about the DP. Friend of mine called me up for a couple of days on a movie, and I said, "Sure." Showed up and there was a cameraman (DP) that I hated. I said, "I quit. I hate this guy. The last time I worked with him he called me an idiot." So my friend said, "Listen, I'll send you up on a scissor lift."

A scissor lift goes up about forty-five feet, has a platform on top on which you put a light, usually for night exteriors. So I went up on a scissor lift the whole night and ran an arc—only came down to eat. My friend knew I'd leave if I had to be on the set.

Advice

If you want to get into gaffing, the best thing to do is look in the Friday issue of *Variety*, find the names of production companies, call them and tell them you'll work for free for a week or so on a film—and then try to get them to hire you. I hate to see people work for free, but you can learn a lot in a week if you pay attention.

Director of Photography

The Director of Photography, or Cinematographer, works closely with the director in translating the screenplay into moving photographic images. He or she orchestrates the lighting, framing, and shooting of the film in close consultation with his three key supporting crew members—the camera operator, the gaffer, and the key grip. Although the Director of Photography does not physically operate the camera on union productions, he or she is responsible for all production photography and anything having to do with the camera(s) and lighting—including the selection of cameras, associated equipment, and film stocks; approval of all lighting and grip equipment; checking and/or film testing sets, set dressing, scenic art, props, actors and actresses, costume, hair, makeup, and so on for photographic purposes; matching camera direction and lighting from scene to scene; setting the camera positions, angles, and moves; determining all exposures; selecting the lenses and composition for the camera operator; supervising the timing of the work and answer prints; and viewing all dailies for quality control.

Laszlo Kovacs

As a boy growing up in Hungary during World War II, LASZLO KOVACS hammered flyers on telephone poles to advertise the village screenings—movies projected onto a white bedsheet while the townspeople watched from wooden benches. Nobody in the village owned a television, and for Laszlo, this was "a wonderful window into a world I didn't know." When he grew up, he applied to the Budapest School of Dramatic and Visual Arts and was one of twelve selected out of three thousand applicants in the cinematography division. There he met another young aspiring cinematographer, Vilmos Zsigmond. They became close friends.

During the Russian occupation of Hungary, 250,000 people suddenly became homeless, and the "free world" opened its gates to the best and brightest—the scientists and artists. Laszlo and Vilmos were able to come to the United States as permanent residents. But once here, they had to make a living. Laszlo ended up working in a forest of maple trees in upstate New York, while Vilmos found employment in the Chicago environs. Neither one saw Hollywood for many years.

Laszlo's first film-related job came about after contacting his cousin in Seattle, to whom he wrote, "My God, this is worse than Hungary. I'm working somewhere behind God's back in upstate New York. If you can't get me out of here, I'm going back." His cousin brought him to Seattle, and together they knocked on the doors of film laboratories, Laszlo's cousin doing all the talking and pointing at Laszlo since Laszlo couldn't speak any English. Finally

Laszlo was given a two-week trial period at a film processing company. Ecstatic, he reported to work, dictionary in hand, and quickly made his talents known. He was given a permanent salaried position and, in short order, was practically running the lab.

Meanwhile, he stayed in touch with Vilmos. Both finally quit their respective jobs to meet up in Hollywood. But it was another four years before Laszlo got a chance to shoot film for industrials, documentaries, and medical films. The director of one of the documentaries approached Laszlo to do a "showcase feature," and it was this work, done for free, that eventually came to the attention of a low-budget film director named Richard Rush. Laszlo went on to do several films with him, including a small film called *Rebel Rousers* starring the young Jack Nicholson. Since then Laszlo has become one of the world's foremost cinematographers. His many credits include *Easy Rider; Hell's Angels on Wheels; Five Easy Pieces; What's Up, Doc?; Paper Moon; Shampoo; Harry and Walter Go to New York; The Last Waltz; New York, New York; F.I.S.T.; Paradise Alley; The Runner Stumbles; Inside Moves; Frances; Ghostbusters; Mask; Legal Eagles;* and *Little Nikita.*

SHOOTING IS like having so many strings in your hand. You know where all the strings are going, and if you need something, you follow that string and garner someone's help or contribution. I like the analogy of an orchestra with two conductors. The principal conductor is, of course, the director. But what the director doesn't do, I have to orchestrate.

What I do is try to create something that's in the air. You feel the electricity, you can't see it yet, but you have to somehow translate all these elements and information so that it comes alive. You're making all the decisions through what the director feeds you. When you're synchronized and connected to the material, it's wonderful. When the director says, "No, that's not what I had in mind," then you're in trouble.

I am emotionally affected by what I see through the lens, and that's how it should be. When the boy is dying in *Mask*, I was crying with Cher, and I wanted to walk away—not to see it.

Criteria: Selecting Films

Who is the director?

You have to audition the director as much as he is auditioning you. And I trust my instincts, my emotions, and my judgment. I usually know in five minutes if we are clicking, even with first-time directors.

What is the story?

If there is no play, there is nothing. You spend quite a few months of your life on a film. And when you finish a film, part of you is left in that film. You put so much into it, you have to think about whom you're giving yourself to.

When I get a screenplay, first I want to read it—like an audience. I just want to see what I'm getting out of the screenplay as a human being and how it is going to affect me emotionally. Then if I feel it is right, I commit myself to it and to the director. You must trust the director completely—it is his film. You help him to make his movie.

It's very difficult to be a director these days because you have to make a movie *in spite* of everything—in spite of the studios, the producers, the production managers. It often seems like nobody's supporting your vision. Once the studio executives decide to go ahead, they change their minds because they have the responsibility and are afraid that if the film isn't good, heads are going to roll. They become paranoid. They become involved in making the film, giving bad advice, instead of leaving the director and the actors alone once they hire them. No director I've ever worked with set out to make a bad movie or to spend all the money in the world. They were all professionally responsible. Of course, it's necessary to have someone oversee the economy of the picture, but this should be done without interfering with the director's duties.

The Director's Wavelength

So now you sit down and find out, "What is your [the director's] movie?" If a director were to say, "Laszlo, here's the script; read it and tell me how this picture should look," I wouldn't even take the script.

Why should I tell him how his picture should look?

I have to find out what's in his mind. I let the director tell me and try to lock in to his wavelength. I try to give the director every latitude. Suddenly, in midshoot, he may change his mind: "Just consider this—

maybe this will be better." Many times when this happens I feel something dying within me. Something is not right, but you let him finish. He has to get it out, good or bad.

When he finishes, you start discussing. Your job is to make him realize—himself—that the first idea, the first instinct, was the better one.

For Martin Scorsese, much of directing is through improvisation. He gives the actors a lot of room, but he steers them. He wants to experiment and see what the actors have and can bring to the story.

As a cinematographer you really have to be on your toes for that kind of shooting. You cannot make it look like a newsreel, as it happens. It has to organically tie into the style that you discussed and the visual look.

When we did *New York, New York*, we did extensive research on old musicals. Marty wants the freedom of improvisation but still wants it to look like it was painstakingly made with great order and great design. So I have to capture these "good accidents" within a framework of very careful, stylized lighting.

My position as the cinematographer is like playing cards. You are the only one who sees what's in the director's hands—you deliver the goods to help him to make his plays.

And you have the whole army of your crew behind you to help you deliver.

The Crew

I've had the same gaffer and same key grip since 1964.

The three most important people are your camera operator, your gaffer, and your key grip. And each has his own crew. You also have your assistant cameramen, and I always say they shouldn't be called that—they should be called "director of focus." In England the first is called "focus puller."

In your crew members, you're looking for the same qualities that you have. The camera operator has to be an extension of your eye, because during the take he is looking through the camera and he's moving the camera and continuously making the compositions happen and ready to include some wonderful accidents.

I usually stand right behind the operator at the magazine point, and the assistant is there, too. And usually the director is physically wedging himself in there, so there's a nucleus of four in that two square feet.

We breathe together and feel together and sweat together.

There's a dialogue going on between the operator and the focus puller: "Too tight, too tight." When I see that my camera operator is in pain trying to adjust, then I know the shot is good.

In my gaffer, I want an understanding of my style, how I like to light and how I see things. Light is the most important factor in creating images. Everything else is in a subservient position. Light creates images. You start with a virgin film in a magazine that has never seen any daylight. You start with black and add light and color. As Truffaut said, "Film is truth twenty-four times per second," talking about the film advancing in the gate. You create the images on this virgin film, with your instinct and feeling, and these are brought together through the people you work with.

There is no storyboard for me per se, unless it's a specific situation that requires it—like a battle scene or a special effects scene. That's rigid, and if you change it, it affects postproduction. The more you listen—to the director and the actors—the more you get ideas for shots.

The Process

When you block out the scene, that's when you figure out the coverage. When do you want a close-up, a two-shot? Close-ups always interrupt a scene. They have the capacity to destroy moments. There again, you have to trust your instincts and, with conviction, be able to tell the director, "I don't believe we need a close-up here," or, conversely, "We should emphasize this moment with a close-up."

Ultimately it's the director's decision, but your responsibility is to feed him all this information.

Not Touching the Camera

In this town, because of the union, the director of photography is not allowed to operate the camera. In Europe, the cinematographer *is* the camera operator.

At first it was very disturbing to let the camera out of my hands. But I learned to live with the American system and to appreciate how important the role of camera operator is. Over the years I've only had three operators. My present operator is Ray De la Mont. He worked

with Vilmos on *The Witches of Eastwick*. But I claim he is my operator! So Vilmos says, "Let me have *your* operator." He has wonderful
qualities, and it's just a question of time before I lose him when he
becomes a cinematographer. I encourage that transition as much as I
can. There are very few "professional" camera operators or assistants.
They all have further ambitions.

The gaffer would be another obvious choice to move up to director of photography. But that very rarely happens, and I'm not sure
why. It would be a natural extension. It may be because he is very
dependent on the cinematographer to tell him what to do. But within
that framework, a good gaffer can take the initiative and come up with
a lot of ideas and shortcuts. And the key grip, too—how to actually
execute a shot or a dolly move or build a track.

Working with the Assistant Director

The director and the cinematographer decide what should happen and how it should happen. The first assistant director is listening
closely to our conversations; he has to be well informed.

A good AD is a blessing. You make certain things happen through
him. He is setting up background movement, timing how long an
actor can stay off the set.

He is the one who comes to the cinematographer when he's
composing a shot and says, "How long is it going to take?" I want to
say, "What am I—a prophet? Predicting the weather?" That's the part
I hate. It's a necessary evil. But I have to give him an estimate because
the actors want to get off the set. The first AD is right there bugging
me: "Could you give me ten minutes' notice when you're ready?" I
have to help him set his timetable so everyone can work at the same
time. I can't just finish my work, sit down, and wait until the actors get
made up and outfitted. By that time an hour would be wasted. That's
why it's very important to work closely with the first AD. Film costs an
incredible amount. You have to try to economize without hurting or
compromising the film.

Production Designer

The production designer enters at an earlier stage of filmmaking
than I do, which I think is wrong. We should enter at the same time.
But they try to save money, just give the DP the minimal prep time to

catch up with the director and the production designer. You usually only get three weeks, unless the film is technically very demanding.

During preproduction the director, the production designer, and the cinematographer—the perfect triangle—make major decisions about the look of the film that are going to be very binding through shooting. So the production designer and cinematographer should collaborate on these decisions before set construction starts.

It is important that the production designer builds a set that I can light and photograph. Usually the production designer is very conscious of that, because if he or she doesn't take my input, then the set may not be photographed in the right way.

Many times we see a house with a perfect exterior, but we don't like the way the interior connects and looks. So instead of doing the interior on location, it is better to build it.

There are some production designers who say, "I'll build this and you shoot it." I've gotten very upset with them: "Hey, are we working on the same picture?" You have to collaborate with the production designer on what best serves the film. Ideally the production designer puts his or her talent to work *for* the picture and consults the cinematographer before going ahead and building anything.

I need to find correct positions for lights on the sets. And he or she also has ideas for colors and tones along with the costume designer. I need to know what colors they have in mind.

The Shoot

Sometime in preproduction, or at least by the end, there comes a point when you actually *see* the film in your mind—hopefully as the director does. And then it just remains to shoot it, which is a totally different process and involves many more people.

I'm very calm and relaxed about how I see the film, but the night before first day of shooting there's an incredible excitement—tomorrow morning it's going to start happening. From tomorrow, every second and every move you make is final; once that camera records that scene, it's history.

By that time the production designer and costume designer are gone. The cinematographer, camera operator, gaffers, and grips are taking over, and the actual process of filmmaking starts.

I don't have to see dailies to know when something works. When you conclude a sequence that is well acted, well directed, and well captured by the camera, there's great satisfaction. Although it's never 100 percent. Filmmaking is a series of compromises. You start with the ideal, but you can never do that; there's always some element that infringes on that. You have to deal with those compromises strongly and rely on your instinct and your feeling. You have to know where your bottom line is.

Final Shot

I'm always very depressed when filming is over. It's like somebody died. That moment always arrives with a major emptiness.

You feel it's something that's born, took off, and has its own life and doesn't need you anymore. And it's going to appear on marquees and in theaters. You know your film is playing, you drive by and there's a big piece of you inside there.

Easy Rider

Easy Rider not only changed Hollywood, it changed people's lives around the world. On a recent trip to Hungary, my niece came back from the hairdresser's and she had told the hairdresser I was visiting from Hollywood. The hairdresser's jaw dropped, and she said, "That's your uncle? Tell him I've seen the film thirty-six times."

And that's behind the Iron Curtain!

Some critics minimized the achievement of whoever was involved with *Easy Rider*—Dennis Hopper, myself. They said, "A bunch of kids got together, got into a mobile home, and went around the country and made a movie and got lucky." This was very derogatory, it wasn't so.

We approached that film with just as much care as any film before or after. We had a shooting script, it wasn't improvised. The locations were improvised because, traveling, we would see something about the countryside, a place where it would be great to build a campfire.

We were such a small unit that we were able to stop spontaneously instead of going to our next scheduled stop. The freshness was there. We would get an inspiration—"This is it!"—and just do it simply, quickly, and wrap.

Easy Rider was one experience that gave me a strong connection to America.

Having Film to Show

That first "showcase feature" I did . . . we shot around the clock on weekends since everybody had regular jobs during the week. And in sixteen weekends we completed this black-and-white film. We all put our own money—what little we had—into this film for wardrobe, guns, horses, cheap lodgings, and some bologna sandwiches.

We asked CFI if they would process the film for a deferral; somehow they went for it. So we could see dailies there—35-mm black and white.

This film had a major purpose for everybody involved. We all needed a showcase—the actors, me, the director. I wanted to get into features. And nobody would consider me with just the 16-mm documentary stuff I had been doing.

I tried to make this little showcase richly textured—did a little night-for-night exterior, day interiors, night interiors, broad exterior, horse chases. We made sure we had a little bit of everything that a major film would include.

In this town, people see what you've done and say, "Yes, that's a wonderful exterior, but can you light?" That was the case after *Easy Rider*. And then after I'd been doing studio pictures, one executive came up to me and said, "You really light beautifully, but can you shoot exteriors?"

This is typical of the mentality of today's executives. It just shows how little they know about filmmaking or the history of the filmmakers they're dealing with. That's most evident too in the way they are starting to "colorize" the great old black-and-white films.

I hate to see black and white disappearing and to see the downgrading of the old black-and-white films—wanting to colorize them. It is a very unnatural act. The business people decide and commit this sacrilege. They have no respect for that piece of art—a classic, rare film.

Black and white requires a unique artistic approach. You're not dealing with different colors, but different tones and shades of black and white. You're making a careful translation of colors into shades, and I think lighting becomes more important in creating the tones, separations, and depth.

In any case, off that little black-and-white western I got my first feature, a low-budget exploitation James Bond–type film. It was when *Dr. No* came out and became an enormous hit and all these low-budget filmmakers were making copies. But that was the beginning of where I am today.

Advice

The union actually has a training program. You can start out as an assistant loader or second assistant cameraman and move up through the rank and file to first assistant cameraman, camera operator, and finally cinematographer.

Or you can stay away from the union and just become a cinematographer through luck and persistence. Which is what I did. I was never a camera operator as defined by the union. I always tried to get work as a cinematographer. When you reach the point of being an accomplished cinematographer, then a producer or director is willing to go to the union to battle for you.

I got to a point where directors wanted to use me as their cinematographer on union films, even though I was not in the union, and they would slip me in with any legal loophole they could resort to. Finally the union people got fed up and resigned themselves to the fact that I was going to be a cinematographer whether they liked it or not, and they gave me a card. Suddenly I became a group one cinematographer.

Initially I couldn't get in because Americans were saying, "How can they come here and work when our own citizens cannot get in and work?" The union was trying and still is trying to protect its membership. Against what, precisely, and whom I've never found out. Because I think that the basic personal talent of an individual is the strongest path into the union. I always believed, "One of these days it's going to happen." Besides talent, the most important thing to have is a great will.

How badly do you want this?

I tell cinema students, "You want it twenty-four hours a day? That's not enough. You have to want it twenty-*five* hours a day." You've got to want it badly, because there's another guy who wants it more than you do—and he'll pass you like a racehorse. I really believe that a person who has talent and persistence and is dedicated 200 percent can achieve what he or she wants sooner or later.

Education is enormously helpful. Gaining experience is essential. I don't necessarily recommend cinema schools. Or find anything wrong with them. Except that sitting in classes is another three or four years out of your life.

My education provided me with a foundation that I am grateful for. The philosophy of the cinema school in Hungary was, "We can't give you talent, but we can help you to discover it if you have it." That's the purpose of a cinema school—to nurture and bring that talent to full blossom. But when you leave cinema school you must gain some practical experience. I cannot emphasize enough: "Keep shooting and shooting and shooting." Make your own mistakes.

I feel very lucky. When you consider the billions of people on this earth, how many can do what they really like to do? Some people work in factories or offices, and they hate it. They wish they could do something else. We are the lucky dogs who can do what we like to do.

I don't want to retire. I think the moment that you do, you're dead. So in between features, I try to fill in with as much work as possible—with commercial work. It's an incredibly good training ground. It's like training to be a fighter. You can go there and keep in shape, and whenever the fight is called, "I'm there, I'm ready."

It provides me with a continuity of experience and a place to experiment. TV commercials often *require* that you come up with new ideas. Ever since I started working in feature films, I've supplemented it with commercial work.

Many people mistakenly look down on them because they are advertisements. But in terms of technique, they include all the elements that you need for a feature film.

The visual language: it is important to keep speaking it.

Camera Operator

The Camera Operator operates the camera and is responsible to the director of photography for composition, focus, camera movement, and anything that comes within the domain of the camera frame. As the sole individual, other than the director of photography, to look through the camera on every take, he or she may reject any take deemed faulty. The Camera Operator is charged with the proper functioning and maintenance of the camera and related equipment, determining correct shutter position and filters, perfecting focus, zoom, and t-stop changes (aided by the first assistant cameraman, also called "focus puller"), and seeing to it that the correct film stocks are available and properly threaded into the camera (aided by the second assistant cameraman, also called "loader"). He or she also works closely with the grip crew to perfect dolly, crane, and boom moves and with the sound crew to ensure that no microphones or sound-related equipment appear within camera frame.

Walt Lloyd

Graduating with a degree in advertising from the University of Georgia, WALT LLOYD intended to make his fortune, then "retire and go sailing around the world." The first time he ventured out to Los Angeles, he discovered the seamier side of advertising—and smog, and he returned to the South, this time to North Carolina, where he worked for a public television station and raised and rode horses. When he finally came back to the West Coast, he found work in a San Francisco commercial production house on the administrative end. In his spare time he would assemble, disassemble, and practice operating the cameras the production house would rent out. Walt discovered that he loved operating the camera. After two years he launched out on his own as a free-lance assistant cameraman. Since then he has been working with the camera exclusively and has been camera operator on such films as *Never Cry Wolf, The Hitcher, Radioactive Dreams, No Man's Land,* and *Less Than Zero* and most recently has embarked on a new career as a director of photography. Subsequent to giving this interview, he received Agfa Corp.'s prestigious Diamond Award for his work on *Sex, Lies, and Videotape,* which won the Palme d'Or at the 1989 Cannes Film Festival.

I USED to take trips up into the mountains of northeast Georgia, and on one of these trips I noticed a bunch of tractors and trailer-trucks up this logging trail right outside Tallullah Gorge. As I got closer I saw they weren't going anywhere. They were stuck. I pulled over to take a closer look because it's really unusual to drive a truck like that up a logging trail.

It turned out that it was a crew filming *Deliverance*. I stayed there for three days watching them, and I thought, If there is ever a way I could do this, what a wonderful way to make a living. Here are grown men and women acting like kids and getting paid for it.

They were up to their waists in mud, lowering the cameras and the equipment down into this huge gorge, and when they wanted to create the rapids, they would just open the gates in the dam above them and the water would come flowing through. It looked absolutely impossible to do. And there is no other business in the world that would have ever tried to do something like that.

It was a bolt of lightning. This was my first exposure to filmmaking—sitting up on the bluff overlooking this gorge and watching the filming of *Deliverance*.

Operating the Camera

I love operating the camera. It is manual, but it is more than that. It is like dancing. There is a timing and a flow that you have to find. You move a camera differently in a very tense and violent argument scene than you do in a love scene.

It is an incredibly technical job. It is also very, very simple. As soon as your eye knows what the film sees, as soon as that realization occurs, then your eye can be the film. When you know how the film translates what your eye is seeing, that's all you need.

You train your eye to the lights, and you learn to put a filter on the camera and what type of film to use. You have an assistant cameraman who can put the camera together and do the technical things. What you need to be concerned with is creating the mood and the environment that will make the scene work.

The DP is running the lighting crew through the gaffer, and the first assistant cameraman is running the camera crew. The operator is in this autonomous zone concentrating on the action and the actors, rather than getting too involved in the politics of running the crew and running the set.

The most important thing is to be decisive. I am one of four people who can ask for another take. The director, the director of photography, the script supervisor, and the camera operator can all ask for another shot.

The most obvious reason to ask for a take is that the shot did not happen the way it should have. More subtly, it is too much of a compromise for you to accept. You may want something to happen in a scene that is so important to you that you have to sell that next take. Sometimes you succeed, and it is appreciated. But you also have to respect the fact that every time you do another take it costs a lot of money. You have to be fiscally, as well as creatively, responsible.

The only problem with operating, if you are working a twelve- to eighteen-hour day, is that you can't take a break. Everyone else can walk off the set, go get a cup of coffee and relax, and you are tied to the camera. Even so, I wouldn't trade it for the world. Being the camera operator to me is the best job in the world. You actually see the film as it is being made.

United Effort

That is not to say that the camera operator is the only one responsible for really making the shot, because it is a team effort.

Your first camera assistant is in charge of the equipment, the technical aspects—assembling it and pulling focus, making sure the focus is correct during the shots. Your second assistant loads the camera and is a support person to the first assistant. He handles all of the paperwork, does the slating in the beginning, keeps all the equipment close. He is the one to tell the production manager when we need more film. And he keeps track of the inventory. That is a very important job.

All this frees me up to operate. But I'm working very closely with the first assistant cameraman as we focus. And if the camera is moving at all, the crane operator or the dolly grip becomes just as important as the camera operator. The move has to be made smoothly, and it has to follow the actors moving. To do that successfully, you need a team of five people working together.

Game Plan

It should ideally be a compilation of ideas of the director of photography and the director. The operator is there to translate and execute that compilation. There has to be a boss. Even if you do not agree with the director, it is your job to do what he wants.

There are plenty of opportunities to discuss civilly different ideas and alternatives. Most directors realize that making a film is not a dictatorial process, that it is a somewhat democratic process. And that it takes everybody to do it. But the bottom line is, someone has to be in charge, and when I want to direct a film and I want the ultimate control, then I'll do it, and at that point I expect to be treated as the captain of the ship.

The director of photography usually hires you. And, more often than not, the camera operator gets no prep whatsoever. He starts the first day of shooting.

As the camera operator, you listen to what the director has in his mind. He may throw out films whose style he thinks is appropriate for the film that we are working on. For *No Man's Land*, for instance, the director said, "I want this film to have a feel like *The French Connection.*"

The French Connection is a very exciting film, and the camera is always moving and jerking and shaking. Which is one of those things that inherently you try not to do. You try to make all your moves smooth. So you try to get the excitement in the camera and not compromise your own idea of what a shot should be.

Where is the line between being a bad cameraman and being an exciting cameraman? You make that judgment.

What is this going to look like when you add music to it, when it is chopped and fast, as in chase sequences?

Is it really important to make the move perfect? Or is it more important for there to be that tension created by people bouncing off the edge of the frame and the frame being filled and spilling over moving objects? This is what's going on in your mind as you try to execute the plan.

Setup

Usually with the dramatic sequences, interiors or houses, there is one camera—the A camera. Many films will have a B camera if, for instance, you have to shoot a dance or a big party scene or drive-by's or an exciting fight scene. Then you can have two or five or nine or as many as eleven cameras running, which is a lot to keep track of. You try to make sure the last one is rolling before the first one is out of film.

The director of photography works with the director in placing all of the cameras. I like to be there when the first blocking is done for a scene so I can walk through with the DP as he is figuring out how he is going to light and shoot it, and the director is trying to figure out how to block it.

I want to see what is going to happen rather than just walking on the set, aiming the camera, and turning it on. I like to take a participatory role. I watch the blocking. I figure out roughly where the camera is going to be. I figure out if there is going to be a dolly move or a camera move. We mark out where the tracks are going to be. The lighting is taking place. The actors go back into makeup. The camera gets out there and onto the tripod or the dolly.

Physical Movement of the Camera

The camera sits on a head that moves the camera up and down, right and left. The head sits on a tripod or a dolly. And the dolly moves the camera physically, up and down, which is called "booming," or it moves it along the tracks. Or if it is a smooth—say, a linoleum—floor, you don't need tracks, you can put the dolly on the floor and move it around anywhere.

So the dolly grip, the grip who actually pushes the dolly and raises and lowers the camera, is really important. He has to see what the camera is seeing *without* looking through it. He has to anticipate actors moving so that he can be moving the dolly when they start moving. He has got to be smooth. He has to do three things at once. It's a difficult job, and it takes talent and grace to do it. A good dolly grip can make a camera operator look like a million dollars.

Capturing Spring

Early in my career, I met a wonderful DP called Hiro Narita. After doing a low-budget picture with him, he asked if I wanted to go up to Alaska on a film called *Never Cry Wolf*. They were putting a wilderness scene together. And they had a still photographer, David Cavegnelo, who was also a naturalist and had shot for the Audubon Society and *National Geographic*. He needed someone to shoot for him, to be an assistant operator type.

I jumped at the chance. Went in to meet with Carol Ballard, the director. Carol said, "I want you to capture spring." I thought, That's a lofty assignment—capturing spring. . . .

He said, "Birds flying, the ice melting, flowers blooming. Capture spring. . . ." I thought, Are you kidding? This was the ultimate

355

assignment. What could be better? Flying to Alaska to capture spring.

We rummaged around in Carol's warehouse and picked out these ancient cameras that I had never seen—CN-3's, which are great cameras for the job—and he had probably every kind of Nikon lens ever made, which he had adapted to these cameras.

We took off for Alaska, landed in Anchorage, and immediately rented a four-wheel-drive van. David had researched and knew that we could follow the thaw up all the way to Nome, which is below the Arctic circle. We would hire a pilot to fly us in somewhere and tell him to come back in a couple of days. Or we would drive in and hike with the cameras in our backpacks. And follow a herd of sheep or a few moose. Follow ptarmigans, eagles, flickers; it was just an amazing experience.

We were capturing spring. But actually what I was doing was having the time of my life and getting paid for it.

Two Systems

There are actually two systems. In the British system the DP controls the lighting. And the camera operator works more closely with the director.

In the American system, everything goes through the director of photography. The director of photography is totally responsible for the technical crew below him—for the grips, the electricians, and the camera department.

It is more of a military hierarchy, but when you consider that it is costing you sometimes $100,000 a day to shoot, you need a military system. And you are talking to somebody who did everything he could to stay out of the military after growing up on military bases—for sixteen years. This organization is necessary.

In the American system, when it comes to the point of blocking a scene and placing the camera, the director of photography will work closely with the director and the camera operator, block that scene, and figure out where the camera will be placed and when it is going to move.

In the British system, the responsibility of the camera movement is left more up to the operator and director, with the DP not taking such an active part. The DP concerns himself exclusively with the lighting.

It is hard to say which is better. It depends on the magnitude of the film and also on how familiar the crew is with each other. If an American DP has worked with an operator for a while, and the operator knows the DP's style, then it will get closer to the British system.

Moving Up

The standard union way to move up to being a director of photography is going from second assistant cameraman to first to camera operator to director of photography.

The other way is through lighting—from electrician to best boy to gaffer to DP.

It is very difficult in the feature field to become a director of photography without paying your dues by coming up through the ranks. You have to learn that you need a certain amount of coverage for every scene. You need your master shot. You need your wide shots, your close-ups, and your transition shots. And there is quite a gap between what one learns in film school and the real film business. You need that exposure to the physical aspect of the camera.

Advice

Read the credits. Find out who the directors of photography and camera operators are and call them. You see names on posters. They are listed in the 411 directory. Call them up and say, "I know your work, I saw your film. I thought it was great, and I would like to work with you as an assistant."

It is very important to work with people whose style you like. It's a waste of time—except to survive—to work for someone you don't like or whose work you don't care about.

Another good way to get into the business is to go to rental houses in Los Angeles. There are about ten rental houses, and they are hiring all of the time. That is how many people become assistants. They start out in rental houses and become expert technicians. Once you become an expert technician, you are indispensable on the set, especially if it is a location movie. When you are out in the middle of Wyoming or Montana and you can tear the camera apart and put it back together and fix it, you become extremely valuable.

I've torn a camera apart and spent hours putting it back together, and through luck, it worked. And I've also spent an hour on the phone, with the camera apart in front of me, talking to the technicians back in Los Angeles as I was working on it trying to fix a problem, so that we could get the next shot. And that is *not* the way I like to work.

Hindsight

I took a long time getting to where I am now. After I saw the crew shooting *Deliverance*, it was almost ten years before I got into the film business. I meandered from coast to coast. And there is nothing I would change. I could probably be a little further along by now if I had come out single-mindedly. But life is not just work, and my life experiences are enriching to my work experiences. It is very important for me to select my projects so that I don't get into a rut.

I'm a little naive and idealistic. I think people work in this business because they love it. I have a different approach than the guy who became a technician because his father was a technician. He is working in this business because he is very good at it. It is what he has known all of his life. It is like the third-generation fireman or third-generation policeman in Philadelphia who has a big mortgage and four kids to support.

Quite frankly, I never want to get myself into a position where I have to take a job. Because for every good job that comes along in this business there are about eight or ten jobs that I don't want to do.

One of the first things I did when I started free-lancing was put a few months' income away, and I haven't really dipped into it too much. I know it is there, and that is what gives me the freedom to select my projects. This is one of those rare businesses, like working on an oil drilling platform in the middle of the North Shore in Alaska, where you work such long hours and are so completely involved, you can't really spend your money. It is very easy to save. And you just have to put yourself in that frame of mind.

More than money, I need a challenge. It is now hard to get on a set where I'm not thrilled about the film or the director of photography. I don't accept every film that comes by, and sometimes I wonder after the film comes out and it's a hit, "God, did I make the right decision?"

But I'm at the point where if I don't feel like I can take some excitement or challenge away from a film, then it is a job. And that is what I don't want this business to become for me.

10
THE PRINT

Once the movie has been shot, the film itself—the product of everyone's intensive labor—becomes the most valued element of the motion picture.

The Film Editor determines the order in which the captured scenes are arranged for final viewing.

The Negative Cutter carries out the precarious task of physically handling the single copy of the "negative" from which hundreds of movie prints will be developed.

The Color Timer must personally guarantee the quality and vividness of the color in the final film product.

The Titles and Optical Effects Coordinator arranges for the proper recording of the names to be shown at the beginning and end of a motion picture and also oversees the use of a postproduction camera, which enables the filmmaker to alter or enhance those images already captured on the film.

Finally, the Projectionist threads the final print of the movie from reel through projector so that the motion picture may be seen by an appreciative viewing public.

Film Editor

The Film Editor selects and assembles the film to create a story progression in accordance with the director's vision. He works closely with the director, viewing dailies with him to determine the selection of images, and with his assistant editor in the actual organization, physical handling, and cutting of the positive workprint. He also supervises the synchronization of voice and sound tracks with the picture and provides guide tracks for the sound effects editors to enable them to prepare for dubbing sessions. Additional duties include designing, preparing, and approving orders for opticals, titles, stock footage when necessary, and viewing the composite answer prints for quality control. He or she also coordinates the work of the sound and music editors and the negative cutter, and in the absence of a postproduction supervisor orders editing supplies and rentals.

Freeman and Carmel Davies

FREEMAN DAVIES and his wife, CARMEL, have worked on most of director Walter Hill's movies, including *Southern Comfort, 48 Hrs., Streets of Fire, Brewster's Millions, Crossroads, Extreme Prejudice, Red Heat,* and *Johnny Handsome.* While Carmel's apprenticeship was served under Freeman's guidance, since giving this interview she has gone on to become a film editor in her own right. Despite the pressures of the business, they have successfully maintained their marriage and raised two children.

FREEMAN: There are about 2,500 members in our union. That includes film editors, sound editors, music editors, film librarians, assistant and apprentice editors. Employment can be seasonal and unemployment is often high. Some make a living on independent projects, editing commercials or the like. Only a couple of hundred film editors work regularly in feature films, usually because they are affiliated with established directors. I was lucky. I didn't just "break in." I'm third generation. I have been working in the lab or cutting room ever since I was a kid. I got a summer job when I was fifteen and spent the next dozen years or so doing all the peripheral jobs, learning the support aspects that let the head editor do his job editing the movie.

CARMEL: I was a research and circulation librarian before I got the chance to become an assistant editor. Arranging, cataloging, filing, researching—the experience was valuable as it was similar to the duties of an assistant editor.

Duties of Assistant Editor

CARMEL: You take care of all the details so the editor is free to make creative decisions. This includes syncing dailies, synchronizing the sound track with the work picture. Making sure that every shot we are supposed to have is accounted for, dealing with the lab during the long process of production. Production may last two to five months.

The lab receives exposed negative daily and develops and makes prints from the negative daily, hence the term dailies. The assistant goes through the lined script and notes what the director has asked for and then double-checks that camera and sound have ordered every take. If we didn't get it for whatever reason, the assistant makes sure we have it or can get it.

A large portion of the assistant editor's time is taken up with handling the thousand and one phone calls that come into the editing room everyday, juggling people, time, and equipment.

There are many people who edit who have never been assistant editors.

FREEMAN: I think those people can miss some things. I'm constantly drawing on that initial exposure to technical aspects I got as an assistant editor. I'm glad I know all that I know from having "not edited" for the first fifteen years of my career. I started working in the lab, so I know about printing and timing; I worked in the sound department, so I picked up some background in sound. A friend of ours, while assisting for the first time, got promoted to editor. She edited two films but has since gone back to assisting, having realized that there's a lot she doesn't know. She wants to go back to pick up some of that technical experience she missed from not being an assistant long enough.

CARMEL: If you work with an editor who has never assisted, you can really tell. They seem to be less capable of troubleshooting and focusing on what is really a problem and what isn't. You're much more self-sufficient if you have a good assistant editing background. Instead of waiting for an assistant to have time to do something for you, you will do it yourself and continue to move forward.

FREEMAN: One editor we worked with, who had never been an assistant, would have the assistant just set up a system. But the assistant he had didn't have a system, kept changing from one way of organizing film to another. When we came on, we couldn't find film.

CARMEL: It was a nightmare. There was 77,000 feet of film, which isn't much, four editors, and three assistants. It took so long to locate footage that you needed all those people to do what should have been a simple job.

FREEMAN: On our last show, we had about 800,000 feet, which is a lot, and just one assistant and three editors. That's how tight and organized our system is. We all had assistant editing experience. The average amount of film shot for a feature is 150,000 to 200,000 feet. I value my assistants, the way we operate, there's very free input. I really want my assistants to let me in on ideas they have or tell me if they perceive a problem.

Criteria for Making an Edit

FREEMAN: I'm not as theoretical in my approach as a lot of editors are. I'll make a cut because it just seems right. Maybe because I spent so many years watching other editors work, editing is second nature to me. I don't think about it or talk about it that much. I just do it.

CARMEL: But Freeman is a perfectionist. He'll work and work on a scene until he gets what he wants. He worries about everything from the lighting to the color tone to the rhythm of the cuts to how a scene affects the film as a whole.

FREEMAN: Nobody said this is an easy job. It's fun, but *not* easy. The editors spend more actual time on the film, frame by frame, than almost anybody else involved with the movie, in some cases more than the producer or director.

From the start, we're put in the position of judging performances. One of the hardest things for an editor is learning to match the intensity and physical action of a performance from shot to shot and take to take within a given scene.

If you have a lot of coverage, and the actors are doing things the same way, the movements are the same, the performances are even, you can cut wherever you want. But if they don't match physically—body, posture, and so on—you have to find a way around what they're doing.

CARMEL: You have to sort of distract . . .

FREEMAN: Cut away from it. Walter called today and said he had a terrible day shooting a scene. The coverage in the morning was going along real well. They were shooting out on the water on a ferry boat and he had a plan of how he was going to cover the scene. Then they went to lunch, and the performance level after lunch changed dramatically. The conditions out on the water changed, affecting the movement of the boat. He called and said, "Tell me what I need. It may not be a problem, but it feels like it to me. The scene's two and a half minutes long, I wish I had had it written as a minute and a half. The actors are taking tremendous pauses. We're getting the right content, but it's overdone."

So we then have to find the balance to make the performance work. And they may have to go out and pick up that shot. It'll depend on what I can do with it. I'll cut it real quick, send it to him, and when they come back, if they need a section that's more compressed, they'll have to re-do it. That's continually happening. Sometimes scenes are overwritten. The same information may be imparted in two or three scenes, so you have the latitude of selecting what scene you want to put that information across in. Or maybe you do it twice.

So physical movement, lighting, and camera work can vary from take to take, and we have to determine how best to match them. If you're cutting on movement, sometimes you want to make the movements the same, sometimes you want to make it jarring. It's all very theoretical until you have the film in front of you, which hands the problems to you.

CARMEL: When you sit in dailies, you'll see a scene and think it's going to be very easy to cut. When you get into it, things you didn't notice turn out to be problematic.

Something being a problem is determined by how the scene is ultimately supposed to play. For instance, when we were doing *Red Heat*, there were lots of situations where we wanted to hang a little bit longer on an actor to add to the drama of the scene, and he would do a little shtick with his eyebrows that blew the moment. When you saw it in dailies, you thought, "Oh, it's going to be so great." When you get in there and are doing it frame by frame, it's the little details that can hold you up. And then again, that's not problematic if you choose to play the character in a more flip manner.

FREEMAN: There's an inherent pacing in the story, in the dialogue, in the actors' delivery at the time they're doing it. If you don't have a lot of coverage, you can't really change that. If you do, you can pace it up. If you're into a certain pace and they're giving you that pace, you can just let it go.

In the bathroom fight in *Warriors*, for instance, I don't think there was any shot that lasted more than sixty feet. There was a lot of action.

And the *boucherie*—the dance sequence at the end of *Southern Comfort*—was interesting. I got the chance to play with time there. There are several things going on at once. These guys are being stalked. You've got paranoia to convey against the backdrop of all that great Cajun bayou dancing footage Walter [Hill] shot.

After the Rough Cut

FREEMAN: It's like writing the drafts of a screenplay. Working with Walter, we joke that editing is the final rewrite. We can take out or add any lines of dialogue we want or rearrange the structure of entire scenes or sections of the film. Walter gives me a lot to work with. There's always great footage. He pretty much lets me do what I want with the initial assemblage. He trusts me enough to give me a lot of control in the rough cut.

CARMEL: There's a lot of room for creativity, given the parameters of what the director has on film.

Interaction with Others

FREEMAN: The cameraman (director of photography) will tell me what his intent is, what he's going for in the overall look of the film. Working with Walter the way we do, they generally don't look at dailies after the first week. It's a very unusual situation; most people don't do it that way. I judge if it looks good to me. If I perceive a real problem, I'll send it to the cameraman and to Walter.

On the one we're currently working with, I've sent very little film to them because I like how it looks. There's a lot of discussion about "desaturating" the look of the film, getting the rich colors out—which takes the contrast and levels it out, and then we do another process that puts the blacks back in. That's a lab process, done by reels. On the film *Tucker*, they flashed every reel a little bit differently, so there were progressively different looks throughout the film. But you can do it only by reel, not by scene or cut.

The look of this film is going to change possibly dramatically by the time we finish everything.

There's a timer who works with the dailies timing who establishes a printing light that lets us have a constant. So we'll know if they're deviating from that and see if we really have a problem. If they're correcting everything for you when they perceive a problem—that is before we see it—it's harder to judge how far off a cut might be.

This last week, an A and B camera had two quite different looks. So I've asked the timer to see how much he can correct to make it look the same. And if they can't achieve the color balance we want, we may just go out and pick up that one particular shot. It's a driving scene done with camera mounts—most of the shots are shot through the window. Depending on what angle you're shooting at, it's going to look different with the reflection of the sun, clouds, different weather on the glass during the day. The shot that didn't match was not shot through glass, and it doesn't look quite like the others. The color timer is getting day to day very even consistency, except for this one instance. The lab gives us a general report if they perceive a problem. But often they won't see a problem because they're looking at the film at high speed and they'll miss it. If they've missed a problem it's our job to catch it and hopefully solve it.

CARMEL: The sound mixer sends his logs to us. The production sound not only gives you your background, but it gives you your performances, which is crucial.

FREEMAN: If it's a chase scene, five times out of ten you're not going to use the sound, you're going to heighten the sound. But performance sound is very important to get. The production sound mixer will often call wanting to know if the sound is good or if we're perceiving the problems he's having. They apologize a lot, they get into noisy areas, and there's nothing they can do about it. In the middle of an industrial plant it's hard to get the dialogue. If there's good background sound at a particular locale, I may use it for the scene it was shot for or for another scene.

CARMEL: We also work closely with the sound editor on specific things we need—special sound effects that have to be created, or a sound effect that will make a transition for us, *or* a performance that has to be changed in ADR (automated dialogue replacement).

FREEMAN: Sometimes you'll get into a situation where something has to be Foleyed. For instance, the shoes that a character may be wearing don't sound right to you—maybe they've got a soft muffled walk and you want a hard sole that slaps, a reverberant sound. That all has to be communicated to the sound editor.

When we have a cut that we're about ready to turn over to sound effects, we'll have a screening with the sound supervisor and his key people, give them input so they know what we're looking for. We get them started in a direction, and they'll elaborate on that with their expertise. If I like or don't like something, I'm free to tell them. The director, of course, will let them know if he doesn't like something. But quite often, I'm more technically oriented toward the sound than the director is. I'll tell the director my suggestions, and he'll say, "Give it a try," or, conversely, he may be very happy with the scene as is. This is on a scene-by-scene basis. You go through the film for maybe a month, month and a half, on the rerecording stage.

CARMEL: We'll have some contact with the first AD when we want to add scenes or shots.

FREEMAN: We'll make a list of shots that we'd like to get in a post-insert shoot [shooting done after principal photography is completed], for example. We'll coordinate with an AD on what angles we'd need, what props he'd have to get, if we need extras, things like that. Where it becomes a mini-shoot.

CARMEL: And the production designer as well. When they've been on location and are coming back to L.A., they have to match new sets to existing sets already shot, they'll need to see footage. We'll pull clips for them and tell them how much of a set or set decoration will actually be seen, so they know exactly what to match if they have to do more shooting. And they also just like to come in and see how their work is looking.

FREEMAN: The way we work with a production manager (other

than negotiating our salary and determining the editing budget) is: He needs to know if a set can come down. Since I'm evaluating whether the scene has been covered, if I anticipate that we might want to tighten something up, we'll instruct him to "save a section of that wall" for the close-up in an insert shoot. He wants to know because he has the place rented and wants to clear it out.

If there are lots of special visual effects, you'll be coordinating with the optical guys, depending on how sophisticated it is. There may be a special editor on the film just for the effects.

An example of dealing with opticals was when there was a readout monitor where the actors were interacting with this computer, and the special effect was to burn in a written message delivered by the computer. The look of that type style was discussed with the special effects people, the director, and the producer—how long the cut's going to be, the timing of the cut with the mock-up of the dialogue, so that they know precisely what to put in. Often you may shoot the actor against a blue screen, and you don't really know what's going to be in the background unless you talk to the special effects people who are shooting the background. If there's going to be movement in the background, I want to know what it is. There's a lot of that kind of interplay within departments if it's a real technical effects show.

On Winning Prizes

FREEMAN: I've always felt that it's pretty hard to judge an editor's work unless you know what he had to work with, what kind of footage he started with.

CARMEL: It seems that, often, awards go to the editors of well known films.

FREEMAN: If a film gets other awards, too, it helps. When a film is popular, the editing usually gets noticed. Which is ironic, because one of the goals of an editor is to do such a good job that nobody notices the editing or how the film is put together.

The Future of Film Editing

FREEMAN: The trend is toward electronic film editing. As we get closer and closer to having random access off disks, rather than linear tape, it will become as flexible as film. It's a different spatial relationship. Right now I deal with a "distance" of film—a length, something concrete in my hands.

My feeling is that if video had come out first and it was in this box, everybody technologically would be trying to figure out, "How can we get it out of that box and look at it in our hands?" It's almost backward.

The decisions are still the same, but I miss the feel of the physical film in video editing. The mechanics of putting pieces of film together take time, but they're just that—mechanical—you can be thinking about what your next cut is while you're making your splice. It gives you more creative thinking time.

If you're making choices on a video machine, you don't have the liberty of taking the time that you might on actual film. The process of video editing demands that you speed up. You're using a piece of equipment that is worth maybe a million dollars, and you're scheduling a time when you can use it. Right now I go in, and if I want to stay late, I stay late. But if I'm scheduled for eight hours on a video editing machine, I've got to think in those eight hours. It's more pressured. It's costing you this many dollars an hour to work on this piece of equipment—you'd better be productive in those hours. The other way there is still a dollar figure attached, but I have more latitude. If I'm feeling creative at the end of the day, I can continue. If I'm having a slow day, I don't feel so bad because later on something's going to start clicking.

I would say in the next five years I'll be editing on video. There's a system now that does have random access, and it sounds terrific. You can trim things without having to re-lay it down. With the digital process you'll be able to randomly drop frames, add frames, extend things in a much quicker fashion. It's very close to film, other than the physicality of it.

Advice

Several times a year, an individual will ask me how to break in. Sometimes they're even already established in some other aspect of film. A sound mixer told me he wanted to break into editing. He's already making, salarywise, what I'm making, and he'd have to take a cut to start all over in a new capacity. His background in sound is helpful, and he could probably break into editing if he's really serious by negotiating to do the mix of a show as well as working in the cutting room.

A lot of people now try to get in by going into a sound effects house, where there's very seasonal, transitional employment, so there are openings. They'll start as a runner. There'll be an opportunity to move into sound effects editing. And once you're in the union you can move around.

There are only so many openings. You should be willing to do anything to be near enough to make the move when an opportunity comes up to work directly on a film.

CARMEL: A lot of assistants worked as film librarians or in film shipping or even in the mailroom at the beginning. You're on the lot, you get to know people. One day everyone is too busy with other things. They need someone to sort through a hundred reels of film, so you come up from film shipping to do the dirty work. They remember you for that. Next time there's an opening in the editing room, they think of you.

FREEMAN: Not too long ago, having a relative who worked as an editor was the only way to break in.

CARMEL: It still doesn't hurt to know someone.

FREEMAN: As far as the temperament it takes, editors run the gamut. Some are very aggressive and forceful, some are very maternal, others are very diplomatic. I think most of them are very patient. You have to be able to work things over and over and over again—and find new ways of approaching the material, try to stay fresh.

Negative Cutter

The Negative Cutter is responsible to the film editor for cutting the camera original negative, the sole raw material from which all positive workprints are made, to the specifications, frame by frame, of the finalized workprint and for the care and condition of the negative. Additional duties include writing up orders for dispatching the negative to the laboratory for fine grains (black-and-white positives used to duplicate negative where clarity, not speed, is important), CRIs, cleaning, treatment, or duping, and overseeing the work of the breakdown operator, who must meticulously break down, splice, catalog, file, and store the negative.

Diane Jackson

DIANE JACKSON started working in "the labs" twenty years ago and worked her way up through the ranks from breakdown operator to foreman to negative cutter. She now owns Reel People, Inc., located in the Technicolor laboratory building, and does all of Paramount's and New World's negative cutting as well as servicing many independent film companies. Among the hundreds of films for which she has done the negative cutting are *The Untouchables, Fatal Attraction, Crocodile Dundee, Coming to America, Star Trek IV, Absence of Malice, Heartburn, Beverly Hills Cop II, Some Kind of Wonderful,* and *She's Having a Baby.*

FOR NEGATIVE cutters, one error is an error too many. There is virtually no room for mistakes. Our job is critically important in the sense that we are holding in our hands millions of dollars' worth of camera negative. If camera negative is torn, scratched, or destroyed, there's no way, unless that section is reshot, to get it back.

What our job boils down to is the sole responsibility of the camera negative. It is not a creative job. It is very technical, and it's critical. I've always jokingly said, "I cannot make your film better, but I can definitely ruin it for you."

When an editor makes a cutting error he can call me up and say, "Diane, I want to get a reprint on scene so-and-so," and I can take that roll of negatives, send it in to the lab, and get him another print.

If I make a mistake, I have ruined camera negative and it's gone.

The Process

The process is quite simply this: On a daily basis, the director, the crew, the actors and actresses, all go out and shoot. And on a given day they may shoot as few as two or as many as twenty rolls of camera negative. That night they turn these "dailies"—the original camera negative rolls, Fuji, Kodak, Agfa-Gevaert, whatever—into the lab.

They're closed up very tightly in black sacks because they're unexposed. The lab develops the negative so that it becomes a product that can be put into the light. They make a positive print off each daily. These positive prints are given to the editors.

The negative is given to us by the lab. The editor screens the dailies to approve them. If everything is fine, he notifies the laboratory.

We, meanwhile, have been breaking down and cataloging the dailies—the negative—into individual scenes. On a given daily, you could have as little as one or as many as thirty or more shoots—for example, the director has said, "This is 32 take 1," and he'll want to take it again and again until he's satisfied. He might go on up to "32, take 20," depending on how many times they have to shoot this scene.

The director and editor decide what scenes they want to print. When the developed dailies come in, a camera report comes with it, and it tells the laboratory which scenes they want prints of and which scenes they don't want. These become the "B negative"—that's unused, it's no good.

Keying the Negative

The negative has what we call "key" numbers on every foot. A given scene might have two hundred feet, and it has a head key number and a tail key number, which we write on a jacket. The jacket is a small piece of paper that protects the negative on which we write, in addition to the key numbers, the slate, and the name of the show. These are stored numerically, from the smallest to the largest.

These numbers that are on the negative are stock numbers on each foot of film. They come from Eastman Kodak that way. In 35 mm there are sixteen frames to a foot, so for every sixteen frames there's a number.

Now the editor who has simultaneously received a positive print of the negative that I'm dealing with is proceeding to do what his job is editorially. When he's ready to cut the negative, he sends us those edited positives, what they call "workprints," which we then key. We write down the first key number of every shot and the cut number. The reel could have eighty cuts, it could have three hundred.

We then go to the box where I am storing the show, have broken

it down and cataloged, and start pulling the negative scenes the editor
has chosen out of the boxes.

Often on one given scene you'll have at least three or four cuts
because, for instance, the dialogue that you and I are doing, there
would be a camera on you and a camera on me . . . I'm talking, then
you talk, and it cuts back and forth.

Once we've assembled all the negative rolls to match exactly the
editor's print, we submit it to the laboratory and they splice it. Then it
goes to timing.

We work up to the point where there's an answer print. The
editor, the director, and other interested parties then come in to approve the quality, the format, and the color.

Keeping Track

Our records have to be explicit. I have to sign showing that I
received X amount of dailies per day, which lets the lab know; they
then have a copy on record showing that that negative was put into my
possession.

If, after I've broken it down, the editor calls me and asks me to
send a piece of negative to an optical house, such as Pacific Title or
Cinema Research or whatever, I have a receipt book that lists the name
of the show, the date, the scene number, the complete key number,
head and tail, whom I signed it out to and whom it came from, which
would be ourselves, Reel People, Inc. And I get a signature from
whomever I turned the negative over to.

When material is returned to me, I take the paperwork off the
board and I check it off, and it better all be there or I'm immediately
on the phone telling them that they did not send me back seven rolls,
they only sent me back six, and somewhere I'm missing a roll.

From the first daily that we receive till the final product when it's
completely out of my hands and in the lab's hands, we are totally
responsible for where every frame of negative goes, for the condition
it's in, how it's put together, and how it looks on the screen.

Slugging the Negative

When we cut a show, more than likely we don't cut a reel complete the first time. There are camera original scenes that are at the
optical house, one thing or another. So when we're cutting, and we

come to a section that is missing, we "slug" it. We put a piece of white 35-mm film in there that indicates negative that has yet to be inserted. Later on, we'll drop in "slugged" scenes.

The Fragile Negative

When the editor and the producers see the final product, a beautiful clean print, they're elated because they know how many times this very fragile material has been through so many people's hands.

From day one, the very first roll of camera negative that we receive, the process starts as far as how careful we have to be in how we handle and store it. We put protection on every roll so that no part of that negative is exposed to the edge of a box.

Down the road we will start doing things like airline versions, or the television version, or a syndication version. So even though a show's been cut, it's done, it's out in the theaters, I still hold on to the "outs and trims" [usable negative] for about six months.

The lab, Technicolor, keeps the final negative print of the film in their vault. It's high security and has atmospheric conditions—very cold and set up to preserve the film.

When I think they've gone through all the versions, I call Paramount or New World and say, "Hey, I'm running out of space, I've got more shows coming in, I've got to get this stuff out of here." And they will make arrangements for it to be stored at Paramount Film Library or with Pacific Title Archives or Bonded Film Services.

They have a librarian who makes decisions on what to keep as stock footage, and they will keep the trims and the outs. They'll shred the B negative—the portion of the dailies that they don't want because "it's no good, it's an incomplete scene, somebody started to laugh in the middle."

But anything that was used in cutting the show, they store.

Way after the fact, two years later, I still have to be able to know where everything is. Even though it's left my hands, it may be in a vault somewhere in the city where they're storing it, I have to have records of what I gave them, so that if I ever need to put my hands on the negative again, I can locate it by going through my paperwork.

I have files on every show I complete, every piece of negative that ever went through any of our hands for the entire time that we were responsible for that picture.

Cleanliness Before Godliness

If I were in most editorial rooms, I wouldn't make it till noon without getting dirty. There's no need for editors to keep their areas clean.

They're under a great deal of pressure, dealing with many more elements than we are—the optical effects, their various prints, the mag tracks, different sound elements for the effects and the music and the voice-over—and their stuff is being trashed around.

I get workprints in here that look like they've been rolled over by tires and coffee poured over them. To be fair, they do try to avoid trashing the print as much as possible because they have to screen it for the director and other individuals. And there are people who'll say, "I don't want to look at a dirty print," which means making reprints.

We have to keep the negative *immaculate*.

You handle the edges, you never put your hands on the negative, *never*. You put your thumbprint on it, the emulsion, it's impossible. You can hand-clean it, you can wet gate it, you can do lots of things, and it'll help it, but it won't be in the pristine state it should be in.

Buried in Negative

Absence of Malice, starring Sally Field and Paul Newman, is a feature I did some years ago. Reel eleven of *Absence of Malice* had over three hundred cuts.

Three hundred cuts for a single reel is a very action-packed reel, that's a lot of movement taking place. That would have been okay, but in addition every cut came out of approximately a thousand-foot scene. In other words, they must have had seven or eight cameras shooting at the same time, just letting the cameras roll.

Out of those three hundred scenes I probably pulled out two hundred, all approximately a thousand feet long, so by the time I got it all set up around my bench I was in a hole. And it took me two days and two pairs of slacks, because you hold the roll in your hand over the bin, and you're holding it to your stomach to keep everything in control, and at the end of each day I had worn a nice hole in each pair of these pants.

Those are the ones you see coming, and you just cringe. You lose money on those. Because you always quote a flat price: "I'll do your feature for X amount of dollars."

Reel People, Inc.

We're a corporation. The name of the company is Reel People, Inc., and I'm the president as well as the owner/operator, meaning I work as well. And during our busy season, our crew consists of myself, my foreman, two other cutters, and two breakdown people.

My foreman does everything that I do. She has the authority to assign work, see to it that things get done on time, and deal with the customers. If I'm not here, my foreman's second in command and has the authority to make decisions.

You earn that position. I was a foreman for Fox Television for 5½ years before I went into business for myself.

Good Money

We have people who came here forty years ago for a summer job and have been here ever since because the money is glamorous, even if you have one of the more menial jobs in the laboratory. Because it's union—we all belong to the Film Technicians Union, Local 683—a person can, without a high school diploma, someday be making $25 to $30 an hour. The reason I got into this business was simply because of money. I was twenty-eight years old, raising a son, divorced. And *then* I realized that I had a business instinct, and that I wanted to get good at this.

Human Error

We are blessed, and I knock on wood when I say that; there has not been one error in this room in three years. But human error exists. And if anybody made a mistake, they would never hear a word from me. I'd say, "It's okay. I want you to calm down and forget about it." And I would explain the situation to the customer.

I have very good people in here, and if a mistake happens, it is just a genuine accident, and I am simply not going to get on them about it. We've all made a mistake at one time or another in our careers. And to get upset with them, to intimidate them, is going to create another mistake. They're going to get nervous, they're going to be overly cautious, they're not going to get a rhythm going again.

Advice

It's almost a closed union. Local 683 has dropped back by over 50 percent in the last twenty years because of videotape. There's a lot of layoffs.

If I were going to talk to some young adult, I wouldn't encourage it. I would say, "Go for tape, go for editorial, go for something other than this end because we're being phased out."

The future for negative cutters, in my opinion, is ten years. There's still life in features. But even that . . . Alan Alda made a movie, *Sweet Liberty*, shot it on film, then transferred it to tape. All of the negative cutters I know, we all have that fear. We all feel—work as hard as you can, make all the money you can, invest it, save it, and try to find another business to go into eventually.

If you *are* in this area, my advice is 1) relax, and 2) realize the seriousness of what you're handling here. Any given roll of negative could be worth a hundred thousand or better. You drop it on the floor, you spill coffee on it, you spill soda on it, you crack it up, you are in major trouble, so you do not smoke in your cutting rooms, you do not drink coffee in the cutting rooms, you do not have your lunch next to you, you have to leave that area. And I have an area where we have a refrigerator, a coffee machine, and a microwave. You can eat in your room even, but make sure that there's nothing on that table, and before you start, wash everything down.

The name of this game is accuracy, right down the line. I've had three John Hughes films where my A negative—I'm not talking about the part they didn't print, I'm talking about the part they printed—was over four hundred thousand feet each; that's a lot of negative. And you put one scene in the wrong box, just imagine what you have to go through to try to locate it.

I feel that negative cutters have always been underestimated, have never been given the credit due them. Granted, I can't make your film better, but when people realize the responsibility that we have, and what we could do if we didn't take what we do seriously . . . we could ruin somebody's major investment.

They've only in the last five years started giving negative cutters credit on the end titles. And it's about time.

Color Timer

The Color Timer is responsible for setting the density, contrast, and color balance of the film in order to match the color from scene to scene and to establish consistency, through the color on the filmic image, in the film's mood and tone. He or she works closely with the director of photography to determine the shades and density desired on the positive print and with the Hazeltine operator, who executes the desired color gradations on the original camera negative print (much as the editor would make editorial decisions on the positive print as a "blueprint" for the negative cutter).

Aubrey Head

AUBREY HEAD took a summer job at Technicolor in 1949 doing positive assembly, found he had a knack for it, and decided to stay. He worked his way into viewing and, finally, color timing, which he has been doing for the last twenty-five years. He is currently in charge of Technicolor's theatrical answer print department, supervising color timers. Among the hundreds of films he has color-timed are *Thief, Altered States, On Golden Pond, Sophie's Choice, Coal Miner's Daughter, Under Fire, The World According to Garp, Ragtime, Heaven's Gate, The River, Blade Runner,* and *Amadeus.*

I DON'T know why the word *timer* is used. It's strange, isn't it? You think of somebody with a stopwatch.

In England they call it "grading." Color grading. Here we call it color timing. Nothing to do with time at all. What the timer does is set the density and the color of the scene.

Once a picture has been cut, as close to answer print stage as possible, we run the work picture for the client—the director or who-ever calls the shots—to determine the "keys." They will say, "We like the mood of this particular sequence." And that will be the key; that will set the tone for color for the entire film.

I take that scene—the key—and have it on the right side, and on the left side I crank through the scope, which would be our equivalent of a Moviola, and I stop and make each sequence blend into that key for the mood and color that they want.

We have three colors, yellow, cyan, and magenta. We combine those. Yellow and cyan make green, cyan and magenta make blue, yellow and magenta make red—and more. Then we can raise the lights. If you go evenly with yellow, cyan, and magenta, raising the lights, you make the whole scene darker on the screen, which is working with density in color.

The responsibility I have as a color timer is to make sure there is consistency in the darkness or lightness and the particular shade of color. Each picture will have a key tone. For instance, in a period piece you might have sepia tones, rusts and browns. A contemporary thriller like *Thief* with James Caan had predominantly cool tones—blue.

Working up through the Lab

You work up through the lab. You have to go through the control end of it where you understand the different steps, from the original negative to an interpositive to an internegative and all the specs of different stocks. All of this background is necessary.

I spent many years in viewing, which is where I really learned color. In viewing I would look at the film coming off the dye transfer machine. Freshly made. I would view it through one projector, and I had another projector on the right side of that through which we would run a reference. This was the reference the client had approved. I had to make color corrections to make this production match the reference the client approved.

It had already been color-timed by someone else. And this was what we called production or release printing.

Each lab has its own timers. In this town there are Deluxe, MGM, Technicolor, and CFI, basically. Four labs, and each one has its own timers on staff.

I am now more in the administrative end. I get involved in timing only when there is a problem or if somebody gets sick. I would say I am more or less a color consultant, and I supervise the timers. I have about ten top-of-the-line timers who work for me; most of them have been with the company over thirty years. Here at Technicolor, it is more or less a seniority thing. You have to be here long enough to acquire the background. It's considered an apprenticeship situation.

The Hazeltine

The average picture has about 1,000 to 1,200 scenes. We make each of those scenes consistent in color and density. When you get a first printing, you can then work on a Hazeltine machine, which is like a TV monitor that reads the negative and brings up an image on a screen. There will actually be a positive image of the negative. We can start off with beginning lights in the Hazeltine—the yellow, cyan, and magenta.

The Hazeltine operator goes through and puts initial lights on every scene. And then it's taken to the printing room to make a positive print with those printing lights.

The Hazeltine operator is a negative timer. I'm a positive timer . . . I work with a positive print. When that negative goes over to the Hazeltine timer, he'll put that positive workprint up on the reference side, on the right side, in a comparator, and he'll wind down this scene, which I've given him notes on. The notes might say, "At 625 feet in, reel 1, scene of two men facing the camera at the bar, that is a beautiful key of that sequence at the bar." Then he'll match the two for density and color for the mood they want.

In my notes, he'll have keys all the way through, so when I get the print it is probably close to the direction I want, but I have to smooth it out scene by scene, and I'll reprint until I get it to where I think it is fine to show the client.

They in turn will look at it and say things like "I think you are carrying the whole thing a little light," or "You are carrying this too warm." You have to interpret what they are saying, since they usually don't know the different colors.

I'll go back and work with the positive print again, looking at my notes from the screening with the creative people, and at 625 feet in, reel 1, two men to camera, I'll put a note down and say, "It is light," or "It's cold," or whatever. Then when I go into the scope to time it scene by scene, I'll put that workprint up to that scene and make adjustments in the computer and send it back down for another print.

This will repeat until the client is happy. Three or four screenings will usually take care of it.

Knowing Color

Occasionally I work with people who try to get something out of the negative that is not there or who think they know more than they do. There are times when the negative itself is underexposed or over-exposed. There is something wrong with the negative, so you can't get what they want out of it.

My best experiences have been with people who are seasoned and experienced and who know what they want. A cinematographer who comes to mind is John Alcott, with whom I worked on *Under Fire*, who has since passed away. There was a shot in that film where the guerilla leader was dead in this room and the light coming in from outside streams in. He completely overexposed that scene to get harsh black shadows against the light streaming in. The man was very gifted that way.

It's rewarding to work with people with that kind of talent . . . cinematographers like Miroslav Ondricek, with whom I did four pictures—*Amadeus*, *The World According to Garp*, *Ragtime*, and *Funny Farm*. He lives in Prague, Czechoslovakia. And I occasionally still talk to him on the phone. He doesn't speak English very well, but I know what he wants. We feel at ease with each other in spite of the language barrier.

Communication between the cinematographer and the timer is very important. And with all the creative people, you have to be able to understand what they want. Even though they don't know exactly how to tell you.

On *Amadeus*, the dailies were shot in Europe. I flew to Saul Zaentz Studios in Berkeley to run the workprint there with Miloš Forman, the director, and Merrick (which is what I called Miroslav Ondricek). The dailies that were manufactured in Europe were very yellow-green and off color in density and not much help. I had to sort of create the color myself.

What I did was take the key from the scene when Mozart is dying, the light from the candle at his deathbed. There was nothing else to go by. You had to use your own imagination as to how it should look.

And I created the "key" for the rest of the film from the light of that candle.

Titles and Optical Effects Coordinator

The function of a Titles and Optical Effects Coordinator is to produce the main and end titles for a film and to shoot the special optical effects. Optical effects are not shot by a camera under production circumstances but are created under controlled conditions, usually by reproducing images on previously processed film with an optical printer. These reproduced images run the gamut from dissolves, fades, wipes, matte shots, superimpositions, and variations of added, enlarged, or reduced images to very complex manipulations of time and space.

Richard Gernand

RICHARD GERNAND started working in motion pictures twenty-five years ago in the laboratories, doing everything—splicing, developing negative, and cutting film—and has been involved in the titles and optical process for the last fifteen years at Pacific Title, a titles and optical house that has been in existence since 1919. Among the hundreds of pictures they have worked on are *Dirty Harry*, *Romancing the Stone*, the three *Star Wars* epics, the three *Indiana Jones* epics, *Empire of the Sun*, *Roger Rabbit*, *Fatal Attraction*, and *Platoon*.

OUR FIRST contact is the editor. He's the person who's actually got his hands in the picture and the one you want to really talk with to get a feel of what's going on. Along with that, of course, the creative and the finance people—the directors and producers—get involved.

On a title assignment, our print shop and art department will cut and paste and make layouts. Then we'll make a copy of the layout for the customer's approval. Once he looks at that and approves it, we'll take it down to the animation department, and I'll make sure that they shoot it the way the customer wants it.

This is such a customized business that you can't say, "Give me a number five," or, "Shoot me three feet of a number two." It is also an extremely fast-paced business; it is all deadlines. They would literally love to bring it in in the morning and have it out at night, which can't be done.

The client will give me approved legal copy from their legal department, with all the correct names and titles. We stay out of the legal process because there's a good possibility that if we make a mistake, we will have to reroll it all over again at our cost. We don't want to be legally responsible for something that important. We stress that when we get legal copy it be perfectly "clean" copy. Then we take total responsibility, and we're off and running.

Then it's anywhere from a five- to eight-day turnaround from the time that we take the type sheet and print up our first layout on the print shop computer to when we send the customer the proof sheet to approve size, spelling, and positions.

We're back and forth there for maybe a day or a day and a half. Once they've approved that, then we go back to the computer again, and it has a capability of printing up a cell (acetate-based) title card, and it'll be black background with clear letters. We'll take that, lay it out in our art department, and touch it up. And assemble it, so that it can be shot on the animation stand properly.

Once the art department is finished with it, it goes down to the animation department, where it is set up on their animation stand and a test is done to determine the proper exposure. At that point, we're ready to shoot.

If it's to be shot as any color title over black, then we can shoot it right there at that moment on original color negative and they'll get their end credit the next day. But if they want it over a background, then we shoot a black-and-white high-contrast piece of film, which will give us the film elements we need to put that same title over a background. That would be an optical process.

Title Design

A title designer creates a concept, title color, type style, does all the preliminary title design work, and follows through with the producers, directors, and editors; they take over the design responsibility, but will work with a titles and optical house to deliver a completed title. Those titles are very expensive, and they look it.

We don't pretend to be title design people, but we have done hundreds of thousands of titles over the years. And if we have an idea of what a client wants, we can expand on it and create it for them.

Last on the List

During postproduction, when the editors are reviewing the rough cut for their picture, or the second unit group is doing fill-in shots or freeway shots or pickup shots, that's about the time they start thinking about titles. Ninety-nine percent of the time what we deliver is the very last thing that gets cut into the reel before it goes to the lab to be answer-printed and readied for distribution. We're under quite a bit of pressure in the sense that the whole picture and their advertising campaign and distribution campaign, especially if it's a big picture, can hinge on final delivery of the titles and opticals.

I am clued into the budget and time requirements and complexity of a job by one or a combination of requests made by a client: (1) "I've got a very small budget," (2) "I've got to have it in a week," (3) "We want the best quality possible," or (4) all of the above. Number 4 is a tough order to fill.

Budget

I've worked with producers who said they had ten thousand dollars total for everything; that was a main title, end title, and all the effects. That's considered small in the sense that most main and end titles, on average, cost about ten thousand, not counting the special effects.

A large job would be into fifteen to eighteen thousand for the main title, another five to eight thousand for the end credit. There's really not a lot you should do with an end credit unless you want to get fancy with it. And then however many effects you include, of course, will increase the cost.

On *Return of the Jedi*, we were responsible for about 150 of the effects out of a total 300 to 350. They used us and a couple of other optical houses because there was so much work; they literally went to everybody in town.

Fortunately I knew the guys at Lucasfilm Ltd., and when it came to the actual titles we did those. And then when they went to foreign distribution we did all the titles for seven different countries, all in the individual names, all the accents—seven different times. It was a big job, the kind you like to have.

The smaller-budget picture might be anywhere from five hundred thousand to a million dollars. By the time they get to us, their budgets are usually pretty much used up, and they only have six or eight thousand dollars to spend on everything.

The End Credits

It used to be ten credits at the head end, your major stars, your producer, your director, and the name of the picture; that was it. And then the end credits were generally the major people, the principal cameramen, and the location people, possibly your cast again, but very limited crew and maybe whoever distributed the picture. That was it, very short.

Empire of the Sun's and *Roger Rabbit*'s end credits are five hundred and something feet long. That's six minutes of credits rolling by. I just finished one called *Powaqqatsi*, the sequel to *Koyaanisqatsi*, which got close to seven hundred feet. That is a huge end credit, and has set the record as far as I know.

They've named everybody who was involved in any facet of the business in every country they were in. Their theory is, they've gotten that much assistance from all these people and they want to give them credit even if it costs them thousands of dollars extra.

Optical Effects

Optical effects are created under controlled conditions. Special and visual effects are done on location or on a sound stage, and they have one or two opportunities to get the shot right. We can do it any number of times.

For instance, they want to shoot a fire at the Bonaventure Hotel. Obviously they're not going to set the Bonaventure on fire. The film company will shoot the Bonaventure, we'll make the appropriate mattes, and by compositing an optical on a special camera and using these different pieces of film element, we can put the fire in the specific window and make the building look charred, create smoke, and so on.

These are called the special optical effects, as opposed to special visual effects, which is what they might do on a sound stage when they physically burn a little miniature town. Once the town is burned, whether it be a miniature or real life, it's gone.

The beauty of an optical is that if it's not right the first time or they want to make the fire larger, smaller, redder, greener, whatever, we just go back on camera and change it.

An example of an optical effect would be a shot of a ship that had capsized and was turned upside down. The film company photographs a miniature of the hull of a ship floating in a tank of water with a solid blue background. Then they take a separate shot of the people who are supposed to be standing on the hull of that ship against a large blue canvas. This is called a blue screen process. We then create a matte, which is a very fine division, a line that you can create to make the two pieces of film come together and give the impression that the people are standing on the hull of the ship.

Another example would be one we did of a car exploding in an underground parking area. The cameras photographed the parked car in the underground area and the live action of the person, who was supposed to blow up, walking toward the car, opening the door, getting inside, and turning on the ignition.

They then turned the camera off, moved the car, littered the place with debris, started the smoke so the whole place looked like it was the aftereffect of an explosion, started the camera back up again, and photographed that "after" of the two shots. We then took the beginning and ending pieces, ran the film down on our optical printer to the point where he supposedly turned the ignition on and the explosion happened, and introduced an explosion by some special film explosion effects we have so it looks like the car was blown to smithereens.

Once you bit-and-piece this thing together, you wind up with a special effect that can't be duplicated in an underground garage.

We've done work for Lucasfilm—all three of the *Star Wars* films and the two *Ewok* pictures that they did for TV. And they'll often use a matte painting of a particular forest or a city or a planet with two moons that we know can't exist. They'll create the matte background, which is the painting, and the matte, which is the high-contrast or hard-edge piece of film that will actually act as our separation. They'll also photograph the live action. We then composite it all into a complete shot.

We also shot the shooting-star sequence in *Platoon* where the guys are trekking through the jungle at night. That was a basic animation process, shot one frame at a time. The animator has the capability of going back and putting a streak or a glowing head on the shooting star to give it a comet-type effect. We will have complete control over the angle and speed of the approach. If the client wants it faster, slower, bigger, smaller, we can make it anything he wants. So if you can't go out and wait for Halley's comet to fly by, we'll make it for you.

Logos

The logo for Amblin' Entertainment was derived from the *E.T.* picture—with the little guy on a bicycle riding across the sky and when he gets to the moon the bicycle slowly stops and at the same time the name "Amblin' Entertainment" animates across the scene.

That was a series of continued takes. Our art department did some sketches and a storyboard, we went back and forth. It really was a concept derived from input from Amblin' people and our people. Once we got it close to what we wanted, we started putting little pieces on film, doing what they call "pencil" tests, little animated tests, and eventually we shot the job. It was a process that took about two months.

Selling the Movie

One thing they do in selling a movie is try to create a look to their titles that also ties in with the theme of their picture so they have consistency in their posters and their advertising in the magazines and newspapers.

For instance, *Romancing the Stone*—that title, no matter where you saw it, was always the same. It was always written out with "Romancing," and then the "Stone" looked like it was cut out of a piece of emerald. The idea was to get that visual impression, so that whenever you saw it you thought of the movie immediately.

For an audience that is not aware of the content of the picture, perhaps a title or even the title design might help persuade them to go see it. Just like the title of a book might persuade you to buy it without knowing what's inside.

What it is useful for is offshoot industries that a film might generate. All the *Star Wars* pictures have a similar design concept, from the movie title to T-shirts and all the other paraphernalia.

Union Representation

Most employees of film optical houses like this are members of Local 659, the cameramen's local, myself included. We're not the same kind of a cameraman who might go on location, but we're still in the camera end. We're just working on stationary cameras, special effects cameras, as opposed to a mobile 35-mm motion picture camera.

We have other unions in the company as well. There is the artists' union, the print shop union, the lab Local 683 union, and then we have our drivers, who are members of the drivers' union.

Advice

Videotape has a very firm foothold in the business now. But the quality of videotape is still limited when you compare it with film quality. This is the consensus throughout the industry. If you have a very involved optical effect or title sequence, working on motion picture film will give you much better quality than videotape.

Someday in the near future, they'll have videotape to the point where the quality will equal that of film, and at that point there'll be a slow transition to everything being on tape.

Commercials are almost all exclusively done on tape. Fades and dissolves, a very simple process, were previously done on film. Now they're doing them on tape for all the TV shows. There's a loss of quality, but on the TV set you don't see it the way you would in the theater.

My advice to somebody new coming in the business is to learn computers, learn video, and learn film. The combination of the three is where this business is going to be. Right now we've got a whole bunch of computers here running our cameras. The guys have learned on the job, but it's taken a lot of training to do that. If a person came into the business fresh with a good computer background, he'd have a distinct advantage.

And eventually computers will be used to run the video cameras, so of course, if you have video knowledge, that will help.

The complicated effects still have to be done on film. And when you're looking at the budgets that these people are working with to produce a motion picture—the average is anywhere from five to fifteen million—to spend an extra couple of thousand dollars to get titles and effects that really stand out, that's a drop in the bucket.

There are some very professional producers who know what they want going in. There are no frills, and they stay on budget. And when you bring a picture in on budget, then you've got the money to pay for titles and the art design for your posters and billboards. And that gives the picture an added push.

Studio Projectionist

The Studio Projectionist operates the projector, screening films for producers, directors, editors, and the various executives connected with film projects at that studio. He or she is responsible for screening the film in focus and at the correct light levels, for keeping the film reels in order, for the maintenance and proper functioning of the projector, and for acting as custodian of the film print while it is in his or her possession.

Sal Olivas

As a youth, SAL OLIVAS was employed as a farm worker before serving in Vietnam and returning to California to live with relatives and look for work. Hanging out on weekends with a friend in the projection room of an East Los Angeles movie theater, Sal learned the job through osmosis. He gained entry into the projectionists' local and was sent out on various assignments, including a one-day job on the Paramount lot. The assignment stretched into weeks, then months. Sal has now been screening films for administrative heads of the film company, directors, and film editors for fourteen years.

I HAD to learn studio procedures, had to be exact and right. Outside the studios, in the public theaters, you can make a few mistakes and no one's really going to jump on you. In the studios, you're working with producers and directors, and they have to see everything exactly right. If there's a flaw in the negative, they have to know it's in the film and not in the way you're projecting the film, so they can reshoot it. If there's a flicker, they have to know they can trust you to tell them if it's in the projection light or in the camera.

Focus is most important. Usually the cameraman [director of photography] is at the dailies, and he knows he's not out of focus. So you have to be right on the ball, as opposed to running a theater projector where you just throw the thing on and if the film is scratched or you put on a wrong reel, you usually don't suffer the consequences.

The Drill

There's a chief projectionist; he's head of the entire department. There's one on each studio lot. He also coordinates working hours.

When I started out, for about a year, I used to work twelve to fourteen hours a day. I'd work around the callboard, where they call you every day to tell you where you're going to work, whether they are going to keep you in that same spot or send you to another studio.

At night I'd work the public theater for five or six hours more. And then, on the weekends, I'd put in a twelve-hour grind at a revival house.

Two or three months after I got to Paramount, they offered me a "house run." A house run means you actually go to where a guy lives. He has a regular screening room in his house, which he uses for entertainment and work. Sometimes you run dailies. Most of the time you run production footage or released or prereleased films or films borrowed from other studios.

The film is delivered by couriers, the film carriers. And we usually ask that if we're going to be needed on the weekend, to please let us know on Friday if possible. But many times they'll want to call you on Saturday. So sometimes you can be held up until six or seven on a Saturday night waiting to hear if they want you. They have to pay you, but still, it's your time that's ticking away while you're waiting.

Whenever I do a house run, I'm treated nicely, and of course, the money's good because you're on the clock. They pay you by the hour, so if I leave the studio at six and arrive there at eight, it can amount to overtime or even double time. It's very good in that respect, but your private life is just shot because you're never home.

I was lucky that my wife was able to handle the hours. She was very understanding. I can't always make it to family functions, even on holidays, because I have to work. Or I may get to stay at home for an hour on a holiday and then leave because my job has me on call.

Secrecy

There's a lot of confidentiality involved with this job. I remember one particular director who's known for his secrecy. He would absolutely refuse to let anyone else see the dailies. And we had an agreement that when the film arrived, I was to lock the projection room door. No one was to come in. Even if it was the head of the studio, I was to stop the machines, tell the director on the intercom that someone was out here who really wanted to see the dailies, and he would come out and take care of it.

One time even I was not allowed to look at the screen. I'm serious. The projectionist was not allowed to watch. The editors brought the film in with about twenty-five feet of "focus" leader attached. The director had one of his editors, who'd already seen the scene, in the booth with me. And the director explained to me, "I don't want you to look at the screen. Put the film on, start it, focus it, then please look away."

So I looked at the opposite wall. And when the film shoots through the port glass, there's a reflection and the reflection hits the wall. So the editor is looking at the screen, I'm looking at the wall behind, and I'm looking at exactly what he's seeing. It was so funny. And it was ridiculous because there was nothing obscene or out of the ordinary in the film. It was just something the director was experimenting with. He just didn't want anybody else to see it.

And he's that way about his scripts, too. At the end of the picture, he sent me a script of the movie. And when I opened it up, it was blank. All the pages were numbered and everything, but it was blank. He gave everyone connected with the picture a blank script, and he signed it as a kind of a put-on thing. Because that's his thing—secrecy.

The strange thing is that this same director was fanatical about trusting only me to project the film. Once, I went on vacation in isolated canyon country. The director went nuts when he found out I wasn't at the studio. He yelled and screamed and insisted they try to locate me and bring me back no matter what the cost. The chief projectionist himself had to volunteer to take my place until I got back.

When the film was finished and scheduled to be shown at an exhibitors screening in San Francisco, the director insisted that I should be the one to personally deliver the print. He said, "I want this man to go with this film on the airplane." He put padlocks on the "Goldbergs" (the film cans) and handed me the key. They had a limo to take me to the airport. The film did not go in the baggage compartment. The film went on the seat next to me.

When I got there, they had a car waiting to take me to the hotel. I kept the film in the room with me overnight. The next day they had a car drive me to the theater where the exhibitors were waiting.

I was in the projection room the entire time. The film never left my sight. When I came back to Los Angeles, the director had me deliver the film right to his house.

That's the way he wanted things done.

Inspiring Confidence

There are certain times when you speak up, and there are other times when you just don't say anything. You have to read the mood, the situation. There's times when they even ask you your opinion.

For instance, screen tests. They might have footage on a number of actors up for the same role, and they'll ask me over the monitor, "Who do you vote for?" I just shout out my opinion. What the heck, they're not going to fire me for making the wrong casting decision.

Here are all these creative minds, the head of the studio and all the executives, and here's the projectionist who gets to put in his two cents. It's fun that way.

Sometimes I get to read a script, then I get to see the screen tests and who's going to be in it, then see the film develop as they shoot, run it when they put the music to it, and finally see the finished product.

I remember watching the dailies on *Flashdance*. We were all saying, "Wow, what's happening here?" Then they put the music to that film, and it just made an entirely different picture.

Nightmare

I have a recurring dream running a film for a two- or three-thousand-member audience, a huge audience. Something happens in the projector, and I cannot get it started. I can't get the right film on, I can't get the thing to run. It's a nightmare. People are waiting and I hear the hum of the crowd and I'm sweating and my hands do not work.

I'll tell you a true-life incident that happened when I worked at a public theater. I was working on a weekend and I went downstairs to get popcorn, and when I came back I'd locked myself out of the projection room while the movie was running.

First of all, we're not supposed to leave the room while the movie's on. Second of all, each roll runs about eighteen minutes, and I stayed talking to the workers and manager at the candy counter for almost that long.

You have to understand, the doors in this theater were solid, they're fireproofed to protect the nitrate film. And I'm locked out.

So, no big deal. I go downstairs to get the manager's key. The manager goes into his desk. There's no key for the projection room door.

Now I'm down to about seven or eight minutes. So we call the owner of the theater, and he says, "Yeah, there's a key there," and the candy girl, everybody's looking for the key. We can't find it. The roll's running low, I know when the scene is going to change. The image will die, and the light will keep going. I can't open the door, and I'm thinking, Let's call the fire department.

Finally I run downstairs to my car and I get a huge lug wrench with a pointed edge on it. I bang on this door until I finally wedge the wrench between the wall and the door. The door pops open just in time to make the changeover. I barely made it, maybe thirty seconds to spare.

It could have been a disaster because when the carbon runs out, it continues to feed. It's on a screw, and unless you cut the electrical source, it'll just keep feeding on itself. When it runs out of carbon it just jams, and pretty soon things start breaking. The film would keep going on the bottom roll, around and around, but the equipment would break.

That was the most panicked I've ever been. A matinee on a Sunday afternoon.

Luck and the Future

I often think how lucky I've been to have ended up here. I had other jobs, factory jobs and the like, and here I am working in Beverly Hills, going into these beautiful homes owned by the heads of the movie industry. And it's something I try never to forget—where I came from.

I've put in time, coming up on twenty years. I worked hard, did my best. I have a family now. I need to be at home more. It's not like a nine-to-five job, never has been.

I live out in the desert. We've got a couple of acres. I'm investing in real estate. I'm buying more property so that, eventually, I can live off my investments.

Also, my union has a pension plan. We're a small union of two hundred fifty guys considering a merger with the local sound union to give us more power. Because of the union, I don't have to worry about health care costs. They paid for the birth of my son. I'm an asthmatic, and I need medicine from time to time, and the benefits have been tremendously helpful to me and probably will continue on into my old age.

Advice

To be starting out now could be very rough. The number of jobs is dwindling. The big companies seem to be taking more and more away from our union with each contract negotiation, every two or three years.

I would say the main thing is to make sure to educate yourself in video because video is the coming thing. It's here now. They're doing so much with it in all phases of filmmaking—projection, editing, these things that high-tech electronics has brought about.

This takes a new understanding and as much experience as you can get before the future catches up with you.

11
THE MAGICIANS

Through their technical virtuosity, the professionals in this chapter create the illusion of things, places, and processes that may or may not bear any relationship to reality. By enabling the viewer to escape the bonds of time and space, they give us a glimpse of the future or the past, the horrific or idyllic.

The specialists in this chapter can create entire worlds that have never existed before or beings that may or may not have any human parallel.

Visual Effects Producer

The Visual Effects Producer supervises the overall visual effects approach to a motion picture and is responsible for each scene that requires special visual effects, namely the manipulation of photography to produce the illusion of reality. He or she works closely with the director, visual effects art director, and the visual effects director of photography in breaking down the script for visual effects and/or special effects and is responsible for planning, scheduling, and organizing their execution. While special effects are actually created on a sound stage or location for the production camera to shoot, visual effects are shot with a special camera and crew and are later incorporated into the film, using mattes, traveling matte photography, blue screen, models and miniatures, opticals, and many other techniques.

Richard Edlund

Born in North Dakota, RICHARD EDLUND moved west as a teenager and got involved in a program that gave high school kids a chance to rub shoulders with professional photographers. An assignment to photograph a navy "shindig" inspired Richard to join up and continue studying photography under military auspices. During a two-year hitch in Japan, Richard rebuilt an old film processing machine, starting a motion picture department at the Navy Photographic Center and experimenting with documentaries. He subsequently enrolled at USC as a cinema major but soon left to "bloody his knuckles on all the doors in Hollywood." His first job in Hollywood, at an optical house, resulted from halfheartedly leaving his résumé at the California Department of Employment. While working with opticals, he also learned product lighting for commercials, namely "how to make a can of deodorant look dazzling and the fine art of beer pouring," and got a chance to experiment with special effects.

Tiring of the commercial world in the late 1960s, he launched into his "hippie sabbatical" period and became a rock-and-roll photographer, doing cover albums for the Fifth Dimension, the Association, Seals & Crofts, and Three Dog Night among others; invented the "pig-nose amp" (an amplifier still used by rock-and-roll musicians); studied Zen; operated a fleet of cable cars in San Francisco; and made some astrological films.

Finally, hooking up with the commercial field again, he developed the "candy apple neon" and "glistening chrome" looks, still used today in animated graphics. He also met John Dykstra and Doug Trumbull. John Dykstra had been commissioned to do the visual effects for *Star Wars*. Doug Trumbull, an acknowledged mentor of today's leading visual effects artists, eventually became Richard Edlund's partner. John Dykstra and Richard set up the San Fernando Valley warehouse, which became the *Star Wars* machinery generator and the original location of George Lucas's visual effects company, Industrial Light and Magic. Today, Academy Award–winner Richard Edlund is recognized throughout the industry as a master in his field. His credits include *Star Wars, The Empire Strikes Back, Raiders of the Lost Ark, Poltergeist, Return of the Jedi, 2010, Ghostbusters,* and *Die Hard,* among many others. He is the founder and president of Boss Films, a visual effects studio located in Marina Del Rey, California.

WHAT DREW me to photography was that it is a way to melt together art and technology. In order to take good pictures you have to understand what photography is all about and what a camera is and why you do certain things with a camera.

Visual effects, where I am now, is a field that is the razor's edge in photography. It is where you are pushing everything to the limits and manipulating images photographically to make audiences believe they are seeing something that they are really not seeing, whether it is matte work or animation or miniatures.

Special Effects/Visual Effects—The Difference

Special effects and visual effects, it's an industry distinction. And it *is* confusing.

The studios used to have their own special photographic effects departments. Matte painters, optical printers, setups for *The Ten Commandments* or for doing the burning of Atlanta in *Gone With the Wind,* were all done at Paramount. Or the effects for *Marooned in Space* were done at Columbia.

They closed them down in about 1960 when there was this spate of street films: *Shaft, Bullitt,* the car chase, the era of the zoom lens. There was no longer any use for special photographic effects, so the term became obsolete. And there were no visual effects movies made for a long time, and/or special effects movies.

Today, what we call "special effects" is the guy on the set who has the fog maker, who pulls the stuff across the floor with wires, sets up the big squid heads and the mole smokers and the fire in the fireplace. That's all *shot by the production camera.*

Visual effects, or "special visual effects," as it is sometimes called, involves photographic composite work, or work that is incorporated into production footage. That is what we, here at Boss, specialize in.

It's part of the whole aesthetic, it wraps around, and it makes sense to do that. It's better, I've concluded, to have a visual effects art director, who deals with the director on all of the scenes that require visual effects and then follows the aesthetics of the production through to the end.

Then you have a visual effects director of photography, who handles the shooting of the plates, dealing with the photographic aspects of the production.

That is the way I've set it up here. And I have taken the credit "Visual effects produced by," which makes the most sense from my position because that is what I've become—more of a producer. It also leaves open the visual effects supervisor credit for my colleagues.

I've become much more of a deal maker and administrator and supervisor over the years. It was inevitable. And the expertise and the hands-on virtuosity that I may have had at one time has been eclipsed by other people because I have an octopus position as opposed to a focused one-job-at-a-time kind of situation.

Star Wars

I had been working with Robert Abel, a very innovative, creative force in the commercial field, developing new animated graphics techniques, when I met John Dykstra and Doug Trumbull. John and I hit it off, and we went out to the Valley to set up this warehouse, which became the Star Wars machinery generator.

I was in the perfect place at the right time with the right capabilities to take on the project as director of photography for all of the special effects.

The VistaVision Camera

We were able to purchase these old cameras called "VistaVision," which had been on the shelves gathering dust for twenty years. VistaVision was a format that had been introduced in the fifties that didn't last very long, and the equipment was lying around. Nobody thought it had any value, so we picked it up for nothing.

We got these cameras and polished them up, and set up a machine shop and a model shop and art department and animation stands and built an enormous amount of equipment for Star Wars with

397

Twentieth Century-Fox money. We spent almost a million dollars before we shot any film.

On *Star Wars*, I took the credit of "first cameraman," and that goes back to my childhood, seeing the "first cameraman" title as opposed to "director of photography." So I took that credit (it means the same as director of photography) and received an Oscar for that.

Getting into the Union

Many years before *Star Wars*, in my optical house days with Joe Westheimer, I'd had a run-in with the union. I was kind of a one-man band in the back room—running three setups—and Joe got busted for having me work nonunion.

I had real long hair at the time. It was the sixties, the beginning of my hippie days. But finally, out of deference to Joe, I got my hair cut. When I went down to the union for inspection, this very Napoleonic character—not a real tall man who wore three-piece shiny suits and always talked down to you—said, "That's not short enough."

I didn't like the fact that having short hair was a prerequisite for getting into the cameramen's union. So I left the union on philosophical grounds.

But when we started on *Star Wars*, I wanted to be aboveboard. I went back to the union and talked to the new business agent and told him I'd been offered this job, that I was definitely qualified for it and I couldn't think of anyone else who was.

And he said, "Oh, we have guys."

I said, "I'm not trying to be smart or anything, but I just think that this project and this particular group of people are unique."

About nine months later, when we had our big robotic boom camera, which panned and tilted and rolled and was all programmable and there was a big blue screen down at one end and all of this weird-looking technology sitting there that had never been done before—we invented it to do *Star Wars*—I knew these guys were coming. And indeed, a tough Local 44 representative and this huge character from the grip scene, all bedecked with IA lapel pins and big rings, came to see what was going on.

Knowing of their impending arrival, I programmed the camera to go down the track, boom up camera, pan, tilt around, and then come back toward them, boom on, swing over, and stop at this particular point right in front of them.

When they came out on the stage, I had this all set up. My attitude was that I was going to be taken in as a DP, a director of photography, or I was going to quit. I was not going through any more hassles with the union. I knew that I was in a good position. There was nobody at this point who could have taken over from where I was going because I had designed the stuff and knew how it worked.

So I punched the button, and it just blew their minds because they saw a whole revolution in technology happening in front of their faces. It shook their foundation, and, in fact, they said, "Fine."

I've had no problems with the unions since then. In fact, when I set this company up, I came down here and was more or less welcomed with open arms by the union.

We are a big hirer of people in town. We are now both helping each other, and the unions have been very cooperative with us.

You can't really be against the unions. Because if you didn't have unions, you would have sweatshops. The producers would work people for twenty-four hours a day and pay them nothing. That is what happened in the 1940s, the grip wars of the forties. They were dropping wrenches off the catwalks. People were almost getting killed from all these problems and making ten cents an hour and frying up in the rafters all day watching a big arc light.

The unions have their place. There are all of these problems, but it has actually worked out on our behalf. When you do hire somebody from the union, you are not going to get some bozo who doesn't know what he is talking about. And a producer can call the union and say, "Give me a crew tomorrow at nine A.M.," and tomorrow at nine A.M. he is ready to shoot. He has the right people, the right equipment.

Finishing the Trilogy

I made a deal with myself that I would finish the trilogy—*Star Wars, The Empire Strikes Back,* and *Return of the Jedi. Jedi* was a very difficult project, both psychologically as well as in terms of brute work.

But I'd made up my mind to leave. It wasn't giving me the chance to do what I wanted any longer. I had a group of people who all wanted to work together, so when I left, that group would join me. There was a long period of "What is happening?" And then there was a dark Thursday up there at ILM when everybody had gotten the word that I had made the deal, when the pen was put to paper.

It was like a fade-out, a long dissolve. And all of a sudden we were packing up.

Boss Films

And here is where Lady Luck was on my side again. I had been talking to Doug Trumbull. He was thinking about retiring from the special effects area and spending time on his own projects. And here was his studio with a lot of equipment just sitting around. He wanted to get out. And I wanted to come back to Los Angeles.

It was finally *Ghostbusters* and *2010* that enabled us to get this studio turned around, rebuilding it. We started negotiating on both simultaneously. It was a very strong and interesting negotiation to put two studios in bed together. MGM and Columbia would be splitting costs; it was a very complex deal.

I formed this company, Boss Films, at that time. You have to set up a corporation to deal with the studios. Union signatory, employer of record, and all of these legal situations. I had about twenty minutes to come up with a name.

Visual Effects—A Ministudio

Visual effects is a very complex process. It is more complicated than any other thing in the movie business. We have forty thousand square feet here. It is like a ministudio.

There is a stage that is 100 by 120 feet. There is a model shop down at the other end of the building, and there is a matte painting department with a robotic camera, all of it electronically controlled. Then we've got a couple of motion control setups. We've got a big cloud tank and an animation department and an optical compositing department and an editorial department and a machine shop and electronics shop, engineering, and accounting.

The crew and the overhead on something like this is phenomenal, although we are very careful about cost control. We've never had less than about fifty-five people on staff since we started this company in 1983, and we've been up to as many as 190.

Competition

I think it's great that we have competitors. The whole essence of America is competition. And if you don't have a competitor, then you start to get fat and lazy. There is usually plenty of work, and we've outbid our competitors on certain jobs and they've outbid us on others.

We have the King format here, which is 65 mm, so we shoot in the biggest film format possible. Therefore our ultimate quality—that is, technical quality on-screen—is higher.

On Working in Los Angeles

In terms of the creative work, you can create the same degree of isolation here as you would in Kodiak, Alaska. You are going into a building, a studio, to work.

We tend to work five-day weeks here and stay away from these six- and seven-day weeks because I think people need to have room, have their own life, and go out and do other things.

Obviously you get into situations where it is overtime and there are crunch periods, but as a general rule it is a ten-hour day, twelve hours during production, because you can't do this kind of work in eight hours. And we've tried it. Occasionally we scale back to eight hours if we have a thin period, but there is a momentum. Also, it is a business of workaholics, and people can't turn off after eight hours.

Photographer

On my tombstone, I think if I had to bring it down to one word . . . "photographer" would sum it up.

Photography is a whole way of life.

Since my high school darkroom, I've built fourteen darkrooms. I finally have my dream house, in which I have built a really nice darkroom. It is like a submarine in there, but it is a very high room and you need ladders to get things up on high shelves.

My thought has always been, I'm not in the business for the money. Although I am motivated by money, obviously, but I've always felt that if you are good at what you do, when you decide to specialize, you then become very good. The better you get, the more money you get. It just automatically happens.

It has worked out that way in my life. Maybe certain occupations have brick walls you are going to run into, but the movie business is pretty flexible, and of course, you are only as good as your last picture, so your luck has to hold out if you are going to hold on to that kind of philosophy.

It is a tremendous responsibility if you think of how much people are influenced by motion pictures. It is mind-boggling to contemplate . . . when you fly from here to New York and look down and see those little towns, or if you look at a map and see all those little black dots and lines . . . that probably 70 percent of the people (and more than that on *Star Wars!*) in every one of those towns have seen movies.

Here you have this little business, motion pictures, that is maybe a five-billion-dollar gross revenue business, not including cable—which is dwarfed by the laundry soap industry.

Film's impact is just immeasurable. It has the power to completely change people around. And even though what I'm involved in with my field is perhaps more environmental—that is, we are charged with the responsibility to make the audience believe that they are in a particular environment—there is that contribution that we make toward the success or failure of that film.

Visual effects cannot make a silk purse out of a sow's ear. If a film doesn't have what it takes—which means a good script, a good story, and the bare skeleton of a hit—it is not going to be a hit. We try to pick the good scripts and enhance them with visual effects.

Advice

My first advice to anyone who wants to get into the business is to decide what they want to do and focus themselves.

If you want to be in costumes or if you want to be a prop maker or if you want to get into photographic effects, you want to do matte painting, whatever you want to do—you have to develop yourself first and know that you have something to sell and then come to Hollywood and persist.

Everybody has a different story of how they got in. I happen to think my story is a pretty outrageous one. To put a résumé in the Department of Employment and get in that way . . . it's a long shot.

Some people start by sweeping the floors. Sometimes we have the ability to bring in people who have budding talent here as production assistants in a nonunion position. And it doesn't pay very much. But at least if someone has what it takes and you can see talent that is worth developing and a personality that fits within the group, then that's a way of getting in.

You make yourself valuable. You create a position.

Visual Effects Researcher

The Visual Effects Researcher researches and develops cinematic theory and practice in order to create or refine photographic techniques, processes, film stock, and the like, to be used in producing visual effects for motion pictures.

Jonathan Erland

JONATHAN ERLAND started out as an actor, lighting designer, and technical director in the British theater. When he came to the United States in 1956, he found that union problems meant he "couldn't eat very regularly as an actor" though he did participate in the last few years of the Golden Age of live television drama with the CBC in Canada. As that era declined, Erland began to gravitate toward the world of industrial design and exhibition, among them Charles Eames's designs for the 1964 World's Fair in New York. By 1975, he had established a small business in partnership with Lorne Peterson, and his work was almost entirely in the industrial world. It was during this time that George Lucas and Steven Spielberg were laying plans to embark upon the monumentally ambitious and technologically revolutionary *Star Wars* and *Close Encounters* productions. In their search for people with expertise in injection molding and other industrial design disciplines, they recruited Erland & Peterson. Intrigued, the pair stayed in the field, Peterson moving north with Lucas, and Erland staying with John Dykstra to establish the research and development department at Apogee Productions, the visual effects house that occupies the same site where Dykstra assembled the original *Star Wars* effects facility, Industrial Light and Magic. Since then, Erland has been constantly involved in researching and creating new techniques and processes that will further refine the visual effects field. From Shakespeare to *Star Wars* may seem a strange journey, but from Jon's viewpoint it all involves "problem solving, imagination, logic, and magic" in the service of telling a story. Though he defies definition, the word that comes to mind is "inventor." He has created processes that are responsible for many of the stunning visual effects in *Star Wars*, *2010*, *Battlestar Galactica*, *Firefox*, *Lifeforce*, *Star Trek The Motion Picture*, *Never Say Never Again*, *Spaceballs*, and *My Stepmother Is an Alien*, to mention a few. He has received three technical Academy Awards (for his Tesselated Front Projection Screen, the Blue Max, and the Reverse Blue Screen techniques, all of which have also been granted U.S. and foreign Patents). Current projects include Reverse Front Projection (a variant of front projection process), Electronic Intermediate (a method for providing electronic postproduction techniques for feature films), and improved methods for discharge lighting (flicker-free fluorescent lights for stage lighting). He has been elected a fellow of the Society of Motion Picture and Television Engineers which recently honored him with the Journal Award. He serves on various committees for the SMPTE and the Academy. Born in England, he is fifty years old and has two children and two grandchildren.

WHAT I do at Apogee is research and development, which covers a variety of research—into film stocks and photographic techniques as well as light sources, special technology for molding plastics, and, well . . . almost anything. The cornerstone of our business is traveling matte cinematography.

Traveling Matte

Traveling matte cinematography, or composite photography, is where we take two or more different images and collage them together into one picture. . . . Which is one way we can make Superman fly. We didn't do *Superman*, but that's a good example. Superman is mounted on a post or pole which is blue, and he's filmed against a blue backing.

This is the blue screen process that dates back to the 40s, to the advent of color film. Blue screen allows us to take the original color negative and split it up into its three component parts. We can then isolate that blue screen area, the pole and the screen behind Superman, and make an opaque matte of it. We then isolate the subject, Superman, which was in front of that screen, and print it onto a new piece of film.

Then we take a counter matte or hold-out matte which is made by reversing the first one we got, namely the blue screen area, and we can protect the image of Superman we just printed by putting this hold-out matte over it. Now we can print an image, say the city of Gotham, on the remaining portion of film that till now remains unexposed. The end result is that we've printed two separate pictures onto the one frame—and the background has become the city receding into the distance behind Superman.

Traveling matte photography/blue screen is a complex process that is still evolving. New wrinkles and new techniques emerge and I've been responsible for some of those new techniques.

Star Wars resulted in a tremendous resurgence in the use of traveling matte photography. It had fallen into disfavor because it is very difficult to do, and if it's not done well, it looks hideous. It can look like cardboard cut-outs pasted together. When we talk about the various techniques and refinements, what we're really talking about is taking that elementary blue screen system and finding ways to optimize it, so that the image that you see is totally convincing.

High Tech as Theater—(Or, The Bent Mirror)

When you take it all the way back to the beginning, all this high-tech stuff has its fundamental roots in a bunch of hairy people sitting around a campfire telling stories at night. That's theater, then and now. Whether it's on a live stage or on a movie screen, it's all theater, it's all telling stories. Shakespeare taught us our mission in theater was "to hold a mirror up to nature," and it's often been said of special effects that it's all done with mirrors, which is partly true—but then we're apt to bend the mirror occasionally!

This is just one other facet of theatrical presentation. I am intrigued by the evolution of this ability to present the story. I was intrigued by that when I was an actor, and I'm intrigued by that same thing now that I'm working in film technique.

It's exciting and occasionally rewarding when you are able to see that you've made something that much more believable to an audience, or made it have that much more impact on them. And I guess what keeps me hooked is that I have been able to see and make progress in that direction.

The Inventor

I have a share in three technical awards. One for the reverse blue screen, which is a process we developed here to make it easier to film models and miniatures that don't lend themselves to blue screen—things that are shiny and would reflect the light.

Instead of having a blue screen, we have an invisible phosphor that we coat onto the model which we then film twice—once in white light, which renders it looking normal, and once in black light, in which that phosphor glows and produces an image of just that object glowing like a light bulb. We use that silhouette image instead of the blue screen to make our matte. *Firefox* was the first film that used the technique. There was a compelling rationale for doing it because it was a shiny black airplane which would otherwise have reflected the blue screen, causing holes to seem to appear in the wings.

At least two of the things that I've worked on start out with the word "reverse"—reverse blue screen, and reverse front projection.

We called it reverse blue screen because that was a way of looking at the problem—turning the problem inside out or upside down to see if there was a solution hidden behind or underneath it. The logic in that is we frequently want the opposite of what we think we want. Instead of taking a picture of something against a glowing background, we really want that something glowing against a "nothing" background. Once you've developed a knack for attacking problems that way, not always but sometimes the solution comes from just looking at it from the other side.

The reverse front projection does a similar thing: it takes existing concepts and existing procedures and rearranges them. We still have a beam splitter, we still have a projector, a camera, all of the same things. We just put them in a different arrangement, and some totally new things emerge out of it.

The other two technical awards both relate to front projection/ blue screen. We're building on work that people have done before— Bill Abbott in that case: Many, many years ago on *Tora! Tora! Tora!* he was doing conventional front projection, and the image that he was going to front-project was wrong. Here he was—stuck on a stage with all of this $50,000-a-day pressure on him—and there was nothing he could do.

So he decided to project blue out of this projector onto that front projection screen and composite in the image of the background later.

As far as we know, that was the first time anybody had done that. He had a wet submarine as his subject, and if it had been a conventional blue screen shot, there would have been blue bouncing off the hull. But with front projection it was all coherent light, and hence there could be no spill.

We took that idea and evolved it to a very high degree into a device that bolts onto the camera and projects an isolated mercury line, which is as pure a blue as you can find in the world. You may have seen *2010* which has this enormous space-walk sequence that was done with blue max. It can produce a much, much larger blue screen than you could ever hope to do, with sanity, with conventional processes.

We also had to upgrade—along with that—the front projection screen itself which had been fraught with problems stemming from the seams. It's made by 3M in a roll two feet wide. Their instructions say, "Just roll this out in strips," like roofing paper. Which was well and good—but when it was rolled out you could see shifts in gain (or brightness) from one section to another. People tried cutting it up into squares and sticking it down in a mosaic. But if you were projecting organic images, like expanses of sky with clouds, the rectilinear pattern of the seams would leap right out at you—they were inconsistent in an organic scene. So what I did there was to design a shape that could be cut on a die, and produce a "tile" that could be tessellated onto the screen, eliminating all the square corners and straight lines.

The research on this was precipitated by *Dune*, which needed to film large expanses of blue screen to be able to provide sandstorms. Subsequently, we've used the blue max on *2010*, *Lifeforce*, *Invaders from Mars*—just about everything we've done.

Research in a Service Industry

So we have no permanent trainees. The business economics is such that the fact that I exist and that this office exists is something of a minor miracle in the film industry, which isn't geared toward doing research. It's an off-the-shelf business for the most part. Only, perhaps the fact that they're somewhat enlightened here and we work in the "cutting edge" of the business requires us to maintain a research and development function. If we don't do research, we're going to be in big trouble very quickly. So we do. But it's difficult to incorporate this activity into the financial side of filmmaking.

Most businesses that have research and development activities going on have a product that they produce; they manufacture it and get income from that to fund the other research.

The film business is a service business: "You bring us your script, we turn it into pictures—we give it back to you." So it's difficult to tell some client, "We're going to charge you for research that may not happen in time to benefit your job, but will benefit the guy after you." That producer's going to say, "The hell with that!"

So the existence of research and development is highly unusual. And having trainees to help would be a luxury beyond our wildest dreams.

Apprenticeship

We do, at various times, take on apprentices. They are apprentices in the program that the cameramen's union runs in conjunction with the Producers Association. They are going to be assistant cameramen working their way up to be camera operators and so forth.

They are sent by the union to various and sundry studios, so they work on the TV shows like *Dynasty*. When they come here, they see a rather different side of the business. They find themselves doing startlingly different things, sometimes getting caught up in some fairly sophisticated experiments. And some fairly mundane things, like careful analysis of perforations. They're a great help—enthusiastic. It's undoubtedly good for them. It's not going to happen to them elsewhere, but it'll give them a better understanding of that area of technology. They're here only briefly because this program rotates them through all of these different environments.

One of the apprentices who spent some time here—David Drzeweicki, twenty-five years old—is a motion picture fanatic. Mad about it since he was a child. He studied film at college and is actually one of two people I know who attempted blue screen 16-mm at college. It boggles the mind, because it's technically very difficult to do, and practically impossible without very sophisticated equipment. And indeed he didn't really succeed, but he tried. His knowledge and interest are formidable.

The apprentice program will provide David with a union card, and then will commence a very difficult time as he has to work his way through a series of categories: assistant camera operator (mostly carrying the boxes and fetching the coffee), where his suggestions may not always be welcome; camera operator, lots of responsibility but still not always easy to have a lot of impact on what's happening; finally, director of photography, with ultimate responsibility for the "image" on the screen and he will get to have a say in how the work is done! A long hard road, and many do not stay the course. The trick is to survive the process with your enthusiasm still intact, still caring as much about the work as you did when you first heard a camera motor purr.

Postscript: *David is now a valued member of the Apogee team. Having availed himself of the opportunity to study motion control cinematography while at Apogee as an apprentice, he finds himself among a select few possessing this extraordinary facility. He has many bright ideas, and his suggestions are welcomed. He still, however, has to carry the occasional box!*

Happenstance and Tenacity

Mind you, in terms of young people coming into the business, I heard the same thing when I was in my teens and starting out to become an actor. What you hear from the beginning is "Don't do it!" I auditioned at the Central School of Speech and Drama, which is a near-lethal experience. Hundreds of people show up there; in those days, maybe thirty a year got in. The first thing that happens is you get sat down and told, "You really don't want to do this. If you're at all wise, don't do this." The process is so intimidating it's hard to see how anybody winds up doing anything.

So I couldn't advise anybody who had the same interests I had, because it's almost entirely happenstance that I'm doing what I'm doing—happenstance and tenacity (which sounds rather like a vaudeville act, doesn't it?—Happenstance and Tenacity).

Whatever it is that I'll be doing in ten years, it'll be something similar in process, I'm sure. What I do . . . you live it. You don't just clock in, do it, and clock out again. It stays with you twenty-four hours a day. Problem-solving, inventing, is constant. What changes is the venue in which you're practicing that activity.

Legitimacy in the Film World

The fact that what I do is not well enough established, nor considered as relevant as I think it ought to be, means that the scope for what I do is somewhat circumscribed. There is no real way to provide the appropriate budget.

It's an essential activity. But in the context of the film industry, when you tell the producer he's going to have to pay this little R&D surcharge, he doesn't see where it plugs into his plan. I take that back a little. Clint Eastwood knew and supported the development of the reverse blue screen because, in trying to do his job, he was aware of the problems of conventional technology. At that point there was no guarantee that we were going to solve the problem. But, certainly, he was an immediate beneficiary of it. But that was unusual; most don't want to hear, "This is interesting, this is new and experimental."

I once wanted to use an unusual film stock that would have yielded a better image—for a client—using an electronic telecine transfer. I could show images of that film, but I couldn't show that film having gone through the whole process and say, "This is a piece of tape using that film. That is what your product is going to look like." They weren't willing to experiment with something whose results they couldn't visualize, so we didn't use it. Because caution and convention are the bywords in this, *apparently* innovative, business.

We are beginning now to come to terms with this issue. What we are going to do is create a research foundation that will permit us to do the kind of research the industry needs to keep it young and vital. There is a precedent for this facility. Many years ago, we had an organization known as the research center, which was part of the Motion Picture Producers Association (which, in turn, succeeded the Academy of Motion Picture Arts and Sciences Research Council). These entities were responsible for many of the developments we now take for granted, such as the color difference blue screen method and front projection. The center was disbanded in the early Sixties, as a consequence of the effect of television on the movie business, and since then we have had no comprehensive research function. We have had to make do with the scattered efforts of people like myself making do with scant resources.

The new foundation will have a much broader base of support than did the old Research Council. While we anticipate the Producers Association will be a participant, we also look toward many other organizations, such as the Academy of Motion Picture Arts and Sciences, SMPTE, the AFI, universities, government agencies, major corporations such as Kodak, Sony, and others who share an involvement with film technology.

Among the functions of such a facility will be providing an aegis under which young people, like Drzeweicki, can work on research projects under the tutelage of pioneers like Linwood Dunne (*King Kong*, and others). It would have been so beneficial to have been able to have some apprentices work with Bill Abbott before he left us, and Alan Gundelfinger, and others like them. In Japan they pronounce such people national treasures, while we do that only with the likenesses of presidents carved in stone mountains.

The advent of electronic imaging and computer-generated imagery requires that we develop an even greater knowledge of the phenomena of film. Do you know that we arrived at twenty-four frames a second by sheer happenstance? When sound was introduced, it was determined that it required a foot and a half of film per second to pass by the sound head to produce acceptable sound quality. This translated into twenty-four frames per second. Up to that time we had viewed sixteen frames per second. In either case, we are shown forty-eight "flicks" per second due to the shutter blades in the projector. The point is that we have never done a study into the psychophysiological effects of various frame rates (aside from the flicker fusion issue which is well documented). We know that television "feels" different, and we know that television is distinguished from film in that it displays essentially a continuously acquired image. We also know that Chaplin's sixteen-frame-per-second silent black-and-white films have a vastly different effect on us than does the modern sixty-frame-per-second Dolby sound, full-color Showscan process. But we don't really understand the psychophysiological implications of these distinctions and therefore how these implications impact on the story-telling, which, in the end, is what it's all about.

We need to learn, we need to know, we need to understand, we need to grow; in short, we need to research and we need to develop.

Special Makeup Designer

The work of the Special Makeup Designer, as distinguished from that of the makeup artist, involves creating the illusion of transformation, rather than the enhancement, aging, or natural modification (from weather, injury, or emotional strain) of the existing features. Examples of transformation would be creating the illusion of running sores or wounds, dismemberment, disembowelment, and so on, or the illusion of a humanoid, robot, or animal or of a human being transformed into any such fabricated creature using varied materials such as rubber, latex, plastics, metals, foil, tubes, reservoir sacks, dental and prosthetics materials, or any materials that can be *safely* combined. The Special Makeup Designer works closely with the director and key makeup artist and confers with the cinematographer on the photographic suitability of the makeup.

Chris Walas

As a kid in New Jersey, CHRIS WALAS loved horror movies and had a flair for drawing, makeup, and props, which he put to use in school theater. In Los Angeles, his first job was in the film shipping department at Disney Studios. The second job he got was in response to an ad in a monster magazine, working at a Halloween mask-making company, which, at the time, also did some film work. After a year Chris had moved up enough to participate in these film projects, but corporate policy dictated that film work would now be eclipsed in favor of full-time Halloween mask making. Dejected, he left the company and started working on low-budget horror films, with such titles as *Piranha, Humanoids from the Deep, Up from the Depths,* and *Screamers*—"making some fish, a lot of dead bodies and severed arms." He eventually attained a reputation as a skilled special effects makeup artist. Today Chris's numerous credits include *The Fly* (for which he won an Academy Award), *Enemy Mine, Gremlins, Child's Play, House II, Raiders of the Lost Ark, Return of the Jedi, Dragonslayer,* and *Romancing the Stone.* He is president of Chris Walas, Inc., located in San Rafael, California.

THERE'S ONE given when doing rubber monsters, and that is that you're doing something that is completely false. There's nothing real about it. It's rubber, it's metal, it's whatever, it's glued on to an actor. It is not real. So when I read a script, I ask myself what elements are realistic about the way something is portrayed in the script and what elements can I bring to it that will make it more realistic.

And there has to be some logic to it. So I have to, in my own mind, build a biology behind whatever it is. How does he eat, how do the muscles form? Would he have mandibles? What kind of environment would he come from?

The Fly

The character is the key. In *The Fly*, for instance, what's happening to this guy is very real, it's a very emotional experience.

We also had to develop its evolution. We would say, "Well, at this point the character is having trouble speaking, so that means the mouth is no longer necessary."

We would work out things like "If he's still walking around at this point, he shouldn't have antennae sticking out of his head," or "That's going too far," or "This is not far enough." Finding that fine line that defines the balance of the character and his physical appearance.

They had no actor when I came on. And just getting the designs down was tough. We had five different sculptural changes in the makeup and several different puppets to manufacture. We had full body suits and some partial suits, partial makeup. A real mixed bag. We had about thirty-five people working under my direction.

In addition to being extremely labor-intensive, the materials themselves just take time. You make a mold, and there's a chemical reaction that takes three days. That's it—you can't pour more money into it and make it go faster; it just won't do it.

We had a fair formulation by the time Jeff Goldblum came on. He was very good in that he tended to suggest abstract emotional things that were more inspirational than definitive. Rather than saying, "I think it should have big fat eyelashes," he would say, "Maybe there's something about his vision that isn't quite normal."

Fortunately the start date was pushed back a little. But unfortunately we only got to see Jeff twice before we went on location, so we were basically working off mannequins. We made complete casts of Jeff Goldblum. I still have a bust of him that I have to finish off, painting it gold and staining it for our CWI (Chris Walas, Inc.) museum, such as it is—which is now spreading out all over the shop. Everywhere you turn there's an old leg or something.

Jeff Goldblum was the best human being I've ever dealt with and the best thing about that job. Unbelievably patient. He wanted to understand, which was the most critical factor, what the limitations were. Sitting in a chair for three hours while makeup is applied to you is the norm with special effects makeup. It's rare to find an actor who tolerates the process, much less is interested in what you're doing.

Materials

We use a lot of dental material; impression cream; dental acrylic, which is a type of plastic; foam latex; foam urethane plastic; myriad types of plasters.

There's no one answer in this field; that's what's interesting about it, and that's what most people don't understand.

It's not a set procedure. After *Gremlins*, Dick Smith called to congratulate me, which was a big thrill. He had been an inspiration. I said, "Dick, I have to be honest with you. We made it up as we went along. I didn't really know what I was doing."

His reply was, "None of us know what we're doing, it's all guess-work, Chris, because everything you do is a prototype, it's a one-shot deal."

You have to be able to draw on a large library of techniques and materials, to research and say, "Yeah, that one material with the weird sparkle to it would look good," and just pull things in from all over the place.

For a long time they were just using theatrical makeup techniques, until the sixties when Dick Smith and Rick Baker started playing around with different techniques. A more inspired awareness of material began to emerge, and more materials were being developed—types of urethane plastics. It was a very formative time, and growth in special effects makeup has since accelerated.

Contrary to some other aspects of this industry, in special makeup no one wants whatever's been done, nobody says, "Give me this thing that was in this movie." Everybody says, "I want something that's never been seen before."

Skin Reactions

Another unchartable area is that everybody reacts differently to different materials.

Lou Gossett, for instance, has incredibly sensitive skin. On *Enemy Mine*, he would almost get hives as a reaction, although that was more from the agitation of removing the makeup than the actual materials.

One improvement on that front is that almost all of the major makeup supplies now have been tested, reformulated, and are hypoallergenic. There's a variety of watery-thin oil-based makeup removers that are very gentle. What's happened more than anything else to help us is that manufacturers are supplying data sheets with hazard factors, which for years and years they didn't do. They gave you the most bizarre concoctions of urethane plastics and told you absolutely nothing about them. The package would just say, "This is the mixing ratio, and it sets up in this amount of time."

We found out years later that this stuff had terrible ingredients in it.

First and Second Wave

I believe I was one of the last ones to come in on the first wave of the new technology. The second wave tends to be people who were assistants to the first wave. And because they came up as assistants, their experience was much more limited. They were hired not to do everything that I did, but to do one specific thing, like make molds. So they're not as versatile with respect to awareness of materials and applications and techniques.

I've tried to set up my company so that everybody can circulate and do a little of everything *if they want*. There are those people who just say, "No, I can't do that," which is fine. It's enormously helpful sometimes, in order to accomplish work, to have people who are very good at just one thing. Many of the young kids who want to break into the business tend to be extremely limited in their scope of thought, and their perceptions are one-shot. They're all trying to be the new Rick Baker or the new Dick Smith. And all they're doing is copying what the other guys have been doing. There's not much original thinking or overview in their approach.

Not that I was that original or broad-minded when I was starting out, but the experiences I had opened me up a little bit more. And these guys, they don't want to be opened up, they're happy making the same severed head.

When I was starting out, it was anything goes. There weren't any laws. I still do most of my own formulations, and that's what has kept my interest for so long. There are so many directions and there's so much you have to know to really be in command of this kind of work.

What was great about the early days was, you could say, "I'm going to think of something nobody's ever thought of before," and you could still believe you were going to do that. Today, it's more difficult to believe that anything you're doing is completely original.

Gremlins

It was a turning point in my career. I had been working out of my garage for a year after leaving Lucasfilm, down to $200 in the bank, when Mike Finnell, the producer on *Gremlins*, approached me. It started out as a very cheap nonunion picture, on the level of *The Howling*, and all of a sudden it became a studio picture.

It was extraordinarily draining, both physically and creatively, to make hundreds of these creatures. I would be worn to a frazzle when Joe Dante, the director, would come up with another idea: "You know, we really should have six gremlins jumping up here . . ." My first reaction was just to go for the throat and kill him and get it over with, and then I'd think, God, he's right, it's going to be better. And I'd spend all night and get those puppets ready.

I incorporated during *Gremlins*. The scale of the picture was so large, it just became an economic necessity.

Advice

Most people, even most filmmakers, don't realize the amount of time you've got to put in on projects like this. Whereas most of the crew comes in at seven in the morning and shoots till seven at night, we have to get in there an hour or two earlier to prep, and then at the end of the day we've got to stay a couple of hours to take the makeup off the actors and to clean up and sort through and put away everything that's been used during the day.

Early in my career, I was told by a special effects makeup artist I greatly admired: "Chris, this is the kind of business where every project takes a large percentage of your life energy out of you, and no matter what you do, no matter how you rest, no matter how you exercise, you'll never get it all back, you lose something in every project."

It was scary, especially at that point, because I still had a few stars left in my eyes. It hit me like a ton of bricks. He was right, he wasn't kidding around. I thought at that moment about the toy industry, having the option of a nine-to-five job. There's some security in knowing you have enough time to go home and maybe watch the news.

You get on a film and, especially doing this stuff, absolutely everything else stops. After *Gremlins* I was a vegetable. I went to buy a gift in a store, and I couldn't even deal with the salesgirl, I had not had contact with any nonfilm, nonlatex individual for a year and a half.

Almost invariably, at the end of any project my system is so weak that I'm susceptible to any and every germ. Last year, after *The Fly*, it was pneumonia, and after *Gremlins* I had a kidney stone and broke my ankle. There's always that little addendum to look forward to.

There are times where you don't sleep for two days, or times where you get three hours, and you can deal with getting three hours of sleep a night for maybe a month of filming or so, but then your energy really starts falling.

My advice is to consider your priorities extremely seriously. On a very practical level, special makeup is starting to be a saturated area now. There are a lot of people who have the fascination, were like me as kids and didn't have any place to channel that energy, and now they're saying, "Special effects makeup, yeah, that's a great place to put it. It's imaginative and I can make good money and make weird things that I see in my head." And that's not the case.

It's extremely hard work, it's labor-intensive, and it's getting very competitive. But there's a lot of independent, nonunion production going on in the horror and fantasy film genre. There's the opportunity to get a tremendous amount of experience quickly, if you're really committed to it, and that's what it takes.

It's not the kind of thing where you can say, "I'm going to be a special makeup artist, and I'm willing to put in my eight hours a day." You have to say, "I'm going to be a special makeup artist, and I'm willing to put in my twenty-three hours a day."

You have to be ready to be abused. You've got to be ready, at first, to work really hard for nothing.

CWI, Inc.

My desire was always to try and develop talent that was available up in northern California and to try to diversify. I love working in San Rafael, because preproduction is really the most valuable time for me.

When they finally sign that contract and say, "Go," we're at 150 miles per hour starting off. We've got to get so much stuff locked in so quickly that we start moving.

And when you work down here in L.A.—I've had my business in L.A. for four or five years—you're accessible. Everybody wants to look over your shoulder, which is understandable, but it slows you down, especially on tough pictures like *Gremlins* or *The Fly*.

Up there we're in a slightly industrial area, there's no problem getting any materials, and we just keep the lines of communication open. When I need input from the director or producer or production designer, I call them up and get videos together, or we meet.

It also takes a large load off the director and producer. They don't spend as much time worrying. What they see is far enough along to see progress. The problem with somebody watching over you who is unfamiliar with the process, is that they see you doing something and they say, "Wait, that's not what we want." And I'm saying, "That's just a mold, that will not be seen in your film." It takes much needed time away from the process.

I can't believe how insane it is in Los Angeles. And there's a part of me that loves being down here. This is the center of filmmaking. This is the only place you can be and really know what's going on in the industry.

It becomes completely overwhelming. A friend of mine put it this way years ago: "Living down in L.A. and being in the movie industry is like a drug," because there's so much activity, there's so much exchange of information, whether it's good, bad, or indifferent. You start reevaluating every step. Especially when you realize how quirky this industry is. No matter how good a product you put out, you know there's an absolute element of chance and luck to getting it to that next step.

You wind up spending more time keeping tabs on the options than on your product, and it's self-defeating to a degree. Hopefully you finally get to a point where you realize you're spinning wheels, you get past that and refocus. Had I the chance to do it over again, I would have reevaluated the path I was on much earlier. I got caught in a snowball effect. My career really took off, and I couldn't say no. I got caught up in "Yeah, now the big people want me, this is great."

The momentum carries you farther than your awareness does, and you suddenly realize, "Well, wait a minute. I don't think this is what life is about, I don't think this is what being a human being is about, and there's got to be room for something else." I just wonder what thoughts bankers have during the day and what it is like to have kids.

Now, in my own mind, at least, I have conquered the major challenges of doing this kind of work. I've already taken almost a year off and written a screenplay with another guy, and I'm starting another one right now.

If I had my choice, I would stop making rubber monsters.

Not that I haven't had a blast doing it.

Postscript: *Subsequent to giving this interview, Chris Walas was hired to direct* Fly II, *the sequel to* The Fly. *He also got married. He and his wife, Gillian, recently had a baby girl.*

Model and Miniature Builder

The Model and Miniature Builder constructs scale duplicates of real or fictitious objects when it is too expensive or impractical to shoot the life-size objects. He or she is responsible to the director and the production designer for researching, (on occasion) preparing the plans, building, and setting up the models and miniatures and thereafter responsible for operating, modifying, dismantling, and storing them.

Greg Jein

In show business "by accident," GREG JEIN was pursuing a career in advertising design/commercial art when, on a lark, he did some molds for a Chicken of the Sea Tuna show at Sea World. He continued to accept jobs fiberglassing props and building rockets and miniature landscapes. A projected three-month assignment at Doug Trumbull's Future General Corporation stretched into eighteen months and led to an Academy Award nomination for visual effects on *Close Encounters of the Third Kind*. Later he received a second nomination for twenty-four months of work on Steven Spielberg's

1941. Since then he has built and supervised the building of models and miniatures for many films, including *2010, War Games, Firefox, Star Trek—The Motion Picture, D.A.R.Y.L., Dark Star, National Lampoon's European Vacation, One from the Heart, Deal of the Century, Red Dawn, Batteries Not Included, The Blob,* and *Star Trek V.* In addition to his film assignments, Greg has also worked for defense contractors such as Lockheed and Hughes Aircraft, and his models and miniatures have been displayed at Expo '86 in Tokyo and Vancouver and at Arco Center for the Visual Arts in an exhibit entitled "The Art of Movie Miniature."

I'M A toy maker. I make the toys that the producers, studios, and art directors decide they want for particular projects whether it be for film, television, or industrial use.

We deal with anything that works, whatever materials are easy to handle and cost-efficient—mainly plastics, metal, rubber to make molds, and then fiberglass or other materials to cast them up with.

For landscape, it's mostly shaping architectural foam, building little roads and terrains out of different-colored sands, making artificial miniature grass out of bristle brushes, scouring pads.

There isn't a formal training program for what we do, although film schools will broach the subject in their special effects classes. You have to do it yourself, just fool around. In the early days, when they could not get this "great all-encompassing shot," or it was not practical to do in real locations, they used models and miniatures. And I've seen some pretty good examples from the "dawn of moviemaking." That was the basic foundation for what we're doing now. Everybody learns by what the guy before you did.

As far as my background, in college I took a few architectural classes and learned the basics of landscape architecture and watched other people build models in a nonentertainment field. I used to go to museums and look at the dioramas.

Close Encounters of the Third Kind

My initial assignment on *Close Encounters of the Third Kind* was to build realistic landscapes that would allow the production company to shoot background plates and composite the blue screen with foreground action. In other words, they couldn't find the right terrain they wanted to perform certain gags on, so my job was to make artificial natural things, like the knoll overlooking the city and the trees. The biggest piece we did was the Devil's Tower miniature that the mother ship lands in front of at the end of the film. When we started work, the mother ship was an incidental thing, but it evolved to become a major prop.

Realistic and Hardware Effects

Effects are divided into realistic effects and hardware effects. Something like *Star Wars*, the audience is thinking, Okay, it's not real.

The audience had to accept as real the miniatures we did for *1941*. They could not be perceived as part of a special effect. That was our challenge—to get them to be totally believable. We built a miniature Hollywood Boulevard and a 1941 version of Ocean Park, an amusement park with a big Ferris wheel and merry-go-round.

I was on that show two weeks short of two years. The scale we decided on was 1½ inch equals one foot, and our park was probably close to 100 by 100 feet. We also made some little miniature remote-control people who could be operated from off the stage.

First Impression

Most people use "miniature" and "model" interchangeably. There's a difference between a model or a miniature made for motion pictures or television as opposed to one made for the Smithsonian. You actually get close to museum models, and scrutinize them 360 degrees around, for as long as you want, whereas you see only briefly on-screen a similar model for a motion picture. You're not going to get a chance to look at it closely, study it. It's the first impression that counts. The requirements are not as stringent. It's still three-dimensional, but the biggest trade-off is, if you're only going to see it from one side, you don't have to build the other side.

Game Plan

If we're breaking down storyboards, we will pull out all the shots that are relevant to the miniatures and then break those down in terms of what the miniature has to do. We then give the director and art director/production designer suggestions based on the practical needs, the time needs, and, very important, the monetary needs.

Many times what they want described in a three-sentence line will cost them millions of dollars. In the script from *1941*, there's a couple of lines: "Japanese submarine fires on the amusement park, breaks the gantry of the Ferris wheel, and the Ferris wheel rolls down the pier into the water." That one sentence involved a lot of planning, time, and money.

Making Models to Scale

We have to make our work so real that people don't notice it. If it's a big-budget picture, the art department will give us drawings and photographs. If not, we'll take photographs or videotapes. If a building exists, we'll measure it piece by piece and scale it down proportionally.

And we'll do that for a whole city block. We're matching a street in rural Abbeville, Louisiana. We're presuming the scale models of the buildings will be about four or five feet high, the challenge being that an audience seeing it will believe it is Abbeville, Louisiana, and not Greg Jein's models.

Working with the Director and Art Director

They'll sit down and tell me what they expect from the shot. For example, on *The Blob* they wanted the film to be atmospheric, very much like *1941*, diffused lighting, low angles.

Lighting can affect our miniatures. In some cases they'll want the lights to pulsate or do special gags that we have to build into our miniatures or, as with *1941*, light up underwater. If it's an inherent part of the miniature, we will build them in. If it's the overall stage lighting, if they ask us about it, we'll give them our suggestions, but it's basically up to the director or the cameraman.

Building a Missile out of a Sewer Pipe

We built the fifteen-foot missile silo in *War Games*. The government would not approve the script, so we couldn't get one of theirs and had to be a little more creative.

The missile we built was actually a big plastic sewer pipe that we detailed out. And the missile silo itself was one of those big cardboard tubes they pour concrete into—it's called a Sonotube and it's what they make pylons out of for the freeways.

Working with Blue Screen

We do work with different cinematic processes—for instance, the blue screen. The model we make—say, the city in *1941*—is what's projected on the screen, what's called the plate.

The script called for a foggy, misty atmosphere. That is very difficult to reproduce when you superimpose a person in front of the image of the model because you've got this atmosphere or mist over the model, but not over the man. There are two separate images with uncontrollable diffusion; the diffusions will never match up.

Things like that we bring up in some of our meetings with the DP or the art director. It's not really our problem because whoever is compositing and shooting it should know that, but sometimes if the DP has not worked with that type of process before, it could get him in trouble.

Statue of Liberty

At the end of *National Lampoon's European Vacation*, Chevy Chase crashes the airplane into the Statue of Liberty and knocks its arm down, so we built a Statue of Liberty with an arm that swiveled.

We sculpted a three-foot-tall statue out of clay, then made a rubber mold and cast it. The final version was made out of fiberglass.

After the show, they rented it to NBC, and that's the Statue of Liberty you see on the nightly newscast.

The Union

Our local is the carpenters'—Local 44. When you work on a union feature you can't do certain things. You can't paint or mold your own models. In some cases you can't wire your own models because those are all other unions. We're not even supposed to move them because that's a teamster's job. So on studio pictures, we get people whose work we're familiar with who are qualified and have the "cards" to do the painting and all the rest of it.

We got into a bit of a flap on that in *1941* because we did our own stuff and they came down on us because it was a high-profile picture. But they couldn't penalize us because we were working for Lucasfilm. They're under the Bay Area local, which lets you do everything from sculpting and clay, which you're not supposed to do in Hollywood, to making the molds to actually painting them.

The Future of Models

Models will have a healthy future. Although some people might disagree, computer graphics won't be able to take care of most of the problems, at least not for the next twenty, thirty years.

Computer graphics work well in futuristic films like *The Last Starfighter*. If you're doing buildings of the 1840s, computer graphics don't have the capability.

For instance, when we built the *1941* miniature, we had to build it 360 degrees around because the director wasn't sure where he wanted to shoot. When you do something with computer graphics you're locked into the image you choose up-front, the angle and the altitude it's going to be shot at.

And more often than not the director will come in and not necessarily stay with what his storyboard angle indicates. He'll move to the left or to the right or drop down. And you can't do that with computer graphics.

Advice

Model and miniature building is a highly competitive area because there are many kids who build model kits, some of them quite well, and have found commercial and nonunion work. They work a lot cheaper, too.

If you want to work on films done by the major studios, that all has to come through the union. It's difficult to get in because so many people want to. It's possible, however, to work in film without being in the union, even to get nominated for Academy Awards. On *Aliens*, for example, those were all nonunion people.

If you want to get into this line of work, you should just beat the bushes and work for independent production companies first. Even though you don't make a lot of money, you'll get experience and, hopefully, the insight as to whether you can function in this business or not.

Some people are not cut out for the compromises. They'll take too long getting a model the way they want it, which would totally knock the schedule off. You have to know how to shave things so that the basic form is there but not with all the feathers.

First thing I normally do is look at someone's folio, if they have a folio. Some kids will bring in plastic kits they've made. That's okay, but it's just a very basic exercise—to show that the parts and paint are on right. What they should have are things they've done themselves, built from scratch. Samples of how they would finish a model, paint it. A knowledge of electronics is useful to show that they could wire lights.

You must cultivate a certain flexibility. In architecture, the rules are much more rigid. In motion pictures, what you build doesn't have to last forever. You're most concerned with how it *looks*.

It's not necessary to know camera, but you should have some idea of what the final product looks like through the lens.

Although craftsmanship *is* important, and I want to see that someone can draw a straight line, you have to bear in mind that we're in the "first impression" business. At a world science fiction convention in Anaheim a few years ago, Lucasfilm had a display booth with a number of authentic props from *Star Wars*. I overheard a couple of kids, about thirteen, fourteen, saying: "Well, these are fakes, these aren't the ones they used in the show because look, the lines are crooked and the paint's sloppy and there's glue marks on it." The kids thought they had to be like a plastic kit, perfect lines and smooth surfaces and no flaws.

But they *were* the real ones. And they're as good as they had to be.

Creature Design

Creature Design combines aspects of art (sculpture and painting) and technology (internal mechanisms) in creating lifelike "creatures" for motion pictures. A designer must have knowledge of biological functions, shapes, and materials, along with an inventor's imagination, in order to evoke believable performances from his realistic or imagined creations.

Carlo Rambaldi

As a boy in northern Italy, CARLO RAMBALDI was not thinking about the motion picture business. He studied fine arts at the Bologna Academy, where sculpture and painting attracted many young artists. These areas were saturated ground in the 1940s, so Carlo and his friends toyed with the idea of adding motion to their sculptures. No longer interested in realism, they combined abstract forms with surrealistic movement and experimented with the technology of mechanisms.

One day while visiting Rome, he ran into a friend working on a movie production called *Siegfried*, one of the first films with special effects. For this production, he accepted the challenge of creating an enormous life-size dragon almost sixty feet long—completely mechanical.

A chain of other productions became aware of his talents and hired him for more pictures. Soon the field of special effects for motion pictures became his major source of work.

When Dino De Laurentiis moved his production company from Italy to America, he contacted Carlo to work on his 1975 version of *King Kong*. This assignment led to an Academy Award and two more assignments on Steven Spielberg's *Close Encounters of the Third Kind* and his Academy Award–winning title character in the top-grossing film of all time—*E.T.* Among his many other credits are *Alien* (for which he received his third Academy Award), *White Buffalo*, *Nightwing*, and *Cat's Eye*.

I WAS born in a little village in Italy. Farmers who worked the fields during the day drove back home at night on their bicycles. They were always riding on the roads in groups of five to eight people, talking and laughing.

One night when I was six years old I was watching a group of farmers riding down this country road, and an iron wire, a string of metal, caught in one of their wheels. The bicycle collapsed in the street, and the other cyclists ran into each other and crashed. It was more dangerous than funny, but as a young boy I found it extremely funny. It was so funny, I wanted to see it again.

I decided to invent a piece of bent iron, not easily seen, that would jump at the spokes and jam the wheel. I tried to think of a shape that would cling and trap the wheel when touched. When I was seven, I invented just such a shape.

With more boys from my town, I made a number of these specially shaped wires for playing this practical joke. We would place them on the street at random in shadowed spots between streetlights. And we would wait, sitting cross-armed, waiting for these groups of farmers riding home at the end of the day. The wheels would touch them, the wires would grab the wheels and jam the spokes, the farmers would fall on top of each other, and all of us young boys would take off running.

This went on for several nights. The big question in the village became, "Why does everyone fall every time we get to this spot in the road?" No one ever discovered our little trick.

If you analyze the mechanism of this invention, you'll find that it's extremely logical—you have a base, you have an action and, of course, a reaction. These three elements work together to achieve a final result.

This was the first example of how I was tuned in, even at an early age, to the logic of mechanisms.

King Kong

King Kong is not really an invention. *King Kong* is a reproduction of a giant gorilla.

We started searching in the zoos for the right kind of face, and I found a beautiful gorilla in the San Diego Zoo. Nothing was really invented in *King Kong*; what we did was reproduce that San Diego Zoo gorilla.

Of all the body movements in the new *King Kong*, none were mechanical, other than the giant arms and hands. Most of the film was done to human scale. You know—a male mime in a gorilla suit.

The true challenge of *King Kong* was to re-create the facial movements mechanically, in an emotionally expressive fashion, through animation of the mask the actor wore. Most people think that if there is a man inside, it's the man operating the gorilla. But the face of an actor cannot convey its expressions through a mask. He used only his eyes until we could invent a way to make his mask more evocative.

To shoot the whole film with a giant mechanical Kong would have taken six years of shooting and cost approximately $200 million. Quite ridiculous. So the use of the mime in a gorilla suit was the economical answer.

We did, however, build giant hands and giant arms for important sequences. And what determined the size of those elements was the scale for the actress; from the height of the actress, they developed the size of the hand. A lying-down Kong was built for the scenes in the hold of the ship. And for the death scenes, a supine dead one also was created. A gorilla is so very different from a human being, we had to use transparent resins to make his eyes realistic, and this was the first large-scale use of synthetics to simulate the texture of gorilla fur.

By the time I created another Kong for the sequel, *King Kong Lives*, instead of using different heads for the different expressions, just *one* head was built to do everything. The technology had been somewhat perfected by then.

Oscar

They gave me my first Academy Award for *King Kong*. The statue was for me a sort of "materialized applause" that indicates you have done a certain level of quality work. I am not the type to say, "Oh, my God, I'm so thrilled . . . I'm going to faint." But I must confess, it was a great pleasure.

Close Encounters of the Third Kind

After working on the film *White Buffalo*, I went back to Italy, where Steven Spielberg contacted me. I did not know Spielberg at all, but apparently he had seen *King Kong* and wanted me to design an extraterrestrial for his completed movie *Close Encounters of the Third Kind*. All he was missing was the alien that appears at the end of the picture.

I drew my idea of what the being should look like and sent it to him. By phone, Steven told me he liked the drawing. Then he asked me to give him an estimate for my services.

So I gave an Italian version of an estimate, you know, and asked for $30,000. And Steven had no reaction, you know, on the other end of the line, no feeling at all. And I thought maybe I had asked too much. Then he quickly answered, "That will be fine."

I wasn't aware of the level of costs in America. In Italy $30,000 makes a fortune. This was a remarkably low figure in American terms.

I sculpted and built the extraterrestrial being in Italy and sent it over here. During the shooting, once in a while, Steven Spielberg would yell out to the others on the set, "Okay, everybody, pay attention! Here comes the extraterrestrial from Italy!"

Design of the Creature in *Close Encounters*

Scientifically, the design of the alien in *Close Encounters* is more true to reality than E.T.

Chances are that an extraterrestrial would look more like the *Close Encounters* alien than the little creature in *E.T.*

E.T. was built to appeal to the children and was a manifestation of love. We initiated the creature as a toy invention rather than an expression of scientific hypothesis.

As for the alien in *Close Encounters*, I felt that if we ever encountered an extraterrestrial, it would probably have a thin shape. And since an extraterrestrial would be many more years developed than humans, his brain would be a lot more developed than ours, so the head would be larger. And if the cerebral container was enlarged, the eyes would grow apart as well.

And imagining a faraway planet with very little earthly gravity, our creature would not need a strong neck to sustain the weight of his lightweight skull, so we'd grant him a lithe, lovely, thin neck.

And I imagined a population that would speak with signals and sign language, so ears would not be developed as much. And in a world where sounds and smell would not be important, a very small nose would suffice.

Imagining a simpler, more sophisticated form of nutrition, a very small mouth apparatus would be sufficient. Long thin arms and long thin body. Even the legs wouldn't be very strong because in a more developed technology, people would be walking less, and legs would not be as developed.

So these are the principal concepts that gave birth to the creation of Puck, the alien from *Close Encounters*.

And this began a very important relationship between Steven

Spielberg and myself. We are both very much interested in other worlds.

E.T.

Spielberg had started E.T. eight months before contacting me. At first he thought making a mechanical creature would be a simple problem. He put about twenty makeup artists in charge of creating an E.T. creature. And these makeup people did their best.

They worked eight or nine months and spent about $800,000. Spielberg was in England and couldn't really supervise the work. When he returned to start the film, he found a horrible creature that didn't work well mechanically. So he brought me in to reconceive this troubled creation. We had to build four different E.T.'s, so we asked for ten months.

For the concept of the film, E.T. had to be ugly. Otherwise there wouldn't be any reason for the little girl to be afraid in the very beginning. I wanted to find something unusual, out of the ordinary. And I found inspiration in this thirty-year-old painting I did when I was concentrating on my painting. For the innocence in the facial expression, I found inspiration in the facial proportions and eye shape of a Himalayan cat.

The origins of E.T. arise from these two elements.

You see a cat. Cats have eyes with lines that go upward at a forty-five-degree angle. This makes them very aggressive. I used the same form in bringing up the nose, and I gave the eyes another inclination. By raising the nose, we are getting away from the feline face. That horizontal plane increases the effect of innocence.

Another thing that was achieved in the eyes of E.T. is the expanding of the eyes. It is a very small detail, and most people wouldn't catch it. But when E.T. got drunk, the irises expanded.

It also had to have a mechanism very similar to the human body, with eighty-five points of movement, which is really the number of movements in the human body. The wrist is two movements. And even the head would be an extending neck, up and down.

So an electronic E.T. was designed with eighty-five sophisticated movements. To correspond to the needs of specific scenes, we created another with forty points of movements, a third with twenty, and a fourth for the long shots.

The long-shot body suit to be worn by an actor was used for about 8 percent of the filming. Some critics said a midget could have done everything. That's just not true.

I kept these major secrets in the mechanics of E.T. so that they would not get in the hands of other people.

Secrets

The secrets of my work are very connected to the human anatomy. You can make a mechanism with one hundred levers, but as you perfect it, the number of levers and cables will decrease and synthesize, becoming simpler. The result will be more efficiently achieved.

The problems in the mechanics of the face, which I began to solve over twenty years ago, used to require no less than about fifty pieces. But the longer I have worked on this problem, the more I have obtained a synthesized mechanism. Now the pieces from fifty have become twenty with a better result, with greater efficiency.

I'm not saving this secret because I'm worried or jealously guarding my inventions, but it is only right that if a person wants to show himself as a creative inventor, he must do his own training and inventing, instead of copying or learning from someone else in his particular field.

That is why I don't teach or give advice.

Hiring a Team

Each production is different. But a given job always requires a responsible crew of high quality capable of accomplishing work in a timely fashion.

If a product doesn't work due to an irresponsible worker, that worker can jeopardize or ruin the project, and the production would have the right to sue me.

Whom I hire depends on the type of work and the amount of time given. For example, E.T. had eleven people working for five months. King Kong had two hundred people. Depends on the quantity of work and deadlines.

To build E.T., I hired a sculptor, mold makeup artist. Maybe two sculptors, three mold makeup, four for the internal mechanism, and a tailor for the body suit. These are the principal elements I usually hire. If there's some electronic or computerized needs, then there will be somebody in that specific area I can hire. Usually someone on my crew knows a little bit about everything, but they're very good at one thing.

Often we have to contact someone for a specific task. For complicated things like the hands and face, I design some pieces and have others made, separate pieces.

The assemblage is done only by me, and by me alone.

The mounting of an effect is the most important part. If you cannot put something together well, you can destroy the whole effect. So I take that final responsibility.

The public knows that it's a mechanical creature. But it's important that the mechanical actor doesn't reveal or expose its mechanized nature.

If E.T. makes a movement as softly and gently as a real person with his arm, the audience won't even think of a mechanism. If the same movement jerks, even just an infinitesimal jerk, the audience will understand that the mechanism is imperfect, and this is a disappointing downturn for the psychology of the audience.

The Collaborative Process

There are filmmaking characteristics that bring more value to one of my creations: camera position, lighting, and, of course, acting performances and editing are very important. These are the four major characteristics that help an effect to be its best. Unless I see something that I know will not work, I usually leave these other elements to our diverse professional collaborators, who do a fine job of accomplishing their own share of the work.

Alien

Mechanically, they're the same. E.T. could have been a criminal if you put a knife in his hand.

Similarly, even the alien in *Alien* could have been a lovable creature. Pretend an alien walks up to you. We play happy American music on the sound track. Now it's not scary because the music creates a good atmosphere.

The monster of *Cat's Eye* is a terrible monster. It's like a small gnome. It fights with a knife against a cat. It's very short and dressed like a medieval clown. The face is horrible, but he moves very playfully. He's introduced in the film as a kind of dancing criminal, so we're not sure how to feel about him. It all depends how something is presented with camera and music.

The painting concept for *Alien* is from a Swiss artist by the name of H. R. Geiger. They found him through his previous renderings of creatures for the movie. The director saw the paintings, and the expression of the monster was what he was looking for. Geiger drew further profiles of this long head, and then we constructed a three-dimensional model sculpture. And from that, the whole monster was developed.

The mouth definitely is the killer point—the double jaw. The monster was also filmed extremely well. The audience doesn't really see the monster entirely. You're just made aware of its fleshy appearance. But the filmmaker makes you feel the presence of this monster psychologically, even if you don't see it. You feel it there through the photography and editing, and that is how the maximum tension is achieved that truly terrifies an audience.

If you see a dark hallway and there's an opening door, you don't know who's going to come out of that door. When the monster appears, I think the fear has a drop because once you see it, then you *control* it. Fear predominates only when something's beyond your control, only when you don't know what to do.

So Ridley Scott uses the opening-door system of suspense, and the monster appears so rapidly. This way the viewer has no time to relax. The monster does damage in a flash, and then it's over. If a monster appears slowly, in many more frames, you're much more able to perceive it and adjust to its threat. These psychological consequences are very important to the effectiveness of my creation.

The idea that the alien is different every time you see it is another reason for its effectiveness. The unpredictability of its stages of transformation is another frightening element.

In truth, anything can be terrifying depending on how you present it.

On Directing

I could direct a film, but my temperament wouldn't allow it. A director must be strict and severe. That is not my nature. A director has to have patience. It bothers me to say something twice. It's against my nature to repeat *anything*.

Advice

First of all, you should have an artistic background to do what I do. Without an artistic background you cannot really invent these things. The mechanisms I produce are also a form of sculpture. If you don't have a sense of form and sculpture and anatomy, you cannot do this kind of work.

Sculpture and mechanics must always work together. You have to have an artistic base and be extremely self-critical of what you do.

I will never teach at a university or give lectures to students in a formalized setting. A chef could never create another chef like himself. In fact, if the truth is told, he doesn't *want* another chef to be like him.

I think every artist always has a secret he will not give away. Not even to the best student.

12
THE SOUND

Everything you hear during a movie—dialogue, background sounds, or music that enhances the emotional impact of the film—was selected and recorded by a crew category in this chapter according to the needs expressed by the director.

Production Sound Mixer

The Production Sound Mixer is responsible to the director for recording all production sound, synchronous and "wild" (nonsynchronous dialogue or location sound effects), and for the quality of the mixed and recorded sound during production. He or she operates and maintains the mixing console, recorder, and associated equipment, keeps the sound reports, and prepares the recorded tape for shipment and delivery to the sound transfer studio. As head of the sound crew, the Production Sound Mixer hires the boom operator and cable man, selects or approves the selection of all sound equipment and raw stock, supervises the loading, transportation, setting up, and dismantling of all sound equipment, and oversees the placement of microphones on stands, beams, and actors by the boom operator. The Production Sound Mixer is also charged with protesting any take in which he or she deems the sound quality faulty or inadequate.

Jim Webb

JIM WEBB did news and documentary sound work in the 1960s. These roots in live production led to a series of specials on musicians for PBS. From there he went on to feature films, working with Robert Altman on *Nashville* (earning a British Academy Award) and *The Wedding*, among others. His production sound on *All the President's Men*, which spectacularly captured newsroom chaos, garnered an American Academy Award. Among numerous other films he has worked on are *The Rose, The Onion Field, True Confessions, One from the Heart, Hammett, The Outsiders, Country, Flashdance, Down and Out in Beverly Hills, Legal Eagles, The Milagro Beanfield War, Colors, Moon over Parador,* and *Beaches*.

I N THE old days, when sound men were more of a big deal, if you didn't like something, you could stand up and yell, "Cut! Cut!" That is a rare event these days. And I would be reluctant to do it. Cut a shot and you had better have a good reason—like your tape recorder blew up. That lack of sound awareness is sad. . . .

If they give you a chance, you can contribute as much to the mood of the film as the cameraman. I wish that more directors, particularly art directors, who help select locations, were more informed about sound and valued it more as a production value.

There are probably only half a dozen to a dozen directors who value the sound track enough to care about the noise level on locations. And overall I don't think most people would know a good track if it came up and bit them in the leg. When you ask someone how the sound in dailies was, the usual response is something like "Well, I heard all the words."

The Job

A production mixer records all the sound that he can during shooting. That includes everything said in front of the camera and, additionally, any atmospheric sound that is not immediately on-camera—whatever he can get there on the set that may be needed later on.

Later on, in the rerecording process, a team of three mixers who handle dialogue (mostly mine, hopefully), music, and sound effects will combine these respective tracks into one final and complete sound track. That is why on Academy Awards night you'll usually see *four* guys walk up there, because it will be three rerecording guys and the production mixer. They judge it on the entire sound job, and sometimes it is pretty hard to separate who did what. It is a team effort.

Boom and Cable

I pick my own crew. I will not do a film without a boom man of my choice. The boom man, your main "mike" man, is *the* guy. I give him the set. I say, "You stay and keep your ear in there while I'm putting the system together, find out what is going on, and come back and brief me." My stuff is only as good as the placement of his mikes. We *must* complement each other.

I reflect this in the credits. My credits (when they allow me input) will always say, "Production Sound"—my name and the boom man's name. Not "Mixer" and "Boom."

The boom job in my estimation is one of the two toughest jobs on the set. He has to know everybody else's job. He has to know the lighting because you can't put the mike where it will cause shadows. He has to know lenses because he can't dip the mike into the frame. He has to know the lines in order to know where to point the mike. If the camera is going to move, he has to know where the dolly grip is going to go, otherwise it could run over his foot, or he could end up in the shot. He has to be physically strong to hold the microphone boom pole out there sometimes four or five minutes. It is very tough, and there's a high burnout rate.

The cable man does all the things that the mike man doesn't. He is really a utility person. If you've got a little playback, he does that. If you need to run the wires, he does that. If you need somebody to hold a second mike, he does that. He's the grunt, the private who's out there making it work for the rest of the troops.

Mikes

If you get down to basics, the primary equipment is a tape recorder and microphone.

Microphones are tools, like different kinds of wrenches. You use the right tool for the particular situation, and you tend to carry lots of tools with you. You've got lavaliere mikes and shotgun microphones and regular microphones and ones that come apart and come together and can be hidden here and there. I have my own equipment, and it makes little difference to me whether it is a studio picture or not because I only work with my own equipment.

Robert Altman

I went to work for Robert Altman because I had some multitrack experience and he was looking for a way to shoot movies using multitrack recording so that he could have all of these actors overlapping dialogue and not worry about it.

Altman was the first to commit to multitrack as a total system all the way through a film. It was portable. It ran on AC or DC. We even had it on Greyhound buses shooting scenes while the buses were moving. It was a completely self-contained system.

I like to get it while it is happening, out in the trenches. And the way Altman shoots, you have to get the sound as it happens and not depend on postproduction. Normally you would shoot a scene a line at a time, using only one track, and movie audiences are pretty much conditioned to hearing one line at a time.

Altman feels that if you walk into a bar and you hear a guy talking, mumbling, the way I talk, that is *real* life. It drives some people crazy because they can't concentrate on the plot, they're too busy trying to figure out who's talking. In an Altman film, actors will overlap as they are talking. You hear off-screen as well as on-screen dialogue and subconversations going on.

Many of his films started with little or no script. 3 *Women* had a one-page outline. There was no formal script, and they dealt with the story each day, one day at a time.

When *President's* came along, one of the reasons I got the show was because of the big newsroom scene. They were going to use what they called "deep focus," split diopters, so you could see and hear things going on in several rooms simultaneously. They reasoned that

438

if I could record all these simultaneous conversations in *Nashville*, I could do something similar for them. It turned out they didn't quite need that much sound. But it got me the job.

The Conversation

Coppola's *The Conversation* is a landmark movie because it brought sound to the audience's attention. To acoustically pick up a conversation two blocks away is a physical impossibility. But it makes great fantasy.

I just wished Francis had a little more insight into the value of a production sound track. At that time, he felt that whatever problems he had with a production track could be fixed later in postproduction. I feel looping is a poor way to do it; you lose in performance. An actor coming in after the picture is shot, on a sound stage, is not even in the environment where the scene was acted. If I can capture it as the actor does it, it is almost always better. It is more "of the moment."

Zooming

In a sense, I "zoomed" unsuspectingly on a picture called *California Split*, where we used the multitrack.

The shot was a long room with three desks in it, one behind the other. The idea is that the camera is going to zoom from the front desk back to the last desk.

Using three tracks, one for each mike, I put a microphone on each desk. The gal in front was talking on the phone, the guy in the middle was talking in Spanish to somebody sitting at that desk, and the desk behind was the conversation between George Segal and the guy who was playing the insurance agent.

We ran the dailies in multitrack, and I discovered that, as the camera moved through these people, I could dial through the tracks at exactly the same rate of speed that the lens was moving, and the effect was a "zoom microphone."

The Console

Jack Cashin, Robert Altman's engineer at the time, and I designed a board that had four monitor busses, so that different people— for instance, the director, the boom man, the script supervisor, and myself—could hear different mixes of whatever was being recorded.

Altman would want to hear the main characters, so I would set his earphones up on that particular monitor buss to hear that group of people. Then a second assistant director would say, "Give me the background guys," so I'd set him up on a second buss. And the boom man would say, "I don't want to hear any of that, just give me my microphone."

Now prior to shooting I would listen to each to make sure they were all working, but many times I recorded some people "blind" by just watching the meter and sampling them.

When we built the new board I added a "solo function." To use a musical analogy—say, a group of musicians—if you push a button, it would correspond to a particular microphone attached to the violins; you push another, it would correspond to the horns for the instant that you hold the button down. I wanted to be able to do this for the production dialogue. Since we monitor in mono, which makes it difficult to figure out what is coming from an individual mike within the total mix, it would help in assessing the individual components of the overall mix.

I would go through the mikes while the scene was going on and listen to each one in turn. But by the time the scene ran, say, a minute, and I'd gone through them once, I found I'd heard each one once but I hadn't really heard the scene in its entirety, and who knows what happened to that microphone after I left it and went on to the next one?

It turned out that the solo didn't really help me because things were shifting around too fast, which is the difference between music and movie sound tracks, Altman style.

With music, you've got a group of musicians in a studio that are all tied off, and they all stay in one place. But in an Altman movie, you've got microphones that are constantly moving and changing in acoustic relationships. So I found it better to just sample them before the shot and make sure they were all at least working, and then do a kind of monomix in my headphones, which often sounded like the Tower of Babel.

The option *not* to use some of your material becomes as important as the ability to use it. If you decide it is in the way or you don't need it, you simply fade it out in postproduction. For instance, in *Nashville*, there is a scene at the "Pickin' Parlor" with two things going on at the same time. Robert Doqui, an actor, is having an argument and is busy getting up and leaving. Henry Gibson is seating his group at the table. You have a choice of tipping the scene one way or the other. You want to hear more of Robert Doqui, or you want to hear less of him and more of Henry Gibson, you can make that choice in the dub.

We started out with just a few principals who carried the main dialogue, and then we would mike little groups of people: extras, a guy talking to his girlfriend, a waitress taking an order. Later, because all these tracks existed, you could create a left, a center, and a right as seen on-screen using sound and bring up whatever you wanted to emphasize. The board is your tool for controlling the sound levels. The word *stereo* is really a misnomer in that sense. It is multitrack. You are laying down tracks with as *much* isolation as you can get so material can be picked up and positioned later in postproduction or thrown out if it is not any good.

Straight Time

Straight Time was based on a book written by a convict in jail. I interviewed with Dustin Hoffman for the show. The first four or five chapters are nothing but pure sound descriptions, all the sounds that this guy hears while he is in his cell. From the birds to the jailer to water sloshing . . . I had a list about two feet long.

I actually went up to Quentin with a tape recorder and mike, spent two days inside the south cell block where this guy had heard those sounds, and they were all still there. I recorded birds up in the top, the sound of a guy walking down each cell as he went along, I went out into the yard and recorded the wind blowing through the concertina wire, although I'm not sure anybody could identify what it was. Background sounds of the yard, the mess hall, all the things that you find in prison. Dustin loved them, and many of them were used in the sound track of the movie.

Tones and Shades

One of our responsibilities is to get "room tones" or "outdoor tones." They are *very* difficult to get because the crew is trying to get on to the next shot. You have to shut them up and make them stand still. It is the longest thirty seconds in everybody's life. Nobody can stand completely still. They are all fidgeting.

You need to record that silence, to fill the tracks where the sound effects cutters have cut lines and there are little gaps they have to fill with the "tone" of that environment. It is an editing tool, to fill in those dead spaces with living silence.

Looping

You want them to use your track because you think that is the best for the picture. And yet I've had to say to an actor in desperation, "Look, if you don't talk louder, you are going to wind up having to loop this movie [replace the dialogue in postproduction]," which is a terrible thing from my view, of course. It means I couldn't do my job. Whereupon the actor will turn to me and say, "What is wrong with that? I can work on it. I can make the lines better. I can polish the reading." Some actors do mumble, so it's necessary to polish their performance later. Some of them don't want to loop it and make more of an effort to get the dialogue across during shooting. But inevitably there are some things you just have to replace. Either the reading wasn't there, or you want to change the reading.

Peanuts

I've done whole pictures outdoors where it's hard to control environment. *Long Riders*, for example, was shot in Georgia because they thought Georgia looked more like Missouri in the past than Missouri does today. And they grow peanuts in the central Georgia plains.

Peanuts need to be dried when harvested. They're collected and thrown in these big dryers, which run twenty-four hours a day. The sound is not unlike an air-raid siren. You can hear those suckers a quarter of a mile away.

We had to shut down the ones that were close, and we tried to point the microphone in the opposite direction from the others. But you are talking to a farmer who needs to get that crop dried and out the door. He can't just sit on it. I guess they threw a lot of money at him, bought the crop or something.

Getting Work

It is about personal relationships, like every other phase of the business. But just because you've won an award . . . I can remember going for an interview once and saying, "I've done two or three Altman movies," and the guy looked at me and said, "Okay, what else have you done?" And I'm thinking, God, that wasn't enough. What do I say now?

It takes years to build a reputation where people will call you to do jobs. It's a *long* haul. One or two hit films doesn't guarantee anything.

In terms of the process itself, I would like to see more communication going on between postproduction mixing personnel and the production crew. There are still many areas that can stand more scrutiny, education, and awareness.

I've never really been bitten by the bug to do something else. I'm satisfied with what I do. It often feels like a chore, but if the film and the sound track come out well, it's worth it. I feel good that I can make a contribution. And I feel it is an artistic contribution.

Boom Operator

The Boom Operator is responsible to the production mixer for operating and maintaining the microphone boom, or "fishpole," along with the attached shotgun ("directional") microphone. He or she positions the microphones to pick up the voices, sound effects, and/or music at the perspective desired by the mixer. As the "man on the set" in terms of sound, staying close to the director to determine his sound requirements, the Boom Operator provides the crucial link by capturing the production sound to be recorded by the production mixer. The Boom Operator works closely with the camera, electrical, and grip crews to ensure that the boom, the microphones, and the mike shadows do not appear within the camera frame.

Forrest Williams

FORREST WILLIAMS came to Hollywood with a degree in theater and film and a die-hard desire to be involved in "the business," his ultimate goal being to direct. He hit Hollywood "with this rosy-cheeked attitude that, of course, you want to help me, of course you'll want to look at my student film, of course I'll direct your next feature." The first door that opened up for him was working at an equipment rental house that specialized in sound equipment. There he learned the "grass-roots technical end of sound" and accumulated enough days to get into the sound union. He continued working in sound, gaining experience as a cable man before becoming a boom operator, on such films as *The Rose*, *Witness*, *Escape from Alcatraz*, *Death Valley*, *Americathon*, and *Damien—Omen II*.

T HE BOOM is a fishpole that attaches to the microphone. If you ask me, "Is it heavy?" I'll tell you, "It breaks my back, lady."

Fortunately a roll of film only lasts eleven minutes in the camera. It's not a matter of being muscular or well built, it's more like a long-distance race. Endurance counts. You start to shake, but you just have to ignore the pain. The only way you can hold a microphone over your head is wanting to do it. Not wanting to screw up. You don't want to make a shadow. You want to do a good job. And it costs a lot of money to roll that camera again. Every time they have to retake a shot, it's anywhere from a couple thousand dollars to tens of thousands.

When shooting exteriors, the pole becomes even heavier with the added weight of the windscreen over the microphone.

Cable Man

When you join a production crew, the first job in sound is as a cable man—seeing that the equipment is maintained and looking after the needs of the mixer and the boom man, which can be anything from "Get me a glass of water, boy," to "Put me in the shade." Today the title is "assistant sound technician." And they make my day easier by working a second mike on tough shots.

That's standard procedure, to take the low-man-on-the-totem-pole job first and observe as long as you can. Once you've learned enough doing cable man work, then you make a move yourself. Hopefully you don't have to wait too long for some guy to say, "I like you, Forrest. Why don't you be my next boom man?"

Pecking Order

There are cliques, there's a pecking order that exists from the cameraman all the way down to crafts services man. I was very naive about production work, so I got out there expecting everyone to pick up a line, share the work. Doesn't work that way. I can't touch a light, he can't touch my microphone, I can't touch his camera. It's very segregated and very competitive. It's an army, and the general is the director. And the second in command is the director of photography. That's whom your allegiance is to—the DP.

The Job

The boom operator's responsibility is to be on the set at all times, never leave the set from the morning's "call time." The most important thing you can do is get your cup of coffee, say "hi" to people, walk on the set, and listen to the director. He's the guy you follow around, you stay in his back pocket, and you walk with him through the set.

The first shot is always a master. He'll line up his shot, and you've got to be listening to him. And while you're listening to him, the wheels in your brain are turning and you're thinking, Okay, if the actor's going to be over there, I've got to put a microphone here. You decide, on the basis of how the director is blocking and what he's saying, where you're going to plant your mikes or how you're going to swing the boom around the set.

My recommendation is to develop a rapport with the director. If you don't have that, then you have to go through that god-awful chain-of-command crap—go to the assistant director, who goes to the director, who goes back to the assistant director, who goes back to you. And by the time it gets to you, third or fourth person, you may not get the answer you need anyway. If there's a question regarding sound, the man to go to is the director because he has the answers.

The only time a director will initiate getting into the nuts and bolts of sound is when he comes up to you personally and says, "Forrest, we've got a long shot here, and you're going to have to rig the actors." He knows way in advance what his shot design is, and rather than going through the rigmarole of rehearsing the whole scene and waiting till the last minute for us to find out that we have to put a body mike on the actor, he'll just tell us—which is really helpful as far as knowing what equipment to break out.

445

You have to observe the director, try to read his mind and know exactly what he wants to do. And once he's said his piece, not only do you have to know where to put your mikes, you have to know where the camera's going to be—and if the director of photography uses a certain lens, you have to know how that affects the scope of the shot. You have to know lighting because how the DP lights the set will affect where you put your mikes. There is also the grip and electrical department. Without their help you can have a miserable time. A good boom operator has to understand the work required of the grips and electricians. If they are confident, you know what you're doing, and the day goes smoother.

Problems

The most obvious problem is when the mike dips into frame. That's what the average viewer is going to see and what gets blamed on the boom operator.

It is the camera operator's responsibility to tell you when that happens. He's looking through the lens, but you have to be aware of when the boom comes into frame or even the shadow of the boom. If your subject's close, you'll have fewer problems, but if it's backed off and wide, you may have the Coliseum to worry about. In confined spaces, low ceilings and a wide shot force you to keep your microphone up close to the ceiling, and you might have to make a lot of swings with it.

There's always a plan A, plan B, and plan C. If plan A doesn't work, where you're using a good strong recording microphone near the actor's mouth, you go to plan B, where you plant a microphone somewhere. If you can't plant one because either the camera will see it or it won't be in an optimum position to hear the dialogue, then you go to plan C with radio mikes—which the actors don't like because you have to hide them on the actor's body, and if the actor has sheer clothing, that's a problem, too. You have to be ready to make these changes at a moment's notice, as discreetly as possible.

Any element—climatic or environmental—is a problem with sound. The biggest problem in sound is background noise. Nature we can contend with—rain, birds—that's just there. People talking, planes overhead, are all headaches. In a western, you don't want to hear a freeway nearby or a jet going over.

Windbags and Mikes

There's no such thing as an exterior or interior mike. The difference is in the protection devices called "zeppelins" or "windbags," made of certain materials that keep the wind from hitting it. These microphones are very wind-sensitive, so you have to protect them at all times, which makes the microphone heavier.

A shotgun microphone has a narrow field, and it can pick up someone's dialogue farther away. So it's used most often with exteriors—say, a western. You're filming Mt. Whitney, they want to hear James Arness a hundred feet away.

A shorter-field microphone has a wider span and doesn't pick up the farthest things. It's a close-proximity mike, and it keeps a cleaner sound.

Every microphone has a specific job. Whatever the director determines the shot is going to be determines the kind of microphone you're going to use. The mixer determines what his favorite kinds of mikes are. As a boom operator, you work with the tools he wants you to use.

The standard industry microphone is the directional microphone. It either has a narrow, straight-ahead recording ability span or a semi-wide field.

Hand-held mikes like the entertainers use have a wide recording ability. It has to be close proximity. If you pull the mike away from your body, it's of little use.

The kind we put on the bodies—the little peanut microphones—are omnidirectional. They have a flat recording capability, recording whatever's closest to it, usually the mouth. It will pick up someone else's voice close by, but not as strong.

Signal to Noise

To hear more clearly everything that's being recorded, a boom operator should wear a headset. The microphone then becomes an extension of your ears. The human ear is an extension of your brain. I can be in a noisy room, a party, let's say, and be talking to you. All I'm hearing is your voice, even though all around me there are people talking. Because my brain only wants to hear you.

A microphone doesn't have that capability. A microphone hears everything. It can't separate sound. If you were out in the middle of a quiet meadow and you were recording, you could turn the knob up forever until you could hear the grass grow. But the sound of an airplane will also be exaggerated proportionately.

So if you want a party sound, what you do is tell everybody behind your actors to pantomime. Then later you lay over a wild track of the extras' murmurings. That way you can play with the dialogue and keep the background sound for the dubbing.

Background noise is what you want to control. The textbook usage is "signal to noise." The signal is what you want to record, the noise is what you want to eliminate.

The mixer and I are responsible for that background noise to the extent of mentioning it to the director. If we hear something in the background and the director didn't catch it, we say, "You may not like that cut because you had a car go by in the background." They may not have heard it. From then on the ball is in his court. He may do another take or say, "We don't have time, let's keep going."

Trends

The film industry, as far as keeping up with sophistication in sound, is way behind. The government has marvelous sophistication in sound. The CIA has mikes you'd never see—plug 'em in your nose or teeth.

I think there's some great motivation to refine sound. It would simplify a lot of things, but I don't want to stab myself in the back and agree to it right now! I'd love to see some major monies spent sophisticating all the equipment in the industry. Not necessarily eliminating manpower because I think for every machine you invent there's got to be somebody to push a button on it.

It would take some of the glamour out of it. But there are times I would kill for sophistication on a small narrow set when I have to swing this thing around and be yelled at for half an hour by a belligerent director.

How good it sounds is the bottom line. The microphones we use today are what you want for optimum-quality sound. Radio mikes you put on an actor are a great tool, but you have inherent problems with them all the time—clothing noise, where you put the damn thing without it being seen, and then you have radio mike frequencies. Sophisticated equipment just does not exist right now, and I don't see it happening for maybe another decade—as far as possibly eliminating my job!

Oil magnates and real estate entrepreneurs buy their way into our business and call themselves filmmakers. What in hell do they know about the nuts and bolts of making a picture? The old studio bosses—Goldwyn, Cohn, and Warner—they may have been grouchy old farts, but at least they knew what had to be done. Today, young corporate executives from some parent company will make across-the-board cuts in manpower and wages without a thought about why that job exists. If an executive were to ask my advice, I'd tell him or her to forget the three-piece suit and the expensive lunches, spend time instead on a production from start to finish. Watch how it's done. Recognize what the needs are and where the wastage exists. Films aren't made in air-conditioned offices—*deals* are.

Aspirations

The realities of this industry hit me hard the first year of working in it. People were either rude or nice. The rude ones set me straight. They told me to make up my mind: go for one thing and fast.

I didn't choose sound as a career, it sort of chose me. But fate has a way of being a blessing. My first location assignment as a cable man was on a western where the electricians would grumble jealously while I was wrapping spaghetti-thin cable and they were wrapping cable thick as pythons in one-hundred-degree weather in Kanab, Utah.

There is a drawback in this industry. Once you pick a certain career or *seem* to pick one, you're labeled as such. Years ago it behooved the studio to keep everybody in a caste system. Below the line and above the line were separate, and never the twain shall meet. Actors didn't hobnob with the techs, unless you were a Clark Gable who went fishing with the grip.

They're merging together more now, although not as much as I'd like. Young guys or girls getting out of film school may not get that first crack at selling their scripts or making films. They just want to get into the business. That's what happened to me.

If you're creative and you have an idea and you love movies, it's only natural that you'd want to make your own. Whether it's little student films or home movies, major studio productions or independent nonunion features, the desire is there. Someday soon, hopefully, I'll be putting my own ideas on film.

Satisfaction

I think it was William Goldman who said, "Directing is hard work, but it's not hard work like Van Gogh painting, it's hard work like coal mining." Operating the boom *is* hard work, but I take pride in hard work.

And I like the responsibility, the learning and the rapport you develop because of that responsibility. I get an immense sense of pride when I see something on the screen and I know that all the work I put into it was on that screen, not looped—which means replaced by the actor at a later date—but the original track is on there.

And you know you had to fight, scream, kick, bite to get it on there. Not screen credit, none of that. But the job is done and done right and appreciated by the director or the producer. Knowing that my work is physically on the screen and you feel it there throughout the whole movie.

Postscript: *Since giving this interview, Forrest acquired the rights to a novel,* Song of the Wild, *and adapted it as a screenplay.*

Supervising Sound Editor

The Supervising Sound Editor is responsible for the quality of all the sound on the final sound track, excluding music. She or he oversees the work of the editors on sound effects (postproduction recording and editing of all artificially created or natural sounds other than music or dialogue), dialogue, Foley (the postproduction synchronization of body movement sound plus sound effects with visual images) and ADR (automatic dialogue replacement, also called "looping," referring to any voices taped, recorded, and incorporated into the film in postproduction), and coordinates their work with the work of the music editor and rerecording mixers.

Cecelia Hall

CECELIA HALL left her childhood home in St. Louis to study art history in London and Milan. During these several years her interest in film further developed, and upon her return to the United States she set out for Hollywood intent on becoming involved in some aspect of film, hopefully as an editor. She found her first job as a negative cutter by culling the Yellow Pages and calling up film companies "cold." Later, she and a friend bought a 16-mm Moviola together and started getting small jobs, mostly editing trailers and reediting foreign films for distribution in the United States. In the process she learned all aspects of postproduction, schooling herself the "low-budget" way.

She discovered she loved sound editing at a time when no one else was interested in doing that work, and continued in that area. Since then Cecelia has been involved in sound from editing to recording to mixing, and now works exclusively as a supervising sound editor. The sound tracks for which she has been responsible include: *Top Gun* (for which she received an Academy Award nomination), *Witness, Beverly Hills Cop I, Beverly Hills Cop II, Star Trek The Motion Picture I, Star Trek II, Star Trek III, Star Trek IV, Pee Wee's Big Adventure, Pee Wee's Big Top, Nuts, Distant Thunder,* and *Harlem Nights*. She is presently designing the sound track for *Hunt for Red October*. Cecelia became the first woman president of the Motion Picture Sound Editors, an honorary society, in 1985 and currently serves on the executive sound committee of the Academy of Motion Picture Arts and Sciences.

F OR THE most part, people feel that the emotion is going to come out of the music. In some cases that's true, in some cases it's not. The climactic eight- or nine-minute scene at the end of *Aliens* has no music—there are just sound effects. That says a great deal about the director, the producer, and the supervising sound editor—their understanding that that's where the emotional power and impact lie.

In *Top Gun*, we had the challenge of a movie that was about jets—a movie, essentially, about "a boy and a plane." And it was crucial early on in the film that we make people believe they were really experiencing and feeling the airplanes, but that we *not* wear them down and turn them off.

That's a very delicate line. It was very difficult to achieve and achieved only by trial and error. We dubbed and then we looked at the film, and then we dubbed some more, took it to theaters and looked at it, and came back and dubbed some more.

There were moments in that film where I felt we should go with the music. The music would take off and be very dynamic and exciting—you were on a roller-coaster ride.

Other times, in situations of danger or threat or anxiety, it was important to go with the sound effects. We were extremely lucky on *Top Gun*; we had producers and a director who loved sound effects. Tony Scott, the director, was totally committed to the sound track.

Tony's a very dynamic and imaginative guy who wants *everything*—the music, the sound effects. He was always pushing us right to the brink. As opposed to the usual situation, in which the sound editor wants to hear more sound effects, in this case I found myself wanting to be a little on the conservative side. Tony was right. When I saw it in the theaters, I was glad that he had pushed us farther.

It's what makes sound exciting. You have the opportunity to do anything—it's very expressive. You can use your imaginative powers to create a specific mood or contributory atmosphere. I think sound editors are just coming into their own in that regard.

I recently read an interview in which the director came to his sound editor and said, "You will be my symphony. You will create the music and the rhythm of this film with sound effects." The film he was talking about was *Raging Bull*, which I think stands as one of the definitive, great sound tracks. Under the best of circumstances, people who do what I do look at it in that way and hope they will get the opportunity to compose a whole track, to contribute in such a significant way.

Sound Editing

For years we were credited on films as "Sound Effects Editors."

Six years ago, I turned in the credits on a picture I was supervising and listed us as "Sound Editors" (as opposed to "Sound Effects Editors"). The head of labor relations called me and said, "We can't list it that way, and that's as per your union." So I called up the union and said, "Look, this is an anachronism."

Sound *effects* is a very limiting term. We do *all* the sound. Who does the dialogue, who does the Foley, who does the ADR, other than "the effects"? It's as if you're doing cartoons and all you care about is the pops, the doors opening, and minutiae like that.

After a terrific brouhaha, they finally went with "Sound Editors." Although it seems a relatively minor triumph, it's a much more all-encompassing term, and a thought whose time had come. Sound editors needed to think of themselves as contributing to the larger picture.

What I try to do is address the whole result and that includes mixing as well.

The responsibility of a supervising sound editor does not end when you walk onto the mixing stage. Today the dynamic of the mixing stage is very different than it was fifteen or even five years ago. The relationship between mixer and editor is, ideally, a true partnership. It's an opportunity for both sides to bring their different areas of experience and expertise together for the benefit of the film. You work together to establish an overall concept and approach. We coordinate with the music editor, who is usually very helpful in letting us know where music is scored in the movie, what kind of music it is, what, generally, the composer has in mind, and so on.

I see myself as being partially responsible for shepherding that whole process. That's something you need to gauge as you're doing it. You need to know when to give them your input, and it is equally important to know when not to. But occasionally everyone, the director, the picture editor, the sound editor, and the mixers all seem to be of the same mind. They all understand the exact intent of the moment. You feel that everyone is working together to make the same movie, though it doesn't actually happen that often. But it's those moments that make all the hard work seem worthwhile. They're rare and magical.

On-the-Job Training

My training has been akin to being a plumber's apprentice. You learn on the job. I don't say it's the only way, but I have strong feelings that it's the best way.

You can sit in classrooms forever and understand the theory—that's important and crucial in other aspects of this business—but I think the most important educational experience in terms of what I do and what picture editors do is to *look* at films and to understand why they work or why they don't work.

Ass End of Filmmaking

The Motion Picture Sound Editors have given sound effects awards for thirty-five years. But in the minds of the producers and powers-that-be, sound was seen as less important. Also, you're kind of the ass end of filmmaking. You're the last stage in the process, and by that time they're usually out of money and time. Sound had been one of the aspects of filmmaking that many producers and directors didn't understand. Luckily that has changed.

In the last three or four years the attitude toward sound has changed tremendously. That change has been one of the most dramatic and positive results after producers and directors recognized the potential of much of the new technology.

Coming into Its Own

In the last ten years, there were some specific projects that warranted and demanded a whole new approach and new concept of what sound could potentially be.

One of the films that did that was *Star Wars. Apocalypse Now* was another one. It was one of the first examples where the audience suddenly felt the sound move around them and go over them in a very dramatic sense. That was the beginning of a real revolution in this industry in terms of how sound effects were viewed.

I came in at the beginning of that revolution. It was a very exciting time. Other films that had that kind of impact were *Black Stallion, Das Boot, Never Cry Wolf.* These are films whose sound tracks succeed in pulling you totally into the movie—involving you to such an extent that you forget where you are and you become part of that place and time. I remember watching *Das Boot.* The movie engendered such a feeling of sympathy—you really can empathize with their frustration, you want them to make it. It's a fabulous script and beautifully directed, no small accomplishment. But the track is very much responsible for pulling you into it, the claustrophobia and heat and pressure, and the machinery—you're on that submarine with them. It's one of those perfect marriages when picture and track come together to create something very powerful. Again, those moments are very rare.

In some respects the pendulum may have swung too far; some of the more recent films have gotten a little out of control. The sound tracks are overblown. They seem to overwhelm and almost dwarf the stories. It's as if the filmmakers are trying to compensate for the lack of a good story with flashy visuals and sound effects.

I saw the newly struck print of *Gone with the Wind* recently. It is a beautiful sound track. All it needed to be and nothing more.

Supervising Sound

The supervising sound editor oversees the work of the ADR editor, the Foley editor, the effects editors, the dialogue editors, any additional sound designers and Fx recordists.

Initially I'll have a meeting with the director to determine how he or she *sees* and hears the sound. This is an important time because once you get into it, the schedules are now so tight there won't be a lot of time to talk about concepts and overall approaches.

Then what we do is look at the film with the director. That'll be an all-day marathon where you'll go through the whole film together and discuss it in detail. That's the way it should be done under optimum conditions.

Automatic Dialogue Replacement

ADR stands for "automatic dialogue replacement," or "looping" —any voices taped after the movie is shot. And it specifically covers two things: redoing an actor's voice—redoing his performance later on the ADR stage—and additional nonsynchronized voices, or "walla," which are used for backgrounds, wild lines, whatever.

Walla

We record the actors and try to fit something that they were saying into the mouths of the background people. It is called Walla as in "walla, walla, walla" meaning miscellaneous gibberish that's going on.

It's one of the factors that plays a crucial part in establishing locale and time, giving you the nuances of where you are. For example: in *Beverly Hills Cop* we were in Detroit, so the people that were hired were specifically people from that part of the country, or people who could do an accent from that part of the country.

In *Witness*, it was important not only that the background people be speaking German, but that they speak a certain kind of low-German dialect—and that was extremely well-researched. It's a very delicate aspect that you don't pay much attention to, but if it's wrong, you notice it.

In the case of *Top Gun*, the people who looped the film spent a lot of time researching what the technical terminology would be for the people in the background scenes, in the radio rooms, at the command centers, in the aircraft hangars, and on the deck of the carrier. We had a technical adviser on the sound stage with us. Again, even there, the accents became very important. And fighter pilots I talked to told me that, for years, everyone mimicked Chuck Yeager's accent!

Foley

Foley is the postproduction synchronization of body movement sounds with the image track—people moving around in a restaurant, footsteps. Additionally, many effects are created. What you do on the Foley stage is physically re-create everything that you see on the screen, and you do it in a room with open pits that simulate the actual surfaces of whatever you see in the film.

On a Foley stage you'd have a concrete slab for sidewalk, you'd maybe have one that was linoleum tile and one that was ceramic tile, and one that was marble because that sounds different from tile. There would be maybe four or five different wood surfaces: one would be open slats for warehouse or wharf/pier sounds, and a couple of versions of solid wood floors. Then, gravel pits, dirt pits, additional empty pits that you could fill with whatever—hay, grass, and so forth.

What we do is screen the film with the Foley editor and with the people who are going to "walk the Foley"—generally, two people who make all the physical movements.

At intervals during each reel (it usually takes all day to do this) the Foley editor makes elaborate notes and the two people make notes on what they will need. In the case of *Top Gun*, for example, all the activity on the top of the carrier was re-created, so we needed a lot of metal, a lot of cables, winch sounds, specific metal impacts with definition, and such equipment.

In *Witness*, we did a lot of work with water. There's the scene in which Kelly McGillis takes a shower. Things that you might not notice became extremely important to Peter Weir, the director, subtle things to help create a very delicate mood. In another scene Harrison Ford is in the bedroom and it's raining, and we had cut in a lot of rain sounds.

We wanted to heighten the sense of isolation, to reinforce the feeling of "stranger in a strange land," using a variety of "liquid" sounds. So, in addition, on the Foley stage we did individual water drips, water hitting the window. In the last several years, Foley has become increasingly important as the technical quality of films improves and also as a major creative tool, as evidenced in such films as *Roger Rabbit* and *The Abyss*.

Quiet films are much harder to do than noisy films. Car chases and world wars and destructions are busy and difficult and time-consuming, but not nearly as challenging. Because when the screen is quiet you can hear everything, so the technical quality has to be right on the money. The mood has to be correct.

Witness was set in 1985, but it was about the Amish, who choose to live in a time warp of sorts in a pretechnological, rural environment. In order to convey a feeling of another era, we used a lot of tracks that had been recorded fifteen, twenty, twenty-five years ago. We were careful to avoid anything that had an optical hiss on it, which old sound effects often have. We also used some newly recorded effects that technically had a very good sound quality, to give the film a delicate, spacial feeling. But we used things that were older because often they had exactly the character we were looking for.

Unless a track is downright unusable, "character" is always more important than "quality." Good taste, hopefully, will always triumph over technology.

Authenticity

Authenticity in all aspects of filmmaking has come about as audiences became more sophisticated; they won't let you get away with faking it anymore.

In terms of sound, there were probably people watching movies in the thirties and forties who heard birds in the background and knew they weren't the right birds, but the unreal aspects of film were taken for granted. But filmmakers today are much more concerned with details and specifics of creating a believable environment. What we have today is a much more self-conscious kind of filmmaking. It doesn't necessarily make them better movies. In fact, sometimes it's as if the filmmakers are hoping the technology will somehow make up for the lack of a good script.

A Good Sound Track

When I look at a film like *Platoon* or *Runaway Train:* by some standards they're not perfect jobs, but they accomplish what they need to, which is to bring the audience into the film, that is, to involve them emotionally and not take them out of the film by distracting them with the technological wizardry of the sound track.

I'm really an old-fashioned girl with Puritan ethics about film-making. I hate wasting money. I'm as appreciative of a sound track that's been very economically, but very effectively done as I am of a track that I know they've spent months preparing and millions of dollars on.

Room with a View is a perfect example. It's a delicate, quiet, elegant sound track that is perfectly matched to its time and place. The film works, and the sound track works, and the sound track helps make the *whole* work, which is ultimately what it's all about.

Top Gun and *Witness*

Top Gun appealed to the tomboy video kid in me that was thrilled and excited to go to Miramar and see the jets and be there when they were taking off. All that stuff you don't get to do when you're a little girl, and all the toys you don't get to play with.

It was also a perfect example of synergy at work. The sum of all the parts was greater than all the individual aspects.

I took a five-man recording team with me to Nellis Air Force Base outside of Las Vegas, Nevada, one of the largest fighter plane bases in the world. We were there for three or four days recording the Thunderbirds, the air force flying team. They were very accommodating, and probably did a bunch of stuff they weren't supposed to do—they did very low fly-bys for us.

Technologically, *Top Gun* was the most demanding film I've ever done. We used the most varied, different kinds of equipment; it was done in the latest state-of-the-art manner. It was released in the Dolby Stereo "Split Surround" format, which is a system that allows you to feel movement not just around you, but going from one side of the theater to the other—which was perfect for the planes. The visuals demanded that kind of superenergized, dynamic sound track.

Witness demanded very different sensibilities. It's not that I preferred doing one over the other, it's just that a film like *Witness* offered a chance at orchestrating the whole sound track and becoming a much more integral part of the music track as well, and having sounds evolve, as opposed to their being superimposed.

But regardless of how I might feel about a film—emotionally, philosophically, politically, morally or intellectually—I try to keep a purely professional approach. It would be wonderful to work only on projects you like. But I think it's good to push yourself into places you might not think you want to go. It makes life interesting to be a part of creating something you're basically at odds with . . . and besides someone has to make the house payment.

On Being a Woman/Editor

In terms of what I'm doing now, being a woman is a real advantage, but in the early 70s when I started it was still truly a man's world. When I first got into sound—which is much more technically oriented—the field was extremely chauvinistic. It was a difficult period, but one that I'm grateful to have had. I learned a great deal, especially the need for a sense of humor. And the men that I worked with were very supportive and encouraging.

I think I always knew I would have to work extremely hard when I came here. I anticipated that I was going to be kind of the underdog in a working situation.

At this point in time, it matters very little what sex I am. It is clearly a situation where people are professionals. They're there to do the job. I think most of the people I work with and work for don't care what color I am, don't care if I have green hair, or how many heads I've got. They care only that I know what I'm doing, that I can meet the schedule, and make the deadline.

This is going to sound sexist, but I think women do well in this industry for lots of reasons, not the least of which is that they generally have a slightly better ability to see the forest as well as the trees. They have the ability to look at the whole situation and get an overall perspective. I think they deal with stress better. In the long run—they have better stamina than many men do.

I won't suggest that *all* women have nurturing instincts, but *many* women do. People who get into this business and succeed almost have to be nurturing. Because it's not just a matter of taking care of individuals, but there's a very strong sense that you're taking care of the film.

Everyone brings their ego to this business; if you don't have a very strong one, do something else, because it's important to have the courage of your convictions. You're going to be put to the test all the time. You have to believe that what you're doing is right, and you have to be willing to defend it.

But you also have to be willing to know when you're wrong and to understand that *ultimately* it is *his* or *her* film, the director's or the producer's, whoever is calling the shots—not *your* film.

There's this attitude that women have in my generation—"Well, it's important that it's done right, so if you don't get the credit, it's okay, you have the personal satisfaction of knowing that you did it"—which is too self-effacing. But, to a degree, that's a healthy attitude. To succeed in this business you have to have that flexibility. People have to understand that the film gets the glory, and that it doesn't matter too much who made a particular decision. You have to be happy with the personal satisfaction because you're going to spend so much of your professional life not getting the accolades that you know you deserve and, as Pollyanna-ish as this might sound, you have to be happy knowing that you've done the best that can be done.

And that aspect of it is easier for women. I think women are by nature good team players—particularly in a supervising capacity.

Advice

If I were an editor coming into the business now, the first thing I would do is learn about all the new editing systems. And I would educate myself in as much of the new technology as possible.

It's important to understand what the advancements are technologically and to be up on the latest equipment—they're tools of the trade. There have been a tremendous number of technological advancements in sound, basically due to the record industry, which has promoted growth: they're constantly figuring out how to make better records and how to get a better sound reproduction.

Anything that allows you to do your job faster and more easily is certainly an advantage, because the less time you spend on the mechanics the more time you have for creatively contemplating what you're going to do. It gives you more time to look at the *whole* project and try to make changes. And the schedules are so short now you barely have time to get the film cut, much less go back and finesse it.

And, on a lighter note, editing is *very* physical, *very* dirty—that's why editors walk around with those little white gloves on: they are absolutely black by two o'clock in the afternoon. So I'm all for the technological advancements being made in this industry, simply because everybody will be cleaner!

In addition to learning as much of the new technology as possible, approach this business with a willingness to take any kind of job that will give you an opportunity to learn.

Aspirations

I hope I have my name on something I'm extraordinarily proud to have done. And I hope that, on some level, I'm reasonably proud of the majority of things I have my name on.

There's nothing like Monday morning quarterbacking. Some famous director once said, "You never finish a film. You just stop working on it." And *everything* that I've ever done—when I see it after a year, or five years—sure there are always things I wish I'd done differently. And I hope that that's always going to be true. Because if I don't see things that I can improve upon or things that I would do differently, it means that the education process has stopped. And when the education process stops, my life will be over.

Rerecording Mixer

The Rerecording Mixer is responsible for mixing the production dialogue, music, and sound effects tracks into one homogenous composite track and for any "sweetening" or addition of new sound to the final sound track. He or she operates a mixing console, sets filtering controls in the service of a balanced sound, selects and places microphones, and times the sound track synchronously with the visual track. The Rerecording Mixer and crew work closely on the dubbing stage with the director and editor to determine desired sound qualities.

Robert "Buzz" Knudson

ROBERT "BUZZ" KNUDSON played minor-league baseball with the Giants for nine years but decided he'd "better go to work" when he got married. His father, who had been an electrician in silent movies, got him a job in film production. After a year he decided he'd try postproduction and started working as a recordist at RCA. Eight years later, when RCA went out of business, Buzz went to work at Todd-AO, where he has subsequently mixed over two hundred films and won three Academy Awards in sound for *Cabaret, The Exorcist,* and *E.T.* He is currently president of Todd-AO, one of the largest rerecording studios in Hollywood.

W HEN THEY record on the set, all they record is the dialogue. When it comes down to the final print, there's always more to it. There's music and there's sound effects, plus dialogue, so that all has to be added.

When the picture's edited, and the effects editors have built all their tracks and the music people have built their tracks, they come to a studio like ours and it's mixed together.

Hopefully, we can start the picture without the director having to be here physically. We do a "predub" with the sound editor. He or she is our link to the director since they're usually closer to the director—at least at the beginning of the mixing process—because they've been through numerous "spotting" sessions with him, getting the director's input and taking detailed notes on what he wants in terms of sound—more music in one spot, something Foleyed in, dialogue replaced, and so forth. The sound editor stays with us throughout the mixing process to protect his side of the show.

We first integrate the original dialogue with all the replaced dialogue—that is, the ADR or looped dialogue. We listen to that, don't record it yet, then we add the Foley and balance that against the dialogue. We again listen, but don't record. Now we blend all the sound effects against that. When that process is finished we do a "final" mix, which is when we record the composite—dialogue, Foley, sound effects, music. The best way to do that is to have the editor, my crew, and the sound editor collaborate on the mix.

We'll then call in the director, run it for him, take notes, and fix it while he's there, which speeds up the process. If he were here while we were doing all that preliminary process, it would take forever.

It can take anywhere from a month to many months to mix a picture. Billy Friedkin will take ten to fifteen weeks, Spielberg will take five to six weeks, Streisand will take eight to nine weeks. It depends on how meticulous they are.

My first feature as a supervising mixer was *Cabaret*, for which we won an Academy Award. I was working with two excellent old-timers: Dick Tyler and the music mixer Art Pianadossi. I was very naive. When I got a notice in the mail saying I had been nominated for an Academy Award, I didn't know what it was. I walked into my boss's office and said, "What's this, Fred?" That's the honest-to-God truth.

Then the next year I got one for *The Exorcist*—two in a row. By that time I knew what it was. I had the good fortune to work with William Friedkin on that. With the exception of *The French Connection*, I did all his pictures. He knows what a good sound job is, and he won't stop until he gets it. Where there are compromises because of time and scheduling on other pictures, he has the clout to take as much time as he needs.

The Exorcist was probably the longest mix we've ever worked on. Whereas some guys are making you do things over and over again because they don't know what they want, he's a stickler because he won't settle for less than perfect detail. We did Mercedes McCambridge's voice over and over, played it forward, backward, every way but sideways.

Friedkin used volume when it was effective. He didn't make the whole show loud. *The Exorcist* was a show that went from practically zero sound to just crashing in on you for impact, and then settled down again. He used phone bells ringing loudly at one point, along with the devil's voice. He didn't inundate you with sound throughout. Everybody wants their shows loud now because they've been tricked in the theaters. They used to dub a picture at a nice, comfortable level in the past. When it got to the theaters, they played them low, people complained. So now, by dubbing them loud, they think that will solve the problem. It doesn't. They play them so loud, it drives you out of the theater.

Working with Spielberg on *E.T.* was a completely different experience from working with Friedkin. He has a tremendous knack for knowing what's good and what's bad, quickly and instinctively. He doesn't dissect a movie. He won't worry about a footstep or this or that. If it all works, it works. He goes for the overall effect rather than lingering on detail. When he feels something's right, he doesn't play with it over and over, it's "Thumbs up and let's get outta here. . . ."

Having worked with a number of different directors, there are very few who have the security to follow their instincts like that. They don't know when they've arrived, don't know when to say, "This is it, it's never going to get any better." Many of them continually fix and fix and fix. I think everybody loses their effectiveness after too much of that. But it's their nickel and their movie. If they think it can be better, we'll try.

You have to know how to deal with the clients. They're all different, and you have to swing the direction they're swinging in, otherwise it's tough. I know a lot of good mixers who can't do it. There are mixers who are probably better than I am, but they let their egos overwhelm them. I've got good mixers nobody will touch unless I force them onto the sound stage with them.

Dialogue Quality

We've been in sound for forty years, and the actual dialogue quality is worse now than it was then. They shoot on freeways. They don't bother when they pick a location to see if there are any sound problems.

When they used to do the sound all on stages, there was some quality control. And they had more time because the schedules were twice as long. They'd let the phone man put the microphone in, light around it. Now they go ahead and light, tell him to stay out of the way, and the guy's forced to put his mike up on the ceiling somewhere.

You can fiddle around with the sound later on when you're mixing, but the looped portions are rarely, if ever, as good as the original tracks. There are some new advancements that have come out in dialogue. We can now take noise out without degrading the dialogue as much as we used to. Subtle differences. But there's still no free lunch in sound. If you take noise out, you're also taking quality from your dialogue. And good directors know that.

Advice

There's no training for this. If you want to do this, you come to work for a place like ours and you wait for all the mixers to die off or retire, or if they expand and they think that you can do it, they put you out there and give you a chance.

Mixers are in the sound technicians' union—Local 695. You have to get into the union to work in sound, which is hard. More people want to get into mixing because the money's good. Timing's important. If someone wanted to get in, and we could use them, and we were in a busy time of year, we could get that person in.

Trends

There's a lot of pressure. It's just such a grind. You start at a quarter till nine and you work until midnight, a lot. I'm not complaining, because I could go sell shoes if I didn't like it.

The other problem now is that the budgets are such that they don't give you the time to do a good job. They get it in, you get it out—that's what it boils down to. There's a compression factor. They take so much time in production and postproduction, and when they get to us there's no time left, no money left.

I feel sorry for new directors who come along; they're pushed by the studios, and they don't have the clout to say, "Look, I need another week," and so forth. They just make them finish, and that's not fair to them or us.

I predict in the next ten years, and I could be wrong, that sound effects and dialogue editing are all going toward tape. It's cheaper. The budgets are such that any time you can save some money, they'll go for it.

Composer

The Composer composes the music score for a motion picture in order to heighten and intensify the emotional tone of the film. He or she works closely with the music editor in the execution of the technical aspects of this task and, once the score is composed, with an orchestra or other instrumental grouping, synthesized or real, and the scoring mixer on the scoring stage to record the film score.

Bill Conti

BILL CONTI's father and grandfather were both musicians. At a young age, Bill was playing the church organ. Throughout his childhood he studied keyboards and the bassoon, and by the time he was in high school in Miami, Florida, he was playing in the school orchestra, had his own band, and played in saloons at night to make money. When he was accepted to Juilliard's prestigious School of Music for graduate studies, he began writing music in earnest.

Today, Bill Conti is one of Hollywood's most prolific composers, his scores encompassing feature films, television, commercials, and documentaries. He has received an Academy Award for Best Score on *The Right Stuff* and two Emmys. He also received Oscar nominations for Best Song for *Rocky* and *For Your Eyes Only.*

MUSIC TO me is like breathing. It is like eating. I've never known any different. When your life is music, all the other things don't exist. It is so much a part of you that it is not special.

I'd figured out back in my Juilliard days that I wanted to write the kind of music that people would hear and give you either immediate approval or disapproval, and you could do it as a living, rather than being a composer who *taught* music for a living.

I wanted to be a composer in the baroque sense that I made my money by writing music. I knew that there was no marketplace for string quartets and abstract pieces. Film and television seemed to be the most natural place where a composer could write music and get paid for it. So at Juilliard I was leaning toward studying dramatic music, which I could use in a later career of film composing.

One of my teachers became composer in residence at the American Academy in Rome, and he offhandedly said, "Why don't you come and visit me in Rome?"

And I guess you don't say that to an Italian boy. I sold everything and bought one-way tickets for my wife and myself on a boat to Italy. And saw the teacher maybe twice and stayed there for seven or eight years. Both my daughters were born in Rome.

I found myself in Rome playing music at nights in dirty places, making five dollars a night, at age twenty-four or twenty-five.

Ghostwriting

I drifted into ghostwriting for other composers, doing arrangements, orchestrations for film. A young person does not need the money as much as he needs the credit. I got really discouraged about making no money and getting no credit. So I went to Milan to do records. I did about twenty albums, arranging/producing pop-oriented music. Then I directed the Italian version of *Hair* for a year on the road in Italy. And then while being a music consultant on a movie, I was asked if I would like to be the musical adviser on another picture that was coming from the States to shoot in Venice. It was *Blume in Love*.

I spent a month in the Piazza San Marco with Paul Mazursky, the director, and the crew. And I was on the Grand Canal sipping a cappuccino with the still photographer, Alan Pape, who said I ought to check out Los Angeles.

I could not imagine why I would ever want to leave Italy, which I was just completely in love with, but when we returned to the States at Christmas to show the grandparents our two girls, I made a side trip to Los Angeles. And never went back.

It amazed me how well people do film music work in the United States compared with other countries. A great musician is always a great musician, and I'm not saying that we have better musicians or filmmakers here. I'm referring to the music business and recording music for movies.

The film music business is better here than in Europe, and I speak from having done it in both places. I've done films in Rome, London, France, all over, and the musicians there are fine, the filmmakers are fine. I'm saying that we do *more* work. Therefore we have a higher proficiency level in the technical areas. As a musician trying to record the music in a proficient technical way, Los Angeles is Mecca.

There is no question that the way of life in Italy is better for me than any place I've been. And there is no question that all the money in the world is here.

In 1973, looking for work, I was sleeping on Alan Pape's couch, no money, no car in Los Angeles. I rode a bicycle to the studios. I had come over in January by boat and had return tickets to be used by the following January.

Paul Mazursky had a New Year's Eve party. And at that party, he asked me to do *Harry and Tonto*. So I cashed in the boat ticket, put everything I owned in Rome in storage, and did *Harry and Tonto* and thought that that was the big time. I made $6,000. Family of four, Twentieth Century-Fox. It was great.

Rocky

I temp-tracked the music on a little picture called W. W. *and the Dixie Dancekings*, which got me the job to do *Rocky*. John Avildsen, the director of *W.W.*, remembered my enthusiasm on *W.W.* without any money and asked me to do *Rocky*. He said, "This is a folk hero, and if I had my way, I think Beethoven's *Eroica* Symphony best depicts it."

I said, "Of course, yeah, it does to me, too, John, but this is a package deal, and I can't hire a zillion people and have the score running." So I took those ideals he had in mind and remembered that it is the streets of Philadelphia and remembered the *Eroica* Symphony and tried to come up with that same kind of feeling.

Now the *Eroica* Symphony is not to be said in the same breath with anything that I would ever do for the rest of my life. But the idea is . . . a classic feel. Not the greatness of Beethoven. John wanted people to feel uplifted as he feels uplifted when listening to the *Eroica*. That was what I was going after.

Rocky running up the stairs, that "Go for it, man"—everyone got that. That was an accomplishment; that was what I tried to get across. It doesn't always happen that what I try to do comes out.

Of course, I got a little help. There was a picture going on.

In terms of coming up with the music, John Avildsen said, "We have to actually make them think that Rocky can win this fight." I knew the end of the movie. I knew that Rocky lost. I'd read the script. But John wanted to know, "How can we at this point make the people think that he has a chance?" Because if I told you the story in four sentences, you would say, "There is no way he is going to win."

So what is the job of the music? Let's make the people think that he has a shot at it, that he should go for it, go the distance. That was my assignment. And in the area of problem-solving I do my job well.

"You Need a Hit"

In this business you need a hit. You can work a lifetime in the business and if you are not connected with a hit, people not only don't know who you are, they don't care.

After 1976 there was some notoriety from *Rocky*, and I conducted the Academy Award orchestra in 1977 because the producer of the show liked what I could do, at least on *Rocky*. I'd done a hit, but I could as easily have just done one picture and disappeared. Through 1977, the pace picked up. I was nominated for an Academy Award three times, and I won one with *The Right Stuff*.

I was going to go on vacation when I got a call to do *The Right Stuff*. They had a composer on the project but decided to go in another direction. Two weeks later we began scoring. That is a *three*-hour movie. Then I began writing during the day and scoring at night.

Phil Kaufman was trying to tell the personal story of the astronauts, and the hard part was depicting that in the midst of the tremendous historical scope of the American space movement.

I hooked on to the image of rockets going off circling the earth, trying to relate that to the story of these astronauts.

The Oscar

The Oscar was wonderful. You are just blown away because, in this business, that is the biggie. There are life-timers who have passed away, and you say, "He should have." But none of the should-haves count anymore. And it is a great feeling to have won one. You don't have to accomplish that anymore.

Doing a good job 100 percent of the time is the way everyone works. They try their hardest. I don't know anyone who lays back. But in everyone who wins, there's some kind of lucky thing there coinciding with all of the votes at the right time.

The Game

Doing a score for a film—some are faster than others. Most people do it fast enough. You get it done in time, or you won't be in the business. You can't simply not show up.

I don't think speed is a criteria or a negative or a positive in terms of quality. You have to have a degree of proficiency in terms of speed to get there on time.

All writers write on deadline. They have a play date. The TV show has an air date, and the film has theaters that are booked.

In terms of the game, I happen in postproduction—scoring. Here we are in the fourth quarter. We're the last creative element along with the effects and the color correcting and the negative cutting.

By the time they get to us, the schedule's shrunk. No one waits in this town for anything. So you do a score in one, two, three weeks. Six weeks is a long time in this town. Rare to find ten weeks for the composer. So I've got to deliver fast.

Film has got horrible faults, technical things, camera noise in every scene.

Now, that is not the only reason for music—the technical stuff. But it is *one* of the reasons for music. In the silent movie days, one of the reasons the piano player sat down was because the projector was in the same room. And you hear the racket of the projector. So music has two functions.

Two Functions of Music

Music can smooth out cuts. There is a scratchy sound in the scene: "Let's have music." It can tell you what the actor is thinking, where the story is supposed to go. It can perform that Greek chorus function. This is the technical thing. Information.

Now the other reason for music, of course, is the fantasy. We care about the tear in the eye. Whatever it takes. And music has the ability to do that.

What music means to every individual is always different. She cries when she hears, "Don't let your sons grow up to be cowboys . . ." and the other guy hears Mozart's 39th Symphony and there is a tear in his eye. Not everyone is going to look at a Rembrandt and a Warhol and have the same kind of tear. But we need someone to do that.

Baroque Composer in a Romantic Age

Only dilettantes can afford to have writer's block. We are professional people.

I'm getting back to that baroque sense. Everyone in our business is a working craftsman. We are living in a romantic age where "I" the individual is more important than anything.

But in the baroque world, the burgher's daughter is getting married. "Would you write me a mass?" "Sure, give me four guilders. Here is your mass."

Here is where the screenwriter gets offended. The script comes in and the producer says, "Bring in what's-his-name to punch up the dialogue." Or, "This action isn't moving here, I need a better thing. Bring what's-his-name in—he does that. Let him do a rewrite." And it can happen to the composer, too. They bring in someone else if they don't like the score. Now the person who thinks he is an artist in the romantic sense—whatever he does is divine inspiration—is going to be offended.

The people who work in film are trying to make a product, trying to sell a product. Van Gogh wasn't trying to sell a product. Da Vinci didn't sell a product.

We are working in the baroque sense. That's not fair to say to Bach, but I'm trying to take you back to an era where music was written on a transactional basis. I'm the guy to write the music. Why? That's my preparation. I know how to write dramatic music for film and television.

You don't go to a guy who claims to be a serious composer. He is going to write a work, and it will never be heard again. It will have a premiere performance, and that is it. That is fine. He can live in that world. Is it better? This is apples and oranges. It is not "better than." If he can live four hundred years, he'll even find out whether it happened or not.

But there are other people who aren't into that. They are into touching and feeling and writing music and having people laugh or cry or hate it or love it, and it doesn't have to be just hard rock, electric weirdness. It could be "Make it sound like Mozart." There, you've got it. "Make it sound like Schönberg." There, you've got it. This is what we do.

The Process

What is running around in my head is what I've got to do. I have to sit down to do the physical work of putting it on paper. You can do constructs and first notes and "Oh, yeah, this could follow this section." You can do that in your head. But then you have to do the labor, you have to sit down and actually deal with the thing.

So I don't listen for pleasure except on Thursday nights when I go to the symphony. And I don't listen to music in my car.

I'm into everything. I don't care what it is. I think it is all great. Music is valid from Willie Nelson to electronics to classical. All of that. I've got electronics in the back room. I've done a couple of electronic scores, though I won't do the hands-on. I hire the pro electric guys. But I know how to do it. To keep the education where it is supposed to be. And I dig it.

I don't believe in inspiration. I think if God gave you any talent, it is there in a minor degree. We do a lot of hard work. I think the guy who is going to work on it harder than the next guy is going to get ahead. How many talented little nine- and ten-year-olds—then talented eighteen-, twenty-year-olds—are there being raved about? You get into your twenties and thirties, you don't hear people calling you a genius anymore.

The subtext. That is the fantasy. That is what we do, we carry a heavy ball. Did your talent make you do your job well? I don't have the answer, but I can't sit around waiting to be talented. Or be inspired. Because things will pass me by.

If it is not coming today, there will still be ninety musicians sitting there tomorrow. What shall I tell them? That I didn't get an idea? So you work through it, and you've worked through drought so long that there are no more droughts.

Working with the Film

I see screenings of the film to get into the minds of the filmmakers. They don't deal with what I deal with: music. So I have to have them talking to me, thousands of words, and if they won't, then I force it out of them before I can write. I'm not going to write what I feel about this film. I'm going to write what I feel about this in *their* terms. If the guy doesn't like violins, then I don't write violins.

Logistics—I'm working from a timing sheet. You get timing sheets from the music editor. To the hundredth of a second. When it goes "bip," I'd better be there because that's what the plan was.

Advice

We have a few composers in this town who are very qualified, very prepared. And then we have those guys who know one or two kinds of music. They are called "stylists." You want it to sound jazzy? "So-and-so does that. Call him." Don't ask him to do classical. Why? Because it's like calling a pitcher to be a designated hitter.

To learn to be effective with one kind of music is to count on someone liking the way you are effective musically. If you think that you just want to do an electronic score with your little synthesizer, you might get lucky. You might win an Academy Award, and you might work as a film composer. And your style could be in at that time. When your style is passé, if you don't change, you won't be working.

Whereas if you know how to write music from a schooled traditional sense, the great dramatic music that has been written—Wagner, Verdi, Puccini, all of these great operas and great tone poem writers, like Strauss—you will have something to offer film from a studied sense, a classic sense. With a complete musical education, you can do more. I can say, "Mozart would have been effective in this way," and then I can switch to Schönberg or Beethoven or rock and roll or jazz.

People are always going to fall in love, die, and go through the whole gamut of emotions that human life offers, and other people are going to want to tell stories about that on the screen. Therefore, if you know how to handle those traditional emotions and dramas, you could do it with kazoos. You could do it one hundred years from now in whatever medium they want you to do it in, provided that we are all still living, falling in love, dying. And being happy.

Music Editor

The Music Editor is responsible for executing all the technical tasks necessary to aid the composer in creating a motion picture score. He or she takes detailed and meticulous notes on music cues, sets up the film for scoring by delineating on the positive print where the music and film are synchronous, and ensures that scoring sessions go smoothly and to the satisfaction of the director and the composer. Thereafter, the Music Editor physically cuts the recorded music into tracks that will be mixed into the film along with the dialogue and sound effects in dubbing sessions.

Richard Stone

RICHARD STONE, son of a pianist and grandson of a music critic, studied cello with the renowned Janos Starker at Indiana State University but, discovering he didn't like performing, switched to music theory and composition. Upon graduating, he worked in radio as a classical programmer, all the while being fascinated by movies. The first time he saw *Jaws* "something clicked," and he knew he had to become involved with film music. Pulling up stakes with his wife, Richard came to Hollywood, where he got a job at an animation company, first wiping off cells, then working in the editorial department as an apprentice, which got him into the editors guild. There he rubbed shoulders with the music editors and learned the basics of music editing. About this time, he met the president of the largest music editing company in Hollywood, who took him on as an assistant. He eventually became a full-fledged music editor and has now done the music editing for numerous films, including *Witness, Agnes of God, Body Double, The Black Stallion Returns, Maxie, D.C. Cab, Pretty in Pink,* and *Ferris Bueller's Day Off.*

WE'RE RESPONSIBLE for all the technical aspects of getting a composer's ideas into the film, from the very moment of the composer's and director's conception of those ideas through the scoring process and the dubbing process and on into the finished film.

After we screen the film, we will have an initial meeting called a "spotting session," where the music editor, composer, film editor, director, and/or producer get together and, scene by scene, decide where each music cue will start and stop and the nature of each music cue, what it's trying to say and what it's composed of thematically—in other words, how it's meant to help the story.

Many people don't realize that the composer is really a musical slave to what the director or producer is trying to express with the film.

There are far more restrictions placed on the film composer than on someone who is writing music for a record or for a symphonic performance, so much so that the director has the power to throw the entire score out eventually or to ask the music editor to change it substantially, which often happens.

At the spotting session, I'll number each music cue. For instance, "2M-4" will be the fourth piece of music in reel two. This includes any existing songs or other music that's in the film. After that, I will get a dupe of the film—a black-and-white copy—and I will make very detailed timing notes of each cue for the composer. For example, 2M-4 will start when Barbara opens the door at 0 seconds. At 1.2 seconds, Barbara says, "Hi, Bob." At 2.7 seconds, she finishes saying hello and moves her head around. Notes like these for a whole film can grow to become a notebook two inches thick.

The composer will take home these notes and a videotape of the film and write the music. On the notes, I'll also include little reminders to the composer for each cue of what was suggested in the spotting session. For instance, "It was suggested to use Bob's theme when Barbara opens the door and build to a huge crescendo at the end of the cue when she kisses him."

The composer will write the music based on this, and then he'll give me indications of how he wants the film to be set up for the scoring [recording] session.

The composer conducts the orchestra while watching the film projected on the screen. More and more this is done on videotape, but it's still mostly done to film. I will put marks on the film delineating points of time for the composer to be synchronous with the film. For instance, if he wants to hit a downbeat at four seconds into the cue when Barbara opens the door, there will be a warning mark on the film. We also work with a digital metronome "click" track, which is a way to become even more synchronous with the film.

The music editor works with all this technology and is also a musical troubleshooter, making sure that scoring is proceeding correctly and that the director is happy with what is being recorded.

Very often we find ourselves in the middle of a political situation between the director, who wants one thing, and the composer, who wants something different. At some scoring sessions, the director has come up to me and whispered in my ear (so as not to have the composer hear him) that he doesn't like a particular piece of music and that I should be prepared to change it later. The composer is also often asked to rewrite or change the music during the recording session, usually under tremendous time pressure.

After the recording session, I will take all of this music, which is mixed down from the twenty-four-track recording onto three or more tracks, and physically cut it into "music units" the way a sound editor cuts down sound effects. This is taken to the dubbing stage and mixed into the film along with the dialogue and sound effects.

At the dubbing sessions, which can take anywhere from two weeks to six months or more, we slowly go through the film, mixing all the dialogue, effects, and music together. And at that point, I am usually asked to rearrange the composer's music to get it exactly the way the director wants it. It could entail substituting one piece of music for another, or if there have been editorial changes in the film, all the music will have to be cut down or expanded to compensate for the changes that have been made.

There is never a point where the film is absolutely finished until it gets into the theaters. The editor and the director are constantly fiddling with it. So all during that time, there are corrections to be made in the music. After the dubbing is complete, the film will usually go out for a preview. Then they'll make more changes and come back and redub it with those changes. This process may repeat itself several times before the film is released.

The Temp Dub

Apart from this whole process is what we call a "temp dub." Very often, before they even hire a composer, they'll screen the film for a nonpaying audience with a temporary score. They'll call on a music editor to provide this temporary score from preexisting scores, sound track albums, or other scores that the music editor has worked on. From this the director can find a musical direction, find out what role music will play in the film. The temp track also serves as a common language or blueprint for the director and composer, and can clue the composer into what the director is looking for. Often the director will either be in the dark as to what he wants, or may think he wants one thing and find out through the temp dub that that's not what he wants at all. He may want another musical direction, another style.

The music editor can be very helpful in the overall architecture of the score. In many cases, the decisions that the music editor makes in the temp dub influence which composer is hired for the job and how *he* writes the music.

For temp dubs, I have a backlog collection of favorite "stock" music for various situations. But it's not cataloged at all, except in my head. To do so would be very time-consuming. When I see a rough cut of a film for the first time, I generally have a feeling for what style of music would be right—what cues from what films will be right in what spots. This is similar to the way a composer will have certain formulas that he uses to score a film. These formulas go all the way back to opera. They're very simple formulas: tremolo strings for tension and rippling melody over strings for love, things like that. Musical clichés that haven't changed in five hundred years and that people are still using today.

Frequently, the director will live with the temporary score for three or four months through a number of different previews. He will hear it over and over again. So, by the time the original permanent score is written and performed, it's foreign to him.

A smart composer will try and stick closely to a temporary score, if he knows the director likes it. Often the temporary score has a longer "prerelease" life than the final composed score. It is not uncommon to have the final score composed two weeks before the picture is in the theaters. In that sense, the temporary score is probably the most important creative process the music editor can be involved in. Sometimes the director and the film editor will choose much, if not all, of the temp music, but it's been my good fortune to have worked with many who have let me make most of the decisions.

On musicals and rock-and-roll pictures, it's the music editor's job to keep track of all the versions of all the songs, which can become time-consuming and detail-oriented, depending on where the master recordings are coming from and how many there are. Songs are becoming increasingly important in films, mostly because of music videos and their influence on the way people are watching movies and making movies.

Body Double

Technology is changing. When we did *Body Double*, the music was dubbed directly from the digital master, and as far as I know, that was the first major studio feature to be done that way.

When you transfer a digital recording, there's no generation loss. So *Body Double* ended up with an absolutely spectacular-sounding score because of Brian De Palma's vision of dubbing it that way. It's already becoming more and more popular to do it that way, and in the near future that's the way all films will be done.

Budgeting for Music Editing

Some producers don't budget anything for the music editor. It's possible to make a film without one. In Europe, the film editor does most of the things a music editor does. To a European director, the "art" of filmmaking is more in the actual acting and shooting. Americans place a greater value on all aspects of postproduction, especially music.

It makes sense there would be more music editors in Hollywood because, traditionally, American music is a lot more synchronous with the film than European film music. It's more a Hollywood idea—to write a three-minute chase piece of music for a three-minute chase on the screen. In a European film, they would simply put up a loop of fast music and then fade it out. An American composer would fit every cut with a different instrument or do something musical to emphasize the rhythm of that scene. Also, there are about sixty music editors in Hollywood, and a handful in New York, simply because there's more demand for them here and the budgets allow for it. European films do not budget for music editors.

A Restrictive Art

Restrictions appeal to me. I have an aversion to too much free form. To me, art is only art when you have to create it within certain confines. If you're building a sculpture out of clay, you're not building it out of snow. You're restricted by the medium. From my viewpoint, writing music for the sake of writing music is not as remarkable a feat as writing music when you're a slave to the picture. Making something wonderful out of that is truly remarkable.

It is now possible to score a whole film on one or two instruments. *Starman* is a good example of this. And more and more films are being scored with synthesizers because it is usually cheaper that way.

The exception is a film like *Witness*, which used five synthesizer players and the ultimate sound was grandiose and wonderful. You would think five players would probably not cost as much as a ninety-piece orchestra, but these five players were the top five synthesizer players in the world, and they also had the latest equipment in Hollywood in that room.

The challenge for Maurice Jarre was to keep the synthesized sound in an orchestral/acoustic framework. The barn-raising scene took from nine in the morning to midnight to put down on tape. Each track was done separately and overdubbed and overdubbed and overdubbed, which gradually built up all the layers. The final result was spectacular, the result of a very long, very slow and expensive process. Lately, even in television, there's a discernible trend toward synthesized scores.

Advice

My advice would be to talk to the good music editors in town. Tell them about your background and that you're willing to work hard and see what they can do for you.

The turnover is so great; so many apprentices become assistants and then become editors, and then their careers take off. People are always looking for good apprentices. The problem is that a mediocre apprentice may stay an apprentice for a long time. A good apprentice will very quickly become an assistant and then become an editor. Good people are hard to find and to keep.

Musicality, detail orientation, and organizational ability are necessary qualities. And if you want to get ahead in any kind of postproduction work, conscientiousness is vital—following up on things, returning phone calls, reminding people of things. And that all comes out of love for your work.

I know very good music editors who have no musical training whatsoever. They know nothing about classical music. All they do is count. They don't know an E-flat from an F-sharp, but they're excellent music editors because they can feel it, in much the same way that Ella Fitzgerald and Frank Sinatra can't read music, but they're the most musical people in the world.

Like most other jobs in the industry, the hours are abominable. Anywhere from a minimum nine-to-six day up to twenty-four hours. I get into situations, for various reasons—studio desperation, deadlines, previews—where I've had to work around the clock, although the average workday is probably about ten hours long.

Aspirations

As a musician, while I get credit as a music designer and the director will compliment me on picking the right music for a scene, when it's time to score the picture, the composer is the one standing on that podium. It's his music that the orchestra is playing, and I'm sitting next to him operating the clock.

It's frustrating to see myself as a technician at that moment. And that only renews my determination to pursue a career as a composer.

I will be the luckiest person on the face of this earth if I get to the point of being a working composer and making a living at it. If I could do anything over again, I would have spent less time playing the cello and more time studying composition. And I would have come to Hollywood much sooner.

Right now, I'm trying to point my career in the direction of music supervision and composing, making more creative decisions, being more of a consultant and less of a technician.

Postscript: *Since this interview, Richard Stone has become a full-time composer with four feature films,* North Shore, Summer Heat, Never on Tuesday, Pumpkin Head, *and several movies of the week and television episodes to his credit.*

Scoring Mixer

The Scoring Mixer records and mixes the music played by a live orchestra or synthesized instruments during a scoring session. He or she works closely with the composer to achieve the desired sound quality, operates the mixing console, and oversees the work of the assistant engineers and stage hands to ensure that all microphones are properly tested and positioned and that all chairs and headsets are ready before the scoring session. The Scoring Mixer also records, if required (as for a movie musical), a "prescore," a temporary music track, to which film will be synchronously shot, incorporating any prescored music into the final scored track, and supplies any additional music tracks that the music editor might need.

Dan Wallin

During World War II, DAN WALLIN served in the U.S. Naval Air Force and studied in their technical schools, which enabled him, after the war, to get a first-class commercial license and to work in radio mixing the big bands of that era. From there he moved into mixing for film and, since 1954, has mixed over one hundred pictures, including such memorable scores as *Camelot, Finnegan's Rainbow, A Star Is Born, Woodstock, Deliverance, Somewhere in Time, Sweet Charity, Who's Afraid of Virginia Woolf?, Nuts, Baby Boom, Out of Africa, Prizzi's Honor, The Dead,* and *The Right Stuff.*

I RECORD the music for the picture with a live orchestra and mix it down to usually three track mags; that's what they use in the dubbing room.

It can be extensive if it's a musical. *Camelot,* for example, took a year from inception to completion.

For musicals you do a "prescore." This is basic on every musical unless it's a live thing like a *Woodstock.* In *Camelot,* we used a complete full orchestra just to do the prerecords.

And then, after all the shooting and editing are done, you get the final print. You score to that, and you also fill in the prerecords with orchestra or whatever is required. There's no prerecord on a regular feature. It's all done on the scoring stage after the picture has been cut.

Working with the Composer

The composer will tell you what kind of a sound they're doing—if it's a synthesizer combination or if it's a rhythm score or whatever—so you can be prepared, because it's quite a bit different to do a Bill Conti score like *Baby Boom* as opposed to an Alex North score.

Alex is more of a classical composer and stays in that venue very much, so I know what to expect. Bill Conti, by contrast, surprises me. I never really know what to expect. Sometimes I come in thinking I'm going to get a classical score and it's a rhythm score as well as classical, a good mixture.

Finding the Balance

What I'm concerned with is not the individual notes, but the balance. An orchestra has a center balance to it, and after you get to it you know pretty much where everything is going to go, how it's going to happen, what kind of music it is.

Finding the balance means the strings are at the right level and the woods are at the right level and everything is in the right space.

They usually run it down a couple of times so you get your balance. It's my responsibility to find that balance, but I'm obviously doing what the composer wants; I can't go off in a direction of my own.

And it's my responsibility to make sure that the orchestra's recorded cleanly and delivered to the dubbing room in the format they want it in. And to make sure the musicians get out on time. If you have a ninety-piece orchestra sitting in there and it's a four-hour call, if you go overtime, the overtime money is enormous.

The Scoring Session

The mixing console receives all the sound; each microphone comes in on a corresponding part, and you set the level and put in the equalization, whatever it needs, and echo. This is my table of operations.

The key to it is preparation beforehand. You've got to lay all the mike cables, all the microphones, have them all tested, make sure everything is in place.

A lot of record people come into scoring in the way they're used to in the music industry. If it's a nine o'clock call, they come in at nine or at nine-five. That's too late, and they get in trouble, and it costs a lot of money for everybody. My training is traditional motion picture training. We're completely ready to go an hour ahead of time. So if anything unusual occurs, we have an hour to make it right because we're set in every other area.

It takes about two hours to get ready for a full orchestra. The two stage men are here first, setting the mikes. They'll sometimes start the night before by kind of sketching it in. I'll come in an hour and a half ahead.

In an ideal session that goes as smooth as can be, we do from ten to thirty minutes' worth of music in about a four-hour period. The average on a feature is three minutes an hour. If it's wall-to-wall music, that's a lot of scoring time.

Problems

The frustration is when things don't work. For instance, a lot of synthesizers have to be driven with clicks, and often if there's a little glitch, it upsets the programming in the synthesizer and you have to stop and start over again and find out what's happening in there.

Or breakdowns—everybody starts getting very nervous if you say, "Wait a minute, wait a minute, we can't get this in sync." Or if you have a big orchestra—the clock's running, the composer knows he has only so many minutes to record so many minutes, and then you're wasting his minutes, so that makes him pretty angry.

That's why I'm such a bug on being prepared and going as quickly as possible—to take that kind of pressure off the composer so he can do his thing.

The Ignored Category

The production sound mixing crew has an Academy Award category, but the scoring mixer is not included in it. And that is a very sore point for me. For example, in my opinion the reason *Out of Africa* won the Academy Award for sound was because of the music. But it was, of course, the production mixers who received the award.

I tried for years and years to get the scoring mixers included. I said, "Well, why recognize a production mixer but not the scoring mixer?" Their reply was, "It's traditional, and he's dealing with live sound."

I said, "What do you think the scoring mixer's dealing with? One hundred people out there live, and getting it in a certain time. It is an artistic venture and should be included."

It's a political thing, and it's involved with the Academy and some former heads of sound departments who have their dubbing mixers they want to keep happy. The scoring mixer doesn't really work on those studio lots, so who cares about him? There aren't enough of us to get any voting block together to get ourselves into that lineup. There's only five or six of us.

We have no clout whatsoever. It's not just sour grapes because I do both; I also dubbed a tremendous number of pictures.

The sound award includes the dubbing mixers and the production mixer. There's four dubbing mixers and usually one production mixer, so it's five. And they say they just don't want to give any more away. They don't want to have six, so screw the scoring mixer.

Advice

My background was somewhat musical, which really helps, and engineering.

I think some of the universities now, like the University of Southern California or UCLA, cover scoring a little bit in their media school. But basically it just takes a lot of experience.

My advice is to get as much experience as you can, although it's now very hard to get experience. You used to be able to get it in radio very easily; that's how I got all mine with the live orchestras. They would send you out as a junior engineer. Give you these little portable mixers and microphones, and I'd go to the Palladium or places like that where they had live orchestras and set it all up myself, clip onto a phone line, and when the time came to broadcast, I started broadcasting live mix.

The way to learn today is to start as a stage man first. Then you learn placement of all the microphones, which is critical to an acoustic recording engineer. And in terms of real good orchestra recording, learning that less is better than more. The fewer microphones you can use to do the job correctly, the better. Because the more you put in, the more microphones you put on strings, the smaller and harsher they start sounding, as well as getting intermodulation [two or more instruments being recorded out of phase]. If you can do the job, say, on thirty violins, in terms of the coverage, with two microphones rather than four, you're better off.

Basic orchestra, say, a seventy-piece orchestra, I would probably use about twenty-five microphones, and then with the percussion you would add another six. Then, if you start adding synthesizers, you add on more microphones.

From stage man, you can move up to assistant engineer and then to scoring mixer.

Satisfaction

Mixing the orchestra, I love that. And I love the classical orchestra best of all.

Some guys have the idea that synthesizers are the hip modern sound. But what they're doing is an imitation of what the records are doing, so to me it always seems bogus and not really happening. When a composer does his thing, with a real orchestra, it's really wonderful and exciting.

The difficulty on the job is that you're dealing with people who are very emotional. Composers are very emotional, and musicians, too. Although I must say that the musicians are the most together group, most professional people in Hollywood. Really unsung heros. You can put any kind of music in front of them and they play it beautifully, instantly. And then they go in there and do a score in three hours, in one rehearsal and a take. I mean, who else is that professional? Nobody.

It used to be that composers would ask for mixers, but the people who are running film companies now are not very knowledgeable about how important that is. They just see dollars and cents, so they say, "No, you're going to go over here because it's cheaper." Only a few composers have the strength and the clout to say, "No, I'm going with Dan no matter where it is," and succeed.

The Quality of Sound

I would say for the last ten years it's been sliding toward the computers and the bookkeepers who are running the studios. There are some artistic heads, but basically you get down below the line in that area, it's just dollars and cents. It wasn't that way when I started. There's a lot of people who don't know anymore, that's the problem.

I had Jack Warner hiring me, he knew about sound. He was one of the first in sound with *The Jazz Singer*.

Sound recording has advanced so much, it's almost ludicrous how wonderful it is, but the quality of sound getting on the films is worse than it was thirty-five years ago. I think it's because everybody is so sound effects–oriented. They think you don't know what a helicopter sounds like. They have a big beautiful music cue on a helicopter, and of course, the helicopter wins every time.

Who the hell gives a shit about a helicopter? You should hear the helicopter at first, and then when it gets into space the music should take over. That's the dramatic thing, not the helicopter. You establish and then let it go away. That's not the way they do it. They have to loop and roar the damn thing through every time.

They're sound effects crazy. When a door is slammed, it sounds like the whole building's going to fall down. We're not in the business of reality anyway. It's an art form and should be treated as such. Either the sound or the music should give way. A car chase, like in *Bullitt*—when the car chase started, the director stopped his music, period, and it was all car effects—that's great. But in a romantic or a war sequence, I think it's much more dramatic if the music gets a chance to take over.

Sydney Pollack is one of the few directors who has wonderful taste in that area. In that flying sequence in *Out of Africa*, you heard a little taste of the plane now and then, but it was basically a music cue. It worked, everybody remembered it.

I don't think it has to do with lack of respect for the audience or anything like that. It's simpler than that, it's a matter of ignorance and going with the tried-and-true way. They'd just never ever try it another way. When you see a car, make that engine blast, that's it.

It used to be a balance before. Pictures are unbalanced now. It's like an orchestra has a balance; there's a lead instrument, and then you have your background instruments.

The way they dub now, it's just a big roar.

13
THE FURY

The Unit Publicist and Still Photographer provide the materials that create the public's perception of a project and, hopefully, a frenzied anticipation in the potential viewing audience. Through skillful use of news releases, candid photographs, and other media-related items and strategies, the men in this chapter create a mystique that enables a film to be enthusiastically identified by the public.

Unit Publicist

The Unit Publicist is responsible to the producer and the financing company for publicizing the motion picture in the various media—print, radio, television, cable, and so on—during principal photography, with the goal of building an audience for the motion picture. He or she prepares the publicity campaign, writes and plants "blurbs" and feature stories about the production and the "stars," acts as a public relations representative in terms of filtering what can and cannot be made public, sets up interviews with individuals in the cast and crew for the media, writes the biographies, stories of the production, and any related material, and collaborates with the still photographer on the photographs for the production press kit.

Stanley Brossette

STANLEY BROSSETTE grew up in a small town in Texas thinking that going to Hollywood would be like "coming to Mt. Olympus." He arrived in Hollywood in the early sixties and, while working at a Chevrolet dealership, met a couple of press agents who had a "one-step-above-shoestring PR office." Excited by what they were doing, he offered to work for them for free just to learn their business—and was hired as a full-time employee at approximately $15 a week. While there, he met a former MGM publicist who encouraged him to apply for a job in the publicity department at MGM. He got a job as a messenger boy in the publicity mailroom. Working his way up under the old MGM apprenticeship system, he became a publicist and has now been practicing his craft for twenty-five years. Among the artists he has worked with are Elvis Presley, Barbra Streisand, Eddie Murphy, Goldie Hawn, Burt Reynolds, Sally Field, Cher, Natalie Wood, Lily Tomlin, Sylvester Stallone, Clint Eastwood, Shirley MacLaine, Dolly Parton, and Raquel Welch. His many credits include *Nuts, Children of a Lesser God, Beverly Hills Cop, Smokey and the Bandit, Suspect, The Golden Child, The Cannonball Run, Best Friends, The Best Little Whorehouse in Texas, Rocky II, Semi-Tough,* and *Hooper.*

To GET to the core of what a publicist does—it is to somehow do something that will sell tickets to the movie. We are the link between the film unit and the press and, by extension, the public. If we're not here for that, then we're here as hand holders.

Over the years there have been so many complications and layers added that the goal is frequently all but forgotten. Sometimes publicists are charged with keeping bad news from the press—if, for example, they're reshooting scenes, having problems with the cast, or are enormously over budget.

As with all marketing, one promotes what is promotable. *The Golden Child,* starring Eddie Murphy, for example. He is gold in Paramount's coffers. You want to make the world aware that Eddie Murphy, after a long absence from the screen, is going to be back soon in *The Golden Child*, his next big picture. Make them aware of *that* and build some anticipation, and they'll be there to buy tickets. Beyond that, you can take the elements of the supernatural and the special effects and publicize that to create even more excitement—drawing in those people who, perhaps, are not crazy about Eddie Murphy but might pay to see other elements.

Some movies don't have people in them you can sell. So you may try to publicize "the hottest love scene ever" or the fact that this is the first big western in years or some other aspect.

People are rarely interested in producers or directors, other than the obvious Hitchcocks or Spielbergs. They are interested in "stars." That's one thing that's never changed. Even if we don't have many movie stars, we have rock stars, political stars. Movie stars used to be our royalty. One wonders and will never know if Clark Gable or Joan Crawford would have become as big as they did without the studio publicity departments behind them. People say we don't have movie stars like we once had. But we don't have the publicity machines we once had.

Then and Now

I grew up in the forties, when there were big publicity departments. There were dozens of stars, instantly recognizable. Every studio had a stable of stars, and you knew all about your favorites—Greer Garson, Betty Grable, Humphrey Bogart. These people were bigger than life. Very few people today are "bigger than life." By and large they are recognized, even by their most ardent fans, as mortals. In the thirties, forties, and even the fifties, movie stars were gods and goddesses, which probably meant they had impossible standards to live up to, as did their publicity departments. I understand that publicists and other crew people were more in awe of stars in earlier decades—more respectful, understanding, and forgiving. Quite often today actors are perceived as business associates and equals, although an unhappy superstar is still known to shake up a sound stage when things aren't going their way.

Many actors today feel they have very little to live up to other than delivering a clean performance. They don't want the burden of a public private life.

Back then, I am told, in addition to the publicists who were assigned to movies, there were publicists assigned to particular stars.

You were assigned Clark Gable, Lana Turner, or Esther Williams. And you just worked your tail off to publicize them.

Beyond that, there were subdepartments; they had one office that just handled fan magazines. They knew all the editors, all the writers, were constantly pitching stories and setting up interviews. They had a department just to set up fashion layouts for *Vogue, Glamour, Mademoiselle.*

It all changed in the fifties. Maybe things never recovered after the war. The prevailing theory is that things began changing when the "stars" started gaining so much power. While stars were gods to their public before the war, they had no power with the studios' heads—or relatively little, considering how famous they were outside the studio walls.

When Louis B. Mayer commanded that the stars be there, they were there. No Burt Reynolds or Eddie Murphy or Raquel Welch would say, "I don't feel like coming down."

As the studio system got weaker and the stars gained more power . . . suddenly the stars were free-lancing, and they were bigger than the studios. Studios would compete for the big names, so the stars would go to the studios that gave them the most money and power.

Now the stars could call the shots. Their prices started escalating. And they had much more control over their own destinies. Now they told the publicity departments what to do instead of the other way around.

Studios no longer had actors under contract, so they didn't need *huge* full-time publicity departments. By the mid-sixties, they were just hiring unit publicists on a per-picture basis. Paramount, for example, used to have a staff of unit publicists, in-house, who would work on one picture after another because they were making fifty pictures a year. And you'd protect the studio and stars at any cost, because that was your home, and the actors were rather like relatives. Now there's not that loyalty.

There are so many "stars" nowadays who haven't been trained to be stars. Someone came to town three weeks ago and they're beautiful and suddenly they've got a picture. They're big, but they have no one behind them, which is all the more miracle anyone becomes a star. Because there isn't a huge department pushing them.

They may have a private press agent whose only function these days seems to be to protect them and to keep people away from them.

So the star doesn't know what to ask, and the directors are young and don't know how to utilize publicists to make them look better.

Diplomat

The "star" of the picture, quite often, is *not* the actor. If you're doing a Francis Ford Coppola picture with no big names in terms of actors, *he's* the star.

If you're wise, as in any job, you gravitate to the power. Your number-one function—day by day—is to keep the star happy, whoever the star might be. If they want publicity, then you get it. If they don't want it, then you keep people away.

There's an art to keeping people away. You can tell someone "no" and leave them satisfied and with their ego intact, or you can tell them "no" and leave them disgruntled or bitter.

While your primary obligation is to the film company that hires you, I feel you serve them best by serving the press. I was once at an interview where the star literally tried to kill a member of the press. I believe I served that actor by preventing the murder!

Sometimes the press objects to your being there, either consciously or subconsciously. They consider you a censoring device.

There was a day when you *had* to be there. No star was left *alone* with the press. A few actors don't want you present. Most do. But you should be there very quietly, just know when to pour the coffee. A few younger publicists don't know that because they didn't have the studio training. They think they're there as a third and equal party. There can only be so many stars in a room. To borrow from Cher, "Somebody's got to run the toll booths."

MGM Training

I never dreamed I could go to work for what history regards as the greatest studio and its renowned publicity department! During my earnest days in PR, I had become familiar with the name Howard Strickling, MGM's head of publicity, now deceased, who was also Louis B. Mayer's right-hand man. Greta Garbo, Spencer Tracy, Clark Gable, Joan Crawford, Jean Harlow—all their images had been formed under his auspices.

Back then each department had a big mailroom, and I was hired as the office/messenger boy in the MGM publicity department mailroom. I was thrilled.

I was fortunate to be taught the "MGM" way by veteran publicists and became an apprentice within a year. Once you became an apprentice, they assigned you to an older, established publicist. You'd go to the set and watch how they worked. I was trained by people who had handled the legends. That kind of training simply doesn't exist anymore.

And then I became a junior publicist. At that point, Elvis Presley was under contract to MGM. Colonel Parker was his manager, and since Elvis was one of MGM's most valuable "properties," people would do anything to please the Colonel. Well, all the publicists had been trained exactly the opposite of the way the Colonel was managing Elvis's career. Most people were looking for publicity and interviews, but Elvis did no publicity and had little press on the set. I guess MGM figured I hadn't learned to do publicity the normal way, so it would be easier to learn the Colonel's way.

I ended up doing the last eleven of Elvis's thirty-three pictures.

The Production Press Kit

One of our major tasks is writing the press book, which includes production notes on the film—the plot synopsis, background of the movie, interesting facts and biographies on the main people involved both in front of and behind the cameras. If you're a critic for the *Los Angeles Times* or the *Milwaukee Journal*, or if you're going to interview one of the cast members, you'll get a press kit to help you understand the project. This used to be *one* of our jobs but is now often the primary function.

All studios used to require (and some studios today still require) that the publicist write feature stories in which there are lots of quotes. These are known as "canned" features, which smaller newspapers sometimes print word for word.

It'll start out, " 'I'm sick of riding horses,' says John Wayne, who wears a three-piece business suit and drives a Ferrari in his latest film." These are now required less and less. These days they like biographical features—long bios on the players with lots of quotes thrown in.

We prepare these materials. It is then up to other publicity department people to edit and distribute them.

The Bottom Line

All publicity departments, as big as they may appear, are skeletons compared with what they used to be. It used to be that the selling of the picture would begin with the unit publicist, and then it would build, build, build until the release of the film.

On many movies now, no publicity is wanted during production. Or there tends to be a little spate of publicity when the picture is filming, and then there's a dead period where the public doesn't hear anything, and then there's a last-minute spurt of activity.

Expectations are generally lower these days. They feel if they just get someone on the *Today* show and a *Los Angeles Times* interview, that's publicizing the picture.

The bottom line is you're not necessarily getting paid to publicize the picture, you're getting paid to do what the power figure on that picture wants you to do. Sometimes, though rarely anymore, the power comes from the studio publicity department, more often from the producer, director, or star. Of course, you must always make everyone feel that you perceive *them* as the power figure.

It's frustrating when you have a picture for which you could get a lot of breaks, could have *Today, Good Morning America*, the cover of the *Los Angeles Times* Calendar—and you're not allowed to get anything. It's just a damage to your ego because you would like to be flashy and at least have all the other publicists in town saying, "God, you're doing a great job on the movie."

Then again, a really rewarding experience might be one where you are able to take a very small project that does *not* have Harrison Ford or Meryl Streep, is not a $50 million picture, a picture where Garbo is *not* making her comeback—a little picture with no big name, just young unknowns or character actors—and you're able to get a few decent breaks, to create some awareness.

Dealing with the Crew

There are only two people on the set who have nothing to do with making the picture—the still photographer and the unit publicist. We have to develop our own individual ways to get the time and attention we need to get our work done.

The crew doesn't need us, but we need them. For example, if it's a special effects movie or has unusual elements, you'll want to interview some of the crew. For instance, *Entertainment Tonight* was dying to do the animal/bird trainer on *The Golden Child*. That's about as close as they could get to Eddie Murphy at the time!

Life is rough without an assistant director's goodwill. If you have *Life* magazine coming tomorrow to cover a certain scene, you have to keep checking with the AD to make sure they're on schedule. Suddenly, at midnight, they switch things. Maybe you've got *Life* coming to interview Clint Eastwood. And without you knowing it, they've given Clint the day off. If you've worked well with the assistant director, he will call you at midnight at home and tell you that.

The unit publicist must operate with the constant awareness that the production work always takes precedence over publicity. Even if we have *Today*, which is an enormous break and could enhance your box office, the least important production problem is more important than getting an interview done for national television.

We're an intrusion during filming, and part of the job is adjusting to that fact. But we are about the only crew member really concerned with the movie after the cameras are put away.

Hype

I'm often asked how much truth there is in Hollywood publicity. Probably more now than in the past. But I've never known a good publicist or press agent who felt obligated to stick to the truth 100 percent.

The name of the game is to get things in print or on the air.

Exaggeration is part of our craft. If you're writing a biography on a sex symbol who is five feet eleven and a half, well, you know you're going to make it six feet. I guess it depends on the era, how far you would stretch that.

Publicists and Press Agents

You have to be a member of the publicists' guild, Local 818, to work on a union movie set. And most independent publicists and press agents also have to belong because they practice their craft on a movie set.

I am not a press agent; what I do is publicize the movie. The press agent, on the other hand, usually handles a particular individual—an actor or actress, even a director.

There didn't used to be private press agents. There were no big PR firms in the beginning. Why would you need them? You had a hundred people in a publicity department taking care of you, but as the studios got weaker, private press agents emerged. A lot of them had been studio employees. Many of the big PR moguls in town started as office boys at MGM.

Advice

Unit publicity is a small, perhaps dying, profession.

One of these days the studios are going to say, "We've had ten pictures in a row that have wanted no publicity. So why are we hiring ten publicists at a decent wage? We could have one publicist easily doing two or three pictures."

And indeed, many companies are not putting publicists on pictures, or they're having one in-house publicist do three or four pictures simultaneously. Because all they care about is getting the press kit written.

I've never given an interview before this one. I think perhaps I'm the only person not completely enthused by screen credit. I'm old-fashioned in that regard. The idea was that MGM or Columbia or Paramount was so great—and their stars and pictures were so wonderful—that to even admit they *needed* publicity was a contradiction.

I think publicists should still be invisible parts of the machinery. We need to remember that we are a service profession. And those who don't wish to render service should seek another career.

Still Photographer

The Still Photographer is responsible to the producer and the financing company for taking photographs during the shooting of the movie to be used in any publicity campaign and as a record of the production. While he or she does not work directly *with* any of the cast or crew, the Still Photographer must work *around* them in a manner that minimally intrudes on their work while compiling photographs that will be used to entice a viewing audience—thus, often, working in tandem with the unit publicist.

Ralph Nelson

RALPH NELSON's interest in photography was sparked by watching the Walt Disney *True Life Adventure* series as a young boy. He felt then that he could pursue his interest in nature as a photographer and later attended Art Center College of Design in Los Angeles as a photography major. His first professional work appeared in such magazines as *Life, Time, Newsweek,* and *Playboy.* Ralph subsequently became the first staff photographer for the ABC television network, a position he held for two years. He left ABC to work as a unit still photographer on a film directed by his father, a move that qualified him for entry into the cameramen's union. He has over fifty motion picture credits, including *Tucker, Top Gun, The Karate Kid, War Games, Gremlins, Nine to Five, Return of the Jedi, Back to the Future, Dragnet,* and *Indiana Jones and the Temple of Doom.*

Early Training Ground

My early work as a free-lance magazine photographer—*Time, Newsweek, Playboy*—was excellent training because although I am hired by the production, the end users of the bulk of my work are most often the magazines. And in my days at ABC I was in friendly competition with the photographers at the other two networks to create photos that would be used on the weekly magazine covers. That competition, which prompted us to think in terms of an editor's needs, plus the earlier training at Art Center, was very important when I began to work as a unit still photographer.

Definition

I am hired by the production company, or the film's distributor, and am responsible to the producer and the production company for providing photographic coverage of all aspects of the production.

My work includes photographic coverage of the action, both in front of the camera and behind the scenes. In addition, I set up portrait "galleries" of the actors.

The Equipment

I provide all of my own still equipment to the production on a rental basis. Most of my work is shot with 35-mm cameras. I use three 35-mm Leica range finders, and eight Canon 35-mm single-lens reflex cameras with thirty lenses ranging from 15 mm to 300 mm. Many of those lenses are duplicates so that I can shoot both color and black and white simultaneously. I carry two Polaroid SX-70's for continuity stills [a continuity still is a Polaroid of some element within a scene such as hair or wardrobe that must be matched exactly later in the shooting schedule. Pieces of the same scene can be shot weeks or months apart, and the Polaroid provides reliable reference].

For portrait galleries I also have an eight-by-ten view camera and a Mamiya six by eight medium-format camera as well as a complete set of studio strobes.

In addition, while shooting scenes, I use a "blimp," which is a piece of photo equipment seldom used by photographers outside of motion pictures. It is essentially a soundproof housing custom-fitted to the camera to silence the sound of the shutter and motor drive, which allows me to work silently during a scene.

In the early days of film, still equipment was far more cumbersome and film was slower. The still photographer worked in a completely different manner. The production would schedule separate days for the still photographer, providing him with his own crew and the sets and actors. He was then able to re-create the scenes from the film and to set up for portrait sessions. That kind of accommodation has been made unnecessary by today's faster, lighter cameras and faster films. Also, today's production schedules are far too tight to allow for that kind of luxury.

"Kill Rights"

Many actors, especially major stars, often have contractual "kill rights" on any photos that I take of them during production. This means that after reviewing my work, they are allowed to "kill" any photos they don't approve of as a way of insuring that bad photos are not released. I am generally a harsher critic of my own work and will kill more than they do anyway, so I'm not offended when they make kills.

By insuring that their interests are protected, they are more comfortable with the photographer and more cooperative. As a photographer who is a proponent of kill rights, I am probably in the minority.

Trust

If there is one thing that I would say is as important as being a good photographer, it would be a sense of personal integrity. Without the complete trust of the people with whom I work, I would be working under a tremendous handicap.

Although some of the best moments that a photographer captures are private, it is important to understand the difference between moments that have publicity value and moments that invade someone's privacy. It can be a fine line, as some people are more private than others. You must develop an intuitive sense of knowing when to create photos that you feel may be published and when to back off and not shoot, even though you know that what you are not shooting could be important. One photo taken indiscreetly can destroy the trust, and once lost, it is seldom regained. I don't know of any really successful photographers who don't understand this.

Choosing the Moments

Not all scenes in a film provide great moments for stills. It is not only unnecessary to cover every scene, but it may be a nuisance. Knowing what is needed, and planning ahead to cover what is important, is far more efficient than the shotgun approach of shooting everything in sight. Shooting everything is not only a waste of film, it can slow the production. It is just as important to know when *not* to take pictures. Crews are often working under difficult circumstances and will be far more inclined to work with you if they know you only request help when it is really important.

Eyelines

If an actor can see you during a scene, you are in his eyeline. It can be very distracting, especially during a difficult scene. Any movement within an eyeline, or eye contact with the actor, can be very disruptive. Unfortunately, the eyeline often provides the best vantage point for stills. Great care must be taken. I try to avoid being there if

I can, but when that isn't possible, I do my best to minimize my presence. I will remain motionless during the entire scene, even though I may have finished my work, usually with my camera covering my face to avoid eye contact. Sometimes even that is not enough, and I will leave the set during the scene and then request that it be restaged for the stills only. The advantage is that I then have the full attention and cooperation of the actors and don't have to worry about being a distraction. The disadvantage is that it is more time-consuming when each minute is very costly. So that type of request must be made sparingly with the need for stills balanced against production cost and schedules.

Film and Processing

There is no set amount of film that I am required to shoot. I may shoot from as few as two to as many as forty rolls of 35-mm film on any given day. I shoot both black and white and color, in most cases shooting both during the same scene to service both the magazines, which use color, and newspapers, which use black and white. It is possible to make black-and-white prints from color, but the results are not as good.

All film supplies are provided by the production company. The film is submitted daily to an outside lab for processing. Black-and-white proof sheets are made for key people to approve and make selections. Most of the color is shot on transparency film. At the end of production, key sets of photos in both black and white and color are selected, and black and white prints and duplicate color transparencies are distributed. Although I can make recommendations of photos, the final selections for the key sets are made by the studio photo editors.

Unit Publicist

The unit publicist is the person with whom I work most closely, and a good one can be one of my greatest assets. As they are in constant contact with the newspapers and magazines, they know the photo needs of the editors. They can also stimulate an editor's interest in the film, and some of the better ones generate photo ideas that stand a good chance of being published. I attribute some of my best work to a team effort with a good publicist.

Advice

For anyone thinking of working as a unit still photographer, I would offer a great deal of encouragement, tempered with a generous amount of pragmatic advice.

Your talent must be matched by persistence and patience if you hope to get into the union. A little nepotism can be helpful but does not guarantee entry. I know of several cameramen who have tried in vain to get sons and daughters in. And although it may be useful, it is only good to help you get your foot in the door. Once in, you are on your own, and only as good as your last picture.

If you aren't a union member, you need not even look for work at the major studios. The option is working nonunion. They generally pay much less, and there are neither the benefits (medical insurance and the like) nor the protection typically provided by unions. On the other hand, working nonunion can be a way of gaining valuable experience while working your way into the majors.

When looking for work, *be prepared*. You should first of all be a competent photographer, well equipped for film production work. It would be a mistake to try to find work before you are ready, because Hollywood is a small town where word travels fast, and if you do a poor job, it may be far more difficult to get a second chance.

It is an industry always difficult to break into, but one that has great respect and a constant need for talent and professionalism.

14
THE SALESMEN

The individuals in this chapter help determine when, where, and how films will be shown to the moviegoing audience.

The Acquisitions Executive may acquire an already completed film for distribution by a studio or distribution company.

The Distribution Executive will sell the film to exhibitors and decide the geographical pattern for release of the film.

The Marketing Executive guides a team of salespeople who will advertise the movie to the viewing public.

The Theater Owner is the last link in the chain that leads from the mind of the filmmaker to the audience member's seat inside a darkened theater.

Acquisitions Executive

An Acquisitions Executive is responsible for acting as liaison to independent producers for the purpose of seeking completed films or proposed independent productions for distribution by a studio or distribution company. He or she must solicit screenplays owned by independent producers, as well as independently financed films, and negotiate the acquisition deal. For films acquired prior to production, he or she must supervise development, casting, production, and postproduction, according to contract approvals.

Henry Seggerman

Best known as the man who discovered *Crocodile Dundee* for Paramount Pictures, HENRY SEGGERMAN began his career as a film programmer for the Bleecker Street Cinema in New York City. He subsequently worked as a copywriter for Diener/Hauser/Bates and a script reader for Warner Brothers and MGM/UA before being appointed to Paramount's film acquisition department. Advancing to vice president by late 1986, Seggerman was involved not only in acquisitions for distribution, but also in co-productions and script development, as well as acquisitions for Paramount Television (most notably *A Room with a View*). Seggerman worked briefly as senior vice president of production and acquisition for Stephen Friedman at Kings Road Entertainment, and is now vice president of acquisition for Fries Entertainment. He holds a master's degree in cinema from New York University.

IN A way, it's the superglory area of film executive work. You sit there for ninety minutes, you say, "I like it," you make a deal, and then if it scores big, you're a hero.

You didn't have to wait two years and work on the script, slowly plodding through the process. It's more like "I'll take it, let's put it out there." Bingo! One hundred eighty million dollars.

Of course, in reality, there is an enormous amount of hard work that goes into the process.

Creating the Position

When I first started, producers would call up the head of sales. Studios would assign junior production executives to scout out acquisitions. It was a reactive kind of job.

The producer would find out whom to talk to, show it to them, lobby, maybe talk to the head of the company and try to make something happen. I decided to get a little more aggressive about the whole process and make it just as organized and comprehensive a field as production executive work.

As soon as the faintest glimmer of information came out that there was an independent film being shot, or about to be shot, even just a thought of doing it, I'd call the producer and say, "Hey, we're in the business of buying films, and we'd love to get all the information on what you're doing and read your script." I'd be totally up to speed on what was going on with the picture. I would even approach a producer when he went on location in preproduction, scouting. I'd call him in his motel room.

Crocodile Dundee

In America, the major studios tend to attract talent. So a lot of the best independent American filmmakers will be attracted to the majors, or to companies that will fully finance their pictures for the purpose of distributing them, such as Island Pictures or Cinecom. From the viewpoint of acquisitions, these no longer become viable films for acquisition because they're already married to the financing company.

For this reason I was looking outside of America for pictures to purchase. I had been watching Australia, and I knew who Paul Hogan was. I knew that Hogan was a star from his TV shows, which didn't really get exposure here but were shown very widely in the U.K. and Australia. I knew that he had done the tourism spots, although his name wasn't in them. And I knew he was very popular in Australia, England, South Africa, and other English-speaking territories.

Paramount always felt that foreign-language films were a difficult sell, although they did handle a few foreign-language films here and there. So I concentrated on the United States, Canada, Australia, New Zealand, and Great Britain.

About fifteen years ago in Australia (around the time of Peter Weir's *The Last Wave*), things just started developing. The Australian government put in a tax incentive to encourage the making of pictures, so it became a territory where there was a lot of production.

When the Australian production team of *Dundee* announced it was making the film, I sent telexes to them asking, "What's going on? I hear you're making a film with Hogan. Maybe we will prebuy the film. Can we see a script?"

They were playing real hard to get, even arrogant, because that's the Aussie style. And they knew they had something hot. So nothing happened at first.

They started filming. I came to New York where they were shooting. One of my spies told me exactly where they were. So I went down to the set and stuck my finger in the chest of the producer, John Cornell, and said, "So how are we going to make a deal to buy your film?" Just like that.

I had a sixth sense about this movie, so I just assaulted him right there in the street. Eventually they took me out to lunch and even invited me to the wrap party. I kept the heat on my colleagues at Paramount during the months that followed, and my boss, Barry London, clinched the deal.

I knew they were doing something special and had captured some kind of magic. Of all the Australian pictures that I had heard about and knew about, including *Gallipoli*, which Paramount had bought a couple of years prior, I knew this was the one that had a shot at being a hit.

It's a classic fish-out-of-water concept with the Australian outback guy in this big megalopolis. There was also a kind of harking back to the films of Frank Capra, *Mr. Smith Goes to Washington* and *Mr. Deeds Goes to Town*, where you had the wisdom of a rural character, against all odds, succeeding despite the overly sophisticated attitude of the people in town. One of the great things about Australian films in this era of slickness (and a lot of films in the early eighties from Hollywood were very slick and cynical) is this sense of traditional entertainment.

That's the way it often happens with a surprise breakthrough hit. When you haven't had an action film in a while, along comes *Mad Max*, and it re-creates the genre so that now you can have *Robocop* and other highly charged, visual, brilliantly shot and edited action film succeeding at the box office.

For instance, there weren't too many courtroom dramas succeeding around the time of Australia's *Breaker Morant*. Now you've got *Nuts* and *Jagged Edge*. Australian movies start to breathe new life into genres that have been neglected for a while. They bring back trends that are pure and part of film history, the kinds of movies that have entertained audiences over many decades.

It's unfortunate that in today's commercial marketplace, the term *genre* generally means teen comedy or horror or something exploitative. Obviously, when you look at a movie and think about its potential, how you're going to market it, what genre it fits into is a legitimate question. But beyond that, genre can be the pathway to an invaluable historical perspective.

Unpredictability

I firmly believe that unpredictability and "unpigeonhole-ability" are extremely important when the audience discovers an independent film.

I enjoy being able to say, "Wow, I've found this great movie, you should buy it and distribute it," but there's another discovery process, which includes the audience. It's one thing for a moviegoer to see that Robert Redford and Meryl Streep are in a movie and then decide to plunk down six dollars to see that movie. It's another for them to say, "I'm going to go see this independent film." There's a kind of unpredictability that's very important. In the process, *they* discover the film.

Consider the fact that almost every major studio rejected *Crocodile Dundee*. Every major studio rejected *Chariots of Fire*. *Crocodile* made $180 million, *Chariots* made $70 million, and had no major stars. Every studio rejected *Halloween*, which made $40 million. *Porky's* was almost put on the shelf by Fox before it made $100 million.

Another perfect case is *The Gods Must Be Crazy*. Even after that film made $25 million in Japan and was number one at the box office in France, *every* distribution company in this country rejected it. And then two years later, after it was finally acquired by the Classics division at Fox, it went on to make $30 million.

So when buyers out there look at the films and say, "What genre is it in?" And they say, "What film, six months ago that succeeded, is it like?" Invariably, they'll turn it down. You can count on that.

Even films that are financed by the studios often fall prey to the same lack of perspective: *Airplane, Saturday Night Fever, Purple Rain, Star Wars, E.T., Flashdance*. The list goes on and on of executives financing a movie, putting their label on it, looking at the movie, not thinking they have anything that special, and then it goes on to make a hundred million dollars.

I only want original films if at all possible. If it's so obviously in a genre the audience has seen recently, and so obviously just like some other movie that came out last year, they instinctively recognize it as a knock-off and they stay away.

Originality is what counts, even in the way a familiar genre is rediscovered. Only Jamie Uys could have made *The Gods Must Be Crazy*. That's no copy of a Hollywood film. In a way, it's an homage to Chaplin, Buster Keaton, and the Marx Brothers. But it's been distilled with a totally unique, personal vision.

Filmmaker's Selection of a Distribution Company

The important thing is for the producer or financier behind the movie to believe that your distribution company offers something special and unique and will not treat the film like some programmer.

The harsh reality is that there have been in-house, totally financed studio films that have suffered the same fate as mishandled acquisitions—problematic marketing, booked the wrong season for reasons that don't make sense. So it's important for the producer and the filmmaker and the financier to evaluate the type of distribution program that is being presented.

Very often this will involve a commitment of P&A [prints and advertising] and distribution costs to support the film, in addition to the minimum guarantee offered for the rights that are being acquired. The more sophisticated a producer is, the more he'll be involved in the process and consider it to be part of the negotiation with the distribution company.

Look at the most effective and talented in-house film producers and directors, like Woody Allen and Stanley Kubrick and Saul Zaentz. The level of input they have into the release campaign is extraordinary. Woody Allen, for example, has total final approval of every aspect of the campaign.

I think that it's very important for the filmmaker to find a home, a place where his or her film will be handled with the care and attention it deserves. They put three years into making it, they mortgaged their house, hit up on Uncle Morty, squeezed a few presales out of the foreign market. Who knows what they did to get this film made? It wasn't easy. They don't want to see the film flushed down the toilet at distribution.

Artistic versus Commercial Success

I think it's a mistake to create such a hard-and-fast dichotomy. I believe that artistic accomplishments contribute to commercial success.

I don't think *E.T.* would be the number-one film of all time if Spielberg's sense of drama, or the particular way it was shot with a kind of warm Norman Rockwell feeling, had not been part of it. Those elements are artistic accomplishments.

With a film that is geared for exclusive runs only, a sophisticated film, the critics tend to be very supportive. And when the film critics support a movie, even if the subject matter is a "marketing negative" or it's in a foreign language, the critics will create an audience among the sophisticated markets and people will go to see the movie and it will make money.

There are companies in the business of acquiring those films that succeed artistically, and they milk them for every last moviegoer who might want to see them. Especially now, with seven majors, five minimajors, half a dozen art film distribution companies, half a dozen exploitation distribution companies, video companies—giving you money to release films they think will have strength in the video market. I don't think there is a lack of attention paid to artistically successful films that are not going to become blockbusters outside of the exclusive-run audiences. There's more than enough support for those kinds of movies. There just isn't enough quality product out there to feed the many diverse distribution outlets in today's modern marketplace.

Advice

As I said in the beginning, this job of acquiring independent films for distribution used to be done by some production executive or a head of sales who would, on a reactive basis, be called by the producer and sort of look things over. It was a very informal thing. Things are very different now.

Now you have to get hold of every single trade publication from areas of potential interest—Australia, Canada, the United States—that listed where films were starting, like the "Outtakes" section of the *L.A. Times*, the "movies in production" section in *The Hollywood Reporter*, and a score of places where they announce films starting production. Keep looking, calling up the Chamber of Commerce to find out production office numbers. Call them on day one. Get a Rolodex and fill it with numbers until it's like two big wheels about the size of Toyota wheels.

If a film goes into production and you know somebody involved: the director, the producer, the executive producer, sometimes the production manager, just call the people you know and say, "Hi, it's me again." And they know that you're an active buyer. And they know you represent the immense opportunity to get films financed and distributed. But most of all, keep an open mind. Look for originality. Avoid the trap of comparing what you see or read to last month's box-office hit. The moviegoer wants something new just as much as you do.

Distribution Executive

A Distribution Executive represents the filmmakers and the financiers of the film to the exhibitors (theater owners) by negotiating terms of the "licensing" of the movie to exhibitors so that they may show a given film to the public during a contractually-agreed-upon period of time for a prearranged share of the box office receipts.

Leo Greenfield

LEO GREENFIELD is nearly legendary in the field of motion picture distribution, and small wonder when one considers his list of accomplishments. He was brought up in New York City, son of a dentist who (because of "an accident that left him with a broken arm and a very curious mind") purchased a small movie theater in Brooklyn. By the time Leo entered law school, his father's "chain" of Brooklyn theaters had expanded to five, one of which became Leo's responsibility to run. Soon Leo became a salesman for Universal Pictures and rose to branch manager in Albany, New York. From there he went to work with Buena Vista (Disney's distribution company) and continued to rise in the world of motion picture distribution. Since then he has held positions in the highest levels of many prominent movie companies, including (at one time or another) Cinerama Releasing Corporation (general sales manager), Warner Brothers (president of domestic distribution),

MGM (senior vice president of worldwide sales). He is also co-founder with Sir Lew Grade of Associated Film Distribution, an independent film distribution company.

Why There Are Distribution Companies

MOST OF the major film companies have distribution divisions. Distribution companies exist for a variety of reasons. They allow you to control the fate of the picture you have made. You can select, through your company, those venues in which you wish your film to play. You can also control how the picture will be released. For instance, if I have a very delicate film, such as *On Golden Pond*, years ago *Charly*, or that great British film, *Chariots of Fire*, I can determine how it will be released . . . when, where, how, and why. . . . I will determine what the advertising campaign will be like.

But if I am a producer of a film or the owner of the copyright of the film, and I turn it over to another company to distribute for me, that company ultimately has major controlling input—unless one is a Spielberg or a Lucas or a Stanley Kubrick. Stellar producers/directors such as they will have a strong hand in sharing the ultimate distribution and determining the publicity campaign they prefer.

Now the door swings two ways. If one has a film and turns it over to a distributor, producer/distributor, major studio, whatever the nomenclature, you know that picture is going to be played. And you know that you have a powerful company behind to distribute it, as opposed to you have your own little distribution company or you're an independent distributor, so you may not be that fortunate. So now it's which way do you want to go? The task of the independent distributor is becoming more and more difficult because of the power of the major studios and their distribution apparatus.

A Case in Point

Going back thirty years, I was in Cleveland, district manager for Buena Vista serving a very important circuit. I called the circuit buyer about a Disney film I was selling. We have it available, we're releasing it across the country, at Easter. The guy says "I can't play it." I said, "Why can't you play it? Disney at Easter, the kids are home from school, ten days?" "Wait a minute, buddy, I gave you Christmas. Now it's their turn—I'm going to play *White Eagle* from Warner Bros." I said, "You have to be kidding me, I'm here with a bona-fide big picture, Disney, big campaign, important film, what the heck is *White Eagle*?" He said, "You don't understand. I gave you a holiday, and I got to give Warner's a holiday." That was his relationship with the various major companies.

Now along comes an independent with a very good film. He can't get Christmas 'cause it went to Disney. He can't get Easter 'cause it went to Warner's. And who knows about the Fourth of July, what company it will go to? So the independent, unless he has a super-blockbuster or unless he has a picture that can cut such a swath or is so unique, has difficulty breaking into the market properly and getting the ultimate buck to which he may be entitled.

We had to kill ourselves in 1980–81 to get *The Muppet Movie* properly released. We had to prove every step of the way that we had an important picture. And we were told, Well, you can't play it here because of this major playdate, and you can't play it here because of this other major company's playdate. But eventually, because of the power of the picture, the tenacity of the sales organization, we literally kept calling and banging and would not compromise.

Licensing

Licensing means selling to the exhibitors. It's what I do. The everyday phrase we use is "selling a picture."

You don't literally "sell" the picture because the copyright vests in a production company or distribution company who legally owns the rights to that picture. So all one can do as a distributor is license that film for a given period of time. It's much easier for us to say we "sell" the picture to a theater, we "sold" the picture to AMC or Cineplex Odeon, but we don't, in the strict sense, sell film, we license it. We grant a license for the theater to exhibit the film for a given period of time with certain payment terms. It's really a license, but we say we're selling it.

Now the exhibitor is the person who controls the plant or the theater where the film is going to show. He will be granted the license to show it, for example, for a four-week stint. And what he will pay you for something like that often used to vary according to the theater's location and who the exhibitor was and that sort of thing. Those payments no longer vary. But they did at one time.

Runs and Clearances

You see, at one time we had this system of what was known as "runs" or "clearances," whereby a theater in a given area would have what we called the *first run*. That exhibitor showed the picture for a given period of time, and after a number of days—fourteen, twenty-one, or thirty—it would then go to what we called the *second run*. Hypothetically, if you got 50 percent for the first run, you didn't get 50 percent for the second run, but 40 or 35 percent. And then you went down to what may have been in the major city, a third run. So 50, 40, 35, 30, or 25 percent would go to the distributor.

That no longer holds true because now distribution employs anywhere from 1,000 to 2,500 theaters on a national break. And generally the terms are the same right across the board because there is no longer an availability difference in runs. People no longer have to wait if a picture opened first in Westwood or in a Broadway or East Side New York city run. In the old days, they might wait anywhere from fourteen to thirty days before they could see it in their local theater. That no longer holds true. You just break it right across the board. You have anywhere from fifty to ninety runs in New York City. We used to have three waves in Los Angeles. It's now one wave, fifty to sixty theaters, boom.

Screens and Circuits

There are (exclusive of drive-ins) roughly 25,000 screens across the country at the present time. Notice I didn't say "theaters." I said "screens." And that includes the small or the multiplex theaters.

And if you have an important picture, you may get 2,000 of those screens showing the film at the same time. Ten percent of all the screens in the country—*Rambo*, for example, opened in over 2,200 screens. So you can fairly easily gauge a film's commercial success by the size of audience that movie attracts nationally on a "per-screen" basis.

There is what's now known as a series of relationships, whereby a distributor selects theaters in which he would like to play his pictures on an annual basis. In that way the distributor knows he has a home, and the exhibitor knows he has a source of product, providing of course, there is no legal reason not to do so.

In addition, the various distributors select specific "circuits." It is, to a degree, to the exhibitor's advantage. He knows that come hell or high water, he would get this company's product, and his opposition will get another company's product, and they are willing to live by that.

Despite all of this, percentage terms are higher than they ever were before. The distributor has a higher rate of percentage. And a distributor will try to strike an accord with a circuit. And while he cannot necessarily deliver his product to every theater, within the orbit of the circuit, each circuit has a lynchpin theater in which the film must play. The distribution company knows that, in a given period of time, there will be an important theater or theaters available. The exhibitor knows that he will have access to top product.

This is now a business of "circuits." A circuit is a chain of theaters under one ownership. While circuits were always present, we always had quite a number of independents or quite a number of what we call "buying combines," whereby a distributor could offer a buying service for 100, 125 theaters in a given area, in the environs of New York City, Los Angeles, Orange County, and so on.

All of the new construction essentially has been done by circuits. Many of the older theaters were operated by circuits. I think AMC has 1,300 to 1,500, United Artists nationwide maybe 1,500 theaters, General Cinema 1,200 or 1,300, Cineplex Odeon around 1,300. These days, after you have dealt with ten or twelve circuits, you have "sold" 90 percent of the United States. You've licensed 90 percent of the country.

Now you come down to very important money circuits. Loew's Theatres has only 500-odd screens, but it's a powerhouse because of locations; their geographical hub is New York City and New Jersey. And they build wonderful theaters.

It's about the quality of the theater and its grossing ability.

A Short History of Distribution

You don't have to sell a movie anymore, because in today's market your venues are somewhat preordained. As discussed, many companies have loose alliances with exhibition circuits and their affiliates. The only question may be in which particular theater the picture being released will play.

I cannot tell, as Nixon would say, "the exact point in time" when the change took place. It's been a gradual change.

But what we used to do, and what is still done, is you would screen the pictures. You have a screening for all of the exhibitors. There are certain states that require screenings. We always had big screenings. If you're in New York, say, you invite every circuit owner or independent exhibitor in the greater metropolitan area, those theaters served out of the New York branch. You would say (hypothetically) on Thursday, July 5, at ten A.M., we are screening picture X in such-and-such a theater. This is your invitation. And that's the invitation for the exhibitor to see the film and consequently license it. The picture not only sells itself, but this sprang up because of what we call "bidding." Let's go back in time and you will see the evolution. Let me give you a bit of history. And whoever ultimately reads what I'm going to say will find it full of holes, with exceptions, but I'm only dealing now in basics and not in specifics. I am giving you a general background.

Pictures were sold or licensed in bulk. One company would license, say, fifty-two pictures a year, another forty-eight pictures a year, yet another sixty-three pictures a year to the exhibitors. But the exhibitor never saw them beforehand because the company salesmen came around with what we call a "press book." And they showed you a photograph or a rendering of those pictures they claimed they would produce. So you bought them in bulk. But the circuits did not have to buy them or play them in bulk because the circuits were owned by the production companies. Paramount Pictures owned Paramount Theatres, Warner Pictures owned Stanley Warner, RKO owned RKO, MGM owned Loew's Theatres across the country. So the smaller exhibitor, the independent, kept protesting and protesting. And finally the distributors agreed that they would sell the pictures in blocks of five, where they would license five pictures in a group and the exhibitor would have the right, if he wanted, to buy group one or group three. He had to buy the five, and was granted a 20 percent cancellation clause, which meant that he could license the five pictures in that block and eliminate one of the five. If one was an independent exhibitor, there were very few cancellations ever made. The little independent exhibitor or independent circuit or buying combine continued his protestations. Then came a famous lawsuit that resulted in a "consent decree," whereby the producer/distributor agreed to divest himself of his theaters within a two- or three-year period. So RKO had to sell off its theaters, Loew's had to sell off its theaters, the Stanley Warner circuit was no longer owned by Warner's, and you now had a degree of competition.

Said the independent exhibitors: This is wonderful, but how do I know that I will still be able to get my product? How do I know that you won't license it to the theaters of which you are divesting yourselves? We want to bid, bid, bid. And Supreme Court decision stated that this might be unreasonable and unfair to the independent exhibitor because these major theater circuits controlled everything. Nevertheless, the independent exhibitor was given the right to bid against opposition theaters.

A lot of amazing things happened. The independents began to win films, business got better, and the distributor made more money, because by a film so licensed, the distributor could not adjust a bid. A bid was a bid was a bid, and the terms were firm. *Before bidding*, if a film was licensed for 50 percent and it did poorly, the terms could be adjusted to a lesser percentage, but they couldn't be *under* a bid.

Now "the bid" is the number of weeks you offer to play the film, the percentage splits, and whether or not you would offer a guarantee or an advance—that is, "I guarantee you will earn no less than $25,000, and I will play the picture for eight weeks, two at 70 percent, two at 60, two at 50." Or "in advance" was, "I will *advance* you $25,000, and I will play two at 70 percent, two at 60, two at 50," and so on. In this way, bidding evened things out among the competitive exhibitors because nobody really knew what his competitors were going to offer.

Verifying the Box Office

The United States government verifies the amount of money brought in by the showing of a movie. You have to pay tax on your income, but we also have what is known as a "checking service." A few independent companies sprang up whereby you sent in a man, literally with a clock in his hand, and he clocked the number of people who came into the theater. You only did this on a reasonably important picture. And in order to insure the honesty of the man checking the film, generally he was quite elderly and unemployed. The reason for this was, you couldn't buy him off. You could say in those days, "Here's fifty bucks, go out for dinner," and if his supervisor came along and found out he wasn't there, he would be terminated. Now here's a man, poor guy's unemployable, right? So it was in his best interest to stand there and keep clocking. That was known as "checking."

Now the circuits couldn't or wouldn't cheat because their employees would have to become part of the fraud. Their employees would know that the number of dollars taken in were not faithfully reported. And you could have a system whereby the ticket taker could return tickets to the cashier, who could resell them. But if you tried that, your employees now became your partners. Sure, here and there there was cheating. There is no doubt that for a while in the history of the industry, there was what you might call "underreporting." But there are safeguards the distributor has today. And the biggest safeguard is that the U.S. government can, at any time, ask a theater to verify income the same way they might ask an individual taxpayer.

Now, in addition to ripping tickets, which is largely ceremonial and isn't done to prevent resale anymore, you have something that's almost foolproof. In a lot of theaters you get a little white piece of paper like a slip in a supermarket. It's a computerized receipt. And nobody *has* to tear your ticket anymore.

Marketing Executive

A Marketing Executive conceives and executes a plan for selling a given motion picture to the moviegoing public in a way that will persuade them to see the movie.

Sidney Ganis

SIDNEY GANIS, son of a New York cabbie, developed an early interest in entertainment when he got hooked by a theater workshop at age twelve. As a teenager, he responded to a *New York Times* want ad for an office boy needed in a show business publicity office. When the rejection note came, he left it on the kitchen table, where his uncle Phil, a restaurateur with acquaintances in the entertainment industry, happened to read it. One phone call from Uncle Phil, and Sid had the job. Within three years, he was introduced to the publicity chief at Twentieth-Century-Fox who brought him on board as a staff publicity writer for the "advertising, publicity, and exploitation" department there. He rose quickly from copywriter to press agent and was eventually put in charge of placing publicity in seven New York newspapers and all the wire services. He has since worked in various publicity and marketing areas at Columbia, Seven Arts, Warner Brothers, Cinema Center Films. He headed marketing for George Lucas for seven years, working on such films as *The Empire Strikes Back* and *Return of the Jedi*. He served as president of worldwide marketing for Paramount from early 1985 until September of 1988, when he was named president of the motion picture group for Paramount Pictures Corporation.

WHAT YOU call an "epic" to us in marketing is a "big, important movie." *The Untouchables*—we went in and sold it the way we sold *The Longest Day*. Special qualities, great stars—a film that you shouldn't dare to miss—because if you do you'll be missing one of the more significant movies of the year.

We use the vehicle of publicity, the media centers, to feed upon themselves. In other words, if we can convince New York journalists to come and see a movie way in advance, because we think they'll talk about it to their other media friends, then we'll do that. We'll build an inside interest in the film prior to getting it out there.

The Job

Our job is to get people to line up on opening day to go see our movie, then to tell their friends. The "tell their friends" part we have no control over, but the first part we have absolute control over. It's up to us.

We have to get to the public—through a television commercial, or a story in a newspaper, or a film clip on television, or a poster in a theater lobby, or a handbill in a shopping center, or a promotion with McDonald's.

What we do for a living is to say, "Excuse me, there is a rather fragile product out there that is not going to be around all that long—if you don't have a look right now, you're going to miss it . . . please have a look."

After that first weekend, it becomes a more complicated and strategic job of reminding moviegoers in a world where there is a tremendous amount of product to choose from, that our product is more important than anybody else's. That involves spending money on television and print advertising—and creating whatever dynamic you can come up with. To *go*. But also—*stave off* the competition.

Crocodile Dundee II opened against *Rambo III*. We dealt with *Rambo III*. But then we had *Big*, we had *Big Business* and others coming in through the summer. So we had to remind people, "Yeah, you can see all those, but make sure you see ours first."

Release schedules are the unsung heroes of my end of the business. It's hard for people to understand that if you open a movie at the wrong time, in the wrong week, you can kill it. But it's so enormously important to make sure that strategically you're opening on the right day—in the right week. Against no competition—which almost never happens. Or, more realistically, against competition you can deal with.

We know right now [early June] what other studios are going to release through Christmas and into next year. But . . . that changes from week to week. In other words, we all look at each other's schedules; strategically we try to outsmart each other. It's a gutsy, highly competitive business. We all know each other, we're all friends—and we're all incredibly competitive with each other. Though we are personally fond of each other.

There is a general belief that sequels are easier to market. But the one thing you have to remember about sequels is that, though audiences are *willing*, they are easily turned off if what you're showing doesn't make sense to them in terms of the original.

The other thing is, if the material doesn't look special and new and different—even as a sequel—that also can turn them off. Marketing a sequel is not necessarily an easier job. The great thing about working at Lucasfilm was that we had the opportunity to concentrate on one film for an extended period of time. Right now we're working on *eighteen!*

Planning a Marketing Campaign

At Paramount there are more than a hundred people who create a marketing campaign with me. That's the marketing staff of this company. It's a very complicated, difficult process, with absolute, exact planning as the mandate. We must do it with total precision—as it relates to the release date, the product, the competition. We have to be able to strategically understand *how* to buy television for the product, *what* programming to buy, the *content* of the commercials, what a *trailer* should look like, what it needs to *communicate*, how *much* do we say, do we *tease*, how much do we *not* say?

In what direction is the publicity campaign going to go? Do we take actors out on tour? Do we bring the press to Los Angeles? Do we have a junket somewhere in the country? Do we do one-on-ones—the way we did with Paul Hogan—which turned out to be extraordinarily successful back in the days of the first *Crocodile Dundee* when very few people knew of Paul Hogan.

One-on-ones because Paul Hogan is "homespun"—easy to communicate with—let's bring him "home." Let's take him to Cleveland, Ohio. Yes, it's going to take longer. A junket takes a weekend.

So . . . off we went with Paul Hogan to fourteen cities, city after city, with Hogan coming *into* the neighborhood and talking to the radio personalities and the press—one-on-one.

Trailers, Commercials, Posters

A trailer can be one hundred percent effective because you're appealing to an audience that is already there. A moviegoer is a moviegoer. The best place to find moviegoers is at the movies. The best place to give them information is while they're sitting there waiting to look at a movie.

De Niro seething on the steps in *The Untouchables* . . . first time we saw it, great scene, very dynamic, that's what we want in the trailer—that's his anger, passion, danger, special person, De Niro—larger than life. Turned out that we were correct. The reason I know we were correct is that the audience remembers it.

Relationships, action—you use them in different ways in a trailer. When you're defining an "action" audience you're thinking usually of a male audience, usually a younger male audience. That doesn't mean we won't show action in a commercial that is slanted to a female audience. Because we will, though we may temper it with something that has specific appeal to women.

Sometimes we want to communicate a specific idea. Maybe we don't want to be diverse, we want to be very narrow.

Commercials cover more ground, because the impressions you make on television are national impressions. But the impression you make in a movie theater is to the five hundred, or two hundred, or ten people in that theater.

The commercials and trailers are similar in that, if we agree on a concept, then that concept in one way or another will be put out there in a consistent format.

Posters . . . are things that filmmakers can look at, and be critical of, and change, and diddle with, and change the color of, and change the position of the hand, have a gun or not have a gun. Eventually the poster does become useful in that it translates into the newspaper advertising look. What the poster *is* usually becomes the newspaper ad. Posters are not nearly as important these days as they used to be when movie marketeers would create gigantic billboards—things they called twenty-four-foot sheets. Driving along the street you look up—and see the poster.

The Press

The Paramount marketing department consists of more than one hundred ambassadors of goodwill. We have to foster good relationships with the talent, the critics, our home office colleagues, everybody. We are a service organization. We service everybody associated with the movie, from a guy who worked on the production as a cable puller who happens to want a photograph of himself, to Siskel and Ebert. We need to have good relationships with all of those.

We're willing to supply the press with information they need to meet their needs. Not that we expect them to be uncritical of our product—but we do expect them to be fair with us in the way they handle our product. For instance, if we say that a review date for a film is one day before the film opens, we don't want to see the review out there four days before the film opens. But timing the reviews sometimes becomes important; sometimes we *do* want a review out four days before the film opens—depending on the product.

Critics . . . I think we've made them important to us. We quote them all the time. We use excerpts from their reviews in our advertising. But we're probably doing that because we don't have enough confidence in our own good work to *not* use them.

Traditionally, critics have been used to point out what's great about a movie. There always has been this controversy about whether, in fact, anybody pays attention to what we put in the papers about what the critics say. Does anybody care that some critic says "The best action film of the year so far"? Is that motivating? Does anybody care if a critic says "So and so's best performance ever"? Don't know. Probably not. But we use them. Out of our own fear of what might happen if three less people go to the movies—when we tap them on the shoulder with our campaign.

Target Audiences

There are four quadrants—very briefly, men and women over and under twenty-five years old. Those are the four targets. Then there are the most frequent moviegoers—the teenage audience and a college audience up to twenty-five years of age. The targets, depending on the product, fit into either all or some of the quadrants.

Here you go: *Crocodile Dundee*, older men and women as the target audience. *Crocodile Dundee II*, everybody. *Beverly Hills Cop II*, men, younger and older. *Children of a Lesser God*, women, older.

We believe in demographics and test marketing as tools. We're very interested in knowing what an audience will think of our trailers before we put them out, so we test market them. We send them out through an outside research company. They put the trailer out into the field (in an unfinished form) and get reactions from potential moviegoers. That information comes back to us. And we're very interested in what people have to say about the material that we're planning on putting out there.

First and foremost, the biggest tool we have in this business is our own instincts. That's why we're in show business. Show business never works off "stats." In the back room the stats are important, but when you get right out there with the product: not stats—guts.

It's as important to us to know what an audience in New York or Chicago thinks as it is to know what an audience in Yakima, Washington, thinks. The level of sophistication of an audience changes as you move toward the center of the country or the southern part of the country. Southern audiences are more willing to accept action films of a certain variety than a more cosmopolitan, sophisticated sector of the country's audiences.

Working with Lucas

He's extremely open to other people's opinions. And when he's heard them, he then makes up his own mind. He pioneered some radical ideas about marketing. Big merchandising tie-ins are not so radical today. But he invented it. In his contract with Alan Ladd, Jr., who gave him the means to make *Star Wars*, he said, "Okay, thanks for the means to make *Star Wars*, but I want to retain all the merchandising rights." *Really* radical back then. And Laddie gave it to him, and as a result of that Skywalker Ranch exists today, to a large degree, based on the revenue from the merchandising of *Star Wars*.

Art and Commerce

They don't have to clash. Art and commerce can serve one another. Artists have to understand that they're creating their art in a commercial situation. If they weren't, they'd be creating their art and flashing it in front of themselves in the bathroom mirror. Art and commerce can come together gently. It's not appropriate and it is inexcusable for an artist to say "too much commerce" unless there *really* is nothing but commerce. This is about commerce *and* art.

Advice

Learn as much as you possibly can, all the time. From before you get into it to the time when you've been in it twenty-five years. Keep learning.

Listen. Be aggressive. Don't be obnoxious. Move right up to where that fine line between aggressive and obnoxious exists and make an impression. Aggressiveness is a totally appropriate way of describing what a person has to do to remain potent in this business. We're all competitive—it's a rough-tough situation. But we're all reasonable with each other. We play by a set of rules that are competitively appropriate.

But, most important, keep learning. If you want to get into the business and you have some idea of a way *in*, then know everything about that way *in* before you approach the entrance.

There was a time when I thought seriously about leaving the business or, in fact, kind of staying in by opening a restaurant. I think now, many years later, that would have been the biggest mistake I could have made in my life. Just as they say in the movies, "Once it gets into your blood, it's in your blood." And it's in my blood and I love it. I wouldn't have it any other way.

Theater Owner

A Theater Owner owns and operates a public building for the purpose of exhibiting motion pictures to a moviegoing audience. He or she makes profits from the sale of tickets at the box office and food/drinks at the refreshments counter in the lobby.

Henry Plitt

As a soldier during World War II, HENRY PLITT was brought back to the United States on a "hero's tour" to sell war bonds from the stages of theaters. He was assigned to the Paramount circuit—at the time the largest theater chain in the world, with 1,700 theaters—and before his return to duty, he was invited (should he come back "in one piece") to join their executive trainee program. After the war, he took Paramount Theatres up on their offer—several weeks' stint at the Brooklyn Theatre in New York doing everything from usher to cashier to the "guy in the street who tells you to have your wallet out and money ready." From there, he was put through a rigid training course in New Orleans and then through theater management school in North Carolina. Next came an assignment at the United Detroit Theatres, a Paramount-owned circuit, again doing a smattering of everything in theater management from real estate to confections, and a district managership in Ohio soon followed. His final assignment as a district manager for Paramount Theatres was in New Orleans, where he moved up the ranks to become president of that circuit, covering eight southern states. In 1958 Henry was brought back from New Orleans to New York to run ABC's distribution and syndication arm—ABC films (United Paramount Theatres owned the American Broadcasting Company at the time)—and he turned around the faltering company in the next seven years, making it a successful enterprise. In 1965 he returned to running the theater division of ABC for seven years, then bought the northern half of ABC's theaters, followed by his acquisition of the southern half in 1978, which translated to all of ABC's theaters (at one time known as Paramount Theatres, Inc.) becoming Plitt Theaters. During all this time, he had kept a hand in producing and decided in 1985 to pursue it more fully. He sold Plitt Theaters to Cineplex Odeon and is now actively producing pictures under the Plitt Entertainment Group banner, as well as developing and guiding a venture called Showscan—a revolutionary method of film projection.

THE THEATER manager, who used to be "Mr. Show Business" in his town, is now a guy who opens and closes a store.

When I was starting out, the life of a theater exhibitor was very exciting. First of all, we had what were known as "first-run" pictures—which meant that a producer in Los Angeles who felt that the best launching of his picture could come from Henry Plitt in New Orleans would see to it that his picture was released in our theaters.

The studios at that time didn't have the extensive advertising and marketing people they have today. And you, as the district manager, would view the picture in the screening room and come up with ideas on how a picture should be sold and what kind of campaign you should have. You *and* the studio advertising people would coordinate your thinking and activities. Then came the time for the exploitation of the picture, which is when the theater manager began to play his role in how the picture was sold.

We no longer have that single first-run release of the picture. What happens now is that the picture, for example, is released in forty theaters in Chicago simultaneously. None of those forty theater operators is prone to go out and attempt to put on a campaign in his city for that picture because he has thirty-nine other compadres doing the same thing. And as a result, the responsibility for the advertising and the exploitation has fallen into the hands of the studio's advertising and distribution departments.

They in turn farm it out to agencies. The agencies, in some cases, are very good—in some cases, very lax. You might find a documentary-type picture being advertised on *Cheers*, where there's no relationship whatsoever, where the audience that *Cheers* generates has nothing to do with the potential audience that documentary-type picture would generate. It's gotten so divorced from the source, from the people who actually see the public buying tickets, in spite of all the computer readouts and additional monies spent on advertising.

The theater manager today is concerned, not unlike a restaurant manager or shoe store manager, with a number of things. The physical building he manages has to be suitable for occupancy. He can't have roof leaks and people sitting there with their clothes getting soaked or pieces of the ceiling falling down and hitting them on the head. He has to have his sidewalk clean so people will feel inclined to come in. The house has to be cleaned overnight, so that it's spotless in the morning, and enough time scheduled in between shows to clear up the spillage. He generally has—and it's very important—a concession counter.

A concession counter puts him in the grocery business very quickly. He has to have people vend behind the concession counter with a variety of confections that will be appealing to the public. He has to price those concessions so that they are generally higher than the local Thrifty store and to make a sizable profit because when the final count comes in, you'll find that the exhibitor is not making his money from movies, but from groceries.

We're in the grocery business.

We weren't always. In the early years of show business, what we grossed in the theater had a great deal to do with what we did to sell that picture. The gross ranged from seven to fourteen cents per patron who came into the theater. Today the per-patron ratio is up in the dollar-and-a-half range. So you can see what an impact all the items they now sell behind the candy counter have. In the old days, you had a candy counter, which was a little glass case. It was not the important thing, it was an adjunct. The important thing was the picture, the screen, the projection, the sound.

Now the projection and sound are still very important. People do go to where they get the best viewing and best audibility. When *Star*

Wars opened in Los Angeles at the Avco Center in late May of 1977, it did a business beyond everybody's expectation. But it opened at the Plitt Century Plaza on the sixth of July of that same year, and all of a sudden the business at the Avco fell apart. We didn't have a better location, we had a worse one. We had parking problems they didn't have. What we had was beautiful projection and fantastic sound, and the public found their way to our door.

In this industry, your projection and your sound must be given very high regard. When you stop to think, a man directing a picture will shoot a scene seven times. That's minimal, it's usually more like thirty. The normal viewer looking at dailies doesn't even see what made him do it over and over. But the director saw something—a piece of sunlight, something that to him when it appeared on the script would make a tremendous difference—and he wanted it done precisely and done right.

Now you get it in the theater, and you've got a projectionist sitting up there half-asleep, the focus is out of whack. This guy shot the thing seven times. The *worst* of the seven was better than what you see on that screen. It's such a waste. I think the theater manager should feel some obligation to the filmmaker and the film, not to mention it's just good business.

The theater manager also has to be something of a banker because he's got to see to it that tickets are in the ticket booth, that his prices are appropriate, that the money is drained from that booth in appropriate fashion so that it isn't stacked up to the point where somebody walks up to the counter and puts a gun in the window. I read last week a theater had a Brinks truck come by to pick up their money. One man sat in the truck, the other went in, came out gun in one hand, sacks of money in the other, and got robbed—$161,000. No theater should allow that much cash to stack up. That money should have been "bled" from the box office, from the safe, and from the physical property eight times before that kind of accumulation took place.

Reports

In addition to all that, the theater manager has reports to prepare. He has the manager's weekly report. With the advent of computers going on-line to central offices, a lot of the work a manager used to do in the early days he doesn't do anymore because it's all being fed in. Every time a ticket is punched, it's not only being recorded where it's punched, but it's going into a central computer that's forwarding it to the home office.

Nevertheless, he still has to fill a weekly confection report because there is no such thing there as running inventory in confections. If you took the amount of sales you made last week that were reported to you, and you deducted that from the inventory you had the week before, in five or six weeks you might find out you didn't have any inventory because it had all been stolen! You have to take a physical inventory at least once a week and, in some operations if they are having serious shortages or losses, every night.

So this theater manager's a pretty busy guy. He's got to get into the newspaper when the picture's playing—it's on at seven-thirty, it's on at nine-twenty. The business of coming in the middle or late is much higher than it used to be because now they insert screen ads before the feature, and if you get there in the beginning, you're now exposed to all that junk for ten to fourteen minutes before the picture comes on. It's pretty boring, and it isn't what you paid your money to see.

Retrospect

I can only say, in retrospect, that I find the job of theater manager today and tomorrow very unattractive, and that I found it extremely attractive yesterday. The best illustration I can give you is with a picture released years ago by Allied Artists, who were a very minor company, called *I Was an American Spy*. It was taken from a *Reader's Digest* story by Claire Phillips, who was a prisoner in a Philippine prison camp during World War II. I was a district manager of eight southern states at the time, and I drove into Texarkana, Texas, and met with the manager and, as I did all the time, looked over his bookings. We got to *I Was an American Spy*, and I asked him what he was planning to do with this picture. He said he didn't know. So I said, "What's the synopsis?" and we looked at it. I said, "Let's hold a screening for all the former prisoners of war who live in Texarkana." Now how were we going to find out who and where all these prisoners of war were? We decided to go to the Veterans Administration. They didn't have any record of who had been a prisoner. So I said, "Can we put a notice on your bulletin board?" figuring they had people coming in there all the time. They said, "Yeah, you can do that, but if I were you, I'd go to the American Legion." So we went to the American Legion and went through the same process. They recommended we go to the Veterans of Foreign Wars. So we finally put a notice on their bulletin board. We held a screening on the Saturday morning prior to the opening, and the place was jammed. We opened that picture to a staggering amount of money. Now Allied Artists saw these numbers and called up and said, "What the hell did you do?" We told them. They then pulled all their dates, made a deal with Claire Phillips, and took her around the country on personal appearance tours. And out of nothing, they had a picture. This was the thrill of being an exhibitor in those days.

Jerry Lewis was in a film, *Don't Raise the Bridge, Lower the River*. I had girl pickets walking along with sandwich signs on the bridges in Chicago where they open up to let the boats through, advertising the film. We did something for every picture.

My test of what a manager could do to sell a picture was what he could do that was costless. It's no big trick to take twenty spots on the radio, to take a full-page ad when a third of a page would do or, in the age of television, to get a lot of TV spots. That's not exploitation, and that's not selling. Exploitation is going to see the superintendent of schools and telling them you have a picture called *1776* and that you will set up special matinees for their students. We had the biggest gross on *1776*, and to this day Columbia Pictures doesn't know how or why the Oakwood Theatre outgrossed everybody else.

They don't do it any longer because now you don't have exclusive runs. The guy says, "What the hell can I do with this picture? Tom Smith down the block is playing it, and the other guy a mile and half farther down is playing it. And now I'm selling comfort, parking, and confections."

In today's market, the exhibitor is nothing to the studio. He owns a shoe store and opens it up and sells shoes. In the old days there was an energizing competition among the advertising people and the theater people.

Booking Today

The exhibition companies have people who are known as buyers and bookers who go to screenings set up for them sometimes three months before release, sometimes seven days before release. The theory under which the Supreme Court requires the industry to operate is that pictures must be sold theater by theater, town by town, picture by picture. That is nonsense. It's all done by "block booking"—which means if they have a big successful picture but they have three pieces of crap preceding it, if you want to play the blockbuster you have to play the other three pieces of crap, too. The Court doesn't refer to it this way.

We have what we call "stop pictures," and if you haven't included the preceding pictures, you don't get the stop picture. And you *live* for those stop pictures.

There's another thing that goes on now called "tracking." You're the head of an exhibition company, and you make a deal with Universal that in Detroit they're going to "track" you. You've got seventeen theaters, and Universal plays the movie in all your theaters. Now if the next Universal picture that comes out is a dog, you can't tell Universal, "Show this somewhere else," because you are their customer, and as their customer you're expected to take their product. You play the hot and the cold, although you may be able to wrangle over terms. You may say, "This picture's a piece of crap, I'm not going to pay 70 percent for it."

The film buyer representing a circuit has the problem of wrestling over film rental. The film company, not unlike the storekeeper, has a tag on the sale of the film. They have what they call a "national pattern" of distribution, which applies to people who pay the national pattern. Now if a fancy store on Rodeo Drive in Beverly Hills sees this guy from Texas coming in with a big hat and a big wallet, the thing is marked $100,000, he pays $100,000. But if a guy from Beverly Hills comes in and he sees that same thing and says, "I'll offer you $80,000," there's a good chance he'll get it. A film company is pretty much the same way. They have a national sales pattern for a picture. The picture may have opened in Chicago and died. They have to revise their sales pattern, or they won't get it played.

Or there'll be people who are in very important positions. They control markets like New York, Chicago, Atlanta, Dallas, and they have arrangements with film companies. There's so much activity between the federal government antitrust division and exhibition and distribution that I hesitate to get into any specifics. Suffice it to say that each circuit or each theater has somebody responsible for buying a film and, generally speaking, booking the film. And then they have another word called "settling," which means either paying contract terms or reviewing it so that maybe something under contract terms is paid.

There was a relationship between theaters and the film-producing entities in the early days. We were friendly, we did things together.

Today they don't know anybody in the theater business. They know circuit heads; there are maybe twelve important circuit heads in the United States. They don't know district managers or theater managers. And many of them don't even have the slightest idea of exactly who does what when it comes to making and distributing a motion picture.

Acknowledgments

This book was four years in the making, and because of its nature, hundreds of people have contributed time, support, and encouragement to the endeavor. Most of them know who they are, but we would like to single out a few here.

Eric Ashworth, our literary agent, believed in this project from the beginning and never gave up until he found it a convivial home. Our gratitude for his unceasing faith in us, and in the idea of this book, knows no bounds.

Marc Gompertz, our editor at Crown, ever gentle and accurate always conveyed and maintained a clear vision of the final result; and David Groff, who batted clean-up, was master of follow-up.

Others who gave of their time are Marty Bauer and Dan Halsted of the Bauer-Benedek Agency, Joseph Bernay, Alexandra Denman, Lindsay Doran, John Dykstra, Melton Maxwell, Stan Milander, Phil Alden Robinson, Aaron Russo, Penelope Spheeris, Jeffrey Sudzin, and Edith Tolkin.

Those who helped us corral the right interviewees include Doug Collins, Nancy Foy, Tony Ganz, Chris Gerolmo, Jon Levin, Spencer McDonald, Leigh Murray, Rone Prinz, and Karl Schanzer.

Ed Feldman provided access to key crew members and many laughs along the way.

A special thanks to our tireless transcribers Debbie Bishop, Belinda Martin, and Beverly Wright.

We gratefully acknowledge the assistance and information given to us by the unions.

And we would especially like to thank all those who consented to be interviewed. Without their generous participation, this book would not exist.

Index